I'll Never Write My Memoirs

**SIMON &
SCHUSTER**

London · New York · Sydney · Toronto · New Delhi

A CBS COMPANY

First published in Great Britain by Simon & Schuster UK Ltd, 2015
A CBS COMPANY

Interior design by Joy O'Meara

1 3 5 7 9 10 8 6 4 2

Simon & Schuster UK Ltd
1st Floor
222 Gray's Inn Road
London WC1X 8HB

www.simonandschuster.co.uk

Simon & Schuster Australia, Sydney
Simon & Schuster India, New Delhi

The author and publishers have made all reasonable
efforts to contact copyright-holders for permission, and apologise
for any omissions or errors in the form of credits given.
Corrections may be made to future printings.

A CIP catalogue record for this book
is available from the British Library

Hardback ISBN: 978-1-4711-3521-7
Trade paperback ISBN: 978-1-4711-3522-4
eBook ISBN: 978-1-4711-3524-8

Printed and bound by CPI Group (UK) Ltd, Croydon, CR0 4YY

MIX
Paper from
responsible sources
FSC® C020471

Simon & Schuster UK Ltd are committed to sourcing paper
that is made from wood grown in sustainable forests and supports the Forest
Stewardship Council, the leading international forest certification organisation.
Our books displaying the FSC logo are printed on FSC certified paper.

To my ancestors and descendants;
my blood relatives and relatives-in-love

Before

1.

When I told my son Paulo I was writing a book he said, "Oh, Mom, wow—I hope the world is ready for that!" When I told my family and friends I was writing a book, some of them got very anxious and freaked out. They wondered what on earth I was going to reveal. In spirit, I think most of my family knows what is coming: They are used to it. It's not as if the story of my life is going to be a surprise to them. Some of the details might be, but I think they are ready for whatever happens. They know to be prepared. They've had experience hearing about my experiences.

There will be blood, and thunder. I will take liberties, with my life and theirs. Now and then I will take on my own reputation. Those who know me, and are related to me, or close to me, have been warned many times by my actions that I am very unlikely to go quietly into the night, or into the light.

I once wrote and sang, "I'll never write my memoirs." I meant it at the time. I could have meant it forever, but it seems I've broken my own promise—turns out, for some things, there is no such thing as forever. I should never make promises to myself. Sometimes, there's nothing wrong with breaking promises, though. You can't go through life without breaking promises. You need to break a few rules as well. Well, a lot of rules.

When I wrote those lyrics, I'd had a fight with my boyfriend at the time, my son Paulo's father, Jean-Paul, and I would always put those kinds of incidents into song. Fights and arguments make great songs. There is a lot of my life in my songs, and after this argument with Jean-Paul I announced, "No memoirs, no comment." I decided that the only way I would be known from then on was through my music, through pictures, and through art as an art groupie. They would be the only footprints, the only clues to where I've been and what I was thinking. So touch me in a picture, whisper in my mask. All you would need to know could be found in how I look in a photograph, or captured in a song. The rest is mystery.

That was whenever it was, some time ago. I've changed my mind. I do that a lot, and why not? If you are a fan of doing the unexpected, and I am, then it is an advantage to be highly skilled at changing your mind. If you do not want to limit yourself, then be prepared to change your mind—often. If your attitude is, I will try everything once, then even if you have vowed never to do something, eventually there will come a moment where the thing you have banned yourself from doing seems especially tempting.

I will never write my memoirs seemed like a good commandment at the time I made it. Now is the time to break that commandment. Much of my life has been played out in public, full frontal, no-holds-barred, but there are plenty of secrets to reveal. I'm in the mood. This doesn't mean I will spoil the mystery.

I love secrets. They're very important to me. I had a lot of secrets growing up because my mother would tell me her secrets, and my father would tell me his, and I would keep them to myself. I never repeated them to anyone, and I learned the power of keeping a secret, the control it seems to give you. I enjoy those things that belong only to me. My secrets. I worked hard at keeping them, and they are all mine.

I won't tell all my secrets, but enough. Enough for you to think,

I don't believe you. That never happened. I don't care if you don't believe me. The best secrets are beyond belief.

My life is out there. Both in the sense that it is available on the Internet—the photographs, the stories, the truth and lies lit up all over the place—and also in the sense that it has been full of extremes. I have never held back. Why would I? I decided from an early age that the best form of defense was attack, and that taking on the world and living life to the fullest was how I would deal with setbacks and problems. This means you leave behind quite a trail. What you do gets noticed.

Sometimes I read stories about my life, and it seems so much more exaggerated than it actually was . . . and I think, *It wasn't like that!* My life is already crazy and unpredictable, but when it goes into the world, somehow it gets bigger. Sometimes, it's written less extreme, smaller than it actually was . . . and I think, *I was bigger than that!* There is no better way to take control of the stories of my life than to tell them myself in a book.

I'm not intending to correct any versions of me that exist out there. I'm not going to excuse or defend myself in this book. I don't want to spoil any image people might have of me being out of control, demanding, crazy, offensive, indulgent, chaotic, depraved. I can be a pain, but most of all, I can be a pleasure. I might think the legend isn't outrageous enough, but my answer to any suggestions that I have been less than discreet or abusive or just plain perverse is: no comment.

I am simply putting another version forward, one that happens to be the one I have in my mind. What follows is the me that I have made up, rather than the one made up by other people. Whatever people think of me, I want them to keep thinking that of me. I don't even mind if people make up things about me as long as they don't make me look boring or ordinary—as long as they don't smooth me out or reduce me. I don't want to contradict other people's idea of me; I don't want to spoil the illusion. I'm not worried about what people think, because I think people think what they want to think anyway.

I'm not going to try and set the record straight—I'm going to tell things as I saw them, and explain how things happened as far as I am concerned. It's the "which road to take" situation that is interesting to me. The options and opportunities that appear, and why what seems to be the wrong road turns out to have been the right road. Sometimes in the nick of time I would make the right decision and not even know it at the time.

These are my memories. My moods. My moments. My mistakes. It's a book, and it has a cover. So I can do what I want. A book is intimate, which is why it has covers. And if I am going to do a book, I will be very intimate. It's like sex—I'm doing it under the covers. Whatever I say inside, it will have a cover. A front cover and a back cover. It's up to you whether you go inside. If you do go under the covers, don't be outraged at what you find. It's your fault for lifting the covers.

It's my life, it's what I remember, or choose not to remember. I didn't appear here out of the blue on some magic cloud. I went through all this to get here.

Ultimately, achieving something positive in life—leaving darkness behind and discovering the light—is about wisdom, the wisdom that comes from surviving experience. I nearly died so many times, but I am still here. There were lives I lived, and lives I nearly lived.

If you want me, this is me. Not the caricature of me. This is the deeper me, the other me, and then there's another me, and there are other me's I've not even thought of. But I'll get to them. I'll keep following the trail I left behind and find out where I'm going next. I've got one life to work with and I'll squeeze it dry before I'm through.

2.

While I was writing this book I visited my close friend, mentor, and determined free spirit Chris Blackwell at his home tucked so deeply away into the thickly fertile heart of Jamaica, a country of green, green grasses, hanging gardens, chattering streams and unsolved mysteries, you feel like an explorer if you manage to find your way there. The roads around his house are deeply rutted, almost not even pathways, and the roads before those roads that are meant to be better maintained are nearly as bad and packed with potholes and sudden bone-shaking bumps.

When it rains, the dirt roads turn into rivers of molten mud and pull your car deep inside and won't let go. If you make it, you seem to have found somewhere high above the rest of the world, an unhurried oasis of peace and tranquility surrounded by uniquely shaped trees, creepers, vines, bamboo, and palms full of life and vibrancy. It's a clearing in the jungle, high in the sky. It's another dimension, and has probably looked the same for centuries apart from the addition of Chris's house and the grounds.

My close friend Mary Vinson, who married Chris after I introduced them, died in 2004 and is buried a hundred yards or so from the house. She once said that she hesitated when I mentioned she should meet Chris, because she always thought my other friends had something wrong in the head. I will visit her grave and have a quiet chat with her, tell her the gossip. There are plenty of places in Jamaica that are secluded, cut off, fantastically elsewhere, but Chris's home is seclusion to a magical extreme. You can hear the earth breathe.

He likes to keep the roads rough so that he can hear when anything is approaching, about to alter the delicate conditions. Along the way as you jerk and shake along the rutted roads struggling closer and closer to the place he has found, you pass locals living in sheds, huts and lean-tos surrounded by stoic goats and scattering chickens that make you realize how much you don't really live inside in Jamaica. Inside, you only need a bed, a table, and a chair. Mostly, you live outside and grow things to eat, to sell.

I eat some food with Chris, a traditional Jamaican meal, curried goat, ackee, plantain, rice and peas, fresh coconut water to drink, on the wooden veranda of his hexagonal-shaped house set in the middle of the clearing, at the top of a gently sloping hill. Fireflies flicker, crickets sing, the sun goes down revealing a warm, radiant dusk, allowing a thousand giant shadows to surround us.

We talk, remembering when we met, how we worked together, the music we made, the arguments we've had. The scandals I've caused. We've known each other for nearly forty years, and we are as close as you can get without being related. Ask me how close, and I will say we're family. Ask him how close, and he will say we're family.

I've arrived late. He likes to have lunch at twelve, but he knows that's too early for me, and he says two, but he really knows that means I won't get there until four. Especially considering how difficult it is to find your way to his house, off the beaten track enough to elude Google. I make it at four thirty, so in a way I'm only half an hour late. He's quite impressed at my "punctuality." A late lunch drifts toward becoming an early dinner.

There's a smoky, rumpled Rasta man called Lion who lives somewhere inside the vibrant green jungle circling the house. He's allowed to drift around the place in exchange for running a few errands, a gentle mystic man with a hint of something weirdly fierce, beneath twisted branches of yellowing dreads, somewhere between having no age at all and being about three hundred. He gives me what he has in his hand, and I take a puff or two, floating through the smoke, and everything becomes so peaceful but clamped inside the intense grasp of consciousness. I feel our ancestors all around us, forefathers and foremothers, unseen but not dead, their unmeasured energy living through us. We puff a little more and breathe life into our ancestors. The past exists side by side with the present, not behind it; what was—is. Another puff and I sink further into a now time, into the dream we call the past.

Sometimes when writing this book it has been like trying to roll my memory up a hill, and when I get near the top, I lose my grip, and it tumbles down to the bottom, and I have to begin again. After taking in the smoke of what Lion has given me, it feels like I know how to roll my memory downhill. I feel the past awaken. I can remember everything, as if my memories have become as set apart from everything else in the world as Chris's home and land. I can make them out so clearly. They're as big as life. I know where to begin. I can see to the edge of all that there is.

It's time for me to leave. I am always the last to arrive and the last to leave, but Chris wants an early night. Having got me here, he now needs to get me out of here. That's not as easy as it seems. That takes as much planning as getting me somewhere on time.

I don't want to go. I love the sounds here, the smells. I love the company. I love the memories. I love what has happened to my mind since Lion gave it a lift. I could stay here forever, like Lion, who lives on his own, at ease with himself, inside a tree or a cave, down by the lagoon, under the slow-turning stars studding the sky like the biggest disco ball ever.

I am always on the move, but I like to find a spot where I feel secure, and stay there, dig my heels into the dust. I am rooted and restless. I am at peace, but I want to interrupt. I love the quiet, but I want to shatter the silence. It's time to go, but I don't want to go.

I can't help myself. I want more music, more stories, more commotion, more seclusion. I don't want the day to end, although I know it must. Chris begins a game of backgammon with his much younger cousin, also called Chris. This is a clear signal that it's time to go, but I don't want to go. I talk to the girls in the kitchen who cooked us the meal. I tell them about my family, the food we ate, the brothers and sisters I have, being a grandmother. I have so many stories to tell that I have remembered now that I have been touched by the Lion. The Lion has gone, like he was never there in the first place. He's taken some of my memories with him. I'll pick them up another time.

It's time to go. Reluctantly, I give in. I leave the seclusion behind and head off through the writhing, dense vegetation that threatens to come to life in the night, back into the island, back into my memories, before they fade, before they become something else altogether. I go back to where I started.

It's time for something else to happen.

Spanish Town

I was born.

It happened one day, when I least expected it, on an island measuring only 4,411 square miles, a teeming mountainous land of wood and water among a chain of islands in the center of the Caribbean Sea at the western edge of the Atlantic Ocean. That wondrous isle in the western seas.

I came out of my mother feetfirst. I arrived kicking and pissed off, sticky with fury, soaked to the skin. I was what's known as a stargazing fetus as well, my neck fully extended. From the very beginning I was going against the grain and making trouble. Perhaps I was holding on to my mother for dear life, somehow knowing what was about to happen next. I didn't want to leave the one place I had felt at home, where I had been floating for so long, and enter the darkness. Inside, there was light. Outside, instantly, the unknown. The cord was cut. Startled by a strange newness, I didn't immediately make much of a noise, so I was slapped and slapped, to prove that I was normal. I cried out. *I'll show you noise. I'll show you normal.* I shrieked. In my own uprooted newborn way, I probably cursed.

Here I am.

Grace Beverly Jones. As was the custom, I would be known by my second name. Beverly. Bev. Later, when I was four or five, my skin was so charcoal black I would be engulfed when the warm, sultry night fell, throbbing with nature and a slithering hint of the supernatural. My nickname then was Firefly. You could only make out my eyes and teeth, sparkling in the dark.

My new home outside my mother was Spanish Town, the oldest continually habituated town in Jamaica. Five hundred and fifty years of history, starting a few years after the island of Jamaica was first found—"discovered"—by a Christopher Columbus of Italy in charge of exploring and marauding Spaniards. As St. Jago de la Vega, the town on the plains, at the edge of wetlands in the south of the island, it became the capital when the Spanish settled. They gave it a distinct Spanish Colonial layout, with lots of internal courtyards and walled gardens and a Renaissance-influenced checkerboard of streets placed around a dramatic central plaza. Spanish interest in Jamaica waned when it became clear there was no gold, and it became a backwater of the Spanish Empire. It became Spanish Town in 1655 when the British conquered the island. They kept it as the administrative capital and introduced grand Georgian buildings, reflecting the growing empire's wealth and importance.

Spanish Town was the Jamaican capital until the port of Kingston— better placed on the coast thirteen miles away, with more natural vitality—replaced it in 1872. The town's cathedral, built in the early sixteenth century, rebuilt in 1725 as an Anglican church, was the first such building in this part of the world and remains the oldest ecclesiastical structure from the British Empire still standing outside the UK. When I was born, Spanish Town had traces of grandeur but was showing signs of neglect after centuries of colonial rule and the Great Depression in the 1930s; imposed signs of methodical Spanish life, elegant town planning, and aristocratic British influences peeling back to reveal the undimmed Jamaica underneath. It had a faded glory, a shabby gentility, many parts of it cast aside as useless, and was beginning to meet up with the rough, tumbling edges of the capital city as Kingston's population grew.

They say I'm a lot older than I actually am. In the press, on the Internet, they add about four years to my actual age. I'm often asked how old I am—the world likes to know a person's age for some reason, as if that number explains everything. I don't care at all. I like to keep the mystery. I get onstage and tell everyone I am ten years older than they think, and then I hula-hoop for twenty minutes. That's my age—that's how I measure it. I wasn't born wearing a watch, and I never got used to wearing one, and when I was born I didn't know if it was Monday, Tuesday, Wednesday, or Thursday, and I never really know the days of the week now. Days are days, hours come and go, in whatever order, and I keep up with it, in my own way. It's hard to remember things in the right order, but I will try.

Time for me is an energy. I'm another energy, and the two energies wrap around each other. The present can seem as distant as the past, which can seem as close as the present. The most exciting thing is what happens next, even if it has already happened.

Because I never say my age, and rarely have to write it down, I roughly work it out by basing my life on an historic landmark. I mark time by what was happening in the world rather than how old I was. I remember moving to America around the time that President John F. Kennedy was assassinated. Before then, I was living in Jamaica, caged inside a certain goddamned darkness, even though there was so much sun and life. After Kennedy died, I was moving around like a gypsy, looking for the light, for what happens next.

Every birthday party I had after my teens, I always said I was twenty-something. I would know I was thirty-something, maybe forty-something, but never really the exact age.

I didn't grow older. I grew wiser. The world likes to know the age of someone, so I would be often asked. I am honestly never sure, so when it comes to working it out, to work out how old I am, I take something important, like my son's age, and if he is thirty-three, and I was, say, twenty-nine when I had him, then I do the math. So if you ask me now how old I am, nothing comes to mind straightaway. To some extent, it could be any number. Even then I am not entirely sure; it's not because

I am hiding my age, embarrassed or annoyed by it, but because it is not something I keep to hand. It's not the most important thing about me. There are more important things about me than my age that will give you a better idea of who and what I am. I was born. Let's take it from there.

I know just by knowing that the first decade of my life in Jamaica was during the 1950s. The Second World War had finished. It was a few years before Jamaica would win its independence from the British. Many Jamaicans were traveling to the mother country, Britain, to find a new life. To find new opportunities, my parents were preparing to move north, along the East Coast of North America.

My mother was Marjorie, born in 1930; my father was Robert Winston, born six years earlier. They already had two young children when I was born. My mother was extremely fertile and there was no contraception at the time. Five of the children were born in very quick succession; one year, two were born. Lots of juices were flowing. The children kept coming. Robert Patrick was the first boy; later he would change his name to Christian, Chris. Then there Norman Noel, known as Noel. Then, back to front, me, Grace Beverly. After me, George Maxwell, Max. Another girl followed, Yvonne Pamela, and then another girl, Janet Marie. Eventually, there was a fourth son, Randy, born in America, not Jamaican at all, the baby of the family. When she married my dad, my mother was sixteen. By twenty-two, she had six kids. She was a Walters; her grandmother's maiden name, my great-grandmother, was Powell, and some in our family think the first African-American to serve as secretary of state, Colin Powell, might be a relation.

They went to America to get away from her family as much as anything. My mom was definitely stifled by the world she grew up in. She was from a very religious family, among the first to open a Pentecostal church on the island. The very first Pentecostal church was opened in Spanish Town in 1933, three years after the first Pentecostal convention was held in Kingston. This was a missionary venture, a spreading of the word to those who felt estranged from standard religion, because they were too poor, or too otherwise troubled. There was a zeal among the converts based on a determination to be heard and followed; their evangelism was vigorous.

Her uncle was a bishop in this church, Bishop Walters, tight-lipped, with a barren gaze. He was a dominating figure who made the church and its unforgiving belief system the center of the family's life. So I had a bishop grand-uncle whom I thought of growing up as the bishop of Jamaica.

To some extent, his title was self-designated; his was a new untested religion, based on personal calling, its members making up its own rules, following other churches and their categories, so that the leaders became bishops, because that gave them the authority they craved. The Anglicans had bishops; so too would the Pentecostalists. This was one of the attractions of this new religion, that ordinary working people and the lower middle class, who felt snubbed by British and Europe-based churches and their elitism, could claim for themselves a superior religious standing. There were new opportunities for lay and ministerial leadership, which was very attractive. To climb to the top of other religions from a lowly position would take a miracle. Here was a chance to form small communities that could be organized from within, often from within families, instead of having to look to other countries and governments for leadership. There was a whole dynasty of bishops in my family; we are the bishop royal family of Jamaica. I am not sure where I fit into this, although to some extent I have about as much right to call myself a bishop as my grand-uncle Bishop Walters did.

Religion was a way for many Jamaicans to challenge the white-maintained status quo, from eighteenth-century slaves to twentieth-century Rastafarians. It was also a way for those less motivated to resist accepting things as they were. They have every church you can imagine in Jamaica. It's said that there are the largest number of churches per square mile there than in any other country in the world; it seems like there is a church on every street corner. And some religions are more religious than others.

How successful a church is depends how charismatic your pastor is. It's all about aura. It's about conviction. How deeply you believe. My grand-uncle Bishop Walters was an obsessive believer, made religion his whole world and the world of everyone around him. He was in his own way a brilliant performer, and performing is at the heart of the Pentecostal appeal. Jamaicans could identify with that; it is a society of physical performance.

He had an illegitimate son before he joined the church, and he kicked him out, because he didn't fit into his new life. The son grew up in England. We were good friends and I used to see him, but to the family it was as though he never existed. You could easily be cut out and cut off. They take religion to an insane, intimidating extreme, using the Bible, and God, to create a world that they can run in their own image.

Pentecostalism became my religion, as it had been for my mother, because that's what I grew up with. I had no choice. In our religion, according to my bishop grand-uncle, if you strayed, you would be thrown out, into a terrible, hellish exile. They took the Bible literally, all those revamped Babylonian folktales. Eye for an eye, tooth for a tooth. If your right hand offends thee, cut it off. If members of your family do wrong, shun them. Kick them out. Ignore them. "All scripture is inspired by God and is useful for teaching, for refutation, for correction, and for training in righteousness" (2 Timothy 3:16.). The leaders of the religion—the bishops, the pastors—ruled with fear, with a rod of iron. Perhaps they justified it to themselves because in the Bible it says that you have to use the rod to correct a child. We had to read that passage out a lot, as though the fact we were saying it in our child voices made it definitive.

My father's side of the family, the Joneses, were politicians and administrators. They brought the first books to Jamaica and started the library system on the island. His sister, my aunt Sybil, became the head librarian of the National Library of Jamaica in Kingston.

My father was a very good-looking man, and was very strong, mentally and physically. He was a keen amateur boxer and studied at Dint Hill Agricultural College. Farming was a major source of employment in the area; domestic and commercial crops included bananas, coconuts, pumpkins, peppers, and coffee, and there had been sugar plantations since the Spanish arrived bringing sugarcane with them from Haiti. After the

British arrived, the island was turned into one big sugar plantation. The world craved sugar. There was a lack of local labor, and new workers were desperately needed. Africans were found to be excellent workers, experienced with the land, and used to laboring in a tropical climate. Thousands of them were shipped in against their will. To keep the world sweet, Britain took sugar-producing Jamaica as another jewel in its crown, becoming the largest slave-trading country in the world. The cultivation of sugar and the organization of slavery were intimately tangled up.

My father's family were strict in different ways from the religious way—theirs was an army way. My grandfather on his side, his father, Arthur Patrick, born at the end of the nineteenth century, was a sergeant in the army during the First World War. When Britain entered the war, thousands of colonial men were enlisted in the British West Indies Regiment.

They gave land in Jamaica to anyone who volunteered for the Great War. His land was in the cool, isolated, shamrock-green hills that seem to hover under misty clouds, up above Sligoville, a humble, laid-back village steeped in its own gentle rhythms. It was the first free village in Jamaica, divided in 1835, after the Emancipation Act started to free slaves, into small, hilly lots for ex-slaves to live in.

Before then, the area had been a haven for escaping slaves, who had been stolen from the mountains in one land and now found sanctuary in the mountains of another. It was very near Pinnacle in St. Jago, the home of the first self-sustaining Rastafarian settlement organized by the founding father of the movement, Leonard P. Howell. Landless Rastafarians would leave the spread-eagled concrete jungle of Kingston and head for the hills. It was a place that yielded rich crops, including, of course, ganja. It's the spiritual home of the Rastas, seen by them as a sacred site, and you could say what became reggae, and Bob Marley, and the whole idea of "one love" began on that secluded rocky hilltop.

There is something in the air up there, and in the earth, and it remained mostly untouched by the Spanish and the British. It was too remote and hilly to build there. Even the Native American Tainos who occupied the land at the time of the Spanish arrival were situated near the coastline and adjacent to life-giving lowland rivers.

My grandfather had a house in Sligoville among a few other houses strewn about that, from a distance, seemed to be abandoned. There are plenty of dirt tracks that lead nowhere, there are acres of gentle sloping land, and the views to Kingston across the hills and the plains of St. Catherine are spectacular. The island beckons in all directions. It's a less familiar Jamaica for many, away from the heavenly shorelines and the overexposed and protected tourist attractions. The Jones family still has some land there, quietly waiting for us, as if this serene, magical place between the rolling mountains and the wide, wide sky is our destiny. Maybe one day I will think of this place as home. I'll walk barefoot in the grass alongside a river unmoved by time, letting things flow forward in whatever way they like.

As a teenager my father would have to climb up the hill from Spanish Town to his dad's house, ten miles there and ten miles back along a steep, winding road, by foot or on horseback. He would ride up with the horse and walk back, or the other way, walk up and ride the horse back. Once, running an errand, he was late, and to make up time, he rode his horse very hard, so as not to be punished. He made it on time, but the horse dropped dead. His father was absolutely furious with him, and gave him a look that was so angry he said it stayed with him for the rest of his life.

I only saw Grandfather Jones on Sundays after church—we weren't allowed to be exposed to his way of thinking, which was far too free, according to the bishop, and therefore nefarious. We would have dinner with him, but it was always awkward. His stoicism and reserve were frightening to a young child, he very rarely smiled, and was probably incredibly uncomfortable with the circumstances he found himself in, with his grandchildren released for a few hours a week from God knew what. He was very disciplined, focused, stern, and incredibly determined, but was confounded by the rules and regulations of the Pentecostal church. It turned out I am a lot like him. I even look like him, especially when I stare in a fierce, unforgiving way. Eventually, I became very good friends with him.

Years later, when my father himself had become a bishop, with his own church and followers, he would react whenever I looked at him in a certain way that indicated I didn't agree with him about something. "Stop looking at me like my father," he would say, only half kidding. He could see my father's disapproval of his choices and his lifestyle in my face. He could see so much of his dad in me, and that fury when the horse died, it unnerved him.

My grandfather never stepped into his son's church until he was in his late eighties, and he died in his late nineties. He was very against my father becoming a pastor. After he converted, they didn't speak for a long time. My dad did it anyway because he wanted out of his family— even if that meant joining the Pentecostal Church.

The Joneses' strictness was not religious like the Walters'; it was about being the best that you could be. The best politician, the best banker, the best governor, the best professional. It was about making society a better, or at least a better-run, place, rather than planning for otherworldly perfection using the Bible as a grotesque blueprint. My grandfather was very disappointed, to say the least, to see my father go into religion. He was as tough on all of his children, demanding respect, and you can feel how they all hated him for it, for being so inflexible and demanding. One of his daughters never married. She was in love with someone, but her father chased him away. He was never satisfied with any of his children's choices, with whom they married. My dad was as stubborn as him, though, and a fighter, and he got his own way.

Religion as my mom experienced it growing up was not what the Joneses wanted for my father. To such an educated, liberal family, the Pentecostal Church as it evolved in Jamaica from its extroverted America Southern roots—its urgency and lack of decorum appealing especially to slaves—seemed a superstitious kind of religion. It came across more as a cultlike organization than as a traditional religion. It was very much an influence on Jamaica from North America, not from Britain, which meant it broke away from the overbearing colonial influence. But it had its own Jamaican take that was even a little informal compared to the American way—when it arrived on the island, if someone came to a local Pentecostal church barefoot, they would be taken in, and the congregation would praise the Lord. By the time Bishop Walters was establishing rules, no one would be allowed in his church unless they were very formally dressed. The sinners were barefoot; the saints were in their very best clothes, buttoned to the neck. To my dad's father, though—despite, or because of, the dress code—it was an unstable even unruly religion, and opposed to the kind of enlightenment he favored, found in books and via learning.

It did not seem traditional, conservative Christianity, definitely not in the hands of Bishop Walters, but it was a way of establishing an alternative community for people who felt ignored. Established churches in Jamaica dismissed this new arrival as a "clap-happy church," and my dad's dad would definitely have agreed with that. Shamans, clapping to the beat, believing in divine healing.

My father developed an adventurous, rebellious tendency, because he felt oppressed by the Joneses' stubborn need for order and learning. He found it all too orthodox and authoritarian, and, perversely, he had enough space within a relatively liberal upbringing to rebel against his father. The most hurtful rejection of his father he could think of was to head toward this alternative religion, this new, fundamentalist but flamboyant church that had arrived from noisy, unrelenting America.

The Joneses were very British-Jamaican Anglican, very sensible and more accepting of the colonial system, whereas the Pentecostal faith was full of the Holy Ghost, much more mystical and obsessive and consciously or not sympathetic to a rejection of distant British control and superior colonial order where foreign whites were in managerial control. This was their way of dealing with the damage done to the Jamaican psyche by the indifferent British.

I think it became successful quickly in Jamaica because it was a lively mix of two things that had become part of religious convention in a country split between the imported Protestant discipline and an inherited African sense of performance and emotional expression. It was Christian, using biblical symbolism, but it was also spiritual, inheriting traditional ancestral cults. There had been the very Jamaican revival religion that flourished in the nineteenth century, in which

African rituals and Jamaican folk traditions were mixed with Christian belief, and many revivalists easily took to Pentecostalism because of its vibrant energy and faith in the power of healing. Pentecostalism incorporated rituals, spirits, and visions, but without seeming unchristian or unbiblical.

The Jamaicans were very open to the idea of spirits and spirit possession, with their African and indigenous Indian ancestors—they didn't have to travel far from the spirit-filled world many of them already lived in to accept this Pentecostal Holy Spirit. They also gave this more American revivalist religion a little local strictness introduced by the British, but compared to the formal Anglican Church, their style of worship still seemed quite rowdy. They didn't shout like in America or play crazy music and leap around; they still sang hymns, much more traditional and familiar, but in its merciless pursuit of an idea of saintly perfection, Pentecostalism did have a very emotional and exuberant side. The basic premise of the religion was that it intended to turn the sinner into a saint. You achieved atonement and salvation through rigorous ethical piety. To those used to an entrenched, relatively undemonstrative and prim British-style religion, this was very off-putting. It did not interest the Joneses, part of a confident new middle class.

It became apparent that there was a young girl in Bishop Walters's house and no one could get her out of the world of the church, which was very enclosed and withdrawn from the outside. The church needed to establish power over its flock and did its best to limit the number of temptations leaking in from the debased outside world.

My mom became a kind of trophy to local men because she was hard to reach. My dad, always looking for a challenge, made a bet with his buddies that he could get her out of Bishop Walters's sheltered house. Bishop Walters in Spanish Town resembled one of those cult leaders, where if he said to everyone in his orbit *Kill yourself,* they all would. He was very powerful and scary, possibly because he was extremely defensive in the face of orthodox religion, rejecting Pentecostalism as a diluted form of Christianity. He compensated with extra fanaticism, convinced he had discovered the purest, most spiritually transformative form of worship, a serious, relevant alternative to sterile established churches.

You had to do what Bishop Walters said. He represented total authority. And he was my mother's uncle, protecting her from lusty, wayward Jamaicans. Determined to win the bet, and being very enterprising, my father actually changed religions so that he could get inside the new church and its prayer meetings and services, in order to get to my mother.

My dad diligently courted my mom. She wasn't his usual type. She was too skinny for him, but because of this stupid bet he persevered. As a rule, Jamaican men do not like skinny women; they like them plump, full of health, of life, juicy, and therefore very social and lively. We say *mauger*, meaning meager and weak and lacking the required level of power. I am considered mauger—dry and brittle, prone to sickness, a hollow shell—and my mother was seen as very mauger. Five foot ten, a supermodel-type body, size zero—by Jamaican standards, almost a skeleton. But nothing stopped my father because of this bloody bet. It became a matter of pride to rescue this girl who seemed so beyond the reach of anyone.

My mom found the Joneses, my father's family, to be very smug and superior. They were condescending to those they considered uneducated, or even if they were educated but didn't live up to his fastidious standards. My father's father thought no one was good enough for his sons or his daughters. My mom and dad therefore had something in common; my mom thinking, *Oh, well, they think I'm not good enough for him,* and no one could get to her because of the church. The relationship was based on this kind of attraction. They each considered the other out of their league. It became like a Romeo-and-Juliet thing. My mom was not good enough for my dad, according to his father, and they were kept apart by the family. That was the start of the attraction.

My mom and her aloof, unconvinced father-in-law became very close in the end. She was the only one who could soften him. My mom could soften anyone. Some guys tried to rob us once. We had arrived at my aunt Sybil's house in a more peaceful part of Kingston to have dinner. We all sat around in her immaculate front room. I had brought

Richard Bernstein, who did the *Interview* covers for Andy Warhol and designed my first album sleeves; we were doing some filming for a documentary. All of a sudden some Jamaican guy sauntered into the house. He didn't have a gun. He said, "Give me all your jewelry," and held his hand in his pocket like he had a gun. He obviously didn't; it was a piece of wood. It was still pretty shocking, though, and most of us froze.

My mom walked over to him and said, "Oh, sweetheart," and she put her soothing charms on him, flinging softness in his face. Before he knew it the guy was out the door. "Oh," he said, "I better get some of my guys, and I'll come back." Yeah, yeah, right. They never came back. My father slept through the whole thing in the back room.

The would-be thief had a real cocaine face. Jamaican people shouldn't do cocaine. They should stick to marijuana. Certain things grow in certain places for a reason. Cocaine makes a Jamaican crazy. Crazee beyond belief. The Jamaicans should stay laid-back, have a joint, and chill. That's why God lets marijuana grow so freely there. He put the poppy seeds in one place and the coca plant somewhere else. Jamaica had the ganja, grown as a weed, introduced to the island by East Indian laborers in the mid-nineteenth century, immediately taking root as a beneficial substance. It belongs on the island, like it's been brought back to where it first appeared, and grows abundantly among the native grasses, plants, and weeds. It suits the locals' temperaments, as something that seemed imbued with spiritual, medicinal, and religious properties. Leave everything in its place. Don't mix it up. Especially when people can't control it.

My dad tricked his way into getting the girl whom nobody could get because she was inside Bishop Walters's force field, and everyone was intimidated by the bishop. In Jamaica then, you married as soon as you got your period, so sixteen was a bit late for my mom. If you weren't married by sixteen you were seen as an old maid. It seemed as though Bishop Walters was going to keep her for the church like a nun. The women in the church were called Sister. My father reached in, and he actually got Sister Marjorie, and she became his type.

My mom was a natural and very keen athlete, tall and lithe enough to be excellent at running and jumping. She was good enough to be in the running to represent Jamaica in the 1948 London Olympics in the long jump. There was a photograph in the newspaper of her ready for action wearing gym bloomers, and when the church members saw that, she was pulled out of competition. In the church according to Bishop Walters, wearing shorts was not allowed. They were called *batty riders*, for the way they slipped up the crack of your arse. And that was too much for the family. There was an Islamic level of intolerance, an Amish severity.

There was this other man who wanted to marry my mom. He was called Cecil Rowbotham and was from a big family. Later on, the Rowbothams became very close to the Joneses—one of my brothers dated one of the Rowbotham girls—so we stayed lifelong friends. Rowbotham was in love with my mom, but my mom said she didn't go for him because she thought his fingers were too short. Her father was a professional pianist, a leading figure in the performing of mento music, the jaunty, abrasive Jamaican and Trinidadian folk music mixed with swing jazz and storytelling blues that was the precursor of ska and reggae, and long fingers on a man became very important for my mom. Her father had very long fingers.

John "Dan" Williams, my maternal grandfather, had his own dance band playing jazzy mento, and would often accompany the legendary calypso pioneer Lord Fly, Rupert Lyon, known as the Calypso King of the world, and one of the first musicians to record homegrown Jamaican music. They made a number of rip-roaring 78-rpm singles together, including a big local favorite in the 1940s called "Trinidad Carnival Song" an energetic carnival song, with an opening line that went: *Jump in the line / Wag your body in time.* Their songs were full of life and a subversive, madcap comedy. They recorded a song about a really bad meal called "Swine Lane Gal": *Salt lane gal can't cook rice and peas / The bottom burn the middle raw / The gravy taste like castor oil.* Their regular haunts included the Wickie Wackie club in Kingston and the Myrtle Bank Hotel, Kingston's first hotel. My mom found a picture of him in his band, a slick-looking group of handsome musicians looking like they knew what a good time was, or at least how a good time should sound. These guys clearly knew that to perform in the Caribbean you need a certain flourish. This is a place that likes big gestures, and a sense of grandeur.

There is music in our family that goes back a long time, but the religious element turned their back on music as any kind of pleasing show business or fun. My mom's mother became very religious, taken with this ebullient new religion that offered her a role in life, but Dan didn't have much time for God, so he left. That's why they split up. She chose the church. He chose entertainment, and would split his time between Jamaica, Nassau, and America, touring with his band and backing singers, including Nat King Cole. In America, he started another family. He had three sons my mother never knew about, her half brothers, and he died at forty-seven after returning ill to Jamaica from Miami in 1958.

At the time, I was kept in the dark about this exciting long-fingered musical maverick, because my grandmother, his ex-wife, had rewritten her life completely as though he never existed. He didn't fit, he was everything the church rejected, so he was completely exiled. The idea of there being an extroverted, displaced entertainer in the family who made records and got up to wonderful no good in after-dark exotic nightclubs was much too sleazy a distraction from the all-important church. I, though, must have inherited his rhythmical wanderlust through the blood. His banished energy was transmitted through to me.

My parents left for America, my father first, and then my mother, looking to make a new home, or have some space for themselves. They'd had half a dozen kids, and then they sort of eloped, in the sense of running away together, one joining the other later when he had found a new home. We were raised by my mother's mother and her new husband, whose first name was Peart. My grandmother, with her daughter's children in her care, married a man who was twenty years younger, and he, as our step-grandfather, became our guardian. We called her Aunt Ceta, and she immediately ceased to be a grandmother in the traditional sense.

Peart was my grandmother's God-fearing church replacement for the wicked traveling pianist John "Dan" Williams. I don't know if my grandmother divorced my grandfather. In Jamaica, you often simply walked out, and you remarried regardless of the paperwork. In the church, my grandmother's brother was a bishop, and he approved or disapproved of any union. Everything had to go through him. If he says yes, it goes ahead.

My grandmother and her sister were both cougars, marrying men much younger than they were. Up to this day I still wonder how both of them managed to marry men twenty years younger than they. How was this allowed? It seems so unconventional. Even now surely it would be frowned upon. I can't believe they got approval from their brother the bishop. Even though their husbands were in the church, it still seems so unlikely back then. Maybe there were standards I don't know about, which makes the church seem even more like a cult, with its own dubious morals disguised as religious law. It was all very hard-core Christian—marital monogamy was a must, sexual promiscuity a pure evil; independent thinking was curbed. In moral issues, the Bible was the authority. Somehow, though, if you knew the right people, you could slip through the cracks and do what you wanted.

To this day, if I do such a thing, have a boyfriend twenty years younger than me, it is looked upon unfavorably. Very unfair—with men there is no limit, but for women, no way. Men get away with it; they can be ninety-eight, with their girls in their twenties. Women have no chance. But there were my grandmother and her sister back in the 1940s, part of a religion transfixed by the Bible, taking up with men half their age, their marriages sanctioned by Bishop Walters—very strange. I'll never unlock that mystery.

My grandmother and new guardian didn't have any kids and didn't want any. A deformed, abusive atmosphere in the household was rooted in his ambition to impress Bishop Walters, and rise up in the church, or it was part of a very demanding and immature personality. He knew nothing about raising kids and was suddenly saddled with a whole squabbling brood, but he wanted to look good to my great-uncle. He looked up to him and wanted to make sure he was next in line to become a bishop. Family was important as its own community: Everyone lived within a few yards of one another, keeping themselves to themselves inside this new, very lively and persuasive church.

He married our grandmother when she couldn't have kids anymore, but he ended up with five of us after our parents moved away. He took us all in while my parents built a new life in America, so you could say he was a great guy, but he treated us like he owned us. Like we weren't human, just something to have to deal with.

Everyone in a position of male authority in the church was a mas because they were a master, and *mas* was short for *master*. Master, massa, a name rooted in the history of slavery itself, from the masters of the estate. He was Mas P because he was Peart and you used the first letter of their name. This in itself turned him into a kind of gothic monster with an ugly, stunted name. I absolutely hated him. It makes my skin crawl thinking about him even now.

At the time, the practice of parents going away to earn a living and leaving their children with their grandparents was quite normal, but there was nothing normal about Mas P. His way of keeping us in line was to become a ferocious disciplinarian. I think of him as a real sadist who had an apparent excuse to be so cruel because he was our guardian. He didn't want kids, and suddenly he had a handful to look after, so he used religion and fear—real fear—to keep us all in check.

I presume he loved his wife, because it was an awful lot to take on, this bunch of kids all under six. I don't know if he was beaten when he was growing up, if he was taking out his anger on us. I never knew about his family, his mother and father. We never saw them. I don't know if he left them behind for religion. He eventually took over for my great-uncle as bishop. But once he took over he didn't have the position for much longer, only a couple of years before he died.

There were six of us, but only five were living in our grandmother's house. One of us was living around the corner with our great-grandmother, known as Ma. Bishop Walters is her son—it's like a clan, we all live near each other, we are all connected, almost confined to being inside the family. She wanted to raise Pamela, the fifth child out of the six. We were like a pack of little kitties, and my great-grandmother went into the litter and plucked out Pam—Pam was cute! Ma wanted her like a pet. My mom couldn't do anything about it; anyway, she thought it was the best thing to do. It was part of the culture. It still is. Parents who were too young, or couldn't look after all their children, would farm their children out to grandparents—in this case, a very formidable great-grandmother.

"I like Pam," she said, and you didn't say no to the great-grandmother. She was the matriarch, and in Jamaica the matriarchs can be more powerful than the patriarchs. She was still beating the kids with a broom at eighty, and was strong for many years more. She was six feet tall, half Scottish, hard-boned, the daughter of a slave master who got left behind—the owner took the son but left the daughter, who lacked value. She looked white. You hardly saw her pale, weakened hair; she would always keep it tied, and sometimes at night when she was too weak and tired, I would have to stay with her. She passed away at ninety-eight. Pam grew up separate from all the rest—we got to see her only on church Sundays.

We had no idea what Pam was going through. We thought she had it easy, but she probably had it worse because she had no brothers and sisters to talk quietly, secretly, with. I think in some ways she has punished us over the years for not being there with her, even though it wasn't our fault.

Pam missed all of our togetherness. We could hold hands when it got particularly bad. She had no one to hold hands with. It must have been very, very lonely. She doesn't talk about it. She didn't come to our father's funeral. She is still as removed as she was when we were young. Pam was there, but not there.

We were all made to dress differently from other kids from the beginning. We had to be the example for the whole church. As children, we were brought up very much to be seen, not heard. We were examples from when we were little pickaninnies. I always thought that was too much pressure. It's a church celebrating perfection, a cleansing of the soul, and we had to appear unwaveringly loyal. Nobody of my age at that time would dare question the absolute authority of the church or this version we were presented with.

I had to be dressed in little dresses over the knee; I couldn't straighten my hair, which was the fashion then. It grew thick and tangled, and was very painful to braid into the tidiness that was expected. Everything I wore had to be long-sleeved. We weren't allowed to ride bicycles too far from our house. We weren't allowed play after school, because that was seen as too frivolous, and allowed chaotic thoughts to enter our minds.

The church seemed to know everything we did outside of the bubble they created. If we played in the gully after school, somehow— I never understand how to this day—someone would always go and tell on us, even if there was no one around. I always thought there was a big eye in the sky that was telling on us if we did something wrong.

The gully was down at the bottom of a hill that gently sloped down from our house, an area of heath and bush that is now full of houses and is very different. We used to pick berries; there were cows grazing. It was like a Garden of Eden, really; a place where everything tasted and smelled good and you could feel happy. Our innocence could bloom. I could find fun in the gully, climbing trees, finding hiding places, discovering new feelings, feeling something unexplained stirring inside of me. Hiding away from the male authority and the Bible, from being banned from exposure to anything that might be considered worldly.

It was Mr. Philpott's land back then, a local neighbor who seemed happy to let it run wild. In my day it was like a little forest. I would pet a little with local boys in the gully. You show me yours, I'll show you mine. There was tall grass, above our heads, and you could hide in there and mess around with cousins. That was okay then, to a point. Cousins married then. It was very British, really. First cousins would marry. Noel was once engaged to a second cousin. Being in the church made it even more attractive, using marriage to keep everything under the same roof, inside the church.

Being found in a barrel at nine years old with a boy, not knowing what I was doing but knowing there was something to be done and really wanting to find out, led to a two-week deliberation about how exactly I should be punished. It was like the convening of a monstrous system for an inquest into my insolence. How extensive should the beating be, how long in duration, how public the humiliation? A little natural, tingling curiosity about how I was really feeling—not how I was ordered to feel—led to a trial that implied I had broken the law and infuriated their malicious God. The blows came thick and fast.

I was far too young, but you knew when you liked somebody, so you would hold hands, mostly with girls—it wasn't sexual or anything. Girls in Jamaica still hold hands all the time; it's very normal, nothing going on, walking down the street from school holding hands, safely exploring a honeyed closeness.

Whatever we did, however innocuous it seemed to us, or whatever other children were doing, there was this huge accusing eye hanging in the sky watching us and reporting back to our stepfather and the church. They always seemed to know where and how we were up to no good. Perhaps they assumed without ever knowing for sure. Or they didn't care if we were doing something wrong or not. Punishment was their way of keeping us in line.

After all, we got beaten a lot. Serious abuse.

There were tough leather belts on the wall with our names on them that were used to beat us. We would be beaten for what we were going to do even if we hadn't yet done it—beaten in anticipation of insubordination. Each belt was a different weight for who we were and how old we were, but sometimes you'd get struck with a belt above your years—the worse the perceived sin, the heavier the belt. If it got particularly bad you had to climb a tree and choose your own switch, which would then be used to whip you. Mother and Father had no idea of the ferocity of Mas P, and we were afraid to say anything to anyone, because that would have made things worse. He would read letters, whichever direction they went in. Everything was intercepted. It was like living in a prison camp, one where your guardian—your step-grandfather—was your guard.

There was one level of chastisement for playing after school, one for turning the corner of the pages over in the Bible to keep your place, another because you were on the verge of doing something wrong, not sure what it was, but you might as well be punished already, and then there was the beating you knew you were going to get at the end of the day. You'd be at school all day knowing that at the end of the day you were going to get a whipping.

My grandmother was a gentle soul, and she was totally dominated by Mas P. I remember sometimes she would try and get in the way when he was going to hit us and stand in between us, but he was so much stronger. She was afraid to stand up to him. He would brush her aside with one arm. If she ever disciplined us, she would hit us with a cloth belt—nothing painful at all, something light torn from her dress, a gesture.

Every night was church night—prayer meeting, Bible class, general service. Saturday was a day off; we could crochet, study a bit, visit family, other church people. Sunday, all day God. It never stopped. You couldn't move for God. It was only a word, but what a word.

We weren't really allowed to play with neighbors. My first love at ten, eleven, was my neighbor, but that was us standing at the fence and looking at each other with puppy dog eyes. He had two sisters, and he became a quite famous cricketer—I remember his name as John Prescott, who played for Jamaica, but never made it to the West Indian Test team. Being with him felt really dangerous—we didn't pet or anything, but he wasn't part of the church. My two brothers liked his two sisters, so we would go over the road to play for a short time, out of sight we thought, hoping that God wouldn't find us in our hiding place.

I wasn't supposed to play with my brothers, because they were boys. I was meant to stay put and crochet. I loved to crochet; it was another form of relief. I used to crochet until the skin would come off my fingers, and then I would put on a bandage and keep going. I would make shawls and doilies for the house. My grandmother's tiny sister, the one married to a man twenty years her junior—Mas K—was the one who taught me to crochet. Mas K's profession was making knitted bed covers, so she was crocheting and he was knitting. For all of us it was a method, I think, of putting God away. It was our form of praying.

I had so many brothers I became very much like a boy, but was also very vain at the same time. I was very concerned about my looks. I was a tomboy in a dress, but then I didn't have a choice—I wasn't allowed to wear pants. I was doing everything the boys did in order to have someone to play with; otherwise, it would just be me and my aunt crocheting while baby sister Janet Marie slept. They played with me, but I was the girl. They would put worms on me, they would try and frighten me, so in order to play with them, I had to keep up. I would play in the stand-on-your-hands competition, but I was in a dress. I would be walking on my hands with my dress over my face, showing my panties, and the maid would catch me. I would always get caught and I would get a beating.

Competing became important, to break away from this permanent justice system set up to convict me. I was a very fast runner. I loved jumping, over the bar, across scrappy potholes in the street or into a gritty sand pit. I was good at netball. I played jacks. I hula-hooped—kept the hoop moving around my whole upper body without it falling down, spinning it around and around like it was a form of protection. I couldn't come home with sweat on my dress, because that would mean I had played after school, and that was not allowed.

We had three or four people from the church who would do the cooking and cleaning, and they were like spies for God. God's spies telling on us for the slightest misdemeanor. They would get us beaten, so we couldn't stand them.

There was one in particular, Sister Leah, spying on us all the time. She would get us beaten so much; one time we all attacked her because we couldn't take it. We all jumped on her back and started to hit her because we were so upset. She was getting us whipped again and again.

I protected my brothers as much as they protected me. We looked out for one another. If one of us got caught, the others would feel bad that we hadn't protected each other. I would feel bad because their beatings as boys were more ferocious, although I had to watch them get beaten, and that was really bad. I think that bonded us, because it is not something that boys want girls to see. If I was there watching them getting a beating, without clothes, it was a shaming thing, but it brought us together. The girl would get a lot of punishment on the hand, or he would put you over his lap and lift up your dress and smack you that way. Since the attacks on the boys were more violent, I always felt responsible if they got caught. I was supposed to be looking out for them, up the tree, whistling loud enough to get them back in the house. I had failed in my duty. Bev, Bev—why didn't you tell us he was coming?

Young Max was the most rebellious of all of us, and the bravest in how he rebelled. He didn't care if he got beaten (well, he acted like he didn't care). One day, when we were walking to school, he suddenly said, "When we get home I am going to break all the windows." There were plenty of glass windows in Jamaica. He had decided he was going to break all the glass. Something had pushed him to the limit.

We'd say, "You are crazy! If you do that you will be picking whips for weeks!" Being naughty outside the home so that others could see was the most rebellious thing to do, because that would totally break the example we were meant to be setting. Everything had to look perfect from the outside. Max would be determined to make the biggest scandal ever. Nothing would put him off, however much we warned him, even if he knew he would be whipped.

He said he was going to do it. And he did. He said, "I will run," and we said, "Where are you going to run to?" There was nowhere to run. You run and run and run, but sooner or later night falls and you come back to the house and you know what's going to be waiting for you. There was nowhere to run, and no one was going to hide you. It wasn't like Sicily and the Mafia: *Who is hiding this child? Whoever is hiding this child will be put on a ship and sent to America!* Sure enough, though, he would throw those stones, and he would run, and he would get caught, and he would get it worse than ever.

There were very few days I didn't get some form of punishment. It was nastiness. It was humiliating. The God they spoke on behalf of was the jealous, unpleasant one straight out of the Old Testament. This God that was their idol, whom they looked up to, was a petty, unjust control freak, a capricious bully who bizarrely kept regular hours. He didn't seem a very godlike God.

It was all about the Bible and beatings. We were beaten for any little act of dissent, and hit harder and harder the worse the disobedience. It formed me as a person, my choices, men I have been attracted to—all that can be traced back to how I was brought up. It was a profoundly disciplined, militant upbringing, and so in my own way, I am very militant and disciplined. Even if that sometimes means being militantly naughty, and disciplined in the arts of subversion.

There were good things, too—times when the light broke in, when we could turn mounds of dirt into palaces in our mind; but these moments were brief and forbidden seeming, little stinging jolts of pleasure among all this fixed, malevolent sternness, pleasure that was warped in my mind because it would inevitably lead to pain.

The rain would intrigue me, how suddenly it appeared, wet and warm, another surface altogether, another dimension, something that might even cancel dread. It was a hint of another force, something beyond the limits of a world being made up around you by the church, and my grandmother and her petty, brutal husband.

My parents left us behind because they believed it was for the best. I don't remember feeling any resentment that they had left us to suffer this aggressive attention. In many ways, at the time, we didn't think about how horrific it was. It was all we knew, as if it was ordinary, how children everywhere are treated. We had little else to go on. Over time you realize how bad it was, and the problem with that is you feel anger years after the event, when there is nothing you can do about it. It can still control you.

When they went to America, my parents saw how kids there were allowed to grow up, and they felt that it wasn't disciplined enough for them. Maybe that was one of the reasons we didn't join them immediately. But then they didn't know how bad it was for us, because my mother didn't grow up with Mas P like I did—she didn't know that kind of abuse, that level of violence. The bishop was powerful, but he wasn't looked upon with as much explicit fear: He was actually very calm, almost frighteningly calm, as if he could quite easily swallow whole his entire family.

If you saw Mas P, there was something in his eyes that revealed how angry he could get. You can see the spite, the intensity. You can really feel that fire had descended to the earth. It's fascinating that those who put the fear of God in others are often those who live with the most fear—of others, of difference. Those who demand that you conform the most to how they live are the ones who are the most scared and intimidated by life.

I have learned over the years to be able to see in someone's eyes what they are like, if they are prone to violence. You can look in their eyes and tell if they are a serial killer! I haven't seen a serial killer, but I have badly misread a couple of guys. They seemed very peaceful, but they turned out to be pretty dark. Sometimes you don't see it immediately; it's something that comes out when certain buttons are pressed, when you say certain things.

If you looked into the eyes of Mas P in a photo he looks insane. You can see how he wanted power. Or how he wanted to hurt people. Hurt children. My brother Noel thinks he looked as harsh and bitter as he did because he wasn't getting any sex, or if he was, only once or twice a year. At the time, I couldn't imagine his sex life, or anyone else's. He was cruel simply because he was cruel, for no reason.

We were mostly locked inside our closed, paranoid community and we didn't even go outside the church to go to school. The church had their own school. All Saints Apostolic Church, All Saints School, tightly bound together. Everything outside was very alien to us. Even the barber across the street seemed foreign—if you went there you would be grabbed by a ghoul and who knows what would be done to you. This was how it was made to seem, that you must never go into these other places that weren't approved by the church. We had no radio, no TV. It wasn't allowed. Information was completely restricted. It was school, church, school, church, back and forth.

Until you were old enough to go to the public school, you learned the Bible, and nothing else. I know the Bible. Genesis, Exodus, Leviticus, Numbers, Deuteronomy . . . I've tried to forget. A lot to remember as a child, a lot to forget later. It becomes a part of you even if you don't want it to. You try a lot of things maybe you shouldn't to see if it will help get rid of some of that Bible detail you have stuck in your head. You're fighting the Bible you hate to read; you're battling with a God you don't believe in. It never leaves you, once it has been planted inside you with such force.

Once we started to go to the public school, about three miles away, we used to walk between our house and the school, out into Spanish Town, with its dreamlike Emancipation Square still pretending the town was important, the lanes and alleys planned centuries ago busily crisscrossing each other even as they now coexisted with ruins, even slums. The world stretched a little into a new shape, into something other than a biblical nightmare. The walking was freedom because there was no one watching and it was the island, without it being of the church. I remember the trees, the foliage, the larger-than-life plants and luxuriant grasses relishing the climate—you'd see the jerky imaginary faces of animals in the trees and in the shadows.

Real animals with chunks gouged out of them foraged for food on the streets. There were mad mottled dogs roaming about that you had to deal with. You had to work out your route to try and avoid these emaciated terrors. If you couldn't, you made sure you had two or three rocks ready to throw at them. You didn't have a bag then, you carried your books, but God forbid you ever dropped one and it got dirty or torn. They had to be in perfect shape, however hot it was, however sudden the rain, and even if you were chased by starving dogs. If you were chased by the dogs, you had to make sure your aim was good. Throwing a stone in their general direction isn't going to chase them away. You have to hit them. Stop them in their tracks.

Fighting the mad dogs builds character. I run into a lot of mad dogs to this day, so that helped me prepare. It's all connected. From the mad dogs on the way home from school to the mad dogs in the music business.

For us, that was the best time, walking on our own through the brambly lushness of Jamaica, the way plants and scraggly grasses grew in a feisty, random tangle, always something new to explore. It felt like freedom. It was outside the immediate reach of the church that at home wrapped you up in a jagged cocoon. And school was very strict. Very British Victorian. They would have the cane. Our headmaster was from Wales. Big belly, like a blubbery white whale. He would saunter off to get the stick and waddle back, prolonging the inevitable. School discipline seemed less of a burden than church discipline, because it didn't seem as though it was being handed down from God, ruling things from misty afar. It was more pragmatic somehow, not rooted in fanatical fundamentalism.

Once in a while we were allowed to go to the beach with the family, or to eat somewhere—say, Port Royal. I remember stories about how the port used to sink, and then reappear, because large parts of it had fallen into the sea in the great earthquake of 1692. Some said it was because it had been singled out by God. It was known as the richest and wickedest city in the world, filled with brothels, inns, and drinking halls. The deepwater harbor near Spanish shipping lanes and their ports made it a haven for pirates, smugglers, and buccaneers. A hundred years after the earthquake, one of the biggest, busiest cities in the Americas had been reduced to a quiet village. We didn't know the details; we heard the rumors, that it was a ghost town run by pirates.

I remember being very afraid of seeing the mysterious Rastas swarming in packs through the town on their dented bicycles. They were like Hells Angels, except they were leathery, bearded Rastas wobbling a little on bikes with their knotty, dreadlocked hair, which took a lot of patience to grow, which was the point. Their souls were bent and bound into those knots as though their hair symbolized imprisonment and yet freedom.

The Rastas had only surfaced in the 1920s and '30s, but they seemed to have been around since the beginning of time, keeping themselves to themselves, an ancient sign of a mystical, pre-Columbian Jamaica that had been nearly erased by centuries of colonization and outside rule. They would lurk at the edge of vision, as tangible as phantoms, mostly silent, working something out, lamenting their own captivity in Jamaica, nonchalantly loping off into the forest and the hills, possibly dissolving into the rivers and streams. They were used to hiding out, and would abruptly yet listlessly materialize out of nowhere. Now you see them, now you don't.

I had no idea what they were up to. We were told to run when we saw them, and hide under our beds. They were demonized. The church considered them eyesores, drug addicts, a bunch of crackpots who lived in filthy caves. Haile Selassie, Emperor of Ethiopa, wouldn't get off the plane when he visited in 1966 because he was scared of all the Rastas around the plane. They worshipped him as a messianic figure destined to deliver them to a paradise of peace and goodness and greeted his arrival by banging drums and smoking their sacred herb, halfway between sun-cracked warriors and ancient herdsmen. They were visually amazing looking, and I became less and less scared of them, and more intrigued. They had these red eyes that later I understood were from the smoking. Red with weed, the healing hazy fog thickening easily around them suggesting all manner of fluid, life-enhancing rhythm.

They would take over all the land on Spanish Town Road—the road that turned and twisted from Spanish Town to Kingston, where the ghettos spread and they could hide—living in hunchbacked wooden huts, and they refused to pay tax, and they rejected attempts to control them, and they said, *Man is free, leave us be.* They became known more around the time of Bob Marley, but they were around for years before then.

I used to see Bishop Walters, my draconian grand-uncle, standing at his gate talking to one particular solemn-looking Rasta guy, which was very intriguing. He never let him inside; there is always this thing about the gate in Jamaica. You stand and talk at the gate for a long time, but you never let them in. There is a whole book to be written about the gate in Jamaica—an interesting barrier between one state and another, between one stage and another.

The Pentecostal movement in Jamaica and Rastafarianism emerged at about the same time, and they are obviously very different. The Rastas presented themselves as self-determined, spiritually empowered rebel heroes with an anticolonial political cause they represented visually. Pentecostalism recommended moral redemption through transformative Christian rituals, defeating local circumstances by spiritually rising above them. At heart, both are rooted in biblical Christian fundamentalism, both formed self-reliant communities, and both reflected the changes in Jamaica that led to independence. Bishop Walters and his Rasta at the gate clearly had something in common; even if they were in disagreement, they were both talking about methods and aims. They were somehow closer than it seemed at the time. One looked more like you imagined Jesus to look than the other.

Our house was a modest detached bungalow set among other similar dwellings. There was a small, very neatly kept front garden, and a beautifully maintained lawn as perfect as they wanted me to be. The garden was a way of presenting moral tidiness to the surrounding neighbors. There was a working backyard sucked dry by the sun. A couple of lush fruit trees would produce mango and breadfruit. A lavish palm tree spilled out over the roof of the bungalow. Flowers splashed everything with color.

The kitchen was the heart of the house, always full of vegetable shavings and chicken bones. The stove where food was cooked had an air of magic. A corridor ran parallel to the main living room, where the bedrooms and a basic bathroom were. The smartly curtained living room had very pretty tiles on the floor. They're still there, even though my mother thinks they look old-fashioned and has always wanted to replace them with something modern, like patterned lino. When I go back to the house they are a vivid, very solid reminder of all the objects and textures that colored my childhood, many of them now vanished, some still remaining, making me feel charged with both a sweet sadness and a weird exhilaration. Perhaps it is relief that I made it out of what once seemed so forbidding and sheltered, a place of exploitation and oppression, one that now seems so small and harmless, even cozy. I'm never wistful or sentimental when I go back, things getting slower as I get closer, but I definitely feel as though the dreamy past is being held in place, erased of all the nastiness.

Mas P was a very good welder, and he produced lovely ornate iron-work as protection for the doors and windows. I don't know if that's what he did for a living, or how he made money, but the metalwork he did back then is still there today, and, disconcertingly, it is quite beauti-ful. He definitely had a clear eye for practical solutions, reflected in the way he ran the household with an iron will and meanwhile took care to decorate and protect the house.

At night, large moths the size of bats would settle on the walls. You would be afraid to chase them away, because you heard that they were how your ancestors took new form. It was a time and place where ghosts seemed to be always hovering at the edge of our reality, the dead ready to pop up out of nowhere and send shivers down our spines, or even scare the hell out of us.

There were plenty of bushes and thickets in and around the town, where the duppies hung out—*duppy* was the Jamaican patois word for "ghost," but a duppy was more than a ghost or a spook. It was a malev-olent spirit scheming toward some terrible outcome, the very reverse of what it is to be human. I'm not sure I knew anyone who had seen one, but you knew for sure that their heads were turned backward on their shoulders and they carried a chain. And you must never call one a duppy to its face, because to do so gave it power.

To believe in duppies was a definite sin in the eyes of the church. You couldn't ask for any help with how to deal with the duppies. You were left to fend for yourself.

There were a lot of secrets that the adults kept to themselves. We had a separate dining table, so we didn't join in with the adult talk. I was asked to eat with the adults once, because I knew how to do it properly, how to sit and be quiet and next to invisible. All that sitting and keeping still accounts for my restlessness in later years. All that boredom meant that now, later in life, when I get bored I am dangerously bored. In-stilled in me is a desperate desire to break free of whatever confinement I feel is holding me back. The boys were more rowdy; they wanted to eat quickly and go out to play. That never went down well.

It was all very hush-hush, a lot of whispering, and on no account were we ever allowed in my grandmother's bedroom. Even now when

I visit my mother's home, her mother's old room seems very foreign, like some sort of ominous sanctuary. It's filled to a heavy melancholy stillness with buried secrets and hidden energies. The house had a certain smell, from all the cooking, even because of all the dire whispering and judgment, which added to the atmosphere. Houses can be the most dangerous of spaces where even the way the furniture is arranged feels as though it is trapping you there.

I remember my school, and the schoolyard, near the looming Victorian prison and the sinister gallows, a sign of the town's old national importance. There were solid icons of the colonial past everywhere. The square we used to pass through is still there and is a big piece of history from when the Spanish came and then the British. There are a lot of Spanish buildings, very old, elaborate Spanish-type villas, and a Georgian splendor that is very out of place under a hot midday sun.

The narrow alleyways, old cream-colored buildings, and dusty roads, many leading nowhere or out into the country, all very tightly packed into each other, would remind me later of the sinister backdrops used in horror movies. A classic horror movie landscape always reminds me of growing up, probably because every day often felt like it might end up with something nightmarish straight out of a scary movie. There was a venomous, vindictive look in Mas P's eyes when he was about to beat us that was completely monstrous. He conned us into believing he knew everything—he was the all-seeing eye that nothing could escape. It was a look I was to use later in my life when I needed to create a very definite impact in a photograph, video, or film.

The only acting class I ever took was in New York with Warren Robertson, who had been taught by Lee Strasberg, the father of the American Method. He was seen as some kind of guru and had been named acting coach of the 1970s by the *New York Post*. The 1978 book he wrote about acting was called *Free to Act: How to Star in Your Own Life*. One of his exercises was called Sexual Tennis: "Stand a few feet apart and confront each other with your chosen intention. But as you do that, imagine you are trying to bounce a ball back and forth and you can only use your hips and pelvis to do this." One rumor circulating told a story of Warren helping a male student to conjure up feelings of fear by holding a loaded gun to his groin. Warren was pretty committed.

In the classes, I was very shy. Warren could read your mind. I called him a warlock. He was very perceptive. He could see by the fact I sat at the back of the class that I did not want to be in the group; I wanted to be alone. Some people love being in a group. I was never good in gangs after growing up in a gang of boys that I was always on the outside of. I trained myself to work well in isolation. Warren sensed that and told me it was best that I work with him on a one-on-one basis.

He was more than an acting coach. I learned a lot about myself. Working with someone like Warren is about much more than acting. It's about facing up to who you are and how that can be of use when you act. His technique was to liberate you so that you could use everything you had inside you. He would basically hypnotize me to get me to open up. He diagnosed that really I was acting out Mas P in all my performances: the fixed stare, the dominant stance, arms folded, the lashing out . . .

I was always the first in our family to try things, accidentally or intentionally—especially if there was a sense that what I was doing was forbidden. I was the first in my family to drink poison. I don't remember, but my mom tells me that I did it when I was really little, four or five. It was hidden under the bed and it looked like soda and it turned out to be kerosene. I almost died. Frothing at the mouth, blacking out, collapsing under images of Jesus, trembling fireflies, and a vaporous local Rastaman.

Certain rituals stick in my mind. There would be the sudden ringing of a bell and you'd hear the cries—*They're burning the mongooses tonight!* There were a lot of mongooses and they would eat the fruit in the trees planted on our plots of land. Barbed wire would be wound around the tree trunks to stop them climbing, making the trees look mean and creepy.

The mongooses would eat your crop, so you set a trap, and when you caught them, you set them on fire and burn them. It was like a celebration—the bells would ring, and we'd all go out and watch the mongooses be burned to a crisp. Jamaica had a problem with snakes, so they brought the mongooses to kill the snakes. Which they did. So there are no snakes in Jamaica. Bendy-spined worms but no snakes. And then that became a problem because the mongooses ate the fruit, the mangoes and breadfruit that were such an important part of the diet. And then people burned the mongooses. They would shriek like cats being skinned alive.

We didn't have separate bedrooms, so I would sleep in the same room as my brothers. Max was a sleepwalker and I remember at night he would sit straight up. It used to scare the shit out of me. He would get out of bed and start walking. As a child, when it's dark, seeing your brother jerk upright in front of you and walk around the room is pretty freaky.

My imagination was quite vivid when it was dark, with all these thoughts swirling around, and there were no streetlamps. I would be asked to go and get a bag of sugar from the shop around the corner for my grandmother. It would be beginning to get dark. Scared of the old pirates and the smoking Rastas, the charred, screaming mongooses, and the evil eye in the sky, the trees that would hang over tall walls like hulking dinosaurs, the duppies lurking in the woods, the rustling creature faces in the mad patterns of the leaves, my zombie brother walking into walls, and most of all the wrath of Mas P, I would sprint barefooted like Usain Bolt—that was another reason for me to be beaten, because I was barefoot, and I was not allowed to not wear my shoes. I didn't like shoes. They were like chains. I needed to find freedom where I could.

My mind was filled with hallucinations, many of them passed through to me from the church. Pentacostalism is one of those religions where they believe everyone else in whatever religion is going to hell, and they scare the pants off you.

In Bishop Walters's version of the Pentecostal Church, when you are baptized you are baptized in the name of Jesus, not the Father, the

Son, and the Holy Ghost. I did feel as though I had a relationship with God, with Jesus, if only because I was young enough to feel the vicious heat of that hell being talked about. And this was a church that was all about talking—speaking in tongues was proof that you had been saved. It was evidence of salvation. Jesus himself had prophesied that it would be a part of the believer's experience. It said so in the Bible, so it had to be true. Jesus said, "These signs will accompany those who believe; in my name they will drive out demons; they will speak in new tongues" (Mark 16:15–18). The speaking in tongues process was something else that appealed to the Jamaicans' love of presentations that seem larger than life.

When I was baptized at seven, I spoke in tongues, but then again, a monkey can do it. I'm not saying that it is all mumbo jumbo, but as a child you are not mature enough to really understand the concept of speaking in tongues. You hear it in church, you hear it all around you, and there is power in numbers. Everybody's doing it, and as a kid, controlled by fear, egged on by your own sense of daring, you start speaking in tongues.

You're babbling incoherently, making random sounds, you know how to do that, but it feels like it's important and its making you important. Everyone around you reacts as though you are speaking the language of heaven, as though the words are flowing out of your spirit. It's like you get high on it, you get intoxicated. *I got the spirit! I felt it!* It can become musical, with voices falling and rising and the repetition of various phrases—*Yes, Jesus, we love you, Jesus, praise the Lord, hallelujah.* The hidden things of God get revealed.

I didn't know what I meant, but I believed, because everyone around me believed. You do it every day, every day, every day, you hear it at home, at school, at church—the prayer, the laying-on of hands, the spirit—you're told it's a gift, directing you to heaven, and you speak in tongues. You really believe and you really go into a trance. That's what it is, a meditation; you are taken somewhere else, and words pour out of your mouth, your eyes are closed, someone is at your ear talking to you, whispering, *God this, God that, the power of God, it's inside you, it's speaking through you,* and you repeat it, and repeat it, and you get it, you've got it, you believe it, you really do, of course, there is nothing more pure than a child really believing. I believed! I believed it was supernatural. And I believed it was natural, and that it happened to everyone in the world, to the kid next door, to everyone everywhere. I didn't realize that this was not the norm. We weren't let out enough long enough to hear any difference.

I didn't start to doubt God, or faith, or the belief. I never had a distinct moment when I turned on the religion that had been tightly wound around me squeezing the freedom out of me. I didn't have a moment of revelation, that it was all nonsense, or dangerous, or superstitious. I started to want to find out things for myself. I wanted to have my own experiences. And it was in this environment, snagged by all the strictness, that I began to discover pleasure in rebellion—rebelling against authority was not necessarily a method of establishing independence, but it was one of the few pleasures I could find for myself. For me, expected from a very young age to follow the rule or else, being naughty became a great pleasure. I've never lost that feeling of taking delight in a certain amount of mischief.

I remember once somehow I was allowed to stay in Kingston with my dad's sister, Aunt Sybil, the sister of the aunt who never married. It could have been two days, but it seemed like two weeks. She straightened my hair, which almost broke the prime rule; we went to the cinema, where I was supposed to burn in hell sitting next to all these sinners. It was the first film I had ever seen. I have some strange memories of voluptuous visions as I sat in the cinema. The pictures on the screen were so big, eyes in the sky, but wonderful, and from somewhere else that seemed ruled by a better, more exciting kind of magic.

It might have been *The King and I* with Yul Brynner. I don't know for sure, or even whether it was in color. If it was in black and white, it seemed to be in color, new kinds of color, bursting with promise. But I remember it was huge, and watching it was like looking at a dream.

I was overwhelmed. It made me wonder how you could end up in such a world. I was all dressed up, but not for church, and the ugly bristly kink was taken out of my hair. It was seen as a sin to straighten your hair, so every morning I went to school, I had to do my hair to make sure it kept its shape. It was very painful. Sybil said, "Oh, they'll kill me if I let you back home with straight hair," so we had to wash it and put it back to church normal.

There was a delightful naughtiness about Sybil—*I'm going to get you away from these crazy people for a short while and show you a little bit of . . . life!* I never forgot that. This burst of something else, this flash of possibility. I still remember those days so well. It was a big, big, big moment. She treated me as if I was an equal. In a way it made me not so afraid. Everything else was about fear, and that sort of thing can keep you from growing. Jamaica is a land of growth—things grow so fast; it's nature in spectacular, bewitching overdrive—so it was weird to be in a situation where spontaneous personal growth was frowned upon.

Even looking into the boisterous public bar that was on the corner next door to where my great-grandmother lived on the main street in town made me feel like my eyes would melt. The thought of having an alcoholic drink made me think I would burn in hell. The family kept telling us every day that because we had again done something wrong, we were going to be flung into the fires of hell. It was brainwashing. I ended up thinking that if I misbehaved, I would be condemned to hell and lose the power to feel love, happiness, or anything other than cruelty and misery. There was so much fear. Sybil showed me another way—I didn't know how I was going to get there, but I knew it was available. She exerted a liberating effect on me, even awakened in me the idea that I was young, with my own mind, not a smaller, insignificant version of an adult.

Aunt Sybil had been a beauty queen when she was younger, Miss Whatever-it-was, where you ride down the street during the carnival wearing a crown. She did marry, but she was too tough for her husband, because she was very driven. She said she had to read everything she put into the library. An amazing woman—confident, knowledgeable, with such a strong will—and I love her. Sybil is an example of the very strong women who take leading roles in Jamaican life, and she was such an inspiration while my mother was away. I was lucky have such an inspiring female role model in the family.

I was young when I was given permission to occasionally visit her. Eleven, something like that, ten, perhaps. She's now in her eighties, still going strong. They all live long in my family. There's a whole lot of longevity. The women in our family live into their nineties. It's genetic. Sybil was very worldly. She had been to London in the 1950s to study, she liked to drink, she was normal. She went to church, and had some of the Joneses' high-minded toughness and moral fiber, but it didn't take over; it was never taken to the extreme.

Wearing nail polish was seen as an act of rebellion at home, but Sybil showed me it was nothing horrible. My apparent vanity was my worst sin to the church family. I'd want to put makeup on, pluck my eyebrows, paint my nails, as I saw other girls at school doing. If I ever did, I would try and take it off before Mas P came home. Seeing Sybil now and then was a revelation, simply in terms of how you could put on makeup without it causing a catastrophe—it seemed to represent freedom.

My early Jamaican years were an awful lot for a child of that age to process. I split my personalities because of it. To protect myself I would split into different characters. It was the only way to evade that kind of pressure: Hide parts of me that would later emerge as distinct personalities, sometimes with different names.

Eventually I realized it wasn't me who was wrong—it was them. The way it works is: They make you feel that you deserve to be punished. You are somehow encouraged to think that it is a necessary part of life, that you need the discipline. Therefore, you must be worthless, or why would this be happening to you? It is crippling to your self-esteem.

I hung on. I wouldn't let myself be harmed. I didn't want to think that I was weak. I would think of myself as the master. I made sure that I loved myself, because at times it seemed no one else was loving me. That's carried on—it's definitely one of my personalities. One boyfriend told me that I loved myself too much. I thought, *Well, you can love a boyfriend too much, but you can't love yourself too much.* Sometimes you have to love yourself to keep yourself whole.

Something vicious and implacable was being pushed deep inside me and I had to stop it from completely breaking me apart. It was a childhood that was not a childhood. And you end up being detained in childhood longer than you should be, perpetually the oppressed daughter. You take longer than most people to get used to being alive.

There were ways in Jamaica of escaping the brainwashing, but not for long. They would always catch you and punish you. That's what happened to me in Jamaica: I was brainwashed by all this hellfire and damnation, and if I did anything wrong, if I talked back to my elders, or talked to someone I shouldn't have, they would pull out my bottom lip and stretch it and pull it until the skin connected it to my lower jaw would tear. Once I left Jamaica I had to wash all that away, brainwash myself in a way, and for a while it was as though I was washing away the religion, and that viciousness took Jamaica away with it.

We knew our parents were eventually going to send for us—we just didn't know when. There was never a definitive time period. Then, one day, it started to happen. The children began to move to America, pulled away from Mas P and the church.

Chris went first. Then I went. Or was it the other way around? Noel didn't want to go straightaway, because he had embedded himself with friends and in school, and he resisted when they wanted him to go. He didn't want to leave. He was finding his own ways to stand up to the control. My younger brother Max came with me, because he definitely wanted to get out of Jamaica. After ten years, one by one, we were brought to America. My sister Janet was such a baby and my grandmother didn't want her to go. My mom thought it would kill her mom to bring Janet, as they were so close. So Janet stayed behind for a while.

My dad had changed his religion, gotten into Bishop Walters's house, married my mom, and taken her to America. He didn't originally head there, like a lot of migrants did, to carry the message of the church, taking over a uniquely Jamaican modification of an American-style religion. He had traveled to America to work, at what he thought would be a job that suited his talents and enterprise.

He worked in agriculture, and after the war in America they needed people with his expertise cultivating land. He could grow anything, and they needed new food sources at the time. He was full of hope and excitement about a new life away from the complicated family relationships in Spanish Town, but he was disappointed when he got to America that he was not being hired as anything other than a laborer. He considered that he was not that far above a slave, not expected to work as an educated Jamaican would in management or as an entrepreneur, but simply as someone moving earth about and digging holes.

He was in crisis, thinking of his wife and children and how he had moved for a better life despite the opposition of his father. He was a proud man, worried what his father would think, and he became suicidal. He remembers wanting to kill himself, to jump off a platform in front of an oncoming train. He says he was definitely considering it, because he felt he had let everyone down. He was standing at the edge of the platform, a train heading into the station, prepared to jump and end it all, when something sudden and amazing happened. At that point he got what he calls the calling. He had a vision.

He saw Jesus, in some form, who was asking him using words that weren't words, to become a pastor, and open his own church in America dedicated to the healing of mind, body, and soul. He had converted in Spanish Town to marry my mom but had never really bought into the Pentecostal premise, and then, in North America, at the end of his tether, he had this awakening moments before ending his life. He didn't expect this—he had converted to get my mom, to win the bet and get the girl, not to find God. To his surprise, he emotionally and spiritually converted after his vision on the station platform, and took the calling seriously.

My father really did feel he had escaped. Once he made it to America, he found that the Pentecostal Church there was very different from the church of Bishop Walters; it wasn't so exploited for personal power. It was a lot more open than my family's version in Jamaica, and he felt he could correct what he saw as the oppressive elements that had alienated his father and put a barrier between him and his wife. He had his own mission now.

In 1956, after ministering in New York and Connecticut, he founded the Apostolic Church of Jesus Christ in Syracuse, upstate New York. After a few years spent establishing his church and working his way into the local community, reaching out to the unchurched through neighborhood revivals, he felt settled and had a purpose. It was time for his children to come over to the nest he and my mother had built.

I don't know what Mas P thought when I left. I never thought about him. I wanted to forget about him immediately, wipe him out. When he died, more than twenty years later, I felt nothing. I didn't want to commit so much of myself that I had any kind of emotional response. Brother Noel wanted me to think about it from a different point of view, to be released—saved, in a way—but I never could. He didn't want me to think of him as a monster, but to accept that he was ill, or himself the victim. To forgive him. I couldn't. I don't know if that meant I had taken control or was still in his control. The more you try and escape, the more the thing you are escaping from continues to exist. I didn't want to think about it.

Noel's way of dealing with Mas P and Bishop Walters, and their corruption of religion, was that he wanted to go into the church and turn it the other way. Make it kinder, more inspiring, more caringly Christian. He seriously studied the Bible and wanted to transform the churches in Jamaica to which our family belonged. Noel dissected their power. He analyzed it. He wanted to know how it worked and transform it into a positive thing.

We have all reacted to this cult that surrounded us in our own ways. I wanted to be free. Free of myself, almost. Free enough to choose to be lonely. Noel wanted to repair the idea of God. He received a degree in theology, became a pastor in Texas at twenty-six, and later became a senior pastor, and a bishop, and a driven, charismatic preacher at the City of Refuge Church in Los Angeles, with twenty thousand followers. His church is so large it's known as a *megachurch*.

He found other words in the Bible that weren't about God the bully, a supporter of torture and recrimination. God was our protector, which was news to me. Noel needed to uncover a gentle God, to recover some sort of sanity. "Be strong and courageous. Do not be terrified, do not be discouraged for the Lord your God will be with you wherever you go" (Joshua 1:9). In a way he is anti-religion. He doesn't preach to you in the way we were preached to. His Lord is a very different Lord from the Lord that was forced on us. His interpretation is very extreme in terms of our faith. A lot of other bishops and preachers try to get him out—to them he's a blasphemer. He's the me of that world, the me in how I approach my career.

I'm still afraid of walking into the church in Jamaica. It still makes me feel very uncomfortable because of how they all look at you in a judging way. I say to my mom, "I am not going to church in Jamaica," and she says, "No, it has completely changed. It's not the same as it used to be. People can dress up and wear earrings, you can wear pants even!" But it doesn't make me feel any more comfortable, however much has changed on the outside. Even if I can wear pants, I don't trust it after the brainwashing all those years ago.

I went to church with them one time as an adult, but my granduncle had everyone all so brainwashed that it was hard to watch. The housekeeper who looked after my grandmother, Sister Dorothy, still works in the house in Jamaica where I grew up and, even now, comes to Syracuse to look after my mom. She has been persuaded that the television is a force for evil and still will not look at the TV in a room if it is on. She thinks that if she looks at it she is going to burn in hell. Dorothy will contort her body and hide behind her fingers if it is turned on to make sure she doesn't get a glimpse of the hell it is revealing.

They are still under the powers of the long-dead Bishop Walters.

He convinced his followers that they are going to burn in hell if they see something on television—a prime example of people using religion to gain control over other people's lives. I find it deeply disturbing that this still goes on, that someone who is no longer living under the pressure of the bishop still obeys him. It's a power that still causes me to pause, to feel the old anxiety, whatever I have done in my life.

I was successful and famous as a singer when Mas P died. I wanted to send my grandmother money directly, but was never able to until he died. I would pass it through my mother to give to her. Whenever I went to Spanish Town, to visit my mother when she was staying in our old house, if I saw him he would try to back me in a corner. I didn't want to see him, but he would be there, as though he had done nothing wrong, or had raised me as the Bible recommended.

He would try and tell me how I could use my fame, how many people I could reach as a missionary. I never confronted him about what he had done to me and my brothers and sisters. What was the point? Basically, I tried to avoid him. I never trusted that he had shed his venom. Every time we met he tried to reconvert me. He considered me a backslider. A serious sinner.

When my father visited Jamaica he would never stay in Spanish Town, because of the extremism of Bishop Walters. He would stay with his brothers in Kingston. The church was horrified at what I had become, and my father didn't want to have to argue with them. There was enough Jones common sense for him to decide what I did with my life was up to me, as hard as it was for him to understand.

Bishop Walters called me the devil. Whenever I was involved in a scandal that made the papers, I symbolized pure evil. He wrote it in a letter to my mother: *Your daughter is the devil.* He expected my mom and dad to shun me. They never did, whatever I got up to. My dad was punished because of me. He could have been made a bishop long before he was ordained if he hadn't had me to deal with, if he hadn't had a devil for a daughter.

Syracuse, Philadelphia & New York

I crossed the water, feeling no emotion about leaving Jamaica behind. It had never felt like home, and there was little to look back on but confusion and penitence. Our new house in America was in a place called Lyncourt, in Salina, a routine northwest suburb of the industrial city of Syracuse in upstate New York on the shores of Onondaga Lake. We were the only black family in what was mostly a very Italian neighborhood. A couple of families did put their houses up for sale, across the street, next door, when my family moved in. I didn't think about it at the time. Mostly, it was all very suburban and polite, and it looked like a place where you could be free.

Somehow, this comfortable North America of humming lawnmowers and shiny automobiles festooned with chrome looked closer to the over-the-top fantasy I had seen in *The King and I* than anything I'd seen in Jamaica. I'm not sure it was a place buzzing at the center of the flourishing American dream, but it was on the edges of it. There were new highways up in the sky swooping this way and that, and they seemed like they were headed toward adventure. America was in a funny mood at the time, but then, so was I.

I was very glad to be out of Jamaica. I was in serious dispute with my past. I thought, *Whatever happens next, I am going to make sure I do my own thing.* I landed in America looking straight head. I didn't know what to expect when I moved to Syracuse, but I knew from seeing my mother and father come back and forth from America that it was very different. Once my mom was away, she would visit with my dad every so often. I don't know if she started using contraception in America, but the children stopped coming, until Randy arrived about ten years later.

She had changed while she was there—she'd become very showy and stylish. When she came home to visit she was like a film star in my eyes, her natural Jamaican vanity and flamboyance amplified by her being in America at the beginning of the '60s, when things were blooming into color and new voices were fighting through. Her hair would be all straight and glossy, and she was suddenly fashioned out. It was like she was coming from outer space compared to the other women of Spanish Town, who were dressed very differently.

She would be all Givenchy, and very, very on the button for the 1960s—tight dress, stiletto heels, sharp pointy toes, glasses like the tail fin of a Cadillac, earrings the size of saucers. I would see her and go *Wow.* I loved how she looked. This kind of explicit female confidence was a revelation. She was something else. She would make her own clothes from paper patterns, and quickly became a professional seamstress. She would make wedding dresses in the basement of our house, and even now, sixty years later, it's like a dress shop down there, filled with reams of material and sewing machines.

When she came back on occasional visits to Spanish Town, no one from the church said anything to her about this wicked new look. There was a new kind of assurance about her. She had escaped the dreadful reach of Bishop Walters. She was still in the church; she was the star singer, the soloist, and she and my father sort of took on a Hollywood sheen—the pastor and the first lady. She came back fearless. Actually, when she left she was fearless—you had to be to say, faced with such disapproval, *I'm out of here.*

I don't know how fearless I was when I made the move. I was so relieved to be getting away from Mas P and the hell he had made out of getting into heaven. I didn't think twice about leaving Spanish Town. I was somewhere else, and it had meant that my mother now dressed like she knew about films and music and pleasure, and that was good enough for me. There was no way the controlling eye in the sky could follow me here.

I had spent the 1950s in Jamaica, without getting to know the island, because I had been crushed underneath the Bible. In the early 1960s, I was more or less a teenager, and I was in America—it was definitely the right time for me to be there. Eventually, I would find the right place to be as well. If I hadn't traveled in Jamaica, had barely seen the sea that was all around us, a theater in itself, with its esoteric, sunken history, and all that had washed up into the island's gregarious personality, I was going to make up for that now. I was going to move. I was going to make things happen. I propelled myself out of Jamaica so vigorously, I've been rolling on and on ever since.

I started going to Onondaga Community College in Syracuse, which had opened in 1961, so it was shiny new, as if it was also connected to the brash, expectant American dream. I'd already had three years of high school—in Jamaica we started school much earlier than in America—so I was three years ahead of American children my age, and after a short time in high school, I graduated at fifteen and went to college.

Because of my new school, I had a new name. In Jamaica, I was always Beverly. Or Bev. Now I was Grace. That was weird. I was not used to it at all. It's strange to suddenly be called by a new name. I knew it was my first name, but it was never used in Jamaica. They called me Grace at school because it was my first name as it was written down, but at first I didn't even respond when it was used. I didn't recognize it as being me. I was Beverly, not Grace. I was called Bev at home, Grace at school. It took a long while to get used to.

I was laughed at a lot because of my accent. I looked black, but I didn't sound black, or at least not black American. I was considered an outsider and was looked upon with suspicion. I was often by myself, quite a loner.

When I first arrived, there were certain rules I had to follow, because there was still my father, and his church rules. The girls were wearing pants, or dresses with stockings, but I still had to wear skirts an inch or so below my knee, revealing my skinny bare Jamaican legs. I wanted to fit in with my new classmates, at least at first, so that I didn't stick out so much. But a community of insurgent thirteen-year-old girls is not an easy thing to break into, and I decided the best way to join in was to try things that would mean opposing my parents.

I started to wear makeup. This alarmed my dad. He was no Bishop Walters, but he was still a responsible pastor in the Pentecostal Church, and wanted me to adhere to their values. I was in the mood to leave the church behind completely, even though my dad was a pastor, with his own loyal flock, on the way to becoming known as the Shepherd. In a way he was more devout than Bishop Walters, and more loyal to a moderate kind of Christianity, but this meant his children still had to set an example.

I knew this was going to be tough for everybody. It was like my life had been put on hold in Jamaica, and now I could actually start living. I had a lot of making up to do, and I had arrived in a country that was giving birth to the permissive society. Which was doing a lot of talking.

I wanted to challenge my parents—*Do you still like me now?!* I started to sneak in the sinning as soon as I arrived. Flexing my muscles. Sneaking out into the center of Syracuse with Chris, my older brother, and seeing what was there. Getting in later and later. I remember drinking alcohol for the first time at the Lyncourt Grill up the street from our house.

I started with Southern Comfort. It looked pretty and tasted sweet, and I liked what it did to my mind. I drank and drank and drank. I didn't feel it having a terrible effect until I stood up. I fell over in the middle of the road and vomited all over one of those smooth American streets that were so clean it was like you could eat off them, not like the streets back in Jamaica, which, even when they were tarred, seemed gnarled and crumbling, the dark, ancient earth itself barely covered up.

I started to go out to the gay clubs with Chris. My dad was very uncomfortable at the time with Chris being gay. It was one of the worst things for a pastor to cope with in quiet, very repressed suburbia when you wanted your children to set an example for the religious community you were building, to appear pristine and deadly straight within the church family. Pentacostal Christianity is the kind of religion where you command no respect if your own family is seen as being different, or somehow stained.

It was difficult for Chris. It wasn't necessarily a sexual thing—he was simply born very feminine. I felt as close as I could to Chris without us actually being twins. We easily passed ourselves off as twins, though, and I wonder if we were somehow tangled up inside my mother. I was born a little more masculine, a girl with some of the boyness Chris lacked. And he had some of the girliness I didn't have. In Jamaica, this meant he got beat up and verbally abused a lot for being a "batty boy." It's changing now, there is more tolerance, but back then it was the dark ages.

There is a gene, I am sure, in your DNA that traps you inside a certain gender. For people like Chris, from the minute they can walk before they know anything, before they can speak, there is a definite feminine element in their movement. Chris was like that. He was teased because it wasn't clear which way he turned. There is a world where he might have ended up conventionally straight and married. Girls, though, saw him as being too feminine to be sexually attractive, and a lot of straight men are attracted to pretty, young, feminine boys like Chris. Chris did admit to me that he was raped when he came to America by a straight family man. Chris was very delicate and feminine. It was tough for him. He played the organ at church, and I would call him "church gay," or perhaps it should be "church feminine." I think of Prince that way. A whole new gender, really.

He went to a psychiatrist, to try and sort out his feelings. He loved women. He could have had a girlfriend who understood his femininity, but if you are as feminine as he was, then the conclusion is, you must be gay. I don't think that is necessarily the case. Sexuality can be much more fluid than that.

He was forced to choose, and to accept a specific sexual choice. He loved men, because of a fantasy father image he built while his father was away—also, straight men love him. And he was often attracted only to straight men. But then there's no sex, so it's very confusing for him. He walks and he swishes in a feminine way—he was born that way. But his direct sexual preference is not blatantly for men; he has gone with women whom he has had chemistry with. People would ask, *Well, your brother is gay, how come he never got AIDS?* Because he very rarely had sex, with a man or a woman! Closeness and friendship were more important to him.

Mom was much more understanding of his sexuality and tried not to put pressure him. My dad denounced him and stopped him playing the organ in church. Piano playing runs in the family, coming down from my mum's dance-band dad, Dan, my real grandfather. Chris was an amazing pianist from the age ten, a prodigy. He played like the great Billy Preston at age eleven and used to contribute all the church music, help the choir—it was very important for him, this role. My father took that away from him because complaining church members were gossiping that he was gay. Chris was never the same when that was taken away from him.

He would say, "Well, if I'm gay I'll do what gay people do." And I'd go with him to the clubs. Being tangled up, having some of the man in me, I loved that. The man in me—as well as the girl—loved men! I felt I was among my own even as I was so far removed. This was when gay life existed deep in the margins of the margins of the mainstream, a system of rumors, innuendo, and scandal.

Back then drugs were not then around as much, although later Randy did manage to get busted for dealing coke. Dad had to deal with that, which didn't go down well at all. He basically told the police to lock Randy up, he was so dismayed.

I would sneak a little drink, puff on a cigarette that would choke the life out of me, but those were merely early attempts to go out and discover a new world, meet people, different sorts of people, see what they did, good ones, bad ones. I didn't feel disloyal to my parents. I'd been completely loyal to the family I had been given for a decade. It was time to be loyal to myself.

I was crazy about this African-American guy I remember as being called Bobby Rawls, who was a running back for the school football team. His nickname was Half a Man, because he was so small compared to the other players. I was a majorette for the team. I fell madly in love with him—my knees used to melt. He broke my heart: He got a local girl pregnant and he had to marry her. Love then was so passionate, wibbly-wobbly legs and knees, complete infatuation. When I fell for someone, I would really fall for someone.

I remember meeting a particularly bad boy whom I got close to. He was the first boy I truly got to kiss. We would almost climb inside each other's mouth. He was a Native American, Joe Rourke, and apparently he was very bad news, a classic rebel, and I took to him. He was probably of the Onondaga tribe, whose tribal home was in that part of New York State.

Obviously I was in the mood to be attracted to the baddest ass, someone with dangerous undertones, and hanging out with a local Native American from a community with its own issues in terms of where its members fit in was perfect. Joe seemed distantly related to the red-eyed Rastas who used to terrorize Spanish Town with their smoking and cycling.

We were together one night, having gotten a little drunk, and the police arrested him for smashing a window. I got so worked up I kicked a police officer and the cop car, and I was handcuffed and arrested for disorderly conduct. My first official trouble with the authorities. When they tried to take my mug shot at the police station, their camera never worked when I was put in front of it. Perhaps I was too demonic. They tried a few times. It worked when I wasn't being photographed. As soon as they tried to capture my image, nothing would happen. Chris came and bailed me out and somehow made up an excuse about where I had been to my parents.

Our mom was very tolerant and very protective—she would make sure we were safe, but she didn't want Dad to know. She would say, "If you let us know when you are coming home, I will meet you at the corner in the car and it will look as though we are all coming home together." Sometimes she'd sneak us in so Dad didn't see. I was skinny enough to squeeze through a basement window. She understood that all the strictness that she grew up with was no good, and she tried in her own way to break away from it. As long as we weren't hurting ourselves. She knew I had a lot to get out of my system, although I think she thought I would be experimenting with my new surroundings for only a short while. If she had known I was never really going to stop running wild, that it wasn't a passing phase, she might have been less understanding.

I was the first one at college to wear an Afro. That definitely challenged my dad. It was an abrupt way of telling the world: I am not a nice girl! They tried to force me to be *nice* in Spanish Town; well, that failed. I think my father thought I was losing my mind. It wouldn't be the last time he thought that.

The way you wore your hair signified much about your status, identity, and even mental wellness. Well-groomed hair was vital to the church. In Jamaica, it had been braided and tamed. What became known as the Afro, which involved growing out your dense hair, suggested to people like my dad that you were careless, filthy, or even in mourning.

The Afro style was just starting, and I must have seen it in a film, or seen a photograph of the blues singer Odetta, but I knew it was a brand-new thing. I really liked the idea. I instinctively responded to how the first women letting their hair go natural and unprocessed were the daring, artistic types whom I was quickly developing an affinity with. It also meant I didn't have to suffer the pain of educating my tough, nappy hair into neatness.

It was the first real sign of the fact that I now felt, in America, that I didn't have to ask permission to do anything, certainly not change my hairstyle. The Afro was seen as an explicit revolutionary act in the early '60s: To let your hair grow naturally was to embrace your heritage and reflect black pride. I didn't know anything about that. Being new to America, I didn't appreciate the reality of racial segregation. I wasn't consciously soaking up the spirit of change in the air. I just liked how I looked. It felt more realistic, as well; it suited my bone structure, skin tone, and hair texture, and because it didn't require all the maintenance I had been used to in order to obey my elders, it was instantly liberating. It didn't necessarily make me feel blacker. But it made me feel more me. Jackie Kennedy bows were a breakthrough for my mom, but not for me.

We had a big assembly the day I had my Afro on full show. I proudly walked in with this fucking Afro, a tiny brushed-up halo compared to what they would become in the late 1960s, but everyone turned and laughed at me. Older members of the staff stared at me in horror, like I was flirting with prostitution. Very soon, though, three other girls with black hair had one too.

They had all wanted to do it, but they were afraid to do it, in case they were not thought of as attractive, until I did it. There was a photograph of me in the student newspaper with this little Afro. I was already beginning to see how much better it was to be different than being, like in Jamaica, an example to the community.

I was doing my own makeup, my own costumes, and I was trying to dress stylishly. I got addicted very quickly to dressing to impress, even if that meant dressing to bother my father. I would wear two pairs of false eyelashes. Like the Supremes, whose lashes were very heavy, like feathers brushing their cheeks. Mascara was pretty new then, especially out of a tube with a wand. It seemed so exotic. I favored very strong makeup that drew attention to my eyes and lips. Orange lipstick, green eye shadow, even if they weren't made for black skin. Diana Ross's red fingernails seemed to be about three inches long, like scarlet bullets.

I liked the fashion of the Supremes, which seemed to be like nothing I had ever seen before. They were sharply and beautifully decked out in flashy sequins and shimmering gowns, their glossy, stylized hair shaping their faces. They were apparently living the dream, but in the early days they made their own clothes and bought their fake pearls from Woolworths. They were an example I wanted to follow—the most modern thing in the world when the idea of being modern seemed more important than ever. Their dresses were like the old church dresses worn as Sunday best given a whole show-business boost.

I sewed in my mum's basement using the same Butterick and Vogue patterns they would use when they started and had no money. I would cut up old dresses and make new ones from the material. I wanted to look more mature, like my mom, who was dressing somewhere between the Supremes and Jacqueline Kennedy, who was too prim for me.

I wanted to look more like I felt, like someone chasing her own identity, piecing it together both from my upbringing, what I was denied, and what I found looking around me, at women like me, or at women I wanted to be like. I guess this is when I started to exaggerate my appearance, invent what I wore, take ordinary things and customize them, make them my own, so they belonged to no one else. I wanted to be bigger, stronger, more myself. If I had been blanked out in Jamaica, now I was doing everything I could to fill myself in.

I had made myself older because I had wanted to work and make some money. This might be how there are usually a few extra years added to my age; it entered the system somehow. I made myself older than I was to get a job as a telephone assistant as a summer job. I was too young. I had to cheat.

I wore roller skates when I worked, answering the phone as a directory assistant. My employers didn't say anything as long as I did my job. I loved roller-skating. I loved the feeling of speed. Skating gave me my first scar, on the top of my right arm. I was going too fast down a hill in Syracuse, behind my junior high school, and I panicked. I grabbed hold of a branch as I sped past, and some spikes and twigs sliced into my skin. I healed with the broken bits still inside me, and they had to cut me open and take out all the wood. My first scar and my first operation—every scar a reminder of who I was, where I was, and what I was doing. Here I was, going as fast as I could, seeing where it would take me.

My instincts were to become someone else, to be unbound, to be born once more. I was born, I will be born, but as fast as I wanted to go, I brought with me some of the discipline of my old world. I couldn't get rid of it that quickly. Deep down, I wanted to please my mom and dad, as much as I wanted to make trouble, so I concentrated on my studies. I was focused on becoming a teacher. I was top of the class in Spanish. I think that's why my first real boyfriend was Italian and most of the boys I first kissed at school were white—there was that part of me that was European, because of the colonial traces that were left in the buildings and institutions of Spanish Town.

This is why I was strange to others at my school and in Syracuse. Black, but European. European, but Jamaican. It was something I would always have, a mixture of places and accents that I added to as I moved around, constantly relocating myself physically and mentally.

In a sense, my life paralleled that of Jamaica itself; the island gained its independence at about the same time I gained mine. This was because of the many cultures, races, and backgrounds that had come to the island during the previous five hundred years. Something new was always being brought, or started. Out of many, one people.

The funny thing is, I didn't feel any racial pressure at the school I went to. There weren't many blacks there, but I never felt persecuted or harassed. I felt it later, during the 1960s, but not when I arrived. It wasn't on my mind, because in Jamaica, people of African ancestry were in the overwhelming majority. If there was still a legacy of three centuries of slavery, and an insidious, lingering imbalance biased toward the few whites on the island, I never noticed as a child. I was surrounded by family who, in their own way, were successful. In religion, in politics, in business, in the military—the main black population, through entrepreneurship and education, had been given the kind of opportunities to better themselves that blacks in America hadn't received. Though America was such a forward-looking country, the battle for civil rights there was over a hundred years behind Jamaica.

The Jamaicans I knew simply considered themselves Jamaicans, whatever their background. There are nicknames for how black you might be—the lighter shade, the yellow end, the darker one—and people always want to feel superior to someone. I was dark, sometimes darker when I was out in the sun, but there was never a sense of feeling officially inferior. You would be insulted as being dark like the bottom of a pot, but never in a class way, only as a basic insult. It wasn't racial, more about hierarchy within the community, a way of creating status without it having to do with race.

Coming to America, I sensed it was different, but I didn't want it in my consciousness. I didn't want to be thought of as "black" and certainly not as "negro," because I instinctively felt that was a box I would be put in that would control me. I didn't want to be fixed as anything specific. I had been treated as a victim for too long, and now I wanted to be invisible, unmarked, too elusive to be domesticated. Oddly enough, I did this by standing out, often by accentuating details about myself that were down to the color of my skin.

My family brought the first books to Jamaica—at least according to family lore. They were in local government; my uncle was head of the Bank of Nova Scotia. A white friend said, "But they are dark; how did they manage to do that?" Well, they were educated! That's the key—education. In Jamaica, to a certain point, it doesn't matter what color you are if you are highly educated. My grandfather on my father's side said that his grandfather was brought over as a slave, but he had been educated in England, and that made a difference from the beginning. Even though he was a slave, the fact that he was educated meant that our roots were different, inspiring more confidence and drive, and his children and his grandchildren went into politics and banking. In that sense, because he went into religion, my father was the black sheep. That was deemed a trivial way of earning money, and it seemed a backward step.

Of course, in some ways my siblings and I were being treated as inferior beings, beaten and controlled, but that wasn't because we were black. It was because we were children. Once I had the chance to get out of Jamaica, like my mom did, I went out on my own. I needed to stand up for myself. I started looking for people—anti–Mas Ps—who could help me find out everything I could about what went on in a world that had broken free of the Bible.

When I did find someone to help me discover newer experiences, I was fortunate enough that that person was a theater professor at

school, Tom Figenshu, who was interested in literature, the Beats, po-
etry, and theater. In the early '60s, America was throbbing with new
sensibilities, and Tom was so different from what I had been used to
from teachers and pastors at my school and church in Jamaica. I wasn't
even intending to do theater—I was studying to be a Spanish teacher,
to be an interpreter and a teacher of languages. That was my ambition,
still framed within the sensible Jamaican Jones middle-class expectancy
of what I should do. The reality is, when everything was stripped away,
I started out with nothing but a kind of passion, a driving desire. I don't
know where it came from, but I was always very stubborn about it, and
nothing could deter me. I just needed to harness that drive into something concrete.

I saw Tom walking along a corridor at the college and got this instant crush on him. He was only in his early twenties, but he seemed
much older than me, and he had this droopy mustache that made him
seem very artistic. His hair was Beatles long, with a floppy fringe falling
over his eyes. He looked different from other men, as if he possessed
a certain sort of knowledge I wanted to have too. I was desperate to
know something about something, always on the lookout for anyone
who looked like they had access.

There was something about the way he walked, the way he dressed,
wearing round glasses like John Lennon did later. It seemed exotic.
I approached him, because I had found a boldness in Syracuse, and said,
"Wow, I really like the way you look."

He said, "Why don't you come and visit my class?"

How could I refuse? That was the turning point for me.

I entered the world of theater and the arts through a side door. I had
done a little singing in church with my brother, and we had a little singing group, with a girl called Zenova. I didn't sing lead or anything like
that. I always felt that the voice of a woman should be high and pretty.
I sounded more like a man. My mother was a lyric soprano and had an
incredible high, pure voice, so I always thought I was merely the harmony, the lower end, the tenor alto. I never really thought I could sing
at all, because my voice was so deep and manly. My mom was to me the

perfect image of what a singer should be, so it was never my ambition to sing. I could never be as great as her.

It was through Tom that I left Syracuse and began my travels, because he asked me to take part in a summer stock tour he was arranging. The first stop on the tour was at St. Joseph's University in Philadelphia. Summer stock, where small theater companies staged productions during the summer months when traditional theater companies were on hiatus, was very popular on the East Coast, where barns or old mills were transformed into theaters. Soon they would look a little quaint, but Tom was very passionate about the idea, as they had been a great training ground for actors and students.

Summer stock introduced would-be actors not only to acting, but also to the technical side of setting up a show—the idea being *Hey, there's a barn, let's paint it and put on a show!* There was a 1950 Judy Garland/Gene Kelly musical called *Summer Stock,* featuring "Get Happy," where a theater troupe uses a barn as their theater in return for doing chores on the farm. You didn't get paid, but you got digs, and it was an amazing way for me, without any training, to get on the stage.

Tom was very keen that I get involved. He saw something in me, maybe how enthusiastic I was. He came to see my mom and dad and explained to them about the educational value of summer stock. Tom told them he would look out for me. He was very proper in his approach, and they saw nothing to be concerned about. He was a teacher, so they respected that. They were very trusting, but with reason: He said he would absolutely make sure I was okay. I was so excited about the idea, they couldn't really say no.

He put me in a house in Philadelphia with a doctor and his family for the summer. It was all very legit, so my parents were reassured. I lived in the family's children's room while they were away. Tom wrote music and songs for his productions, and he had written a musical based on the *Canterbury Tales.* He pushed me, and said, "You can sing, you can definitely sing." Taking to the stage seemed very natural, because the church is like a show, it's an act; you're onstage, surrounded by other people who want to be taken somewhere, who want to believe in something. You are performing. The singing part I didn't believe in, because I had been brought up to think that singing was only for church, by pure singers like my mom, and I couldn't shake that off. Tom said he loved my voice, and that made me relax.

He gave me such confidence, which was the biggest high I had experienced since speaking in tongues, or since the shenanigans in the gully at the bottom of my road. It was such a thrill to have someone older than me, who knew about things, take me seriously and encourage me.

There were nine of us in the production, each playing four or five different roles—we were called the Ruskin Players. I would play an old lady, all bent and withered, which I took from Ma, my great-grandmother, and a nine-year-old boy I knew locally. I'm good at looking boyish. Without makeup I look more like a Nigerian boy than an African lady, even now. Tom made Madame Eglentyne a drag queen. It was very forward-thinking, to put the characters in drag.

I liked the way his mind worked. He was definitely one of those teachers keen on expanding minds by breaking down barriers, between art and life, teacher and student, performer and audience. He was interested in a form of social exchange that was a revelation to me. It wasn't about the mindless reproduction of knowledge; it was about the meeting with others, the pursuit of freedom and space. It was exactly what I needed to come across at the moment in my life, when I could easily have rebelled to such an extent that it would have led to real delinquency. Instead, it appealed to a sense of purpose that I had inherited from my family, however warped it was.

I loved doing the stage work. It's what stopped me wanting to be a teacher. It gave me something else to think about, in terms of what I could be in life. In Jamaica, in my family, it's like they want you to know what you want to be before you are born. Discovering the stage gave me a way of throwing that out of the window—through the window, so it shattered and there was no way to put it back together again.

With me it was decided before I was born, certainly on the Jones side, that I would be a teacher or a lawyer, that I would enter a proper profession, something that required an orderly mind. With my mother marrying a preacher, all she wanted was for me to marry a preacher. I felt there were enough preachers in our family! I feel the same about music when they tell me to do what everyone else is doing in order to be a success. I say, *No, there is enough of that already.* Sameness is depressing and even dangerous. Let's have something different. I am always going upstream when everyone else is going downstream. This is something that I was born with.

Tom and summer stock tapped into that contrariness. I liked moving around, meeting people, being with Tom. I liked his sense of humor. I liked the long conversations we had about art and theater, Jack Kerouac and John Cassavetes. He was definitely my first mentor. He believed in me when I didn't believe in myself. I inevitably developed such a crush on Tom, if only based on how free and easy he seemed, and what he talked about. I totally fell for him, in all my innocence and lust for new experience, and, inevitably, he turned out to be gay.

After we had finished performing the play, I thought, *Well, I'm not going back home, I don't need no more education. This is education.* Being out in the changing world seemed to be what I needed, not going back to my small-town mom and dad. I wanted to see the world. I wanted to know the world like the palm of my hand.

Angela Davis and Jimi Hendrix were wearing Afros now. The Supremes were a little Las Vegas, but Diana Ross's Afro ostentatiously mushroomed around her head like a woolly cloud with a mind of its own. I was young, but I was Jamaican old—the girls mature earlier in Jamaica. I would have been married with two children by now back home. It was time to find a new family.

Tom had written a song about Philadelphia for one of his student productions, *Kiss Me Kool,* in 1960, about how the city was thought of as being square, an old town not keeping up to date. *Nothing ever happens here in Philly / Living in Philly, what would you expect / But just as long as we live in Philly / Then leave us show a little respect.* By the time I got there, things had changed, and it was my first real big-city experience. Once I had a taste of it, I was hooked.

I stayed in Philly to try and find myself, or more of myself. The Georgian architecture tugged at something in the back of my mind, but mostly, it was the virile skyscrapers punching the clouds that set my heart racing, and how you could have contact with so many new people. I loved the life of the street in the city. The thousands of people all moving around at the same time in different directions exhilarated me. For a while, when you arrive in a new place, you are in a limbo zone—raw, naked, easily moldable—and I loved that feeling. It means you are on the verge of a new life, and I was on the hunt for other lives, new experiences, anything to escape having my mind controlled by others.

The person that I was in Jamaica was not really me, because I never had a thought of my own. I had never made a decision independently, I had no responsibility in terms of my own destiny, so once I got away, that was what became important—being in control of my own destiny. In the big city, every moment you had to make a decision for yourself. This didn't scare me; it excited me. I wanted to remake the world through my eyes. I wanted to create reality the way a child does, something separate from the allegedly civilizing notions of the adults who raised me.

I had to get rid of that old person, but not completely, only the part of me that was under the control of other people. Funnily enough, that part of my life did help me whenever I found myself going too close to the edge. There was something about the idea of prayer, of believing in something, even if you turned that into meditation, into a way of finding yourself. I supposed I would test out the idea of faith when I set out on my own, even as I was turning my back on the way I was brought up.

I wanted to take risks in a way I had never been allowed to as a child. Risks are a strengthening thing, and I took them to strengthen myself. I started to take drugs, as part of that risk taking. If you are a curious kitty, and I was a very curious kitty, you will take drugs however much you are warned not to. If you are warned by people whom you do not trust, because everything they do seems wrong, then you naturally think, *Well, drugs must be a good thing.* I found places to stay, in the hippie communes that were starting to emerge, which were very welcoming, and I set out to explore the city behind the scenes. To label them *hippie* was a way of describing what was happening, but these types of communes had been around certainly since Ken Kesey and his

Merry Pranksters took their famous bus trip in 1964, some of them based on experimental, improvisatory art colonies like Black Mountain College. The self-sufficient Rasta commune Pinnacle, founded by Leonard Howell in the impassive Jamaican hills, was a definite ancestor. There had apparently been hippies hanging around South Street in Philadelphia since 1963.

Hippie communes were the perfect places for me at the time. They had an open membership policy, and attracted the flamboyantly outrageous. They were full of different sorts of people wanting another way of life, to reject mainstream culture, to be rescued from some nightmare or another. I needed to get away from my parents, because they still maintained a link with the church, with the dreadful past.

This was my way of getting out of the Jamaican isolation. I wanted to know everything as soon as I could, even if I had to invent some of it, make it up. I went into things a little protected, getting a little help from others without relying on them completely.

I had an Italian boyfriend who worked in Philly, Sam Miceli. He was a hippie, a thoughtful hippie, committed to changing things, and used drugs not excessively or self-indulgently, to get off his head, but experimentally. He had the long hair that was by now cascading down his back. He worked for the city as a housing inspector, and that was the time when if you worked for the city, you had to have short hair. He would put it in a ponytail, but he was still asked to cut it off. He hated the rules and restrictions put in place by the government, and he was in the newspaper once for protesting about having to get rid of his ponytail. There was real prejudice against people with different beliefs that he considered discrimination. We went on a protest together. He won the case and didn't have to cut off his hair, as long as it was neat.

He was very protective of me. He would come with me on my adventures, helping me when I said I wanted to discover new things. To earn money, I became a go-go dancer in those clubs where lonely men on the road staying in cheap hotels would pay for a little relatively suggestive dance. They couldn't touch you, though. Sam would come and sit in the back and make sure I was okay.

I developed a tendency toward vagrancy. I forged quite a bond with local bums sleeping rough. I was intrigued by the fact they had rejected society so completely. I would invite them into my apartment for a bath and give them food, drink, and some clothes. It was very church of me, because I took from the church the idea of looking after those who had nowhere to go. In a way, those people who cooked and cleaned inside our house, like Sister Leah, were vagrants. They were homeless and were helped by the church and taken in, like adopted children, even if that was a double-edged sword. They were given a home, but they had to work hard for their room and board.

I went on a ride with the Hells Angels once. It was like I sensed meaning in the noise their bikes made. I found the people I was attracted to were attracted to me, because we were all trying to break free of something, looking for freedom. I was interested in interesting people who might be able to plug me into a new world, to help me move into new places. I was on the hunt for them. It seemed like a time of revolution, and I wanted to run with the revolutionaries.

I lived as a nudist for one month in Philly—1967 or '68 or '69, whenever it was—and it was a good summer to sit naked. At home, every day, I walked around with no clothes on. If anyone came to the door, I was naked. I didn't go to nudist camps or anything like that— I basically lived at home as a nudist. In Spanish Town, in Syracuse, they made me wear clothes that covered most of my body from head to toe, like a burka. I couldn't even wear open-toed shoes. Being nude was my response. I was born. I was reborn.

I still kept in touch with Tom Figenshu while I was in Philly. Working in the theater was still my ambition. When he said I should join the actors' union I had to choose a name. There was already a Beverly Jones, which was still the name I was known most by, so Tom said, "Well, try your school name, Grace Jones."

Chris, being Chris, said, "Well, why don't you call yourself Tiesha." They all have names like that now on fame-hunting reality shows, but back then it sounded very strange, like something from *Star Trek*. It was so camp, Tiesha! So I was nearly Tiesha Jones. There turned out to be another Grace Jones, so I put myself down in the end as Grace B. Jones. For a while, that was what I was known as. My checks were made out to Grace B. Jones. Grace, though, had taken over from Bev, and Beverly withdrew deep inside me.

It was a part of the whole getting away from the uniform, the not being able to do things. It was all part of the therapy I was performing on myself. My boyfriend Sam and I moved into an apartment together after a few weeks in a hippie commune. My parents had no idea about any of this. They had waved me off as I left to join the theater, and then I more or less disappeared into the vastness of America.

I used to get arrested in Philly almost every day Sam and I went out. Black or white policemen would see us together in his car, and they would arrest me for prostitution. That was their only answer to why a white guy was with a black girl. The same guys would arrest me all the time, even though by then they knew we were together. Sometimes when Sam picked me up from work, from my dancing, in a hotel, out between northeast Philadelphia and Trenton, New Jersey, I would be stopped by deadpan policemen caped in their bulky black leather jackets and sporting big gold badges. Black, a little insolent looking, wearing loose, gaudy hippie clothes mixed with some figure-hugging leather dancing clothes, bright, shiny makeup, teased up Afro bursting out of my head, provocatively dangling earrings—I must have looked been easy for young, ignorant police officers to typecast.

While I was working at the hotel in Trenton, the week after the assassination of Martin Luther King, there were riots in Trenton, and hundreds of downtown businesses were ransacked and set alight. There were hundreds of arrests, mostly of young black men, and sixteen policeman were injured. I wasn't there, didn't even know it was happening, but clearly as soon as I was spotted by the police, I was public enemy number one.

They were so racist on both sides—the black cops were just as likely to pick me up and give me a hard time. It became harassment.

I never thought it was because I was black. I still didn't think of myself as black, not in the African-American sense. I simply thought they were jealous. I thought they wanted a piece of my action, that they wanted to get into my pants! I thought, *Is this the only way you know how to do it, by arresting me?* It was only years later that it occurred to me it was because I was black.

I wanted so much to be a part of America that I would not let the idea I was different, even in a way that made Americans themselves different, get in the way. I was also determined to resist categorization, because that immediately meant being restricted and definitely meant being judged.

Perhaps it was so overwhelming coming to America that I could not let it bother me. If I'd been born there and really lived it, as a black person, it would have been different. It would have absolutely defined me, but I came into it from a distance. To be honest, I don't know how black America can ever get over how its history developed with this monstrous split. The Jamaican split was much more cryptic; American racial tension seemed like a movie to me. It was something I saw at the cinema, representing people that came from a very different place than me, and I didn't identify with them simply because I wasn't white.

Mostly I was in a good place: I was . . . free, free, free, even if I was being chased by the police. However frustrating the police could be, they were never as soul destroying as Mas P. If you survive a childhood like mine relatively unscathed, you're lucky, and as soon as you can make up rules for yourself, that's what you are going to do, without thinking about what you leave behind.

My parents didn't see me for a long time. I would check in by phone now and then, but I never let them know where I was. They were going out of their minds, but I never fully appreciated that. It's only now that I have my own son and know how worried I get if he isn't in touch with me for a few days that I realize how concerned they must have been.

Finally, after a few months, I wrote, saying I was okay and living in a house in Philadelphia. I kept things vague. I didn't say I was living with Sam; I said he was a neighbor. The whole time I was in Philadelphia they didn't see me. They didn't see me for months, until I suddenly turned up one day on a bike with Sam. We had to pretend that we weren't sleeping together or living in the same place—*Here's Sam, my neighbor from upstairs! He gave me a lift, isn't that lovely of him?* I was wearing these vivid purple hip-hugging bell-bottoms, and a black wig with this straight, Cher-like hair streaming down to my waist. I had left as one thing and returned as another. They were very relieved to see me, and had obviously decided not to give me a hard time.

At the back of my mind, while I was away, I thought, *Well, they're praying for me!* Actually, I wasn't thinking about them at all, to be honest. I put them through hell. I was totally selfish. I had to be to get away and not weaken and sheepishly return home.

I wasn't tripping or stoned when I made it back home. I made sure it seemed like I had been looking after myself, and that I stayed away merely because I had found some work. I had been taking drugs regularly while I was away, though, and had taken acid and been on some trips. Very early on, my motto became: Try everything at least once. If you like it, keep trying it.

The first time I took acid at a hippie commune there was a doctor with us to make sure that it was not done too recklessly. In these communes, your first acid trip was a rite of passage. It was almost an initiation you had to go through in order to be accepted. It was part of a general shedding of your old life, designed to make your past seem very remote. It wasn't about partying—it was part of a series of experiments, under observation almost. These hippie communes were all about creative and personal growth, a celebration of expression, the total opposite of how growth and expression had been stunted in Spanish Town. This was a time when there was a sudden rash of substitute certainties to compensate for the battering traditional forms of authority—parental, religious, and political—had taken in the previous decade. There were new cult religions, emergent self-help movements, and the hippie communities filled with those seeking more abstract, authority-questioning faiths.

The fact that acid was illegal helped create a bond between those willing to take risks in exploring their psyches. It had only been illegal for a short time when I first took it—one day it was legal, and then the next day it wasn't. The illegality gave it a little more allure. It was first made illegal in California in 1966—other states followed two or three years later and the Comprehensive Drug Abuse Prevention and Control Act was passed in October 1970, making it illegal across the United States.

I was very open to trying new experiments in living. And when I took acid, it was as part of an orderly line of people in this rural hippie commune, where they grew their own food. It was the summer-stock spirit taken a few stages further. There was a creek to swim in, and we all slept together, dozens of friendly strangers. Everyone wore what would be seen on the outside as idiosyncratic clothing, and there were no watches, no schedule at all—which was ideal for me. I hadn't really had anything secure on which to base normalcy, so this way of living—one that revolved around sharing, intimacy, being concerned for others—seemed as realistic if not more so than anything else I had been shown. It was, at least for a short while, a real attempt to create a paradise, a joyous center of peace and love and expanded consciousness. And it was supervised; it wasn't a wild free-for-all. It felt safe, which I think helps when it comes to taking LSD.

When the acid came out, there would be a doctor present, the equivalent of a Timothy Leary, with whom I became close friends much later. He was a major, optimistic factor in believing there was a legitimate use for the drug, that it was something therapeutic and transformative. He thought the way it interacted with the nervous system was natural—what he considered unnatural was "four years at Harvard, and the Bible . . . and . . . Sunday School teachings." He'd established the Psychedelic Research Foundation at Harvard in 1960, was dismissed by Harvard three years later, and in 1966 founded the League of Spiritual Development, with LSD as the sacrament. Leary was in favor of these controlled settings, sincerely believing that psychedelic drugs should be approached in a serious, scientific manner for psychological and spiritual enlightenment.

In the hippie commune, with all this outside space, where we would beat overturned canoes like they were drums, you could feel the change, a roll of the wave at the right time for me. I needed to break free, and there was this movement, all about breaking free, happening all around me at the same time, to take me with it. We would queue up, drop a tab, and the doctor would safely guide us through the trip. It was like a clinical trial, with a bit of anarchy thrown in.

Here, again, I was the first in my family to try something, and acid would have absolutely been considered poison by my parents. It is very difficult to explain what happened to me on that first trip, because the only people who really know are the ones who really know.

I remember walking up to a wall and walking into it and it was full of flowers. The petals spun like sparks. A maze of trees headed off infinitely in every direction. Fireflies scattered through the grass. I could hear the earth breathing: There was an eternity between breaths. I became a naked winged woman perched at the prow of a ship, the figurehead of a ship, embodying its spirit, the woman, eyes bright, that they put there to calm gales and storms, and the ship was parting not water but snakes of some sort, serpents and writhing creatures, and this ship I was at the head of would break through; it was wet and turbulent, but not like the sea, and I was slicing through all this mysterious motion, powering through the snakes guiding the ship to safety. Pirates used to think a naked woman onboard a ship was good luck.

I remember wanting to come down because it was going on for too long. Your brain gets tired after a while, all these fantastic images of enormous plasticity, the kaleidoscopic play of colors, all these patterns that seem to have self-awareness. You want to sleep but you can't. A little panic. More panic. You begin to shiver. At what must have been the peak of it all, it was like I was going too fast, like when I was on skates careering down that hill in Syracuse. I couldn't keep up with what was happening, what had just happened, what was about to happen. There was the secret of the universe. Right in front of me. Being whispered in my ear from across the water. Then I fell over on my skates. The world rushed into me. Through me. As if it would take me away with it. The doctor talked me through that. I remember cuddling with somebody. A pulse against my skin. I could see right through whoever was next to me. You couldn't really have sex—it's not for sex, acid. I was too high to do anything sexual. We were all bodies laid next to each other and rolling around, but sex was not part of the trip. It's not physical. It's all for the mind, hints of the vastness of consciousness, how much is in there, and out there.

I remember us all going out for ice cream outside the commune, among all these very straight country people. They were like, *Get your gun—who are these weirdos invading our town?* We bought some ice cream and never ate it. We watched it melt in our hands. It was fascinating to watch the ice cream melt, seeing it beyond our normal, limited, and narrow senses. It was like Dalí's clock. Acid intensifies what is real to such an extent it doesn't seem real. You understand how the universe is not static or stationary but moves all the time. All the local people had this *get the hell out of our town* look on their faces.

It was a super-trip pill—STP—a three-day trip. It was not the strength of the pill, it was the amount of time. You don't know it is going to be three days when you take it. Your whole perception of time is altered. It could have been an hour, a day, a month, a hundred years. It could have been five thousand years. It was now, and then it was later, and now it was beginning. To some extent you dive into reality, not away from it. And you can go so deep into the experience, so deep into what might ultimately be more real than the real, that coming back into this world seems distorted.

I have had a couple of friends who took acid and never came down. They are still on their trip! I have two girlfriends like that; they don't know each other, but they are lost to this world in a similar way. Very sweet, but totally not in reality at all. So nice, but still seeing flowers and solid things melting into themselves. They're stuck having thoughts about thoughts about thoughts.

You have to come down, otherwise you are permanently trapped in a parallel universe. You have to be careful how you come back so that you properly get your bearings. Your ego can get smashed beyond repair if you're not careful. I was lucky really that my first trip was so carefully monitored under the care of a doctor, like a genuine experiment. Otherwise, it could easily have permanently messed with my mind, so you might say it was wise psychedelic usage.

I still walk around having the kind of grandiose thoughts you might have on an acid trip, but without being perpetually inside the trip. That's a good balance—becoming aware of how far your mind can expand but understanding that it doesn't have to expand all the time. Taking acid under supervision taught me to be careful of true extremes. Extreme, but in moderation. Crazy out there, but within reason. Take nothing in your body without being completely fussy. Be very aware.

And that three-day trip taught me to be my own shrink.

I think taking acid was a very important part of my emotional growth, of becoming myself, which was my mission. The mental exercise was good for me. It's like achieving accelerated higher consciousness through ingesting sacred plants, like the old Indians of Mexico and the American Southwest would do in order to expand their minds. The European missionaries would call the visions the Indians had "fantasies of the devil." After all the God I had been subjected to, this was exactly what I needed. My eyes were opened, as it says in Genesis, and I had a better understanding of good and evil than all those hours and hours with the Bible had given me.

Acid helped release me from an accumulation of illogical customs and traditions. In a world that favors mind-dulling substances—alcohol, narcotics, tobacco—it is amazing to sample something that is mind-expanding and that stimulates mental processes rather than suppressing them. For someone who needed to break free of Mas P, the abuser with a holy veneer, it was absolutely perfect.

I am quite psychic. I don't know if it was because of the acid, or if I was born with it. When I am plugged in I can be scary psychic. Knowing when something is going to happen, when not to get in the elevator—I get a strong feeling. I remember telling everyone traveling with me to get off a plane once. We were all strapped in. The plane was taxiing, ready for takeoff. Everyone looked at me like I was crazy. And I said, "Okay, if you want to stay . . . but I'm getting off." The plane never left the ground—there were four attempts, and it never made it.

Stuff like that happens to me, not a lot, but every now and then. If I feel something, I feel it strongly, and I follow the instinct. I think the acid enriched my senses, made them all seem more sensitive. Heightened my emotional and mental processes, or at least made me aware that they could be heightened and accelerated. I think the strong feelings I have about things derive from those acid trips. They do make you into a different person. You see other possibilities.

I was born. Again. This is me. Turn me loose.

I applied to be a Playboy bunny in Philly after seeing an advert in the Philadelphia *Evening Bulletin*. It was one of the few ways a girl could earn more money than standing all day in a shop or sitting down all day in an office. I didn't think of it as demeaning; I wanted to try it out, to see what it was like. Being in contact with people I had never been allowed anywhere near before intrigued me. It appeared to be glamorous and looked like it might be fun, for a while. I thought of it as a way of assuming another temporary identity, to make me even more elusive. I didn't see it as a way of submitting to men, rather as a way of getting more information about how the world worked. And I didn't plan to stick with it for long. It was the kind of job you could move into and move out of: an opportunity. And I was looking for opportunity.

Being a Playboy Bunny seemed a classier step up from dancing in go-go clubs at poky hotels. Ultimately, my goal was still the theater, and not to be stuck anywhere, and the theater seemed to be the best way to achieve that. Being a Bunny was a way of making steady money without interfering with the auditions.

Tom had suggested I model and make some money while trying to do the theater thing. At first, I would commute with Sam on his Harley-Davidson between Philadelphia and New York to go-sees with agencies and photographers. Eventually, I learned to ride myself so Sam didn't always have to bring me. I crashed once, but I wasn't going too fast. There was no new scar.

I would be at New York auditions ready and alert at 6 A.M. The discipline was always there—that never goes away. I can ignore it for a while, but never completely.

There was one African-American photographer, Tony Barboza, whom I used to visit early in the morning to shoot. I stopped by one day with my portfolio, as I would frequently do to get photographers interested. I was collecting photographs of myself as quickly as I could. It was before I got any work, and I was grateful to any photographer who showed an interest. Luckily, Tony also turned out to be a very good photographer with an interest in African history, and he helped me a lot in my early years. My first professional job, for *Essence*, the monthly magazine for African-American women first published in 1970, was through Tony. I am photographed with the psychedelic soul group the Chambers Brothers wearing tight, studded brown leather, looking very badass, like a sister of Melvin Van Peebles.

Tony was a hardworking photographer, as well as a historian and an artist, and he really liked me. He said that I wasn't a classic beauty, but had a very interesting face. He took photographs of me to study my face, but he had time only in the morning to do some tests before his day job. He would take pictures of me in the Afro, wearing dramatic, almost tribal white marks on my face, and sometimes wearing very little. As he would say, I was sweet, but not shy about letting him photograph me nude. I was a nudist! I didn't think there was anything lewd about posing nude. I didn't think of it as being sexual at all. The photos were not dirty; they were very sensitive and exploratory.

They weren't only nudes. Tony took a lovely, unsparing and very peaceful close-up of my face, lips slightly parted in either defiance or invitation, that was the cover of a book called *Black Beauty* by Ben Arogundade. It was one of the first—if not *the* first—professional photographs taken of me, a moment of birth. I am not looking behind. I am looking straight ahead.

Here I am. What have you got?

I sent one of those test nudes by Tony as part of my application to become a Bunny—after all, you needed to show your assets to work there. They weren't pinup photos; they were highly stylized and atmospheric. But you could see what you needed to see.

There was a local businessman called Harry Jay Katz, a very rich, self-made Philadelphia guy, a well-known libertine, bon vivant, and man about town. If anything was happening in Philly nightlife, he was at the center of it, and he was going to open a Playboy Club there after spending some time in Chicago with Hugh Hefner.

He made the papers when he showed his wife the pictures of the nude girls he was going to select to work there. He got about 1,500 applications, and mine was one of them. Few got more press coverage for doing so little. He was ahead of his time in that way. The problem was, ever confident of succeeding in his license application, he had already rented property for the club on a street where all the government buildings were, right by city hall, and the local dignitaries weren't happy. Citing some problems with his liquor license, the police shut him down before he even began. He had to fight, jump through all sorts of hoops, to try and get the club open.

He saw my picture, and he liked it, and I went for an interview, under my dance name, Grace Mendoza, which became a problem for me later. I used Grace Mendoza when I left home after summer stock, in case my parents were looking for me. I didn't want to disappoint them. I didn't want them to know what I was up to. There were little photos of the go-go dancers where I worked in the newspaper advertisements. Even though there was no way that would make it to Syracuse, I wasn't taking any chances. I was in hiding.

After I became well known, as Grace Jones, Harry Katz did an interview, saying I was not Grace Jones at all—I was Grace Mendoza. I just liked the sound of the name, which I think just came from being fluent in Spanish. No special reason, but I liked that it sounded a little Cuban. That's how he knew me. He thought that I had changed it to Jones from Mendoza. He thought he had discovered the real me. As if. Years later, when this interview appeared on the Internet, it mysteriously, instantly infected existing online information about me, saying I was born Grace Mendoza. Once, not long after 9/11, when I was renewing my passport in Syracuse, there was a lot of trouble—the officials, getting their information from the unreliable Wikipedia, had found out about my other name, there was confusion about my age because of the temp job I had when I was a teenager, and the FBI was called in. They figured I must be on the run or something. I was two or three people in one. There were Grace, Beverly, Jones, Mendoza, I was either twenty-one or twenty-five. My mom had to come down to the building where I went to get my passport and explain the misunderstanding. Luckily, she looked like someone you could trust, and she had her softening charms.

My Grace Mendoza dance act was different from the others because I had a whip. I think that was because of the whips hanging from the wall that we had to choose from when I was younger. Each girl had a specialty, and mine was taking charge of things using a whip. I was a demon with the whip. I cracked it hard, with a hell of a bang, in my tight, tiger-striped clothes. I'd bring it between my legs like a snake, wrap it around my neck, flick it fast toward the customers, with laser-eyed attitude, concentrating like a lion tamer. It was about as far from holy as I could get. Grace Mendoza could make your eyes water without even touching you, and on the local nightclub circuit I got pretty popular.

I got called to Mr. Katz's office. We should have called him Alley Katz. He liked the way I looked, had heard about my skill with a whip, and he explained that the Playboy Club wasn't open yet, but that he could use me while he got the office ready. He asked me if I would be his girl Friday, basically his assistant. The way he framed it, my job was to look pretty, act polite, answer the phones, make coffee, and be of general use.

I said, "I don't know how to make coffee."

He said, "Forget the coffee. Answer the phone, greet people. Can you do that?" I reckoned I could.

Later, I would start going to social things with him. He liked having someone decorative on his arm. It was really strange—they were like dates but not dates. We would go places together and my job was to look pretty. I did that for quite a while. I went to see Dionne Warwick with him once. It was all strictly business. I knew his family, his wife and kids. He never tried anything on me. I have no real idea what it was about. I think he simply liked me and wanted to hang out with me. We were just . . . friends. He'd take me home, all very proper, weirdly professional. I'd spend time with him and his family. He kept struggling to open the Playboy Club, struggling with the government, and in the end it never opened. I guess he was in his thirties, a lot older than me, very tall, and I figured he liked having me on his arm because I made him look good. Years later I would walk up red carpets into elite social occasions on the arm of Armani or Versace, and it all started with Harry.

He carried on operating around Philly for years, always on the make, looking for opportunities, opening clubs, trying to make money, meeting celebrities, having his picture taken with Sylvester Stallone, Bette Midler, Tom Selleck. I would run into him over the years, at the Grammys, at parties in New York. A newspaper piece reporting on his antics in the '90s was headlined "The Last Playboy." In 1995, he gained a little notoriety when a woman, a former teacher, Valerie Sheridan, was found dead in his hot tub after a long night of partying—he was cleared of any wrongdoing, but the rumors continued. Then, oddly, it was his son, David Bar Katz, a playwright, who found Philip Seymour Hoffman dead in Hoffman's New York City apartment.

I had another encounter with Philly legends while I lived in the city, an early episode in the complicated relationship I have with my own voice. I didn't think I had a voice at all at that time. I never believed in it as a voice. It was very deep and manly—it sounded like it was coming from another person.

I did an audition for Kenny Gamble and Leon Huff in Philadelphia during the period of going back and forth between Philly and New York on go-sees. I had no idea who they were until much later. They were about to become the monsters of the Philly sound with the Philadelphia International label, their version of Tamla Motown. I just thought it was an audition in front of some local musicians.

It taught me a lesson: to do my homework whenever these chances came up in the future. I walked into it without any idea how important this audition was, that they'd worked with Aretha Franklin and were making an album with Dusty Springfield. They hadn't had their big hits yet, hadn't been anointed the creators of the sound of Philadelphia, but I didn't pay enough attention to what a great opportunity this was.

I think it also had something to do with me not thinking of myself as a singer, since what I really wanted to do was act in the theater. Singing seemed like a distraction, and I treated it as such.

Their productions of the O'Jays and Harold Melvin and the Blue Notes, featuring rich, jazz-tinged strings, prominent hi-hat, and snappier bass lines, pushing the macho rock guitars a little behind the scenes, paved the way for disco. Ironically, the producer of my first album a few years later, Tom Moulton, used some of the session musicians who were part of that pool with the name MFSB (Mother, Father, Sister, Brother) that Gamble and Huff used at the Sigma Sound in Philadelphia. I would eventually return there.

Tom Figenshu took me to the audition. He knew them somehow, or managed to hustle his way in, and he wanted me to record the song I sang in his play, "Rooms with No Sun." It was a lovely song. I would like to sing it now, if I could remember it.

At the audition, I had no confidence at all. It was like someone threw me into deep water and I couldn't swim. Tom believed in me, but it was like I could do it only for Tom. At home, or in front of him, when I sang, I did it without any inhibition. As soon as I got up in front of other people I couldn't do it. I immediately had nerves: *What are they going to think? I'm not really a singer!*

The backing singers, the Sweeties, were hanging around—smoking, laughing, drinking, and looking very casual, like they weren't paying attention. And then as soon as they opened their mouths, these powerful soul voices would effortlessly pour out. I was shaking with nerves, and had to fight to get in character, though I still didn't really know what my character was. The enormous effort I had to put into singing was silly, but there was so much fear I had to conquer. In front of new people I felt vulnerable and useless.

I totally blew the audition. Tom wasn't there in the room with me. It was me and Gamble and Huff and their musicians. If I had known who they were, I would have freaked out even more. I was like this without even knowing how successful they were. The pianist started to play, and I couldn't sing the song. There was this uncontrollable quivering of my voice. A hoarse rasp squirted out and then pretty much nothing. Maybe I should have taken a pill. Maybe a quaalude would have relaxed me. But it was extremely painful and embarrassing.

I wasted their time, and those guys were used to voices, serious voices, singers who shot shivers down the spine. I fell apart. That was the end of that. There was no *Okay, not bad, go away, have some lessons, and come back in a year.* It was like, no eye contact, *There's the door. Bye-bye.* Forgotten as soon as I was out the door. Brutal. That side of the business always was and always will be.

They probably thought I had something on Tom Figenshu. A year or two later they had a huge hit with Billy Paul called "Me and Mrs. Jones"—no relation to me, or to my failed audition. In the meantime, one of my very first commercial jobs as a model was appearing on the cover of Billy Paul's *Ebony Woman* album, Afro still intact, staring straight at the camera, looking like the kind of woman who would never let nerves get the better of her. I don't remember if I did the audition before or after that sleeve, but there is no way Gamble and Huff would have thought that unflappable woman on the cover of one of their label's albums was the flustered, hopeless singer Figenshu had sent along.

Tom realized I had panicked. The Gamble and Huff audition was like a test—and I hate tests. I always did well at school until it came to the tests, and then I would panic, freeze up at the word *begin*. I would have A's during the year in most of my subjects and then fall apart during the end of year exams. Some people are very good at taking tests. I am the worst.

The next time I felt anything like that was when I performed with Luciano Pavarotti decades later—except that time I really prepared for three months, getting ready like it was the heavyweight boxing championship of the world. I concentrated on nothing else. I didn't smoke, and no one could smoke around me. I stopped drinking. I became transcendentally pure. For me it was the equivalent of climbing Everest. I thought about nothing else. But by then I was a seasoned performer and I knew what it took to make my voice work, and how to make it work under the most intense pressure. I had learned from experiences like that abortive one with Gamble and Huff. I had found my character.

———

Even when I was with Sam, I still spent time with Tom Figenshu and looked up to him. There were always boyfriends and lovers, and then at the same time, mentors, collaborators, very close friends helping me who were not lovers. This pattern started with Tom. Certainly I was clinging to the hope that Tom would help me with the ambition I now had to break into theater.

I remember saying to Tom that I wanted to leave Philly. I was running out of patience with the city, bruised by the awful audition, and not making it as a Playboy Bunny. I didn't want to go back home—I couldn't bear the thought of having to go back to my parents, having failed in what I set out to do. I asked him what he thought I should do. I needed to work. My options were: work, in whatever way necessary; continue living with Sam and let him support me; or go back home. The last was not an option. And I was on the verge of leaving Sam, even if he did let me work semi-naked in go-go clubs and took care of me. I wanted to make it on my own and do everything for myself. I didn't want to rely on anyone. I never wanted a guy to take care of me. Help me, yes, but never, ever pay for me.

Tom said, "Well, I am going to New York to look for work; maybe you should move there permanently. Focus on modeling to make some money—you have high cheekbones, a strong look." But he made it clear he did not want to babysit me. Tom knew I was crazy about him. That's when he had to tell me he was gay. I never saw him in a gay relationship, never saw him with a guy, but he made it very clear he was gay.

But he continued to steer me, even if from a distance. I wanted to do theater. I auditioned for a production of *Hair* and was called back many times. They liked my look, but I didn't have confidence in my voice. I opened my mouth, and you could hear the sound of self-doubt. The Gamble and Huff incident had really not helped.

I loved what Tom was doing; he seemed very ahead of his time. He was very inspiring for me, and helped set me in a new direction. He knew his stuff, but when characters like him go from the smaller town to the big city they have trouble. A big fish in Syracuse, making things happen, drowned in New York City. He couldn't make it there. I'd followed him there, but it didn't take long before he wanted to cut me loose. He didn't want me hanging around his neck, and I suppose the Gamble and Huff incident made him lose patience. Maybe he found someone else, a lover, or another pupil to nurture, or both.

One day he was found dead in the street on his own, still relatively young. I have no idea how it happened. It was in the newspaper, very shocking and sudden, no definitive explanation. He seemed to walk off into the distance into a crowd until he was swallowed up and he was no more.

Once I made up my mind—*I am choosing this life, the life of an artist*—I set about figuring out what I needed to do to get to a new place. I always say to my son that to live the life of an artist you must always be traveling to new places and moving around. You need to see for yourself what is out there and make your own versions of what you see. I don't think people see things the same way, so it is important to see the world, and show it through your eyes. And I'd decided it was important to see the world through my eyes, not my mother's eyes or my father's eyes.

I wanted to bust things open and see how they worked. The world became my candy store. I decided I would travel everywhere. I was strong, but I never wanted to feel vulnerable—the link with Tom was what I needed. I don't need the whole church; just one person can make the difference. I needed to be single-minded and on my own, but I also needed know that if I got in trouble, there was one person I could call. Wherever I went, on my own terms, there would always be a sense that there was one person I could rely on if things got out of hand. I was independent, but connected to some form of lifeline.

I moved to New York, after all this driving back and forth from Philly on the bike. I always felt if it wasn't moving, it wasn't happening. If it's not flowing, try something else, find somewhere else, move on. There is no point in banging your head against a brick wall. Sam felt he was losing me. He didn't want me to leave Philly. I think he thought that once I got to New York, I would want something else that would involve someone else. He was very helpful with all the commutes, but there was a moment when he put the reins on me. For me that is always a signal.

The relationship had been going on for so long, in one way the next step would have been marriage and children, but I wasn't ready for that. It was too early for that to happen. It was a tough breakup. We had been through a lot together, and we were good together. It was not the right time. I was not my mother, getting married at sixteen. My family all loved Sam. They thought he was kind and caring, and he was. I needed more than that, though.

He was very hurt when I left him. I didn't know how to handle that then. Sam was always afraid to lose me, but in a way that then made me want to move on. I felt held back, so that the relationship could not be sustained. There was a certain point where he didn't want to go forward, and I didn't want to go backward. I think I learned from that. We could have stayed friends, but he became very bitter, and then it was very hard to stay in touch. I guess he stayed in Philly and did his thing. I had places to go, people to see, discoveries to make.

Even though we loved each other, we started fighting all the time, and then we'd take drugs to deal with the tension. I remember we had some friends in the East Village, and we even tried to live there, but it was Alphabet City, out of the way, almost falling off the edge of Manhattan, and there was a lot of heroin about.

You start to do a little smack on the weekends, you try it out, you hang out with old friends who are taking it, but you don't want it to take over your life. I tried it, but it made me vomit. It wasn't for me, luckily. It wasn't the Rolls-Royce through heaven some people talk about for me; it was annoying numbness. I tried, because I wanted to try everything. *Well*, I thought, *maybe one day I will play the role of a heroin addict. Maybe I should try it.* I was living the method acting technique before I even had a role where I would need to know what it was like to take heroin. Try everything once and see what it's like, just in case.

I was thinking very much about stage acting, more than about film. I got called up for a lot of films, but my accent was too Jamaican. I could not get rid of my accent enough for me to be what they wanted. I had the Afro, but I didn't have that American black accent. It wasn't enough to only have the look. I just didn't sound hip and Harlem enough when I opened my mouth.

My girlfriend Marcia McBroom got every single role I was convinced I could have had if I hadn't had this mixed-up accent. She appeared as the Carrie Nation soul sister drummer Petronella "Pet" Danforth frolicking in a haystack in *Beyond the Valley of the Dolls* in 1970, and I didn't. The director Russ Meyer would always tease her that she had the smallest boobs of anyone he had ever worked with. Helmut Newton would have the same complaint about me. (One of my early nicknames was Olive Oyl, and I was also known as "Nothing in the Middle.") Marcia was in *Jesus Christ Superstar*, one of the people screaming, "Crucify him! Crucify him!" at the end of the show, and I wasn't. Her sister cowrote "Pull Up to the Bumper" with me. Her mother still comes to my concerts and pretends to be by mother. She worked at the United Nations and was a good friend of Malcolm X. Crazy family.

With the theater, I was almost accepted for roles a lot of the time. It was always almost. Almost, almost, almost. I was close, but it wasn't happening. I was doing an awful lot of go-sees for an awful lot of productions needing flower children and offbeat black hippie chicks, but I never ended up getting a role. I kept trying, though. I was unstoppable.

I spent about a year in New York, did the modeling, carried on auditioning. I was with an agency called Black Beauty. They were the first agency I tried, and Richard Roundtree was with them. I stayed with them about a month. They did commercials and catalog work, and I was seen as being too exotic for that kind of work. They said, *Your face doesn't fit. You are really black and your lips are big but your nose is too thin and your eyes are too slanty. You won't get the catalog work that brings in the big bucks.* Even then catalog modeling paid sixty dollars an hour, enough to keep you for a week.

Catalog modeling is awful photography artistically, using the same

light for everybody, whatever their complexion. You would be like part
of a herd—*Next cow, next cow, next cow.* It paid well, though, but I didn't
get any jobs, which was very frustrating. I had found an apartment and
needed to pay the rent. I wanted to do my thing and pay my way and
not feel that I was being preached at by my family. My mom kept saying
I should marry a nice preacher, be the first lady of the church, like her.
That was so far from where I wanted to be.

I left Black Beauty, and I went to an exotic agency called Wilhelmina
Models, opened in 1967 by the former Dutch-born model Wilhelmina
Cooper, and her husband, Bruce, who had been an executive producer
of *The Tonight Show Starring Johnny Carson.* She had been with the Ford
agency and had modeled for ten years, which was a lot back then, appearing on twenty-seven *Vogue* covers. She was one of the last stars of
the couture era, but modern enough to compete with the new British
breed represented by Twiggy and Jean Shrimpton. Faye Dunaway played
her in the film *Gia*, about a lesbian model, Gia Marie Carangi, discovered by Wilhelmina, played by Angelina Jolie. Gia was put on the cover
of *Cosmopolitan* by notorious, powerful fashion photographer Francesco
Scavullo, who would help invent this unspontaneous but positive, desir-
able *Cosmo* look that seemed triumphant but hid harsher truths. It was
all about coldly manipulating vulnerability and neediness to create an
illusion of perfection. It was where phoniness was ingeniously glossed
over to create slick commercial fantasy. Gia had a wholesome, serene
look but a torrid private life, and was one of the first recorded people
to die from AIDS due to her addiction to heroin; the shots of her with
haunted hollow eyes and a body on the edge of emaciation were an
early warning of what became known as "heroin chic."

All the most famous exotic models came from Wilhelmina's agency,
and it was specifically set up for the kinds of girls who were not considered normal. Models like Lauren Hutton, with the gap in her teeth.
Having been a supermodel in her day, Wilhelmina really understood
how hypercompetitive modeling was, as well as how merciless, and
she didn't have the everyday-girl-next-door agency. She had an eye for
unusual new looks, and for different kinds of personalities, the sort that

often lead to trouble. The Ford Models agency had the girl-next-door look. I would be their worst nightmare. I did try Ford, and I was rejected with barely a second glance. Wilhelmina herself didn't accept me straightaway. She kept me working with photographers, and she told me to keep coming back with new pictures. She wanted me to work on my look with the photographers, discover for myself what kind of model I wanted to be.

Finally, she said yes and took me on. She kept encouraging me to find out what it was I was going to be. In order to find it, I went very, very extreme, almost too far. I shaved my head and my eyebrows, which was a big mistake. She was very upset. At one point I used to have a lot of hair that came down too low at the top of my face, almost like a shadow. In my photographs, I would notice this fine down on my forehead. I decided I would get rid of all the hair, not thinking that I was supposed to ask permission. You were expected to check with your agent before you cut your hair. I obviously didn't have the catalog look; I wasn't getting those jobs. I thought it wouldn't matter if I made my extreme look even more over-the-top; I thought that it would actually help.

Wilhelmina was outraged at how brutal I now appeared. From the outside, it looked like quite an aggressive statement. *What the hell did you do?! We can't sell that! It was already too much that your nose is too small, your lips too big, and your skin too dark.* Now I looked ready to kill someone.

She made me wear wigs while my head was shaved, to cover up the impertinence, but I hated them and didn't recognize myself when I looked in a mirror. I wanted my hair short. I didn't like how I had to straighten it when it was longer—the process was very painful—and the Afro was looking passé. I liked how having it short was a threat to people because it made me look so confrontational. I didn't want to make people feel comfortable when they were with me, because I was always wanting to test people, provoke them into a reaction. Ever since I had the Afro in Syracuse, before it had become a fad, I liked how the way I wore my hair caused a reaction.

The biggest reaction came when I cut it to the bone and revealed more of my black skin. It made me look hard, in a soft world. It made me look more like a thing than a person, but that was how I had felt I was treated growing up—as a thing, without feeling, an object, not even human. Having felt that way as a child, it felt normal for to me to shave away my hair and acknowledge that emotionless thingness that had been pressed into me. Without fully understanding it at the time, I savored the response to what I did to myself, by breaking certain laws about how I was meant to behave and look, as a model, a girl, a daughter, an American, a West Indian, a human being.

My shaved head made me look more abstract, less tied to a specific race or sex or tribe, but was also a way of moving across those things, belonging while at the same time not belonging. I was black, but not black; woman, but not woman; American, but Jamaican; African, but science fiction. It set me outside and beyond in some sort of slipstream, and instinctively, I liked that it was a way of expressing that I was flexible, that I could adapt to different situations, and that I was versatile, capable of changing who I was and what I was doing depending on who I was working with and in what context. It was about not being uniform. It was about change, and changing my mind, and through it I could express how I was always becoming someone else.

Shaving my head led directly to my first orgasm. This is because I am fairly sure the man I had my first orgasm with was Andre, my hairdresser from Cinandre, a huge salon at Fifty-Seventh Street and Madison Avenue. It was such a revelation, almost traumatic, the very first, that most of the details have been wiped away, other than the tidal rush of feelings, but a little bit of detective work, rummaging through my memories, has led to Andre as the prime suspect. His salon was where I was sent to make sure that when my hair started to grow back I didn't go ahead and shave it off again. He was someone who Wilhelmina thought could soften the hard edges and at least make me look more like a model than a marine.

At the edge of the Caribbean Sea. April 2015, Alligator Head, Port Antonio, Jamaica. *(Greg Gorman)*

Honeymoon in Bali, looking like it's the 1950s, with my one and only husband, Atila. *(Grace Jones Private Life Collection)*

My mom's mom, who we knew as Aunt Ceta, who raised me while my mom was in Syracuse, on her first visit to America. What a face! *(Grace Jones Private Life Collection)*

Invitation to my mom and dad's 59th wedding anniversary in 2006.
(Grace Jones Private Life Collection)

September 17, 1947
Happy 59ᵗ Wedding Anniversary

Bishop Robert W. & Evg. Marjorie Jones

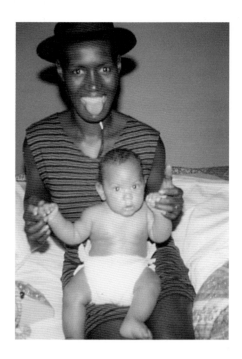

ABOVE: With brand-new Paulo at home in New York on 54th Street. *(Grace Jones Private Life Collection)*

ABOVE RIGHT: Great-grandmother Walters—we called her Ma— watering the garden in Spanish Town. *(Grace Jones Private Life Collection)*

RIGHT: It was arranged that photographs of the children would be sent to Mom and Dad in Syracuse every so often so that they could see us growing up. This one is taken in Spanish Town. Back row, L-R: Chris (then known as Patrick), and Noel. Front row, L-R: Pam, me holding a doll, and Max. We tried to smile to look as though we were happy, but that wasn't always the case. *(Grace Jones Private Life Collection)*

A one-man show. A red curtain, an accordion,
a minimal staircase, one leg up. Voila— theater!
And a Grammy nomination. *(Adrian Boot / www.urbanimage.TV)*

ABOVE: All Saints Church and All Saints School, together the center of my early life in Spanish Town, Jamaica. *(Grace Jones Private Life Collection)*

RIGHT: My supreme mom, Marjorie. *(Grace Jones Private Life Collection)*

BELOW: A Jones family reunion, with Paulo at top left. *(Grace Jones Private Life Collection)*

Ibiza in the 1980s, getting ready to head into the water or into outer space. *(Grace Jones Private Life Collection)*

Hugging the High Priest—a Polaroid of me loving Timothy Leary at some point in time. *(Grace Jones Private Life Collection)*

Lounging in a restaurant in New York, who knows when and where, dressed to solve a mystery. *(John Carmen)*

Acting natural in a 1970s disco setting wearing my specially designed Studio 54 New Year's Eve Norma Kamali unitard.
(John Carmen)

With Paulo,
watching whales off
the California coast,
just after my
breakup with Dolph.
*(Grace Jones Private Life
Collection)*

ABOVE: First lady of the church,
my mom, Marjorie, and my dad,
Bishop Robert Jones. *(Grace Jones
Private Life Collection)*

RIGHT: Bishop Walters and his wife,
Zina, forever in their Sunday best.
(Grace Jones Private Life Collection)

These days they say DJs are God. Back then it was hairdressers who were God. Like Vidal Sassoon. All the celebrities would go to hairstylists like Andre. He was more than a hairdresser. He was an artist and a photographer, very experimental. He cut the hair of lots of models and actresses, and he invented the Farrah Fawcett flick. It was decided he would know what to do with me.

He definitely knew what to do with me.

Andre relished this instinct that I had to find a different place to be, even when it came to my hair, and he treated my short hair like a canvas. It was very short, but there were ways he could change how it looked, and instinctively this was what I was after, constant change. It would be a key part of my overall performance. My hair could be adjusted, changed, edited, in much the same way that later my whole body would be treated.

He was the first one to style my short hair. He was a wizard with scissors. He treated my hair as though he was producing a sculpture, with incredible attention to detail. It wasn't quite the famous flattop that came later, but it was on the way. He let it grow out a little, and then cut what little hair there was into shapes, designs, grooves. He cut a little skier and had ski marks coming down from the back of my head to the front. He shaped my hair above the forehead so that it was very precise. He created partings in my hair by shaving a thin, straight line. He would shave out a groove and then paint it. That was my look, and it became the basis of all my looks, and it is a look you see on so many people to this day, especially rich young black male footballers and athletes. Andre was the first one to paint my naked body, years before Keith Haring would. He would paint white branches all over me.

He was like a magnet for models. Very charming, a trendsetter, he liked trying new things, and practiced photography on the side. Actresses and models found that combination irresistible. Andre's was where you went for the most modern cut, whatever you looked like. He had long blond hair, and he acted really cool, very sure of himself. I hung out in the salon. A few of us would stick around after it was shut and we'd play music and smoke and take photographs.

I suppose it's not surprising that my first orgasm was with Andre. His fingers on my scalp working their magic helped, and it didn't take much for that to lead to great sex. I'd never had sex like that before. It was sex from another era, another solar system. It still started with the mouth but it ended up beyond the body. It made me feel like I was falling backward in time. He was very open-minded and creative, and that seemed to spill over into the sex. He bent me out of shape.

It was so memorable an event, such a life-changing occurrence, that it blasted through time, and it doesn't come to me instantly when it was . . . '77. No, '76. Actually, '73. It was before I did my first album, before I went to Paris. It could have been '72 or '71. Like I say, we weren't wearing watches, we weren't keeping time, or recording every moment like you do now. I do know that it was very quickly after I went to New York after Sam Miceli and started to take some test photographs. That means it was more where the 1970s began than where they ended.

Not only do I not remember the time, the hour, the date, I also don't remember where. Somewhere in space, in a space. I remember there was a before orgasm, and an after orgasm, but other details remain fuzzy. If you don't know what an orgasm is like, when it happens, it finally dawns on you, *Oh, this is an orgasm!* It's like . . . hold your breath, close your eyes . . . AAAAGHGAAASGGHHFHAAAGHGGHHGHAAAASDFF-GGGGAAAAAAAAAGRGRAAAAAAAAAAAAAGGGGGGGGGGH-HHHHHHHHHHHHHHHHHHHHHHHHHHHHHHHHH. It's a heart-attack moment. Am I still alive? SHSHSHSHSHSHSHSHSH-SHSHSHSHSHS-HSSHSHSHSHSHSHSHSHSHSHSHSHSSHSHSH. If I die now, I die knowing the most amazing feeling of what an orgasm is like. We swallowed each other up inside the body of love. Fireflies scattered through the sky.

I was with Sam for such a long time, and I loved him, but I had no idea this was what sex could lead to. Maybe he wasn't patient enough and I took too long to come. With him, it was all very tidy; with Andre, the whole sweaty thing was riddled with surprises and sensationally messy. Maybe there was still a sense that women weren't supposed to enjoy sex, that the sexual freedom of the '60s and '70s was ultimately not about the liberation of women, but a way for men to have more sexual access to a greater number of women. It was not freedom at all, and women who had learned, or been trained over time, to be more orgasmic were still as held back as they had been by inhibitions, fears, traditional female roles.

Maybe Sam was a selfish lover, and I didn't know enough to know that. I didn't even know what to fake, or what that would mean. You don't know what an orgasm's like until you have one. With Sam, I thought, *Well, this must be it,* but I could still feel a sense of frustration—*Is that it? I don't know. Well, where's the big mind-shaking flesh-melting bang?* My imagination and my body told me that this could not be it, that there must surely be something at the center of all this, at the end, that made it more than him going somewhere, and me going nowhere. He was somewhere else, going up, higher and higher, and I was staying put, flatlining.

With Andre, ironically, it wasn't selfish. It was unselfish sex, not unselfish love. He wanted me to experience the feeling, even if really it was because it made him feel good. Then he would tell me how I was the only girl in the world he wanted to give mind-blowing orgasms to. Maybe he had a better sense of timing, in all sorts of ways. I think it took a lot of patience, on both our parts, that first time. And a bit of Barry White and the Love Unlimited Orchestra.

And there were tears, once I had my first orgasm. Tears, because I thought of Sam, and how we had been through so much, and been so close, but this hadn't happened with him. There was also guilt, of course, bloody, messy guilt. Guilt because I was enjoying the outlandish lusciousness of sex. I still cry when I have a big orgasm. That goes down well with whoever's taken me there. I burst into tears, and it is from a combination of pleasure and guilt. But I've learned to take the pleasure and kick the guilt to one side.

Maybe I hadn't had orgasms before because of all that religion growing up. *God is going to kill me now that I've had an orgasm. That's why my heart is beating so fast.* And inside, there was Beverly, thinking, *I shouldn't have pleasure.* Beverly and Grace are pulling against each other at those moments—Beverly is saying, *I don't want to go there,* and Grace is saying, *I want to go there, I really want to go there, let me fucking go there.* It reaches a point of: *No, yes, no, yes, no, yes.* It's a cosmic tug-of-war. A cosmos grounded in divine order versus a cosmos characterized by constant change. No, yes, no, yes, no. Beverly thinks I'm going to die. Grace thinks I'm going to feel more alive than I ever have before. It's a matter of life and death.

I became very close to Andre. We were together for one whole summer, staying many times in his house in the country outside the city. Eventually I found out he had a long-term girlfriend, and had been keeping me a secret, just as she was a secret from me. He had been making sure he kept me away from anyone who might tell me. I found out because she found out about me and came looking for me. She was in a club I liked to go to, Better Days, and she had found out about me and was looking for me with a big knife.

Better Days was on Forty-Ninth Street with a huge circular bar—they played great music, R & B, Stax, Motown, very early, edgy disco when it was what would now be known as cutting-edge. It was a place for hard-core dance junkies, very much a gay club, guys dancing with each other, working up a sweat to a beat that represented threat, and there would be blacks, Hispanics, swinging couples, serious freaks, amazing-looking girls with prominent Adam's apples. A lot of super-charged whistle-blowing, and after midnight it would get crazy in there as though everyone was finding themselves by forgetting who they were. It was one of those clubs creating the template for what was about to come, but the sound system was less sophisticated, the light show fairly feeble, and it was pretty grimy, from when New York was rougher, tougher, more boarded up, but more anxiously alive on the edge of its nerves. The kind of place where a rival might come looking for you with a big knife.

The first Barry White album came out when Andre and I were frequenting Better Days, and we won a dance competition dancing to "Love's Theme," where you could hear disco falling into place when there were still traces of gospel, before the beat got too rigid and the strings too syrupy. Back then, when you danced to this sharply syncopated, rampantly suggestive music, there was trucking, there was the hustle, and if you were a couple, you would be apart—it was club dancing—and then you would come together, not like in ballroom dancing, but raunchier. It became "our song," the soundtrack to our intense romance, the classy strings, the chop-chop wah-wah guitars, the pulsating beat, the schmoozing earth-moving bass. Really, it was the soundtrack to Andre's lover-man seduction techniques—he was a wonderful dancer, moved so fluidly, it was such a turn-on, and it was meant to be a turn-on.

He knew how to manipulate circumstances and take advantage of his position and his talent. He'd been around. He looked the part. His tightly clad hips swung like he knew it, and he wanted you to know it too.

His girlfriend was after me big-time, with a big-deal knife, and a whole lot of vengeance. She was called Clare. That's all I knew about her. Someone warned me to get the hell out of the club, and I slipped out of a side door. It was heartbreaking finding out that he wasn't committed to me—I had thought Andre and I were seriously in love. That country house was where he obviously took his other girlfriends, and I realized there must be other girls. He was spinning plates. Spinning models. We even went to Barbados together, and we did a lot of spinning there.

What was different with Andre was, whether he was faking or not, he had this way of seeming to focus only on you . . . maybe he reminded me of Tom Figenshu, my first crush. We worked well together; it was all very heated, to the point that it was very difficult when I found out about Clare. I hated the idea of breaking up anyone's family, but it went on for such a long time without there being any sign of anyone else. It clicked very quickly between us, seemed very right. And he had that great feel for music, and moved fabulously to it, which turned me on. An experience like that makes you not trust men, and I was very careful after that. Until I wasn't.

Clare stopped eating when she found out about me. She tried to starve herself. It got very complicated, and if I had known there was someone else, I would never have gone with him. Unless I had met her and didn't like her. I didn't know her. It was awful, what he did. We were together for a year and a half. We had to stop. There was nowhere for our relationship to go, even if he had showed me this whole new other world.

I saw Andre a few more times after that, but he was another one of those who simply seemed to fade away, like Tom. Doing their own thing, very gypsylike, and they walk off into a crowd, get gathered up, and are never seen again. They take you so far, and then they leave behind a mystery.

One day, when my hair was cut and sculpted rather than shaved, given style by Andre, my eyebrows back in service, Wilhelmina said to me, out of the blue, "Do you know what? You look like the black Gene Tierney!" Tierney was a contemporary of Rita Hayworth and Ava Gardner. She had these prominent cheekbones, an overbite that she didn't let the executives fix, in the same way she didn't let them mess with her hair, and she played femmes fatales.

Her decade really was the '40s; she was in *Laura* and *Leave Her to Heaven,* one of Martin Scorsese's favorite films. Very striking, unusually sexy, definitely very confident and uncompromising but also vulnerable and prone to serious bouts of depression. She once stood on a ledge outside her mother's apartment fourteen floors up in New York, thinking about killing herself. After twenty minutes, she decided not to jump—she couldn't bear the thought that when she landed she would be mushed up like scrambled egg. That didn't appeal to her. She said, "If I am going to die, I want to be in one piece."

I had no idea who she was at the time. I started to watch her films, and couldn't see the connection. But Wilhelmina could—she said it was in the bone structure, and she got very excited. It made her think that there might be something in me. She said, "She's one of the sexiest film stars of all time." She started to see me in a different way.

She said, "You should go to Europe. They will understand you in a way they won't here. Go to Europe, become successful, and then America will be interested in you." This was her plan: Become big in a place where they get an unusual look, even favor it, and then make the Americans want you. They are intrigued with the new girl causing a stir in Paris. *Oh, we want some of that!* In many ways, considering New York was seen as being the center of the new and advanced, much about the city's fashion industry in the early 1970s was deeply conservative. They waited for others to make a move, and then followed. High fashion to this day is intrinsically conservative.

I could feel that I had to go, somehow find a way. My mom by this time was a lot cooler with everything and the things I was doing. My parents had come to visit and saw I was okay—nothing in the fridge, but that was normal for me. My dad opened the fridge once and the only thing in there was a chicken wing. I said, "You don't understand. We don't need to buy food, we are taken out every night and treated." Every night was a party, and dinner, with photographers and other models. It was a constant stream of nights out. We never needed to buy food; we were out all the time.

I partied every night in New York, and met Antonio Lopez, who at that point was the finest fashion illustrator in Paris and New York. Everything he did captured the energy, movement, and excitement of the city and its fashion. Actually, Paris was a little depleted when he arrived—he helped transform the scene into something connected to Warhol's New York, and he had his own entourage, like Andy. He took some of the art fantasies of New York that were then spinning around Warhol over to the fashion fantasies of Paris, where designers like Yves Saint Laurent were beginning their reigns.

He was described as the Picasso of fashion illustration, giving new life to a then dying art. Very flamboyant, he was from Puerto Rico and moved to New York in 1950, when he was seven. He started out at *Women's Wear Daily* in New York in the late '60s and moved to Paris in 1969. He began collaborating with Karl Lagerfeld, and they ran a kind of salon where models, fashion insiders, and photographers hung out.

I suppose he was bringing a lot of American thinking about fashion, art, and style into Paris, things like pop art, which he sampled in his work, the kinetic jumble of kitsch, street, high art, bold shapes, and cartoons.

I think his moving to Paris was a form of self-exile that I could understand—of getting away from a world that seemed to admire and demand otherness, difference, and specialness, but could somehow only take it pure and unadulterated when it came from somewhere else, as an exotic import. It was like he was chewing up and transforming the imagery that had surrounded him in his childhood, reacting to and exaggerating what he was then ultimately moving away from. His work was all about metamorphoses, and I identified with that. He dreamed up fantasies, and then they influenced reality. There were lots of illustrations he had done in the early '70s influenced by his interest in the risqué singer and dancer Josephine Baker, one of the first major black superstars, where he drew full-bodied African-American women, contrasting their dark skin against the white clothes they were wearing, which came out of the white paper he was drawing on. He said, "If you ever come to Paris, come to see me." They loved the Josephine Baker myth of the black goddess, the sex-mad black Venus walking down the Champs Élysées owning the city with her pet cheetah on a leash.

While I was making my mind up about leaving New York, I had my first casting-couch experience . . . another first for me in my family. I was doing all that running around, trying to getting the theater thing off the ground—all the callbacks, almost, almost, almost. You hear about the casting couch thing, but my attitude was always: no way. I am never going to want something so badly that I fall for that.

I kept thinking, *I am almost there, but one more thing needs to happen, a tenth of a percent of some other energy to solve this mystery of always the callbacks, the callbacks, but never the job. There is definitely potential there. They see something in me.* But something was blocking me, so I decided to leave New York and try another way. I didn't know what, but my instinct was to keep moving.

Before I left I tried one more audition. I thought, *I will give this one a go.* It was for a film called *Gordon's War*, directed by Ossie Davis, starring Paul Winfield, one of the leading black actors of his day. He played Martin Luther King in the film *King*, and was nominated for an Oscar for *Sounder*.

I went to audition for a small part. I had one line. The character, Mary, was a drug runner, a courier, but above suspicion. She was a schoolteacher, dressed nicely, very innocent, with an Afro, because this was a blaxploitation film, and of course she was required to be seen naked now and then. I seemed to have the right experience, between the Afro, the nudity, the heroin, and even the schoolteaching element.

In the film, a black soldier comes back from Vietnam and finds that his wife back home in tough, grungy Harlem has become a heroin addict and that his neighborhood is rife with prostitution. He gets his buddies together to fight the shadowy Mafia-run drug dealers, pimps, and pushers in their fancy furs who have supplied the drugs, the poison ruining lives. It had a pretty funky soundtrack, lots of cool explosions, split screens, freeze-frames, a bunch of sleazy villains, and plenty of exciting car chases. Not the worst film you've ever seen, very much of its time.

I did my audition, said the line, and the director said, "Okay, you've got the part." I couldn't believe it. It seemed too easy. The director said, "Yes, really, you're in, no problem." The producer then sent for me to come to see him in Los Angeles. He said, "Bring your pictures, I know the director says you have the role, but I have to be the one to approve it."

I traveled all the way to his big, beautiful Beverly Hills house. When he opened the door, he was wearing this fancy silk robe, which just about hid a part of him he was clearly very enamored with and couldn't wait to show me. *Oh. And there's champagne. Uh-oh.* And he asks me to sit on the couch next to him. He looks through my photographs. You can read the signs, the way he's talking and looking. Yes, I know the director says you've got the part, but it's really my decision. So come closer. He pats the cushion next to him. Let's have a talk. You could almost hear the slinky Barry White wah-wah guitars and his molten growl creep up behind us.

He's chatting away like its all innocent and nothing to worry about. The next moment he tries to kiss me. I remember I took my glass of champagne and I slammed the champagne so hard in his face it would have stung. I stormed out. I was so angry. Furious. I weighed about a hundred pounds, I was real skinny, but I would have taken him. I turned around and said to him, "Look, if I'm going to screw you, I am not going to screw you for the part. If I am going to screw you, I do it on my own terms." I was so insulted. I was thinking, *I'm good, I can do this, I don't need to sleep with the producer. What an awful cliché!*

I was crying as I left; I thought I'd blown it. I spent all night in despair. More rejection. The next day I got flowers and an apology. And I got the part. I was Mary, the tough, single-minded drug courier, and I did my line.

Later, I was almost the Acid Queen in Ken Russell's full-blown film transformation of the Who's *Tommy*. Again, I thought I was perfectly qualified. I knew acid. I knew how to take charge. There were two black chicks who were really rocking at that time, not doing the normal stuff. There was me, and the other one was Tina Turner. She became the Acid Queen, and I didn't. There was always someone else in the way until I worked out how to make myself the one who was in the way of others.

I loved Tina. She was the first woman I felt that I could be with. I told her that. She just flat-out turned me on. *I could go with you, Tina!* She said, "Oh Grace, you are so crazy." She would say, "But Grace, you don't really work"—because I would simply walk around the stage, like an explosion that hadn't gone off. She would put so much effort into the performing, and next to her it was like I was in slow motion. It was very confusing for her—she sweated and gave it her all, and I barely moved a finger. My Acid Queen would still have been scary. My Acid Queen could have taken over the world, whips and all.

I had a friend, Pola, who killed herself in New York, another reason why I had to get out, perhaps in the end the main reason for me leaving and heading to Paris. You see a glimmer of what could happen to you if you don't adapt and watch out for yourself. It's a world full of anxious, suffering, excruciatingly self-conscious people who cease to exist if they don't keep getting paid—money and compliments—to dress up.

She was also with the Wilhelmina agency, and joined about the same time as me. We were very close. I think after all that time with my brothers, separated from my sisters, I felt like Pola was like a sister; we could be silly together. All my life I have been looking for sisters, as I was always surrounded by boys and separated from my actual sisters. I adopt my best girlfriends and we become as close as sisters.

We shared a small apartment for a while and she had recently shot two major magazine covers that all came out after she killed herself—*Cosmopolitan* and *Vogue* covers. Her face was all over town, days after she had died. *Vogue* was concerned that they were going to put out a cover featuring a dead girl, but they decided to publish the issue. Pola with her big, plump lips staring at the camera, very trusting, very proud, her shoulders sloping somehow sadly. They decided that no one would know that she was actually dead, and she did look so alive. If you did know she was dead, there was a tiny hint that she knew what she was about to do, something broken in the eyes, the lost look of a lost soul.

Pola's real name was Paula Klimak. She was from Jackson Heights, Queens, but with a Brazilian background, decades before Gisele Bündchen and Adriana Lima, and as Paula she was a bit of an ugly duckling, gawky, with glasses, very little confidence. She remade herself as Pola, an absolutely beautiful model. But modeling might not have been the best thing for her to have done, because she was very vulnerable and had issues, some whispered, to do with being raped when she was really young. Her wrecked ego never got boosted even as she was feted and photographed. The business increased the emptiness. The cold, treacherous hypocrisy at the center of it all engulfed her.

Pola was something of an outcast. As models you see each other all the time, you are going to the same go-sees, you are on the same shoots, and you would know right away the gossip. With Pola, no one could believe she was relatively so big—Brazilian big—but getting all the work. She was bigger than the average model, so they had to cut the clothes open to fit her. The models who were starving themselves to get work were outraged that Pola was getting all this work even though they were having to make the clothes bigger. They whispered among themselves sneaky innuendo about what she was doing to get all that work. Psychologically, these jealous models want to kill you. Put poison in your food. *Here are some pills—take a lot, OD, why don't you.* What the fuck? It was a very cruel, indifferent world full of desperate techniques of denial. You had to be very strong to survive.

I was an outcast because of my funny accent, the color of my skin, a strange-looking face according to the New York fashion world, and because in so many ways I didn't fit in. Black, but strangely full of myself. Oddly entitled seeming, which the African-Americans weren't. I was expected as a black model to act a little humble, a little grateful. No way.

Pola and I would hang out together, swapping stories about being the outcast. We were the ones nobody liked. We bonded because of that. But I was not taking the outcast business and all the gossip as seriously as she was. It burned into her. She was very sweet but totally lacked self-esteem. She sought out usually damaging ways to get through the day without feeling more aggrieved and wounded.

We hung out together all the time. Those were the days of the New York clubs before Studio 54; that energy to come was building up in disparate places ready to be concentrated into 54. New York was heaving with nightclubs packed with people fired up and on the hunt for adventure, and I was a regular at most of them.

Le Jardin was off Forty-Third Street in the basement and penthouse of the old Hotel Diplomat. Pola and I loved to go there. It was definitely like Studio 54 before Studio 54. The New York Dolls had played in the basement in their early days. The basement was small and underground, and then in the early hours of the morning, if you needed more room to come down or extend the high, you would head up in the elevator, with an elevator operator, to the tenth floor, still part of the club. That was where I would hang out with Antonio Lopez and Pola and make all sorts of plans for the future, and all the magazine covers we would be on, until it was time to go home after dawn.

It was gay, but there were pretty women there too, because they could breathe a little, and dance without getting hit on—these places were always (probably on purpose) close to the offices of the model agents. David Bowie, Bianca Jagger, Warhol, Truman Capote, John Lennon, and Yoko Ono would be seated on the white leather banquettes surrounded by palms in the corner next to the bar area. Jackie O. and Lou Reed would be yards apart from each other, the wide striving scope of nonstop New York weirdly expressed. What they call the beautiful people, but plenty of wonderfully ugly, unlikely people as well, a toxic mix of those with everything to lose and those with nothing to lose. Movie stars and nobodies mingling as one and the same. It was the nobodies, the real damaged weirdoes, obscure hipsters, gay, blacks, Latinos that made the place, and the city itself, and they were really why the celebrities came, to tap into that erratic, heady energy, and feed off it, using it in how they worked, and played.

I would see Faye Dunaway there, and we became friends and very close years later. There were these monstrously done-up drag queens crowding around Diana Ross, Bette Midler, and Liza Minnelli, desperate to touch their hems and receive their goddess blessing. Beautiful boys everywhere. Exiled Cubans glowing with sweat, dancing the hustle. Waiters in short shorts wearing roller skates. White statues holding balloons. Fruit and cheese in bowls on the tables. Steve Rubell, later one of the owners of Studio 54, was a doorman, taking notes. Talking about it now, it's as if I'm making it up, but it all happened. The '70s, when our hedonism was up in the clouds.

Le Jardin was one of those clubs where you would discover what a disco was if you didn't know. These gigantic speakers slamming the steamy go-getting beat of the city into the room. Amazing DJs flinging you from thrill to thrill and groove to groove, giving life a whole new set of thrilling patterns. Barry White pummeling your senses. Hamilton Bohannon. Betty Wright. Herbie Mann. The Reflections. You could be anything you wanted to be there as long as you were there, and if you were there, then you were cool enough to be there. These places got their reputations because there were fewer people on the inside than there were on the outside. So people wanted to get inside. Great marketing.

A couple of the cattier models said that it was my fault that Pola had killed herself, because I introduced her to her new boyfriend at Le Jardin. He was my friend, and I put them together, but I would still see him at Le Jardin, and they thought we were seeing each other. We weren't, we were only friends. There were all those rumors circulating. I would get very angry with all these models spreading the rumors, but I knew what I knew, and I would never have betrayed Pola.

We were trying to protect her because she was liking the pills a bit too much. We all liked to get high, on mescaline, stuff like that, but she was a little bit more hooked. She was using drugs as therapy, as a barrier, as a way of beating back the demons. For me, it was more experimental, a part of my need to try everything, at least once, just in case it worked for me, and became part of the growing me. My free-spirited approach to drugs was part of a deeper search for truth, not just a way out of my problems.

Pola would get so high and helpless we had to carry her home. She started to worry us. Some of the rumors suggested that there were those getting her stoned so that they could have sex with her. Because she was bigger than other models, she was one of the first models I ever knew who would eat something and then sit on the toilet and purge it out. She was getting very anxious about her size. No one at the agency helped her deal with it.

We all stuck together in those days, helping each other. We would be like each other's therapists, because we never went to see anyone officially. We knew we needed to protect Pola. She was only nineteen, very fragile, you would feel instantly that she needed looking after. We made sure Pola had no access to pills—quaaludes in particular were her thing, and there was one pretty strong, massive purple pill Pola and I used to take.

It had a terrible effect on her—I remember she took this pill at a shoot, and she would leap and jump around, full of beans, and then suddenly fall down in a heap, out cold. It was funny for a bit; then it wasn't funny at all. The pill never used to hit me as hard. Actually, I liked the effect—they were very popular pills, exactly what you wanted when you went on a go-see and needed to look on the ball even if you were a little off the ball. Drugs and sex have this trenchant power where they can open up the mind to what there is beyond the mundane and at the same time drag you into the darkness of the world and your own frantic, fractured mind. On the way up, you get to see all the possibilities in the world; coming down, all the possibilities in the world are wrenched away, and you're slammed onto the damp concrete floor of emptiness. I had to help a lot of the girls through some dreadful depressions and panic attacks, especially when they were either too high or had hit the pavement hard. I'd had my own experiences and was able many times to talk a girl out of some horrible place.

Pola planned her death. I'm sure. There were all these rumors— that she had drunk a bottle of champagne and drowned in the bath, that she walked off a roof of a tall building high on heroin and angel dust, that she accidentally overdosed while trying to numb some pain or another. I found out later what happened.

She would often talk about her father, how he had divorced her mother and then refused to see Pola because she looked too much like her mom. I think that had a lot to do with her getting so recklessly high. A classic case of abandonment bursting into something existentially rotten in the fraudulent world of fashion that superficially appeared to offer solace.

We all sensed that sooner or later she would take too much. She became very unhappy about her relationship with her father. I think this was why she despised men, which sometimes she seemed to, more than that she was raped as a kid. This was all mixed up with some bad relationships—there was one photographer who locked her in a closet and wouldn't let her out—before I introduced her to this guy at Le Jardin, who was so nice, uncreepy, and lovely looking, and very good for her.

One night she told me she was staying with her mom. She told someone else she was staying with me, her mother that she was staying with her boyfriend. She had an apartment by then on her own on Seventy-Second Street, a high-rise building, and somehow she got hold of those purple pills that we kept from her. We wondered how she had gotten them, but when you want to get pills, you find a way of getting pills.

There was also a Hollywood producer lurking around wanting to take her to Hollywood, and he said, as these kinds of guys always do, to put her in films. He might have given her the pills. She took them all. On her own. She didn't show up for work the next day. People were calling me, asking if I knew where she was. I said, "She is with her mom." Her mom said, "She's with her boyfriend." The boyfriend said, "She's with Grace." She had gotten us all thinking she was with someone, but she was on her own. She was found at the window, because, we think, she was calling for help. She had changed her mind after taking the pills. It was too late.

I ran away after that. I was struggling anyway, really. Not as acutely as Pola, but with my own cavorting demons. She was my closest friend, and it was very upsetting, but her death didn't put me off being a model. I had tougher skin, stronger methods of defense, a sense there was a world outside modeling that I was heading for. My motive for carrying on was still to get into theater and cinema. Modeling was still going to be the way I would keep myself, but I would never let it become everything. Something else needed to happen, and I was never afraid to try something new. I liked the sound of a city where Josephine Baker, well known for being naked but for a few well-placed feathers, was a heroine.

3

Paris

I would find a home in Paris, and most of my formative years were spent there. Outside of Jamaica, it is the place I have lived the longest.

First I had to find my way there. No one would pay for me to relocate, so I did it myself. I did a job for *GQ*—most of the jobs I got in New York were for men's magazines. The head guy at *GQ* was crazy about me, so I did a little fashion spread for them. That was all the money I had—to pay for my ticket and my composite of photographs, because on go-sees, you had to bring the composite to leave with the photographers.

And your composite had to stand out from all the others they were getting. Mine was supermodern, to reflect who I was and how I looked. My look was very much born in my own imagination. I had made it up out of my own fashion sense, taken from my mom's style, from understanding the angles in my face, doing my own makeup, and understanding what suited me.

I learned to do my own makeup by asking questions every time a makeup artist did my face. I made sure I never walked away from having my makeup done without learning a little bit more about how to do it myself. This was more interesting to me than turning up and tuning out while my face and hair were fiddled with. I wanted to learn everything I could. I wanted to learn so much so that, if necessary, I could do it all myself, right down to the lighting. It was all about becoming self-reliant—learning how to do hair, makeup, nails, absorbing all the information possible. I felt it was important to know how to do your own thing as a model, so that you weren't merely considered a mindless clothes hanger.

Once I had made my mind up about Paris, nothing was going to stop me. I saved up enough for a budget Freddie Laker ticket to Europe. That was my quite shaky, unformed plan—buy the cheapest flight I could find and leave New York. I had been advised to go to Paris, but had no financial help. Normally, Wilhelmina would send girls to Europe on an exchange with an agency like Elite Model Management, which at the time was run by Johnny Casablancas, who'd founded the agency in Paris in 1972, and they would pay the models' travel expenses. I later discovered that Johnny didn't really want me, so I didn't get any financial help. I was left to fend for myself. I figured if I made it over there, I would make it work, and persuade whomever I had to persuade that I was worth taking on.

I had my book of pictures and an army outfit I had bought cheap at the army and navy store that I still wear now. (I love it—with the chunky pockets on the cargo pants, and the little Italian-green tank on the breast pocket.) I had my army hat, and my mom and I made this long, hoodless cream-colored cape made of a lightweight wool. Before I left for Paris—either to prepare, or say goodbye to America— I tripped on acid for about two weeks. The great sweep of the acid years was still carrying on for me.

My brother Chris had come to stay with me in New York to DJ at the Hippopotamus club somewhere around Sixtieth Street and Lexington Avenue, another 54 before 54. It was one of the great early discos when disco was not yet known as disco. There was just smartly sequenced nonstop music that you danced to, and it was as likely to be Jefferson Airplane as James Brown, the Rolling Stones as Donald Byrd. Harold and the Blue Notes and the Ohio Players used to hang out there.

Chris and I were sharing this rough little flat downtown in Chelsea.

He would prepare his DJ set for the night and I remember having taken this acid, feeling like I was flying around this soundproofed room, like a witch ready to put a spell on anyone who annoyed me. That was my way of preparing to cross another sea and become a castaway all over again. The flight took five minutes and five thousand years, and I landed miles away from where I needed to be without much thought about what to do next.

Still tripping after the flight, I decided I was going to hitchhike from Luxembourg, and I took one of my big photographs and wrote on the back in big black letters: Paris. I had no idea how far away it was, or even that it was in another country. I stood on this big highway—it was a beautiful day. I felt I looked pretty hot in my cape and hat, certainly worth someone stopping for to find out what the story was, but all these sports cars whizzed past me without stopping, totally ignoring me. None of them stopped. I thought, *Everyone in Europe is so rude!*

Eventually, a sports car skidded to a halt. It backed up to me, and the driver said, in English, by the way, "You're on the wrong side of the road. Paris is the other way! I think it's safer for you to catch a train," and he took me to the train station. He helped me get a ticket and onto the train, heading for Paris. I'm not sure if he was being kind or just wanted to get rid of me. I didn't speak a word of French, not one word. Everything got trippier and trippier. The words people spoke—because they were just sounds to me, meaning nothing—took on a life of their own, but pulled me close and closer to Paris. I was determined to get where I was going, and determined to enjoy every second of the experience.

On the train, I met some backpacking hippies, my kind of people, and we talked. I was still spaced out, feeling totally at one with the universe—thanks to the combination of acid and the Freddie Laker budget flight—and totally fearless. I believed that I loved everyone, and that everyone was going to love me. I knew whenever I needed help, it would come to me and get me to my final destination. I had absolutely no doubt, even though I didn't know what I was doing and couldn't understand the language. On the train, I sat on the floor, the hippies played their guitars, and we all sang songs. They were probably singing "Blowin' in the Wind." I was singing "Voodoo Chile." At the station in Paris, the confusion really kicked in. And I really needed to go to the toilet.

The toilets were the most disgusting place I'd ever seen. They were unbelievable and quite shocking. In the public toilets there was nowhere to sit, and you had to squat over this hole. When a woman peed it bounced up like raindrops going in the wrong direction. I had a thing for public toilets that went way back, and I never wanted to use them. I would hold it, hold it, hold it all day at school, until my mom would see me coming and think, *Hold the door, because here comes Bev, and she wants to use the bathroom.* The books I was carrying would fly everywhere and I'd dive into the bathroom. I don't know why I had these issues; I think my mom must have told me about the Jamaican outhouses and the cockroaches, where they were going to crawl. I always had this very dark vision of catching something from somebody else, so I was extremely paranoid. It's a paranoia that has followed me through my life.

It was absolutely awful to use a public toilet in Paris. I never got used to that. The most fashionable people in the world, telling the rest of the world how to dress, and then these black, grungy holes in the ground you had to balance over the top of without getting yourself soaked. You had to have very strong legs. If you were in high heels, you didn't want to take them off, but you didn't want them to get splashed. In Jamaica it was better to go in the bush, because at least there was earth to absorb the piss. In France, it was concrete, it was cold, slimy tile, and there was no way to aim properly. It all seemed so primitive. This was how I arrived in Europe—a tall, very skinny black girl with a cracked American accent, hardly any hair, in army surplus gear, a white woollen cream cape, and a military hat, still feeling the disorientating effects of an LSD trip, astonished at the disgusting state of the toilets at the train station.

Then I had to use the phone. I had decided to call Antonio, because he was my only contact. His apartment was on rue du Rhin and that led to the boulevard Saint-Germain, where the model hotel was—a tiny little place, it's still there. If you look out of the window opposite, there is the very famous art deco café, Café de Flore, which the tourist brochures called the most famous café in the world. It was well known as the headquarters of the existentialists, where Sartre sat writing *The Roads to Freedom.* James Baldwin used the warmth of the café to work on his novel *Go Tell It on the Mountain.* That's where my little room, not much bigger than a wardrobe, was—in the model hotel practically attached to Café de Flore.

It was impossible to use the phone in France. A nightmare. I don't know if they have the same phones now, but back then I avoided them like the plague. Before you'd put any money in, you'd have to read the instructions . . . in French. I realized I was screwed. I thought, *I am going to shoot this phone. I am going to smash it into smithereens.* It seemed to stand between me and my future.

The money goes in and then you have to push a button; the person answers and then you have to push again to hear them. You have to perform about five operations simultaneously. Put it this way, it was not straightforward. I didn't want to seem stupid, so I kept trying and trying, and the person would answer; I'd get the hello and start talking, then the call would be cut off. It was so frustrating. Finally, I asked for help.

It took a while. People had other things to do, and I didn't speak French—the French don't like it if you don't speak their language. I learned that very quickly. Eventually, I got some help and figured the phone out. I spoke to Antonio and felt really good about that. The next day we met up, he was three minutes from the model hotel, walking fast, and I was speeding with a need to get things done. We started taking Polaroids straightaway. He was the most ingenious, free-flowing illustrator, and he was very successful in Paris, which was a special place and a great place for special people to work.

I had broken through so many barriers without even knowing it just by being in the right place at the right time—the right clubs at the right time—and through sheer force of will. Whenever things seemed to be not going my way I always had the courage to break away and try something new.

Antonio loved the new girls constantly coming into town because of the fashion and the vague promises made to them, giving him something else to look at, sketch, dream about. There was an endless supply of the very best, the most determined and excited to be there. I didn't really think I was simply the next girl in line; he had a way of making you seem like the one, his favorite, and in a way, at the moment he was with you, drawing you, he meant it. You were satisfying his need for fresh, anomalous female presence, and he was satisfying your need to feel wanted and understood and even—through the way he drew you and paid attention to you—love.

Every time Antonio drew me it gave me a clue about how to do my makeup and work on different looks, different ways of shading and shadowing. He had been working with Yves Saint Laurent and Karl Lagerfeld since the very early 1970s, and it was an unbelievable way for me to land in Paris. Antonio very quickly sent me on some appointments. He really believed in me, which made me even angrier with Johnny Casablancas later on.

Johnny Casablancas was known everywhere in the fashion world and was extremely influential, and he had a very innovative approach to marketing models and promoting glamour, which helped turn many of his girls into very wealthy household names. His way of selling his models as more than mere models was a big influence on the emergence of the supermodel. He used to say he could take a girl selling vegetables in Utah and have her on the cover of *Vogue* six months later. His whole approach was nothing like the almost puritanical, more protective approach of Ford and Wilhelmina, who definitely had standards; he had a more playboy, rock 'n' roll approach to his relationship with his girls. Wilhelmina would complain that with Johnny, models started to pick and choose what they would do, instead of doing what their agency told them to do.

There was more romance and scandal with Johnny, definitely a mix of the business with the pleasure. The business wasn't only about modeling, either. Unofficially, there was the sense that if you were interested in being a model, you were interested in other, shadier ways of getting on in the world. And when you were a top model, the modeling agencies were always putting you with rich, hungry, horny men. Like a show pony. Until you outgrew your usefulness.

Modeling agencies are where wealthy men look for their female possessions. And a lot of the models took that seriously as a part of their career path. You would go to certain clubs, and certain men would be there, and the ultimate intention was that the girls were there for these wealthy men, because if they were good-looking enough to be models, they were good-looking enough to be taken into that wealthy world—working girls given a legal covering.

Whenever I was fighting a record company or agent over a deal, I would always use that as my default negotiating position. *I don't need to do this,* I would say. *I could marry into millions in minutes.* I never would have done that, though. I never ask for anything in a relationship, because I have this sugar daddy I have created for myself: me. I am my own sugar daddy. I have a very strong male side, which I developed to protect my female side. If I want a diamond necklace, I can go and buy myself a diamond necklace.

My acting coach/quasi therapist Warren Robertson would tell me to put that sugar daddy I invented to one side and let men buy me things and look after me. But I knew I could look after myself. I was always turning things down because I always felt there were strings attached. I would think, *Now I owe you something.* And I didn't want to feel beholden to anyone. But Warren would tell me, "Sometimes you have to let the man in your life do something for you—not to make you feel better, but to make him feel better."

So . . . it is all about them . . .

At first, Casablancas didn't send me out on any appointments. Other girls were being sent out every day. I got pissed off pretty quickly. I was in this toy town hotel, alone, still psyched from the bewitching acid trip, leery about the bleak toilet holes, and I was in a hurry.

After three days of no appointments I decided to confront Casablancas. (I was so impatient; I had a real attitude, or, as I like to think, I could see right through him as just another chancer.) Three is my lucky number—I still like it; it's a good number for me. So after three days, I stormed into his office and said, "What's going on here? I know something is wrong, so tell me what it is. Spit it out. Let's get it over with. Don't waste my time." The acid was lingering and increasing my fierce energy.

Generally, I am the last person to play the race card, because I never think race has anything to do with me—I grew up in a world where our family was at the pinnacle of everything, in religion and politics, so discrimination didn't mean anything to me. Being black didn't hold me back in Jamaica, and I rarely thought of it in America. I hadn't grown up with the idea of racism, with the color of a person's skin being politicized. I wanted to get out there and show myself to people, never thinking they had any preconceived notions before they actually saw me.

But there were all these go-sees I should have been doing, and here is this guy, sitting on his ass—actually, he's sitting on my ass. I was ready to get out there, and he wasn't doing anything. Then he came out with it, and I swear I'll never forget it—and he had to pay a lot for it later. He said to me, "Well, to be honest, selling a black model in Paris is like trying to sell them an old car nobody wants to buy."

Those were his exact words to me.

They hit me like a hammer. I had never before been confronted so straightforwardly about the color of my skin. Until that moment, I'd never in any way felt inferior because I was black. I'd also never used it as any kind of excuse for not making it, or for losing jobs. For example, I knew that catalog modeling was no good for me because of the lighting—I was so black I would come out looking like a shadow next to the studio's white wall. This is why they usually cast lighter-skinned black girls. I viewed all this as technical, rather than being about prejudice. I never even entertained the idea, so I couldn't bear that he was using it on my behalf.

It seemed like a weakness. I remember a black friend who was so angry about the race thing that she would never go with a white guy. I did, because race had never been a factor in my life. I never made a decision based on color, but on energy, on mysterious potential. But there was a sense that black people making it in the business were suspicious that I had white boyfriends. They seemed to think that as a black woman beginning to have success, I should only have black boyfriends, as if to set some kind of example. This really, really angered me—I had grown up with the expectation of setting an example to others, and there was no bloody way I was going to allow that idea to ever get in my way again, and interfere with my freedom.

I had rejection from both sides, really, because I was black—too black for the white world, not black enough for the black world. Once, a friend confronted me about it—actually, she was the editor of *Essence* at the time, and she explained to me that the reason she didn't put me on the cover of the magazine was that I was always with white guys. When *Essence* did eventually put me on the cover of the magazine, it was basically because they had to—by then, I was too much *Grace Jones,* too much "the *f*-word"—too famous. *Oh my God, now we have to put her on the cover; she's achieved something that has gone beyond whether she is with a white guy or not!*

When Johnny said that he couldn't sell me because of my blackness, it motivated me like very little had before . . . and I am very, very motivated. I leaned over his desk like I was on the prow of a ship powering through hundreds of dry gleaming snakes, and I said, "I'm going to make you EAT THOSE WORDS!" And as I left the room, I shrieked loud enough to rattle the Eiffel Tower: "AND I HOPE YOU DIE OF CIRRHOSIS OF THE LIVER!!!"

It was known among the models that he was a heavy drinker—we heard the gossip. Actually, he did die of liver cancer, at age seventy, in 2013—hailed, once all the controversy and exploitation were stripped away, as a model visionary. Well, he was no visionary when it came to me.

As part of our tetchy little conversation, he mentioned Beverly Johnson. She was the biggest black model at the time, with the most magazine covers for a black girl; she was the first black woman to appear on the cover of *Vogue,* in 1974. Johnny said to me: "Not even Beverly Johnson works here—what makes you think you can?" I remember the whole conversation like it was yesterday. The two of us were at war, tossing grenades at each other across his desk.

Beverly was more wholesome than I was, more yielding and carefully ladylike. Beverly didn't shave her hair and eyebrows; she would style and blow-dry her own hair into friendly domesticated sleekness before she went to jobs in case the stylists didn't know how to work with her texture. She would take her own foundation, because the foundation makeup artists had was mostly for white girls.

In America, a lot of the jobs I wasn't getting, Beverly was getting. We would all run into each other at go-sees. Beverly was one of the reasons I left the States. I knew that as long as she was in place, she would get everything—one black model was all they needed—and I would pick up the crumbs. The crumbs were not enough to feed me. I was starving on those crumbs. She was the token black model. They didn't need two tokens—I have never heard of two tokens! And when Johnny told me that even Beverly, with her more natural, less radical look, could not work in Paris, I thought, *Well, I am not Beverly, and even she can't get work. What chance do I have?*

Casablancas made it very difficult for me. He tried hard to shut me down—he really had it in for me. I had pissed him off. I don't think he liked being told he was going to die of liver disease. I could have been a bit more diplomatic, but that wasn't in my armory at the time. I didn't become diplomatic until years later.

I am diplomatic now. I could run for presidency now. I know how to play the game. But it's tricky for me to be diplomatic—it does not come easy. I find it manipulative and insincere. You have to manipulate your own self to get the results you need without actually expressing how you really feel.

It wasn't as though modeling was really what I wanted in life. To be honest, modeling felt so surface to me, so throwaway. It has nothing to do with your soul. It is totally artificial. You jump up, wave, twist your body, throw a pose—this shape, that shape, a little pull on the mouth, a look in the eye, done. If you're lucky, and the photographer agrees. You are in the hands of the photographer. You have to give yourself away. Casablancas wasn't even letting me give myself away.

I was so angry, which is why I cursed him. The idea of joining his agency had brought me to Paris; why hadn't he mentioned the fact that I was no use to him before? It became clear that he never had been that keen on me, and that Wilhelmina was probably encouraging me to try Paris because she wasn't really sure what to do with me.

I was at Wilhelmina's in New York before I left for Paris, and I was coming out of the elevator one day, angry about something; probably having been told there was still no work for me, or Beverly had gotten the job. And there were a couple of guys standing there who said they were starting a new agency in Paris, and if I ever came to town, they would love to have me.

The agency was called Euro Planning, later known as Prestige, and the two guys I'd bumped into were called Stefan and Rogi. I should have gone to them straightaway. They seemed interested in me without fussing about my lips, nose, and attitude. I didn't care that they were new to the scene. I like new. New means they are going to work hard to build something—and that they're not already so big that they can afford to waste people's time.

So after walking out on Johnny and putting the curse on him, I went the next day to Euro Planning. I wasn't scared. Me? Scared? Never! That word does not exist in my vocabulary. I knew that Johnny Casablancas had made the biggest mistake of his life. I had overwhelming confidence in myself and my future. I was going to make him regret it. YOU WILL EAT THOSE WORDS AND YOU WILL DIE! I knew that given half a chance I could succeed. Casablancas's world wasn't big enough for him to completely stop me; in his world I would never have ended up where I did.

Their first three girls at Euro Planning were me, Jerry Hall, and Jessica Lange. Nobody knew who Jerry and Jessica were at the time, but they soon would. A couple of other girls joined very quickly as well:

one from South Africa, known as Este, and an easy-going mixed-race girl from America, more girl-next-door, which didn't work in Paris as much as it did in the U.S.

I had joined Euro Planning just before Jerry Hall arrived. Within a week of my arrival, she had been discovered (at seventeen) sunbathing on a beach in Saint-Tropez by a notorious model scout. He was one of those dangerous, slippery charmers exploiting the model world, half pimp, half booker, with a flaky, magnetic personality, always prowling for new girls that he could control, and sometimes that control spilled over into blatant abuse. He was one of those characters who worked around models because they would then be swimming in a sea of women. And women were their prey, and their pleasure, what they needed to live and thrive, and the girls needed these characters to work and earn. A perpetual paradise for him, very dangerous and sleazy for the women.

Typical that he should spot Jerry and persuade her to try modeling. I was there in the office the day she was brought in to the agency, and it's true what they say—taller than tall, with long, wavy, golden hair stretching all the way to the Sahara, big eyes, flawless skin, legs that went on for weeks, a huge, irresistible smile, wearing these flowing, hippified '30s-style clothes. Then there was the big, creamy hillbilly accent that topped everything off. A head full of hair, and a mouth full of Dallas. We took to each other immediately, probably as a form of protection against the predators circling. Together, we created a force field around us.

We were the beginning of the Euro Planning agency at 3, rue de Courcelles, and the fact they first of all took Jerry, me, and Jessica shows they meant business. They certainly didn't have the same feelings as Johnny about my blackness. They saw it simply as what made me what I was, how I thought, and behaved, which made me potentially a great model, with enough distinct energy to interest the more adventurous Paris photographers.

Casablancas was powerful in his own limited way, and he continued to try to block me. The first week, I got a callback for a big spread at

Depeche Mode magazine. At that time, it was considered a real break-through if you got a big spread in *Depeche Mode* with a top photographer. It turned out Johnny Casablancas owned the studio where they were going to be shooting. He made sure I wasn't going to work in any of his studios, but even that didn't get in my way. There were a couple of photographers not in his world who were fixated on me. And they had names like Helmut Newton. Casablancas had no control over Helmut Newton. No one did. Born in Berlin, he'd moved to Paris in 1961 after time in London and Australia, and by the early 1970s he had become one of the most outrageous photographers in fashion, specializing in hyper-glossed, meticulously coordinated erotic imagery that treated the world as a theater and the woman as an inanimate, spectacular object. Paris, he said, taught him fashion. He already knew sex.

He liked his women to be full of alienness, which I loved, and after many years working for *French Vogue* he was unashamedly after "the sexy." His work got to be branded as "porno chic." You could tell looking at his photographs that he had worked in the 1950s as a society photographer in Singapore and loved the atmosphere of bordellos.

Every time Helmut booked me from my composite it was because of the expression on my face, which he absolutely loved—he saw me as the fearless, high-heeled dominatrix with a man's ass, someone who accentuated and manipulated traditional sexual stereotypes. He would request me, and the agency would get so excited—*Helmut Newton! It's God calling!* I'd be so nervous going to see him. I didn't plan to stay in modeling, but I wanted to be the best I could be while I was in it. I wanted to get the best out of it; I wanted to work with the best. Like Helmut.

There were a few gods, not many, but he was one definitely one of the gods. I would go see him, and he would come out, see me as though for the first time, and say, "Shit, every time I forget that you don't have big tits!" He would be so angry. It was like he was hoping I would have some work done, pump them up with something. No way. He became one of my best friends. He was so damned funny and we would work together a lot. Working with someone as brilliant as Helmut teaches you so much—seeing how he lights something, the visual stories he tells, how he was not interested in mirroring reality but transforming it. His way of working was so powerful and evocative I would never forget.

I loved Helmut's photos—they taught me how to stand, walk, be, even how to look in the mirror and perfect my character. You are always looking in the mirror as a model, either as you get ready for work, being made up, having your hair done, or when you are at home, checking on how you look because how you look is how you earn a living. You need to know how to do that without it undermining your confidence, do it so that you are always learning about what makes you look good in a photograph. Mirror, mirror, on the wall . . . friend and enemy.

It became very hard to think outside the fashion world once I was embedded in it and wanted to be the best. Paris plunged me into the depth of fashion. To the deepest level, and to the highest level. Paris was where the depth was in a superficial world. They were into fashion more than anyone else in the world. They took it seriously, with a tyrannical zeal, but there was also a certain freedom to it, and a luxuriant decadence. It was never boring, always changing. In America, it became very homogenized and commercialized. In Paris, the lighting was darker, starker, a lot stronger—you could tell what the person was sexually thinking from the photographs.

Paris was where the new originated. Helmut, for example, would not have published a lot of his work in the States unless it bounced over from Paris, where he was allowed to do what he wanted. His photos for *French Vogue* were taboo in the American edition. In America, his work would be edited, softened, tidied. It was all about the clothes in New York, not the meaning of the photograph. In Paris, the designers and stylists didn't care how the clothes looked. They didn't care about a little wrinkle as long as the photo was stunning. It was more about the art—the image was all-important. Paris was unbelievably exciting and suited me so much more. The freedom the photographers had was incredible.

Another photographer who took a liking to me was a friend and collaborator of Helmut Newton, Hans Feurer. He had shot the 1974 Pirelli calendar, naked girls wrapped in polyethylene, and in 1983 would shoot the Kenzo campaign featuring Iman swathed in a rich crimson net. He loved shooting details of a model's face and body, focusing abstractly on body parts. His work was very graphic, and he approached his photographs like a painter. This was before retouching and filters, and Hans was fantastic at using natural light, radical composition, and dramatic backdrops to layer a photograph.

When Kenzo Takada, the label's founder, told him he could do what he wanted on that 1983 shoot, he said, "Well, what if I do a close-up of an eye?" Kenzo said, "That's okay." Hans thrived on being given complete artistic freedom, and that was in the air a lot more in the '60s and '70s. You wanted the photographer because of what they had done in their work, so it was stupid to then tell them what to do.

He had a background in sculpture and illustration, and used fashion not as a place to sell pretty things but as a place to experiment with fantasy and otherness, focusing on how wearing certain clothes could transform a person into someone else. His photographs always seemed to be part of some greater mystery he was trying to solve, even when they were in the pages of fashion magazines or advertising a beauty product. He understood that fashion is fantasy and must always include fantasy.

Hans said he never liked women who were clearly in the service of men. We hit it off, and because he was a complicated, demanding person, with very discriminating artistic reasons for wanting to be a photographer, I naturally developed a crush on him. I could learn a lot from him. I think that is another reason I developed crushes on those I worked with closely. I was craving knowledge and, in a way, sucking out their knowledge and experience like a kind of vampire. Imagination was the strong blood I was thirsting for.

We had a very intense relationship, and he liked it when I was very much the dominatrix. I think I was a little too male for us to have actually had a relationship, but we got very close. Strong women fascinated and challenged him, but he wasn't sure how to take the next step. There is a lot about me that is masculine—I am very feminine, but I am also extremely masculine. I've got these two things going on and it is confusing for some men. My way of not backing down offends certain men. I will argue my point. I push the wrong buttons. Hans was interested in the strength of a woman, and sometimes that would mean shooting them in a very feminine way and other times in a very male setting.

He fell in love with my mouth. My first *Vogue* cover, which was actually for *Vogue Hommes*, was a Hans close-up of my mouth, very raw and revealing, with my teeth encased in gold. One of the photos from that session has me rolling my tongue over the gold teeth. I was getting better at knowing what to do with my mouth. He photographed my first *Elle* spread, me in khaki and a beret looking like a stylized version of myself as I'd looked when I first traveled to Paris. He liked to put me in men's clothing, a few years before anyone else did. For one shoot that ended up as the original cover for my first record, *I Need a Man,* he had me wearing a suit and blowing smoke rings for hours on end while he looked for the perfect way of framing my face.

Fashion and style was hurtling through a multitude of changes in the '60s and '70s, catching up with art and pop and pop art, especially in London and Paris. And Hans made sure he was in the middle of what was happening; even now his photos look totally contemporary. You would never know they were taken forty years ago. Photographers like Hans were making up many of the rules for how to naturally, experimentally, and playfully photograph models in real and surreal settings that are still followed today. He is still photographing, always curious about the same elements of a body and face, still in love with mystery.

Paris was filled with these kinds of artists and innovators. It was a place where I could thrive—to such an extent that once the *f*-word thing had really kicked in and I was *Grace Jones,* someone wanted a hit: Casablancas tried to get me back on his side. He was a little underhanded about it. I ended up in his house, brought there by some people who didn't tell me the party they were taking me to was at his place.

He was bobbing for apples (literally) when we got there—it all looked very stupid and contrived.

I thought, *He is bringing me here to humiliate me,* and I walked out. Years later, when he was big in television, his people tried to book me for one of his shows, and they were very persistent. They insisted that I agree. I knew he was still trying to exercise his power and prove that he could get me despite what had happened. I'd spread the gossip about what he had said to me, and how I had flung it back in his face. I made sure everyone knew. It was classic model behavior: *Do you know what Johnny Casablancas said to me?!*

He was still trying to manipulate me and pretend to the world we were friends, that I had forgiven him, or even that I had made it up, and had a tantrum for no reason. In the end, I agreed to appear on his show, but it was basic cold business. He would have to pay. A lot. I would manipulate him, still, because what he said to me was unforgivable.

In Paris, once I'd shrugged off the Casablancas incident, I felt like I had arrived where I belonged. I was what the French needed, and I needed them. Things started to happen. It was as if they needed someone who was so like me it could only be me. The reaction was so positive. There would be a dozen guys lining up in the same room at the same time wanting to impress me. Wilhelmina was right: They really went mad for me. I don't think it was so much my looks; I think they loved how crazy I was. *Let's hire her! She seems like fun!* They wanted to get to know me because I was like an alien who had landed from outer space. People would stop and stare at me on the street as though I were already famous. People in the fashion business wanted to be around me and did whatever they had to do to make that happen—Casablancas hadn't anticipated that. *Let's shoot Grace for the cover of the magazine. She will make our life interesting!*

I learned French in three months flat. I decided to speak it for a month straight, to be with only French people, and to only have one person around to interpret for me. I had studied to be a Spanish teacher, so I had the Latin already. I wanted to learn French so I could understand what people were saying about me—it gave me an edge.

I could tell when someone said something obnoxious and insulting. I knew when they were telling me off, and it enabled me to get inside the French mentality. French can sound romantic even when they are saying "fuck you" and "up yours." They can say the worst thing on the planet about you and it can sound like they are proposing.

I learned the language to deal with their very rude, stubborn ways, and to help some of the other girls. I'm not necessarily saying all French people are rude, it just felt that way to me, and I don't really mean that as a criticism. It's a part of how much they like to take control of things. The rudeness mostly didn't bother me. I knew a bit about rudeness myself. It was okay as long as I knew they were being rude to me, so I could be rude back.

I used to get so frustrated in those early days when I never got butter with my bread at restaurants. Not in France—apparently, French bread is so good it is an insult to slap butter on it. I would throw the baguette at the waiter. *No butter, no bread.* I got really angry. I started to take my own butter with me. I also used to carry eggs with me to throw at the taxi drivers when they wouldn't stop. They used to ask you where you were going before they agreed to take you. Even in the rain. Even when I was with someone who was eight months pregnant.

I said, "Let's get in the taxi without telling him where we are going." We got in, and he said he was not going in that direction. "So what?" I said. "We are in the taxi, she is pregnant, and it is raining." *No, you get out. No, we stay.* He came around and literally dragged us out of the cab. After that I always carried six eggs with me and I would slam them against the taxi if it didn't pick me up, and then scream, "Now you have to go to the car wash!" So I was carrying butter for the restaurant and eggs for the taxis. I was armed and ready.

My very first French cover was for *20 Ans*, a teenage magazine like *Seventeen* in America. I am so black on the cover because there was no sun where we shot. We went to Deauville, a low key, seaside resort in Normandy, on the northwest coast, with this huge wooden promenade.

The beach is so wide you can barely see the sea. Yves Saint Laurent had a home there. The overcast gray skies and diffuse coastal light around there fascinated the Impressionists, but it didn't really suit me. On the cover, I look like a shadow. I am barely there.

When the magazine called to see me, I didn't feel so good about what I was wearing. Something bothered me. My clothes were scratching me. So I took off all my clothes in the office. I sat there naked waiting to be called in.

They took one look at me and said: *Let's hire her! We want Grace! She's too much.* They had never seen anything like it before. If I'd thought about it, I would have thought such behavior would lose me the job—it was a spontaneous thing, but it ended up working for me. Maybe the New York acid was still in my system. I'd been there only a month. *Three days with Johnny. Fuck off, Johnny. No time to waste. Rent to pay by the end of the month. Let's go!* Anyone in my way was going to be knocked out of the way. This was the energy I had picked up as I moved around along the American East Coast. A little bit of momentum in Syracuse, more force grabbed in Philly, and then all of that multiplied in the helter-skelter of New York. I felt I had wasted the whole year there, so I was feeling very impatient.

I never wondered whether it was a brave thing for *20 Ans* to put a black woman on the cover. I thought they figured with all that cheek and energy I must be going places. To this day when I do my Paris concerts they all turn up—they all shriek, "Do you remember that rainy weekend in Deauville and the magazine cover where you couldn't be seen?"

Within three months I got a record deal, and had started recording. I say three months. Everything seemed to be about three months. Though my three months is not necessarily what others might think of as three months. It was simply that everything was happening very quickly. Finally, the speed things were happening around me suited the speed of my mind. I got so much done after that year that went nowhere in New York, which seemed like forever. The world caught up with how fast I wanted it to be.

Jerry, Jessica, and I would basically use our minuscule rooms in the hotel to sleep, and for little else, and we would be out every night—clubs, music, fashion, life. Paris seemed to stay out at night even later than New York. We'd drag ourselves back to the room in daylight after a night out and get ready for the next night out. We were out of our minds on fashion, on Paris, and on having a good time. The '60s, which were all about having a good time and dressing like you knew it, were rushing into the '70s. I developed incredible, long-lasting bonds with the girls I worked with, not least because I also lived with them and we explored new, strange territory together. I have remained friends with Jerry and Jessica to this day, and we help each other and inspire each other. Other models along the way as well. We're always there if one of us needs a place to stay, some help with another ridiculous load of man trouble, or just to share the latest news. We've all been through something particular and—mostly—come out the other side. Modeling—dealing with it, not the thing itself—helped us to take on the world. We're sisters in life—Efva Attling, another singer and model who's become a famous jewelry designer based in Stockholm and the Danish designer Antonie Lauritzen were also part of the group. A crazy group. Good crazy. Young, lustful girls moving around Europe, with Paris at the center, making a living, becoming stronger, discovering new ways to hang out and look after ourselves.

I totally immersed myself in French culture. I would walk around Paris smiling a lot. Stories streamed through every street. It was obvious why it was a city of so many people's dreams. It was cheap, five francs to the dollar. Grimier than it is now. Truer, really, with the fashion dream there to light up the night, burn into the day, and create the legend.

I baptized myself in Parisian blood. Felt glamorous history in the air, got to know the vivid legends: Josephine Baker becoming such a decadent, amoral diva, dancing the Charleston at the Folies Bergère in the 1920s, wearing a banana tutu designed by Jean Cocteau; the cabaret, the glorious excess of the nightlife; the honking, sizzling Paris jazz; the boys dressed as girls; the dazzling dancing girls loving to show themselves off and be treated as artists, not tarts. The great French singers Jacques Brel, Juliette Gréco, Édith Piaf, and Serge Gainsbourg were all melancholy and melodramatic romantics, but also geniuses at representing erotic sensuousness through music. I couldn't resist that combination. The songs weren't only about love, either; there were drunks, and hookers, and despair that needed correcting, or relishing. The singers sounded filthy and wise, and I loved the way they built a world of their own out of melody, drama, and sex. We were looking for encounters without hoping for anything more, without longing for emotional entanglement. We wanted adventure.

All dinners in Paris, I noted, would end with intense discussions about sex. What else was there? A good dinner, fabulous wine, and then talk about sex, and the world is a better place.

Jerry was very open about sex. In Texas, for some reason, the women are very different from those in the reserved American North. Texan women love talking about having sex in the barn—head outside, body inside, so that the rain would be falling on their face while down below they were being ravished in the dry, head soaked wet, the bottom half getting it on in the hay.

I studied the naked couture at the Crazy Horse, the temple of strip-tease, where stripping collided with the avant-garde. I knew the music arranger there, and while I was hanging out, things got a little casting couch with one of the managers. I always hated that, the idea that to get on you would have to sleep with the boss. It made me feel so powerless. And I wanted the power over the men.

Jerry and I would compete for boys. We had this kind of competition going. Our personalities fitted together, but we were also opposites. We liked the same things, and we especially liked the same boys, so we fought sometimes to be first to get there. She would get very jealous. She would ask about a boy we would both be chasing, her eyes flashing, *where were you last night—did you get him?!* Yes, I did, I would admit. *Goddammit, I wanted him,* she'd drawl, genuinely a little put out. It was sibling rivalry. I had never been allowed to play with my real sisters, but now here was someone I could play with. In her book she said we were roommates, but it was a lot more than that. We were close, sisters in love, each wanting the other to succeed, but when it came down to it, if the choice was between me and her, naturally I would choose me, and she would choose her. Jerry and I had a lot of fun together, but we were also rivals.

We would go and buy cheap clothes at a place called the Rag Queen. *Honey, let's go shopping,* Jerry would say. The Rag Queen was not very far from when we lived. It was owned by a German girl, and she used to hunt far and wide for pieces that suited us, but they were never more than we could afford at the time, which wasn't much. She would go on the hunt for clothing that we asked her to look out for—I liked hoodies from the '30s and '40s, to keep my neck warm with the short hair. I didn't want to wear a wig. The short hair was my look, and Paris loved it. I looked natural and unnatural at the same time. They didn't slap a wig on me like they did in America. We used to go on our go-sees in these made-up outfits, and the designers would get their ideas from how we dressed. Lots of designers told us they liked us coming in so they could see what we were wearing and be inspired by it. It made us less passive, a part of the creativity. It was one of the ways fashion finds on the street started to infect the haute couture.

Jerry was tall and fresh-faced, and had all this long blond hair, and I was dark, severe, wore my warm military clothes, and had very little hair. Quite a sight. Chocolate and vanilla. Fairest and feistiest. We did go-sees together, and after a while we didn't want to take the underground. We started to hitchhike for limousines when they were off duty between drop-offs.

Jerry wanted to have fun in an almost ferocious way. We would dress up, and we would look good, glowing with sheer get-up-and-go, in our element as exotics in the capital of exotica. Sometimes we would wear glitter, and African bones around our necks, nothing else, no top, a shred of a skirt. Our boldness knew no bounds, because Paris made us seem like we were always on show.

We'd go out and guys would try and get between us and we would throw them from one end of the room to the other. We weren't interested in anything long-term. Nothing longer than a few hours. Once it becomes a relationship it becomes about control, and back then, we were mostly interested in our careers. We were not looking for boyfriends or for one-night stands, and if we were, we wanted it to be on our terms. We would pick a guy up, not have him pick us up.

We used to go to this great club called Club Sept on rue Sainte-Anne, a really hard-core gay area, run by an ex-stylist and makeup artist called Fabrice Emaer. He was known as the Prince of the Night, and he was very mysterious. You would see him do his thing only at night. There was no sense of a family. He had such elegance and charm, and he attracted a certain sort of personality to his venues.

Fabrice was blond, ageless, could have been thirty, forty, it was difficult to say. Very tall—a lot of the Frenchmen are usually, shall we say, smaller. He wore discreet, elegant suits. He loved taking care of people. He was constantly in motion, and he would float from person to person, making sure everyone was having a good time on their own terms. He had a way of making you feel amazing without getting into your business. This was the nightlife, and he was in charge. That is a real talent. It's hard work, and he did it so smoothly. He always had the right people working for him, and they stayed with him.

Way before Studio 54, Fabrice would mix people with all sorts of backgrounds like an artist. Club Sept had a restaurant on the ground floor where you could chat or play cards after dinner, and a small dance floor in the basement where those who were eating didn't want to go until later. Sophia Loren, Roman Polanski, Lagerfeld, Saint Laurent, and all the top models would have a table—you never had to pay for anything because you would draw in a certain clientele—and then there would be the up-and-coming designers like Claude Montana. (I met Jeanyves Lascombe, my first boyfriend in Paris, while he was working at Club Sept; he was the classic French dreamboat I had been lusting for. We weren't looking for boyfriends, but if one came along who fit the bill, we didn't say no. That didn't mean you stopped seeing other men. I'd have a boyfriend, but I'd have ten others as well.) There was also a vibrant gay clientele, with glamorous straight girls and gays grinding into each other to disco and funk, but this was not a clandestine gay club.

Gays were starting to go to places that weren't only for gays. This was very new; they were coming into the light. They were coming into the world. There was a more furtive gay club next door, and glamorous girls used to go to gay clubs because we didn't want to be picked up. We wanted to go out and have a good time, not get into a relationship.

Jessica, Jerry, and I would go out, and when we dressed up, we looked like nothing else. *Look at us, but don't you dare look at us.* A lot of itches need scratching. We had brazen appetites and desires, enough to crack a man's gaze and bruise his soul. When we went out, if we went to a straight club, every man in the room would approach us. Sometimes they would drink to pluck up the courage, and that would often make them really obnoxious. To get rid of them sometimes we would have to get physical and throw them across the room—sometimes they were so drunk you'd merely flick them with a sharpened fingernail and they would fall over.

At Club Sept there was no sense of a sudden ending to the night, when they would blast on the lights and shout at you to leave, *Time to go*, and you would stand there in the sudden light with your makeup running after dancing all night and your clothes torn from rolling around on the floor. That never, ever happened there, and that suited me. I like to be the last to arrive and the last to leave, and I never want to feel I am being kicked out even if it is seven in the morning. I would leave Club Sept at seven—the clue was in the name—and take the night's vibe into whatever I was doing next.

It was incredibly glamorous, exposing the magic you can achieve with some mirrors, lights, and of course, the music of the moment. This was a disco in heaven, disco as the music of big cities, of the night, of sex. Guy Cuevas was the DJ mixing the classic newly forming disco; hard, insistent rhythms from around the world: scheming funk, hardworking soul-jazz, plastic soul, high-living show tunes, bits of noise and sound, anything that took his fancy in making up a show from records.

The DJ was a kind of sculptor of atmosphere and mood, setting up through sound the charm of possible encounters. The mix of people was part of the magic—in this small space with these strong, sexy sounds pounding into your head, heart, and groin, there were the famous, the lusty, the intellectuals, the chic, the beautiful, the half-crazed, the loners, gay, straight, in-between, over the top, under the radar, the un-decided, whores, models, and Casanovas, the marginal within the marginal, all sorts of heroes of the night, everyone becoming a bit of everything else, bodies coming and going in the shadows. A weird sort of community, sharing excitement, enthusiasm, and one another.

What took place in these clubs was a kind of choreographed dan-ger, cruising as a form of socializing, contradictory pleasures gathered together in a single place. Energy in the margins that would eventually pour into the mainstream. A whole range of sensations designed to make people happy for one night. These clubs were at their peak a rep-resentation of the receptiveness to new ideas that were around at the time; a vivid, breathing, and often sweaty symbol of transition.

It was as though, in this small place, you could somehow change lo-cation on a whim, because of the variety and newness of the music, the varied people, the flashing lights, the sense of what was about to happen because of what had happened the night before, and the night before that. This was very much a time when you could sense the role music and culture were playing in the evolution of homosexuality. It became a fashionable aesthetic; no longer were gays having to keep quiet, trapped in their own places, because now they had more and more places to go, where they were the pioneers, the ones in control, explicitly setting the trends. I belonged in these places, places where you went to perform, to watch others perform—I picked up a lot of the signals that would go into my music in these places.

Out of my mind, but somehow fully focused, I'd sing along in the clubs to my favorite songs, performing karaoke before karaoke ex-isted. You might even see me climb onto tables in the café downstairs from my room, and sing a little. Loudly. That would become my thing: dancing on tables, which I used as a stage, bringing my go-go experi-ence into play, cracking imaginary whips. If I didn't dance on a table, everyone with me would be disappointed. That's still true to this day. It's what seals a night out with me as a good one.

When I was in my hotel hutch getting ready to go out, I would always sing at the top of my voice through the open window and the lace curtains into an inner courtyard that was outside my room. My voice would echo off the courtyard walls and maybe sound a little better than it really was. Este from Euro Planning, who lived in the next room, could hear me showing off, and she had a boyfriend who was scouting talent for a small record company. His name was Stephan Tabakov. He was lean and tall, with these big, popping eyes; he had done a bit of modeling and had a look that was quite striking. He was, naturally, very charming, and was clearly used to hustling, wanting to make something happen. I had a knack for finding these guys who were desperate to do something in the music business. That was not my intention at the time, but I had all this energy, and if that came with a personality, and even a hint of being able to sing in tune, these guys were interested.

Este told her boyfriend, "Oh, Grace knows how to sing!" I was beating her up in a state of alarm when she told him in front of me. "What did you tell him that for?" I asked, thinking I could be heading for a disaster on the scale of Gamble and Huff.

Stephan asked me to do a demo of "Dirty Ol' Man" by the Three Degrees, which I sang a lot, imagining I was in the group. I knew exactly about the men they were singing about. *You can't keep your hands to yourself . . . you can look but please don't touch . . . all you want is another victory . . . you're a dirty ol' man.*

I sang it in a studio called Acousti in Saint-Germain-des-Prés in front of Stephan and the engineers, and they said, "Mmm, it sounds okay, but we want you to take some singing lessons." It was a polite way of saying I was singing out of tune. That was an improvement on the Gamble and Huff rejection, but it didn't appeal to me. I felt free for good of any kind of school. My piano teacher in Jamaica used to crack my knuckles with her wooden ruler when I got things wrong, and she was one of my aunts. The worst pain, worse than the whip.

Whenever I play the piano now I beat it, smash it with my elbows, bang, bang, bang, beat it until my fingernails break. It's amazing how that stuff from your past sticks in your system. That was how I played. I was never going to be gentle, however brutally they rapped my knuckles.

I didn't want to do the singing class, but I reluctantly agreed. Out of curiosity, again. At least the door had stayed open a crack and had not slammed in my face. *Let's see what this is going to be like. If I don't like it, I'll quit.*

Very quickly I started skipping the classes because I didn't like the teacher. She was too stiff and spent too much time teaching me how to breathe. She was the wrong teacher for me, too set in her ways, and they weren't my ways. I found it boring—she didn't excite me, and I do need to be excited. It was all technical and very dry.

Stephan said to Este, "Well, Grace is not serious, so we are going to forget about it." As soon as she told me what he had said, that he was disappointed, some sense got knocked into me. I thought, *I'm being stupid, and too stubborn.* I remembered how silly I felt when I messed up the Gamble and Huff chance. This thing with Stephan could take me somewhere else, not necessarily where I thought I wanted to go, but it might help me on the way there. Overnight, I talked some sense into myself and started to take it seriously.

I thought about what music I wanted to make. I thought about whom I wanted to work with. I started to pull a team together, to really take control. I took off like a high-speed train. I thought, *There are three doors—singing, acting, modeling. What's behind the singing door?*

I took control of the sound of the music. I didn't like French pop music, which was becoming very Eurovision and generic, compared to the disco that was coming through at the time, which felt electric and electrifying. It was both the soundtrack to going out and about going out, what happened as you danced, the people you were with, lovers and strangers, and also what happened after going out. What happened once you had found what you were looking for—another person, or another night on your own, various tensions building. Musically, I knew what I didn't want to do, and it was definitely not the French thing.

French music sounded great before the 1960s, but it didn't sound right after rock 'n' roll, and soul. It had trouble keeping up. Apart from anything else, the French language didn't fit so easily with the new riffs and rhythms.

I was picking up all the nighttime action happening around me like some sort of antenna, and I wanted to feed it through my emotions and transmit it in some way that seemed to make sense to me, and fit right in among that music I was hearing in Club Sept, and what I had been hearing in New York before I left—disco as the beat of man-love, basically, and a sense that dance music was a disguised form of militancy. I wanted my music to have the charged after-hours vigor that home-made French music suddenly didn't have.

I knew I didn't have a natural voice, but I was going to work out how to make it work, stretch it into a new place. If I could have sung like my mother, I would have, but I couldn't. If I could have sung like Aretha Franklin, I would have, but I couldn't. If I could have sung like Chaka Khan, I would have, but I couldn't. That whole period was me finding a voice that I was happy with. And that took a long time—early on, I sang sharp, and I realized producers want singers to sing in a similar key, so that when they mix for the radio, it fits the very narrow, familiar range of what radio wants. It wasn't my key, but I would try and sing there to please them.

This reminded me of catalog work—only now it was not about being forced to use the same lighting as everyone else, but the same key. I had to force myself to conform, and I was always sharp. There was nothing to fix the voice in those days like there is now, nothing to correct you.

I hear my early records now like "La Vie en Rose," and think, *Jesus Christ, I am so off-key!* I went along with what the producers wanted because I didn't know any better, and I stretched and I stretched, reaching for the note with such desperation. I had so much conviction: I was determined to hit that note but never hit it. Someone said, "You are the only black singer we have heard who is off-key, and not flat, but sharp." I wanted to hit that note, and if I wasn't getting there, I certainly believed that I was. That's what you hear on those early records—complete, delusional self-belief.

I thought, *If I'm going to do this, I'm going to be the best* . . . still thinking that I had to be an example. Perfect. The thing was, I didn't want to be a singer, not when I was younger. I didn't like what singers wore. I thought I'd have to wear what they wore if I was a singer. I thought those were the rules. I didn't want to follow that formula, be part of that group. I was totally antisocial in that sense. I didn't want to be a part of the club that everyone else was joining. I always ran away from that.

I felt comfortable going in the other direction. I think it goes back to Jamaica again—I had four brothers and two sisters but, as a form of protection, ended up being a loner. I enjoyed other people's company, but I enjoyed my own company the most. Slowly, I learned to trust others, especially when they could teach me things. I was always attracted to those who were the very best at what they did.

I loved Antonio Lopez's work. I didn't know how important and respected he was when I first met him. The friendship was based on him as he was before I knew about his achievements. I didn't search him out thinking I could take advantage of him. He came to me and invited me in. But he was surrounded by a lot of people who did try and take advantage, so he liked that I liked him for who he was, not what he could do for me.

I became what was known as an Antonio girl. There was a group of us—Jerry, Jessica, Tina Lutz (whom Antonio introduced to the man who became her husband, Michael Chow), Paloma Picasso, Pat Cleveland, Marisa Berenson. He had this eye. All the girls he approached did something special. His girls were not necessarily the pretty girls, or the obviously beautiful girls; they were the girls with balls, with something on their mind. He liked them a little fucked up, which suited me. He liked the freaks and made them freakier. Jerry wanted to fix her nose. She hated the bump in her nose—he said, "Don't you dare!" Jerry and Antonio got very close, and her jealousy kicked in when it came to some Antonio images of me in my portfolio. She ripped them out, and

I was very angry that she did this because being endorsed by Antonio was very valuable in Paris. It helped pay the rent, and that was very important.

We all had ambition, I guess, to be more than models. We wanted to be fabulous in a different way. Once I decided to go into music, for instance, I was obsessed. I wouldn't leave my voice alone until I got it where I wanted. I couldn't bear the thought that it would never sound like I felt inside. Without a special voice I would be very ordinary, and that was never good enough for me in whatever I did. I needed a voice, to speak my mind.

Later, still on the quest to find my voice, I would work with a singing teacher back in New York, a German lady in the 1980s, and she was so much better for me—the total opposite of the uptight Parisian professor, who I'm sure was good for opera, but not for me. When I told her that in Paris the teacher spent the whole time trying to teach me how to breathe, she said, "Ridiculous, you know how to breathe as soon as you are born. Why do you need to be taught how to breathe? This is what I want you to do—I want you to jump on the furniture, leap around the room, and let the note fly!" She was amazing. She treated being a vocal coach like being a therapist and also like a kind of performance. I needed to feel I was being taught by a performer. She taught me so well I could be a vocal coach now.

She used to say, "Let the emotions out, listen to what you are singing, the melodies, believe in that." I turned down so many songs because I didn't believe in what I was singing. I was the first to be sent "Boogie Wonderland" and I turned it down because I didn't believe in it. Can you imagine me singing "Boogie Wonderland"? Preposterous. That song needs a twinkling Tinker Bell to sing it, and I'm much more of a witch with a smear of blood on my cheek.

I said no even though I knew it was going to be a huge hit. Other things are more important to me than simply having a hit, because then you have to live with it—it becomes who you are. People think you are mad if you don't accept something that will make money, because they think it is going to be a hit, and that is all that matters. It doesn't work like that for me. There are a lot of hit songs out there I wouldn't want to have associated with me because they have no soul, no power.

People think I am being too intellectual, but it's not that. It's fine to sing something that isn't intellectual, that is bubbly, and I can do that, but I still need to feel something. I have to like hearing myself. I have to believe that the song can be one I would want to sing forever and not be embarrassed.

I remember working on a song for the soundtrack to the movie *9½ Weeks* starring Mickey Rourke and Kim Basinger. The producer who was doing the soundtrack, Narada Michael Walden, had recently worked with Aretha Franklin. I could never sing like her, but eventually I realized that she couldn't sing like me. It eventually sank in.

A singer is not really meant to listen to herself. By listening, you lose concentration—you cannot perform and listen to yourself. My voice teacher could tell when I was listening to myself. There was too much tension. It's like acting—you are either trying to act, or you really are acting. When you are trying to act, you can see it. When you are acting, it is invisible.

Narada was trying to get me to sing a pretty camp, frivolous song, "The Best Is Yet to Come," in a key I can't sing in. I would love to be able to say I am a vocal chameleon, but I'm not. With certain songs, I have to go through a jungle with a machete in the dark fighting off tigers to get to where it fits with my voice, otherwise I wouldn't believe it. And if I don't believe it, no one else will.

Narada was pushing me to sing it like Aretha and mentioned her, which pissed me off. I said, "This is a waste of time. I can't sing it like that. I'm not Aretha," and walked out. The prima donna, you know, so they say, spoiled and temperamental—but I never like the pressure of someone making me feel inferior without helping me solve the problem.

Wound up, I left for a break, to calm down a little. The Rolling Stones happened to be recording in the same building. Keith Richards was in their studio on his own. I sat next to him at the piano where he was doodling. I said, "I am so upset." He said, "Have a puff on this." Naturally, he had something to puff on, one of his kind of joints, built for his tolerance. I took a puff. It was too strong. Within seconds, I couldn't move. I was paralyzed. I had to be carried out of the studio and taken home in a car. Walden must have assumed I had stormed off. I don't know what Keith thought.

Years later, the same thing happened in reverse. I had been invited with a friend up to his house in Jamaica perched in splendid rock-star isolation on the spectacular tree-covered cliffs overlooking the sweeping sandy bay in Ocho Rios near where my Jamaican home is. I can see the house hanging from the cliff, flag flying above the roof, from my living room. Using telescopes, we could wave to each other. We arrived more or less on time for dinner with Keith and his wife Patti Hansen, an old friend of mine from the Wilhelmina days. It was Patti who had invited me more than Keith. She was very important in his life—she saved him really. We were shown into the dining room and asked to sit down. There was no sign of Keith and Patti. An hour later, there was still no sign of them. I was getting impatient and I marched off to look for them.

I found their bedroom, and Patti was fast asleep sprawled on the bed, and Keith was slumped on a chair knocked out cold with a joint still clinging to his lips, slowly smoldering. The people working for him didn't dare touch it, so it was just burning away. I didn't care about respecting him in that state. I took it out of his mouth and tried to wake him up, but he was too far gone. Eventually he came too, as incoherent as you could imagine, like there were spider webs and sundry creepy crawlies in front of his eyes, and, to his evident alarm, at the center of them, spinning a glitter ball on her head, some phantom of the disco tugging at his mouth. He realized it was me and looked very confused as to why I was there in his home, possibly trying to pull out his teeth. He started shouting at me, "Grace Jones! You should not be here! Get out of here!" It turned out he didn't mean that I shouldn't be in his house, but that I should not still be around as a musician. "You had your day! Your time was up a long time ago!" Patti tried to calm him down. "Keith, Grace is our guest! She's an old friend!" He kept mumbling, about how I should not be here, I was Studio 54, I was from a dead, plastic world. To him, I was disco, and nothing else. I knew better. After all, I had turned down "Boogie Wonderland." Eventually, he passed out again, into another segment of this nightmare. The next time we met, he'd forgotten all about the incident, or just accepted that I was still around, that I wasn't disco, that grotesque aberration. I was more like him, a wanderer, a nomad, at home here and there, with, when it suits, a purpose.

Eventually I heard the song Walden did for the Mickey Rourke film; he had gotten a Canadian singer called Luba to sing like me singing like Aretha Franklin. It was awful. The trouble is, once you go through something like this, it stays with you and is there every time you make a decision. It haunts me, but not as much as the song would have if I had done it.

My German teacher in New York taught me to let my emotions take over, but that meant singing something that meant something to me, that made me emotional and involved, however dark or perverse the subject. Singing is a form of manipulation of the emotions. It's some-thing you even do with your speaking voice—you manipulate a situa-tion, to get what you want. I got that. I understood that. That helped me sing like Grace Jones, which was what I wanted all along.

While I was in Paris, making it a home, another genius, Issey Miyake, turned my life around in the way I like. He was then at the beginning of his extraordinary career. I first met him at an audition in a bare room some-where in the middle of the endless city. It was very everyday. You turn up. You wait with other girls. You go into the room where everyone is. You try on the clothes and walk, hoping you are doing it the way they like.

They all sit around a table, and watch without giving anything away. It's very humiliating. That's why I would never want to be a judge on one of those talent shows. They ask me all the time. Simon Cowell al-ways wants me. I'm offered so much money to do these kinds of shows, but no amount of money is enough to compensate for what appearing on them would do to my soul. They're awful, there's no learning experience, it's demeaning and dispiriting. Sure, it's a part of life, and you have to go through it, but to set it up as something that people laugh at is so damned cruel.

Issey was lovely, though, and he was very fond of African and Indian models, girls not likely to be used by other designers, even the most radical. He wanted the models he used to have a dangerous and ambiguous kind of allure.

He made such a contribution to how I perform, that withdrawn, minimal, underplayed performance. He showed me how to discipline the body in order to heighten the excitement, which was something that set me apart from the standard way that pop singers moved to make their point. He made me realize that to make my presence felt I could stand still, and radiate intense inner life without having to dance around like all the others. I was the countdown to an explosion that was always about to happen.

I found the stillness more powerful. I met Issey when I was thinking about ending my modeling life and become a singer full-time. I had recorded my first single, "I Need a Man." All that energy and discovery, all that strutting American disco fed through the swashbuckling French glamour, and all the lovers I had, my being tangled up with the lingering male genes, it was all there in "I Need a Man," which became an unofficial gay national anthem. He said, "Why don't you sing that song while you model my new wedding dress?" The Paris fashion-show reveal of the wedding dress was always meant to be the showstopping highlight, so it was a real honor to be chosen. It was really my first official public singing engagement. I became known for a while as the singing model.

Through him I learned about theater, Kabuki, and this was a massive influence on how I would present myself as a performer. I had been moving toward it without even knowing it. The powerful, extreme makeup that I favored, the flamboyant costumes and exaggerated gestures . . . Kabuki is an investigation, really, into eccentricity while maintaining something completely pure.

Kabuki's meaning is to act eccentrically, or erratically, and Kabuki gave me clues about how to achieve the spectacular without appearing obvious. I got to it after being in America, and then Paris, and that was the right order—a crash course in pop culture and hippie adventure on the East Coast, a year getting up to speed amid the make-it-here frenzy of New York, a discovery of provocative French passions, and then spinning all this through this dazzling Japanese combination of formality and subversion. It taught me a way of being larger than life without losing control, the way they used their cross-eyed glare and stuck out their tongues to drive away evil meshed with a lot of what I felt about Jamaica and the way I was brought up. I liked the idea that you could repel badness through a look, a held moment. There's an element of the African trickster too, introducing disorder and confusion but paving the way for a new, more dynamic order.

The Japanese influence concentrated the more conventional ideas about performance and entertainment into something very precise and intense. It was a clash of two or three very different forms of energy to produce a new kind of energy that very much reflected and represented my own travels. I think I connected with Kabuki because it was about the enormous amount of compressed energy it takes for the Japanese to deviate from the norm in a place where comfort and formality is highly valued. I had come from a very conformist past, and Kabuki helped me articulate my own form of deviation from the norm, the breaking away from the rigid without it being predictable and shrieky. I could shriek, and in some senses I still did, but I also learned the impact of stillness.

I am not a great dancer. I don't put it out like Madonna. I can dance, but it is not normal—I will stand on my hands, tumble, be a little gymnastic, but in terms of stage, and then performance, and video, Kabuki and Miyake helped me refine a dance that was more natural for me.

Before Issey, I wasn't doing much runway in Paris, which was where the big money was. I was modeling to make as much money as possible, to get me closer to the theater. Paris is like the candy shop of fashion. It's everywhere. Even the most unclassifiable person is doing something interesting. Everywhere there are people trying things, with integrity, even if they remain obscure and neglected. There's something about

Paris, something in the air, in the earth, that always made it work as a center of fashion, this complicated weave of art, frivolity, entertainment, business, sex, illusion. There's something in the place itself, and the earth underneath it, something so powerful you can't mess with it. Hitler left it alone, after all.

Issey took me under his wing. He made me the lead, almost the host, of this radical runway show he organized in 1976 where there were twelve black models wearing his daring new clothes. I would sing and have multiple roles within what was a fashion show remade as a happening. Issey wanted his shows to be more than just fashion, the mundane display of clothes—he wanted theater, scandal, a different kind of event beyond fashion, beyond show business, pure experience, always with an undercurrent of imaginative strength. Even then he was breaking free of the idea of what a model was, and of conventional ideals of beauty.

This show was a fantastic, subversive idea, still ahead of its time. Twelve black models from South America, New York, Africa, Paris, on a monthlong tour of Japan in theaters—fifteen thousand people came to see it. The show was called *Issey Miyake and Twelve Black Girls*.

Who else would think of using only black girls, even now? This was girl power from Mars. I think he liked how as black models having to fight for attention in a very exclusionary world we were more spirited than the norm. Having foreign girls in Japan created a sense of fantasy—instant, transfixing otherness. Wherever I moved I always seemed to bring otherness with me, because I was always in a new place, an outsider. I never quite belonged wherever I landed, moving from place to place, but always acted as though I did, creating a blur between belonging and not belonging.

Michael Douglas and Jack Nicholson came to see Issey's show. They were in Japan promoting *One Flew Over the Cuckoo's Nest*. Of course they took us out after one of the shows. Jack ordered a couple of limos. Jack, Michael, and all the models—it was very crazy.

A couple of the models were a little too starstruck, throwing themselves at Jack. And he was manipulating the situation. There was that Barry White bass in the background. He would sit there with his arms outstretched and big come-on grin, being Jack even then. Before I knew it, girls started to disappear one by one. I found out the next day from my roommate, an African princess who spoke only French, that he was inviting each girl to meet in the car, and each girl thought she was the only one. And one by one they turned up.

I caught his eye and I could tell what he was up to. I wagged my finger. *No, Jack. No way.* I am wired to leave when it is heading that way. It did not seem interesting to me. I was not going to go with a bunch of girls losing the plot. I went home. I had a big word with them the next day! Much later on, many years later, I met Jack and quietly found out for myself what he was like. Actually, we mostly talked about hats, and who had the better collection.

To this day, when the celebrities turn up—Bette, Stevie Wonder, Elton John—I have to warn my band, *Do not let this freak you out.* You get distracted. Even the Queen was not going to distract me. I'd learned to set the example as a girl: *Make a good impression, don't fall apart—there is a proper way to conduct yourself.* Maybe it's a Jamaican thing. No gawking. I thought these models were going to die, they were so overwhelmed. And this was a complicated theatrical show, a musical without dialogue. A lot of cues requiring a lot of concentration. I had never seen anything like it. The way my live shows developed over the years was based on that Japanese trip.

Issey is the only real artist in fashion—smart, sensitive, very humble. Somewhere between a poet and engineer, philosopher and architect, refining centuries of tradition, but always in the future, and somewhere in space, the space he borrowed from the idea of the kimono, and how between the body and the kimono there is only an approximate contact.

He once said that he went into fashion because it was a creative format that is bright and optimistic, and he was there as a seven-year-old cycling to school on the day that the Americans dropped the atom bomb on his hometown, Hiroshima. His mother died three years later from radiation poisoning. She had been severely burned but carried on working as a teacher. He wanted to think of things that can be created, not destroyed, that bring beauty and joy.

He was in Paris at the time of the May 1968 student revolts, which made him question fashion as being something only frivolous and trivial. To Issey, fashion is more than designs, or clothes, or inventions—it is visions, ideas and dreams, turned into wearable, flowing solid objects, shells, algae, stones turned into material. I wear his clothes every day to this day, and even those pieces I've worn for years still surprise me. He once said that his clothes are unfinished, and how they get finished is by being worn for years.

They're clothes you can wear in the street, but they're theatrical enough to wear onstage. They became part of my look, even if I chose to wear just one of his pieces, just a breastplate. He would do things for me, not to market, just for Grace. He knew I liked hoods, so he would do a collection of hoods.

You cannot copy him. You can try, but people will say, *You are copying Issey.* He invents fabric that changes color depending on the time of day. He boils fabric, melts it, uses bamboo and ultrasound to treat his cloth. The way his clothes fold, they form a starburst when you open them up. Unbelievable. He was the first person to give me a chance in a runway show. I'd been to see everyone, and no wanted me. As soon as I did an Issey runway show, twenty-seven people who had previously rejected me for runway came backstage and asked that I do runway for them.

Working with him took me into the whole world of the Orient, which made a big difference to my music and performance. He really liked me, and we have stayed very good friends. We took an interest in each other. I said I was going to stop modeling, and he could see that I was serious about that, that I was interested, like him, in going into spaces where no one else was going. Not a singer, not a model, not a dancer, not an actress, not a performance artist: all of that together, and therefore something else. That's why he set me up as the leader of the show, to help me work out how to be more than only a model.

Working with Issey meant working with the best people, the unique, innovative, edgy women he likes to surround himself with who have something often underestimated in fashion—a great, mischievous sense of humor. Eiko Ishioka, who designed the costumes for the opening ceremony of the Beijing Olympics, was the art director of *Twelve Black Girls*. She worked on Francis Ford Coppola's *Dracula*, because Coppola wanted the costumes to be sets in themselves. She was good at drug-dream vampire brides. I was still working with her on a tour in 2009, and she made what little I wore when I was set before the Queen during her Diamond Jubilee celebration. She once said her clothes were not meant to be comfortable—they were meant to torture the wearer.

That first Issey experience made me focus on what I was and who I was based on the evidence I had—from the past, present, and future, from other people I had been, from other people I would become. He did a whole book, *East Meets West*, about this way of making something from one piece of cloth. I would make something from one person. And that one person was now, much to her surprise, a singer. A disco singer.

4

Disco

Before disco, it was soul music that people danced to; it was funk . . . soul music and funk . . . a saucy, languid Latin swing coming up over the horizon, a place where Miles Davis had taken jazz falling from the sky . . . that's how it was for me. There were clubs where there was music and dancing to all kinds of music . . . and it all came together, in one room, on one floor, under lights that flashed for life, and became disco. It became *Let's go to the disco,* and in the disco there were DJs making music as much as playing it.

Before it was called disco, there were simply dance spaces, party rooms in downtown warehouses and borrowed places over the bridges and through the tunnels out of Manhattan. Lots of places where music you could dance to would be played, creating a demand for a certain sort of venue playing a certain sort of music. The combination of the venue and the music meant that the music that emerged from the meeting of the place and the sound was both the name of the venue and the music—you went to the disco to dance to disco. And you need a DJ to play the records, to choose the range and sequence of the music. The DJ had started to take over the role occupied by the jukebox in the mid-'60s. Disco was the place, it was the music, and it was the DJ and the dancers and then very quickly, it stood for the disco image.

The fact that I made disco music was an accident really. When I made my first records, I didn't think of them as being disco. I made them in France, and the word *discothéque* is a French word, but it did not have the same meaning that it was beginning to have in New York. I didn't characterize them as anything. They were simply songs, with a little bit of soul and rhythm, echoes of singing in church, a sense of something showy whipped up by being in Paris with all the fashion, around the people making it happen.

The first single I released, "I Need a Man," sounds a little churchy in its original state—it could be gospel, and wherever the best disco goes, it never loses that ecstatic feel, that the music that became disco came from soul and funk and therefore gospel. Most of the words had been written by an anonymous, hardworking session guy called Paul Slade. He was in Paris writing English words for French singers who wanted to sing in English. Stephan had put the call out for some words to this track we had, and we chose Slade's because he had followed best the brief we had given him. I helped out with the words, but I didn't know that I was meant to take credit, in order to get paid. I learned that lesson very quickly.

After I recorded "I Need a Man," Stephan in Paris made contact with a New York couple he had heard of called Sy and Eileen Berlin. They were in the clothing business but were going into music, and they became his backers in America. They had the money, and they had formed a management company with the publicist John Carmen, looking after acts like Double Exposure, who released the first-ever commercial 12-inch single, and the salsoul group First Choice.

I remember they once commissioned an eight-foot-tall replica in gold leaf of King Tut's head for First Choice to take on tour as a prop. That's the kind of promoters they were—old-style theater and film show business adapting to the new disco era and permanently on the lookout for new talent. (Eileen was the first to manage a young Tom Cruise in the early 1980s.) At first they didn't have a solo act, and they were looking for something like me. It all clicked.

John Carmen came with Sy and Eileen and he started doing my publicity, propelling my driven, rampageous behavior out into the world whether I was ready or not, where it would become how people got to know me and make their mind up about what I was like. The number one P.R. man in New York in the '70s, Carmen was a publicity magician and made me famous in New York, like he did later for the likes of Donald Trump. Sy and Eileen were super independent, operating a small family-run fashion business. They were starting out in the music business, and they were very much not corporate. That's what I liked about them. They were a little like Euro Planning in Paris—more the underdogs, small, determined to make a splash. They were very enthusiastic about me, but they had a very different vision for me.

Their limited plan was for me to start with disco, which was then fast becoming *the* trend, and then move to singing in Hilton hotels in long glittery ball gowns before getting to Vegas. To me, them asking me to do this was a little like my mother asking me to marry a preacher. Disco in this plan as the new hot thing was the place to start. Doors could open quicker because the rules weren't quite in place; something was forming that you could find ways into. Its home was in New York, inside a very few hectic, inbred square miles.

Sy and Eileen worked closely with a lot of disco acts like the Village People and Bobby Orlando and were in touch with record producer Tom Moulton, who worked out of Sigma Sound in Philadelphia. He had developed the 12-inch disco mix format, which involved extending the rhythmical parts of a track to make the song longer, and better to dance to, because there were no vocals. He made the accidental discovery when a song meant for a 7-inch was instead cut onto 12-inch vinyl, leading him to understand how dynamic and physical this made it sound. Longer and louder. Perfect.

He came up with the idea of the disco break from watching how people dance to music in the clubs, and seeing that their favorite parts to dance to were the instrumental sequences and the extended jamming parts of jazz-funk tracks. They hated it when a record changed and the vibe was ruined. In those dancing situations, music had to flow. This was a very new idea, and before disco became the bad, kitsch disco, a very important moment in the development not only of dance music but of pop music in general and, later, even rock.

Then again, perhaps there were these long instrumental sections so that the DJs could have a toilet break. Eight minutes of music, enough time to make it to the toilet and back. What happened in the toilet that was not necessarily about going to the toilet might then have influenced the kind of relentless mixes that the DJs favored.

Tom would spend days editing tapes together, segueing the instrumental passages into one seamless rhythm, for the gay clubs on Fire Island, where he said he saw white people dance to black music for the first time. These white people were gays, responding to the thrust and thrill of the music. That was the key in a way—the bringing together of two outside appetites into one singular sound, radical new power being generated by society's frustrated outcasts. Then there was the realization that the sound of a record was different for the radio than for the clubs. It all sounds obvious now, but back then it was all brand-new. His thinking helped revolutionize dancing—people would dance for hours on end without a break, working up a sweat.

It was the stark beat, enhanced, and embellished—a little like the way the artist Richard Bernstein exaggerated and emphasized the look of fame and adjusted the color and shape of a face. Richard did the artwork for one of the original "I Need a Man" covers. Sy and Eileen knew Richard, as he had worked on the album cover for their band Black Soul. It was part of the whole thing clicking into place. I had some photos from Paris that Antonio had taken, and these were the ones Richard treated in the way he treated Andy Warhol's *Interview* covers. Around that time we also used some photographs that the wonderful, incredibly modest Bill Cunningham took of me making my way around the streets of New York, long before anyone knew who I was. That's when I was a model working hard to get jobs, as anonymous as anyone. For decades, he pedaled on his bike throughout New York, snapping what people were wearing as they went about their business. He has been fascinated by the clothes that New Yorkers wore since the 1950s. Born in 1929, a few months after Andy Warhol, he was the opposite of Andy, even though he was just as much about and of New York. He didn't care about celebrity, or fashion, and wasn't even that bothered about faces. People being people delighted him—the upper class or the avant-garde—and the idea that being yourself in New York was something special. Accidentally or intentionally, he consistently anticipated new clothing trends, so fashion editors loved and trusted him, and he was uniquely embedded in daily New York life, so the *New York Times* used his photographs as social commentary. I walked around New York a lot, so he took hundreds of photographs of me, just passing him while he was hunting the everyday remarkable. Fifty-Seventh Street was his favorite location, near where I lived. He once said that there, on Fifth Avenue, you could wait and eventually see the whole world pass by. I'm as excited to be part of Bill's New York as I am to be a part of Andy's.

Richard did all the great star covers for *Interview,* which chronicled the comings and goings of the heated-up in-crowd that orbited around Warhol's Factory between Max's Kansas City in the late '60s and Studio 54 in the late '70s. The covers were supersize, the colors saturated. He was Warhol's favorite local artist and would treat celebrity photographs by airbrushing them and retouching them with pastel and pencil scrawls and shadows. It gave the faces a glamorous big-time dreamtime edge as though they were all inhabiting New York embedded in a Hollywood fantasy. Richard was a link between old Hollywood glamour and the more subversive, nebulous glamour of the new underground art scene.

If you knew Richard and you knew Andy, you were right at the epicenter of a hard-working fairy-tale New York that consisted of people like Viva, Candy Darling, Calvin Klein, Halston, Divine, Roman Polanski, Diane von Furstenberg, Robert Mapplethorpe. If you knew how to get in to where it was all happening, everyone seemed to be in the same place on the same trip. Richard was one of those whose job was to capture the trip, and be a major part of it. To be of the scene, you had to be intimately connected with it.

Andy was taking the already exotic and making it even more so, to make sure that there was no doubt that the subjects were worthy of attention. He was fascinated by fame, as an artist but also as a fan. Andy always wanted the famous to look as perfectly impossibly perfect as they could be, which required Richard to build them up into these glorious panels of color. He would treat the newcomers the same, those that were about to be famous or notorious, giving them this instant, colorized glow of fame, with a subtle hint of something brittle, because the clock was ticking. Fame only lasted so long, according to Andy. I had been treated by Richard for Andy Warhol's *Interview* number 24, which showed

Andy taking my photograph with me wearing a Santa Claus hat. Richard also designed the cover of my first album, produced by Tom Moulton.

It was all part of the same sense of making entertainment for a world craving pleasure and escape larger, bolder, and brasher, and more energetically enchanting. The unsettling growing chaos of the threatening, corrupt, and paranoid world out there, all the political scandals and indefinite wars and crises, needed to be kept at bay. Presidents and governments were cracking up; people needed to look after themselves, and create their own new rules and customs.

Richard remixed images of the famous to make the stars more obviously famous looking, from a wonderful fantasy that must never end, and Tom was remixing dance music to make it more obviously about the fantasy of dance, to ensure the rhythm never had to stop. Songs that were three minutes long would now go on longer, and longer, so that the spell would not be broken. The bits that were part of making the song longer started to become more sophisticated, and started to become the best part.

Tom Moulton was given my early tracks that were recorded in Paris, "I Need a Man" with an instrumental mix on the B-side, and then "Sorry" and "That's the Trouble," that we put out as a double A-side, because I didn't want one of them to be a mere B-side. A B-side was seen as a throwaway. I said, "Why am I going to record something you chuck away? It will be a double A, like the battery. High energy." I could never understand some of these stupid rules.

I wrote "Trouble" with a French-Greek writer, Pierre Papadiamandis, who created great, effervescent French-style melodies. He'd written something for a Johnny Hallyday album. That was my first collaboration in music. He couldn't speak English, so he had no idea what I was singing about, and he went by sound rather than sense when we recorded me. My accent was alien anyway, an alien English, and this embellished the alien. I was singing English like I was making it up as a language as I went along. The record went out in New York on a small label attached to Berlin/Carmen management, Beam Junction, which had released Black Soul.

Even then I had made up my mind that I was not going to do the music unless I had some control over it, enough to keep my interest. There was enough going on around me that I was not yet in control of, certainly in terms of writing songs, and choosing material, at least that part I was in control of. You have to start somewhere.

Tom mixed those first three songs to sound more New York and pulsating than they had been in France, and that was definitely toward the coalescing sound of disco, which is a little mathematical, very organized in its own way, to achieve control in the clubs, to create the right mood and movement—and in the end, it still comes out of the church.

Disco in its purest sense means that you will come out of a place having gone into euphoria, feeling that you have rejoiced. That's the sense the disc jockey in the clubs was helping crowds achieve, and Tom took it into the recording studio. Mixing the music to completely control your emotions, bringing you up, taking you down, slowing you down, speeding you up, making you soft, making you hard. A great groundbreaking 1970s 12-inch mix was the sound of an erection—of one shape becoming another. It was obvious that such an idea would come from the gay clubs. Tom was really one of the first, if not *the* first, to take that new idea of manipulating rhythm and pace of the club onto a record that in turn would be played in the clubs.

He had already started work on giving "La Vie en Rose" a disco boost, but he hadn't done it specifically for me. He made a backing track without knowing who was going to sing it, and I was there at the right time, with the right image. He was very sure of himself and his instincts at the time, and because he was clearly the master of this new form he'd helped define, I went along with it all. He was the expert and someone to learn from. I would push myself as hard as I could in order to give him what he wanted. You can hear my determination on the track—the determination that was lifting me into singing, if not necessarily as a singer.

The disco producers were very much the kind of producers who created the track without the singer, and added them at the end. Tom mixed the first three tracks in New York while I was in Paris, and the next thing I hear is that I have a dance hit. I hadn't even heard what he had done. I didn't meet Tom until I went over to New York after the song was a club hit. Sy and Eileen had called me over to do some promotion, singing the three songs I had in the underground clubs.

I had a little crush on Tom, because he was very good-looking, a former model. He was also another demanding, complicated man. As usual I had no idea he was gay. It must have been the man in me, tangled up inside, that always fell for gays, and also for something I didn't have that I wanted to know about. I was living in Paris, so I didn't know much about him.

I would go out to Sigma in Philly to record with him. I think Tom was always a little irritated when I would act a little, as he saw it, precious. Singing there meant overcoming quite a lot of nerves, first of all about whether I could sing and secondly about how it sounded. Tom was very like Gamble and Huff in the studio. No nonsense, the vocals merely a part of the overall effect, and he would expect the vocals to come as easily as the playing of a rhythm. The drummer or the drums didn't need to rest a while before they performed, or need a special drink, so he didn't understand why I did.

I needed to be pampered a little before I sang, even if by myself. Tom thought that was very self-indulgent, but then he underestimated what it takes to deliver a certain kind of performance in the recording studio, one that was done inside pretty much an empty room but that would come across as a great moment and last for a long time. He was one of those producers who like to tinker, and the human element, the actual soul, was not something he wanted to waste too much time on. I think the thing he respected the most about me was my absolute determination to succeed. He thought of me not as a singer but rather as a personality bringing presence to the record. Part of the packaging. Years later, in interviews about that time, Tom would say how annoyed he was that I came across as confused. He said that I was always asking him to come into the vocal booth to help me with the singing. He thought it was silly and pathetic. What he never realized was that this was because I thought he was so hot. It was the only way I could think of to get him to stand close to me. I wasn't so ditzy, apart from the fact I didn't appreciate that there was no way he would ever be interested in me. I wasn't quite man enough for him.

When I heard Tom's mixes I thought my voice sounded really fast. He had sped me up to fit his slick, swinging version of the track. Also, when I did the vocals originally I had a fever, and I was still very shy singing in a studio in front of people. I did the vocals under a table, hidden from sight. Maybe I should have danced on the table. When I heard it, I could tell I had a cold. He treated my voice a little, but not enough to disguise that. It sounded very different from what we had done in Paris. Guy Cuevas, the DJ at Club Sept in Paris, would play it because we became good friends, but I always felt he was not really sure about it.

I was certain that I wasn't going to do any more music in Paris. There was something inauthentic when the French tried to do American or English pop. London was the nearest place where I felt the music scene would work for me, but I didn't go at the time. I think I was put off by the IRA bombings there, which made me think London was a war zone, and by a feeling that somehow London would be too gloomy for me.

Going back to New York once the record was a club hit meant I was going to a place that suited my desire to take my music more seriously, rather than as something on the side. I told the head of Euro Planning to give all my bookings to my friend Toukie Smith. She was the sister of the first major black fashion designer, Willi Smith. Toukie had always wanted to be a model, but her body was the wrong shape for her to get much work in America. Toukie had the big tits that Helmut Newton complained I didn't have.

She had come out to Japan to be part of Issey's *Twelve Black Girls* show. Issey loved her look, and while we were part of the show we became very close. I said she should come back to Paris with me, and because I was now concentrating on the music, I thought she could have my work in Paris. When I traveled to New York for a few weeks I said she could move into the apartment I shared with my boyfriend at the time, Jeanyves. I trusted them both, and at the time she was going out with an illustrator and artist called Jean-Paul Goude. He had become the art director at *Esquire* magazine at the end of the 1960s, and was still there in the mid-'70s.

He was in the Factory orbit, and worked with Richard Bernstein, knew Andy Warhol, and also the writer Glenn O'Brien, who had edited *Interview* between 1971 and 1974 before leaving under a cloud of bad feeling. He had hired Richard in 1972. Later Glenn would host a New York public access TV show called *TV Party,* decades ahead of its time, and edit Madonna's *Sex* book.

I had a fling with Glenn not long after the orgasm eruption with my hair stylist Andre. This was where the Factory world could get a little soap opera, and often inbred. He was very shy, nicely intense, and dry. I liked shy people. I liked talking with him; it was more a mental relationship with Glenn than with Andre. I like both sides. The physical orgasm, the mental orgasm. Glenn and I shared mental orgasms. He had a great, very sophisticated and stimulating mind. He could keep your interest, and you would learn something after you talked with him. I like a mind that takes you into unexpected places. He was very much the opposite of Andre, which is probably why I went there after that macho disaster. No more lover-man, something a little more insightful and intellectually uplifting. At least for a while. I guess these were always the two sorts of men I was attracted to—the man of action, or the man of philosophy. If possible, the man who was both. The action body meets the mind in action.

What Andre did to my hair, Glenn did to my sense of being able to see things in a different light. His friend Jean-Paul had seen me perform "La Vie en Rose" for the Met Gala at the Metropolitan Museum of Art's Costume Institute—he saw me before I saw him, put it that way. He saw me in my new natural habitat. Richard had taken him because he had designed my show, dressing me up as a multicolored luminescent chandelier in a tribute to the artist Erté.

Jean-Paul became more than intrigued with me and how I looked and what I might be like in bed. He would probe Glenn about what kind of men I liked, and what turned me on; he was creating a fantasy about me even before we met. He saw me sing "I Need a Man" in front of a gay audience at a club with a bare torso and a prom dress. There was nothing pretty about it, nothing obvious, it was dramatically exhibitionistic, and there was a tangle of signals in terms of who was what and who was entertaining who. He was instantly captivated. I don't think he fancied my looks. He fancied my spirit.

I was not his physical type at all, really. Bountiful Toukie was, and he liked to make sculptures of her, making her even more voluptuous and proud, but I was too skinny and boisterous. He wasn't my type, either—intellectually he was, but I liked pretty boys. The models. Jeanyves in Paris was like a throwback to the Three Musketeers, suave and dashing. I'm not sure how it worked, but while Toukie was in Paris, she and Jean-Paul started to split up.

She didn't tell me. I thought we were really good friends, although I did a lot of the talking, and she did a lot of the listening. So she never told me what was going on. She knew all my secrets, but she told me nothing. She would just go *mmm-hmm* as I chatted. But they broke up. Jean-Paul said I indirectly contributed to the breakup by helping her model in Paris and letting her stay in my apartment.

Clubs were everywhere in New York, out of sight but there for those who knew where they were, and the first time I sang in public it was Halloween, perfect for me, in New York at the Gallery on West Twenty-Second Street. Twenty-two-year-old Nicky Siano had opened the Gallery in 1972, having consciously designed it as a glowing, throbbing dance palace, and his inventive disc jockeying made it one of the great clubs. His approach to DJing was that of a collagist, cutting up tracks, layering sound effects, suddenly switching the flow, catching you out, lifting you up, weaving a hundred tracks into one so you couldn't hear the join; he was the essence of the idea of the DJ as an improvising composer and dedicated showman. He would say, "When the crowd gets off, I get off," and he wanted to make them scream.

John Carmen had been nagging him to put me on at the Gallery. Nicky said later that when he finally met me at Sy and Eileen's, after I made sure I made quite an entrance wearing an extravagant headdress, legs and arms akimbo, he was entranced because I was so exotic. He invited me to perform at his club.

The Gallery had a very small stage—really just a part of the floor—

as was usual in those early underground clubs, and the audience was crammed into a tiny room. It reminded me of a couple of the drag and strip clubs I used to go to in Paris with Antonio, where it was so full it seemed like there were bodies on bodies, some of them so close they were penetrating each other, lubricated by their own sweat. The stage was so small you couldn't have a band, so you would use playback, like I had seen at the drag clubs in Paris. I also thought that unless you could get a band to play the music as great as on the record, there was no point. The music was beginning to be made electronically—machines were increasingly being used, especially to generate rhythms—so it seemed wrong to have a band and try to reproduce it. These drag shows proved to me that you would not miss the band as long as you put together a show. The show was important for this sort of music, not musicians playing live. There was no room anyway.

I was criticized, because people thought I was miming. This was a real no-no. I would go out of my way to make sure the audience knew I was singing live—I would talk in the middle of a song, I would ad lib, I would throw in something different, to make it obvious I was live, and the rest, the playback, it didn't matter as long as I was for real. It was inexpensive, too, not to have the band.

I had my three songs. That was the extent of my repertoire. They would play the extended Tom Moulton instrumental mixes as an introduction to make the show longer, and to build up tension. I wore my Darth Vader Miyake; that was my uniform, mystery in layers, so you could take a layer off, and then another layer, eventually stripping down to a skintight bodysuit. I came with my fashion feel and the whole Issey sensibility, the theater I had learned from Japan, the stillness and bareness, and went for it like a bat out of hell. I was aggressive about the minimalism.

I had learned that stillness was a better way for me to appear. I wasn't so great a dancer that I was going to wow people with movement. I never try to do what I know I am not the best at. I couldn't dance but I knew how to walk and how to freeze. I had done a whole season of Parisian catwalk and *Twelve Black Girls* in Japan. I also used anything around the stage as the stage, so I wasn't hemmed in. I would crawl all over the place, hiss at people, bark in their faces, and pretend to slap people sitting near me. No one had seen anything like that. Rumors shot around the city—*You have to see this girl, it's outrageous, disco that cuts into you, show business that threatens you. She's as mad as hungry tigers.*

An actress, Tara Tyson, who later became branded a Manhattan socialite after she married the Greek shipping magnate and technology pioneer M. Michael Kulukundis, came along to one of the shows to see what the fuss was about. That was the start of a lifelong friendship. She had small parts in TV shows like *Charlie's Angels* and *Starsky & Hutch,* and had appeared in off-Broadway productions with titles like "Foreplay" and "Porno Stars at Home." Andy photographed her, and she was also a favorite of the beauty-loving superstar photographer Francesco Scavullo, who was responsible for the classic *Cosmopolitan* cover look. Usually, this was the glamorized very white all-American look, but there was a photograph of the black model Naomi Sims on the cover in 1973. It didn't break any new ground, but it was an interesting moment that suggested another possible world.

After Tara married, she gave up acting because her husband did not like her working—the thing I always said I would never do. I once found her at a party locked into her bathroom giving an exclusive one-woman performance for the likes of Al Pacino and Christopher Walken. They were entranced. She had a lot to give, even though her husband didn't want her to. She was a dynamo. She once got in a fight with legendary restaurant hostess Elaine Kaufman at her literary clubhouse, Elaine's. Elaine scratched Tara's face, punched Tara's date, the costume designer Jacques Bellini, in the face, and then kicked them out, claiming Tara had bumped into her with a cigarette and set her dress on fire. "Not my face," Tara shrieked as Elaine scratched her. "I thought she was a transvestite," Elaine said in her defense. Tara was my kind of girl, from my kind of New York, and she loved the way I tore up the stage.

I would have dry-ice fog rolling around the stage, at about waist height, to appear out of and sink into like an animal on the prowl. Because there was no real stage, I had a chair as a prop. Very French cabaret. Leg up! That's all you need. When the stage is tiny, or nonexistent, ask for a chair, and stick your leg up. Voilà—theater. One spotlight on your face. That's all you need to generate mystery.

Nicky then went out after me dressed, somewhere between accurately and madly, as Diana Ross, as if the whole thing was about having a tongue in your cheek. That made me think! It was like in Paris—you can learn a lot about performing in a small, dark space by watching drag queens stretch credibility. I was working on my routine, building up the parts. A little bit of Kabuki stillness, a warrior slash of drag debauchery, a dash of black humor, shoulders out of a gothic fantasy, a load of tease. And repeat. Perfect.

Nicky was one of the first real DJs-as-stars, turning the process of playing records into a flamboyant performance. The decks and the booth were a kind of stage, and he was one of the first to make the idea of mixing records together an art. He was a big influence on Frankie Knuckles and Larry Levan, who was a light man at the Gallery. Nicky later became a resident DJ at 54, before he was sacked after four months for— so they said—excessive drug taking. Some say it was because he played the whole of "Trans-Europe Express" by Kraftwerk, all seven minutes. A bit of both I think—too druggy and extreme, and too interested in less obvious music. Fifty-Four quickly became more about the hyped-up theater and horseplay than about new music; the creation of wild, limitless fun was becoming a very serious moneymaking business.

I think at its best in that New York period when it was being invented as something radical and noisy, disco was some of the greatest music ever. It had conviction and was as much about resistance as it was about escape; it was being invented by very creative and driven people. It drew variously from soul, funk, gospel, pop, rock, jazz, and musicals, and the breaks and segues introduced a very innovative approach to musical structure.

Obviously because of what it became, how it turned very fast into a novelty, it seems ridiculous to point out that in those years before 54 it was actually an experimental enterprise. Disco was damned and there was the anti-disco movement, and for decades before the retro-disco of Daft Punk and company there was a phrase "dead as disco," but you went to those clubs to feel great, and those early disc jockeys were setting in motion a lot of the ideas that traveled through house and hip-hop and the freer versions of disco into the twenty-first century.

You have to separate the commercialized style of disco from the underground places where the ideas first appeared. Disco got a terrible reputation, like it was anti-music, but its beginnings were in many ways more radicalized, inclusive, and open-minded than rock. It was as much an assault on the corniness and narrow-mindedness of rock as punk. Where it ended up was the fault of the white, straight music business, which drained it of all its blackness and gayness, its rawness and volatility, its original contagious, transgressive abandon.

Those early New York club DJs were astonishing in the way they manipulated sound and emotion. The excellence and detail they put into spinning records was breathtaking. They were the originals, and their spirit is at the heart of the success of dance music as an international phenomenon. It took time, really, for that idea of the DJ as superstar to take hold, and once disco went from being a subcultural phenomenon with no real faces or identifiable personalities into the mainstream, it didn't work, because it didn't really have an identity. By the time it made it into the mainstream, the formula had been reduced to a very banal 4/4 rhythm, lacking muscle and erotic accuracy; the scintillating cut-up technique had been smoothed away, and the kinds of personalities who tended to front the tracks were usually quite middle-of-the-road or gimmicky. This was before Madonna took her version of the New York club scene around the world—she softened the edges, toned down the drama, moistened the excess, sheathed the flirtation, but in the outside pop world, it still seemed pretty racy.

Why did disco become so hated? Some say it was because almost everyone started to go disco to chase the dollar. Everyone jumped on the glitter wagon, from the Muppets to Kiss. Rod Stewart took it to bed. Ethel Merman even did a disco album when she was seventy-one, first track "There's No Business like Show Business!" Where could it go after Ethel Merman?

The funny thing is, the first critique of my voice on "I Need a Man," where I was trying to be theatrical and a little Broadway, said that it was like a combination of Ethel Merman and David Bowie. Maybe more because of my androgynous look than because of how it really sounded. Being a man and a woman all tangled up. I sang so low people thought I was a transvestite—there were definite suspicions that I was not a girl.

On my first album, I was doing pounding disco versions of the classic Broadway songs—maybe that's where they got the idea from for Ethel. I sowed the seeds of disco's own destruction even as I helped disco become disco. I did "Send in the Clowns," after all. It was Tom's idea. I don't know if it was a gay thing, but I was happy to sing them. I knew and loved these songs because of my theater training, and any good vocal coach gives you those songs to sing to understand technique.

"La Vie en Rose" was not disco. It's not the formula. But in the early days of disco there was more variety of music that would be played, not least because there weren't that many disco records in the beginning. It was like a throwback to that, when there were different sorts of tracks being mixed in with the more blatant dance records. What counted was the mood they created.

In the disco era it became the song to finish off the night, when the clubs would play something romantic before the lights went up, a last round of fantasy, to slowly come back down to earth. All around the world. It was a mainstream hit everywhere except America.

The first person to play "La Vie en Rose" on the radio was the great and natty New York City radio personality and DJ Frankie Crocker, who made a name for himself by playing an eclectic range of music, from Led Zeppelin to Barry White, salsa to Bob Marley, Streisand to Lee "Scratch" Perry, crossing genres and color lines, before the barriers came down. He was the first to play Donna Summer, and no one played Queen before he did. He called himself the Chief Rocker; Hollywood became his middle name because he was so flamboyant and an absolute expert at grabbing attention. He was also known as the black Elvis, at ease in Studio 54 or Harlem. He had a hatful of nicknames, was adept at changing identities to suit different settings, and was a template for the show-off star DJ, driving around in a powder-blue Rolls-Royce, wearing a suit of the same color.

There were, he would say, seven wonders in the world. But if there were eight, he was the eighth. You can hear early forms of rap in some of his suave, seductive patter, a direct inspiration to those New Yorkers who created hip-hop—*I am going to put more dips in your hips, more cut in your strut, more glide in your stride. If you don't dig it, you know you got a hole in your soul. Tall, tan, young, and fly.* He's featured on the Sugar Hill Gang's "Rapper's Delight."

Frankie was responsible for defining WBLS, the early black progressive FM station in New York, becoming its program director in 1972. He was the kind of self-loving program director who would feature himself naked and smiling with groomed Afro and lover-man mustache on a huge billboard advertising the station—"If you want the best in New York, listen to Frankie." It wasn't just jive, though. He had a real belief in the power of music to change things.

He would play the disco just breaking out of the local clubs interspersed with classic R & B: Stevie Wonder, Aretha, Wilson Pickett, Marvin Gaye, and Isaac Hayes. He understood that a black audience wasn't all the same, one single mass, but was a malleable collection of different tastes and desires. This was when DJs for black radio stations had a vital community role, as preachers, leaders, and reporters, communicating ideas, not merely playing music.

He was an idealistic show-business renegade, but he loved the ladies. Love Man was another of his names. On his show, which I appeared on a few times, he would pretend to take a bubble bath with a female guest, complete with sound effects. I had met him at the Hippopotamus Club, where my brother Chris worked, and he was a deadly charmer, with an eye for white girls. He liked that I worked in the modeling industry and could always introduce him to my friends. I loved his boasts—"Before me there were none, after me there shall be no more"—and took on board his method of making an entrance. Then again, I like to think I taught him a thing or two as well.

He would go out to find new records, not wait for them to be delivered to him. He was always on the hunt. By 1976, he was so powerful and black, having built up enough of a faithful following to have become mayor of the city, that there was an attempt to undermine him, with allegations that he took drugs and money to play certain records. He was convicted, but the decision was overturned.

This was when radio was central to the American cultural experience and the shaping of popular music, and being played by Frankie made a world of difference, because he was famous for breaking new acts at a time when black artists were barely making pop playlists.

I still had an apartment in Paris and I still had a boyfriend there. I had nowhere to live in New York. It was after "La Vie en Rose" that I moved back to New York. Sy and Eileen put me in a dinky New York hotel called the Wellington, and that's where I lived until I found my first apartment. They advanced me the rent. They were really taking care of me—Tom Moulton always thought it was too much, and he hated how they fussed over me in the studio. I was in New York at the right time, especially if you consider that I was living in midtown when Studio 54 opened. Studio 54 wasn't uptown and it wasn't downtown. It was, geographically, midtown. In truth, it was its own town.

The underground, downtown clubs weren't palaces of dreams like Studio 54. They didn't look like cathedrals filled with beautiful people; there were no exotic corners and secret rooms. They were seedy. There was a lot of sweat. The floors were soaked with spilled drinks and body fluids. There were holes in the wall that led God knows where. People passed in the night and never met in the day. No cleaning ladies doing the bathrooms. Funky spaces. Quaaludes, mescaline, acid, pretty much pre-coke. No liquor license, so you'd smuggle your own in, or take a pill, a little something to lift or distort your spirits. A bit of confetti, a few balloons, flashing lights, to make it all seem pretty. You wouldn't know what it was really like unless you stayed to the end, when the lights went up and you could see what a shitty hellhole it was. The lights go up, and the fantasy is spoiled. You need to keep the fantasy intact.

Disco was seriously dressing up soul and funk, going somewhere to be seen, where the beautiful people went—Halston, Calvin, Liza,

Bianca, the whole fashion world finding a fantasy that supported the fantasy they were committed to. The underground clubs in that part of Manhattan, where the streets have no numbers, were where you went to hear newer, edgier music that wasn't so much about fashion. They were places for the more serious social dancers. Those early underground places, like the Loft, the jewel of the private parties, came out of gay rights, hippie happenings, Afro-American rent parties in Harlem—before it all became so commercialized.

Studio 54, on West Fifty-Fourth Street between Seventh and Eighth Avenues, became the disco of all discos, those places to be seen, fashion displays with music, possibly because it was inside a theater, an old opera house with ceilings almost a hundred feet high. It took about seven years for the idea of what became known as disco to go from a few needy, speeding downtown revelers getting together in a stark, unpublicized warehouse in the middle of nowhere for raucous worship of rhythm to it being the overpublicized center of the celebrity universe.

A private insiders' party, a close, small community, became monstrously public. It was going from a place where it was really tricky to even find the door to get in to a place where those desperate to get inside would crowd around the roped-off entrance. So you knew exactly where the door was. This was where disco became more full-on, and ballooned into the outrageous and, ultimately, the camp. I suppose I arrived naked so many times it was partly my fault. But at the time, Studio 54 seemed like the place I had been heading for since I had left Jamaica—not the promised land, but some sort of grand playground where I could really forget about those whips and prayers. It would become a new place with rules and rituals to break free from, but for now, I was speaking in very different tongues.

There was Studio 54, and there was Max's and the underground clubs. Two approaches to glamour, one for the fashion people, one for the more intellectual people. One was more political than the other, but I was comfortable in both places because they were both about difference, filled with different people, and I liked difference. They represented different ways of developing the spirit of the '60s as one decade of change mutated into another, one into pure escapism, the other more experimental and almost academic in its pursuit of musical perfection. The two grooves coexisted within a few New York City blocks of each other. Punk and disco were becoming themselves at the same time within the same small area of Manhattan. It was a very small community, New York. The club scene, the art world, the music people, the fashion freaks, the energized, dislocated misfits, the gay spirit, different generations, various tribes with no name, all overlapping and interacting and spiraling off into new shapes.

Studio 54 appealed to my sense of outrage; the underground clubs appealed to my sense of exploration and adventure. It was the two sides of me—or two of the many sides—craving freedom. Fifty-Four offered a self-indulgent, excessive, even amoral form of freedom, and was a place where I could let it all hang out; the underground clubs satisfied the explorer in me seeking new discoveries. The key was learning how to balance these two sides—the irreverent me who'd turn up at a nightclub like I was the circus coming to town, and the me who was always interested in invention and innovation.

Before Studio 54 became notorious, it was the epitome of a certain kind of divergent identity shape-shifting, so there were the beautiful people, the poseurs, the fantasists, but there were also those with more cerebral urges. It was about the mix of people, all in one place. But the club's logo, after all, was the moon snorting coke off a spoon. Nothing was hidden. It was right out there in the open. You can't imagine America without drugs of one form or another, without its drugstores, rock stars, dealers, bored housewives, or bankers, and Studio 54 blew that notion up your nose so that you couldn't miss it. Made it so obvious that the country was on drugs, or it wouldn't make it through the day, that it became a problem.

Up high in the seats above the stalls, because this was a theater, you could disappear into the shadows and get up to whatever. Up above the balcony, there was the rubber room, with thick rubber walls that could be easily wiped down after all the powdery activity that went on. There was even something above the rubber room, beyond secretive, up where the gods of the club could engage in their chosen vice high up above the relentless dancers. It was a place of secrets and secretions, the in-crowd and inhalations, sucking and snorting. Everyone was in the grip of what seemed like an unlimited embrace.

Celebrities headed for the basement. Getting high low-down. Not even those who got inside the club could all make it into the basement. You'd stumble into half-hidden rooms filled with a few people who seemed to be sweating because of something they had just done, or were about to do.

The music was magical and the DJs were crowd-grabbing showmen. All the best DJs wanted to work there; the sound system was the very best, and they had their own special horseshoe-shaped booth to control things from. It all contributed to creating this special atmosphere, and at its best democratized pleasure: The anonymous drag queen could dance next to the international superstar and there was no difference. The lights were integral, so that as the music became more animated so did the lights. These were rave parties years before there was such a thing. Everyone got on famously.

One of my best girlfriends at the time, Carmen D'Alessio, was there at the beginning of Studio 54. We were very close and went dancing together all the time in those places for the few for whom the idea that dance music could have such spellbinding nighttime momentum was growing. The blend of space, light, and sound, the hot mass of bodies, the obscure but definite sense of occasion, and above all the music constantly released this feeling that anything was possible. You could dance on your own just for the hell of it. I would go all dressed up and come home with my designer clothes in tatters from all the activity and movement. Going out was a very physical thing.

I went to see the premises of Studio 54 with Carmen before it opened. She found the place, in the daytime, when you really had to use your imagination to realize what it could look like at night, with the lights, people, and noise knocking it into something else. "Look at this place," she said. "It's fantastic!" The first thing I did was check the acoustics—singing at the top of my voice—and because it was a theater and had been a TV studio, it sounded fantastic. Carmen knew what she was doing.

Andy called Carmen the number one jet-setter among all the jet-setters focusing on New York as the essential center of pleasure. He said she had the best list of everyone beautiful, young, and loaded. She was hired by 54's owners, Steve Rubell and Ian Schrager, to promote the club when it opened in April 1977, but obviously she would say that she created the whole idea of the club.

Ian was very quiet, not seen around much, but he had tremendous energy and paid very close attention to every little detail. He was a fan of Walt Disney and wanted to create a fantasyland for adults, a Magic Kingdom for hard-core sensualists. Steve was louder, always seeming a little drunk. Always spitting quaaludes into my face when he spoke, but sweet and lovable and into his family. They were still in their twenties, and the whole thing ran away from them. Oddly, they also went to college in Syracuse, my adopted American base, their hometown, where within a few years I would be celebrated in the city's equivalent of the Walk of Fame somewhere between Alec Baldwin and Lou Reed.

Steve and Ian wanted their club to reflect back and outdo the actual excess of the city, be a continual stream of big, juicy parties, and Carmen knew how to arrange that. She was a genius at event planning and turned the whole thing into a rampaging concept. She brought to bear a mix of the PR ingenuity she had learned from working for designers like Valentino, and the things she had learned from going to the clubs in New York about what made an almost dangerously great night out: erotic energy, and the classic New York melting-pot mixture of personalities and ambitions, where there would be gays, blacks, Latinos, whites, straights, transvestites, celebrities, nonentities. It's like an acid trip without taking acid, where you are provoked to such an extent by all the metamorphosis going on around you that it seemed the dressed-up, turned-on people really did have horns growing out of their skulls; that there really were centaurs, angels, and devils; and that the music was the sound of sex, foreplay to orgasm, first kiss to the little death.

What went on was in some way a harbinger of the haywire shamelessness of reality TV—minor celebrities fighting among minor celebrities to avoid losing their fame, demented role-playing, the not famous doing whatever it took to get some attention, the truly famous and aloof and immune watching it all as a kind of sport for their amusement.

It was really a place where you had these big, spectacularly designed parties, as though every night was an opening night. There really would be a naked black man leading a naked woman on a white pony through a curtain of gold streamers, pagan-style events with real circus animals; Armani welcomed with a drag queen ballet; cakes in the shape of Elizabeth Taylor presented by a marching army of decorated Rockettes. Carmen popped out of a cake at her own party, something I am very fond of doing to this day. Crowds would gather outside to get in, and if you were gorgeous enough, more than famous enough—although gorgeous *and* famous was the golden key—you would pass the door policy. Some would be desperate to do whatever it took to get from the outside to the inside, and then if they managed that, to get from the outer circle into the inner circle.

For the actual, original opening night Carmen sent out five thousand invitations promising a special gift. So many people turned up that legend has it that Cher, Woody Allen, and Warren Beatty couldn't even get in. They say Frank Sinatra didn't even bother to get out of his limo once he saw the chaos around the door as people fought to get inside.

Once you found yourself inside, 54 was a kind of heaven or a kind of hell, or both, of highness—the highness of drugs, of groomed, glistening noise punching out of massive speakers, of flash dancing, of close, thrilling association with the famous and infamous, or explicit displays of public affection. As you partied, in the sense of blowing your brains out, Donna Summer, Gloria Gaynor, the Village People, Sylvester, Chic—and I—sang their songs. Andy Warhol said that when it was really fun, you expected someone to be murdered.

What went wrong was that Ian and Steve didn't follow the New York rules as decided upon by the establishment. There would be more people outside than inside. It would be packed outside, and you would go inside and there would be all this space. And this made getting in even more of a priority among those people who were really never going to get in, because their faces or styles didn't fit. I think they turned away top people, because Ian and Steve didn't give a shit who you were. They knew how to achieve the right balance of people, the mixing of the famous and the unknown. They had an instinct about who would not fit in. They knew the kind of people they wanted to let in who would be part of this "personality salad," and they knew who to turn away to avoid wrecking the flavor. And you never knew why you weren't allowed in; you were simply turned away, thinking, *I'm good-looking, I've got money, I've got a new tux.* Never enough. It wasn't about that. If you weren't clearly bringing something to the party, some kind of personality that couldn't be missed, then you were never going to get in.

And in the end, those who couldn't get in, who felt they were missing out, decided to exact revenge. Some very important people or their sons could not get in. *You think you have power?* they said. *We'll show you power.*

I think the powers that be were definitely alerted to the place by those who were rejected, either because they couldn't get in or because they were sacked by the club for some misdemeanor or another. There was no way such a place dedicated to the most extreme form of pleasure could continue to exist without upsetting those on the outside. It was such an unreal place, and eventually it clashed with reality.

After the peak, the heyday of 54, which marked the end of the underground and the beginning of what decades later, deformed by democratization, became structured reality TV, *Big Brother, The Bachelor,* and the party island of Ibiza, you would come out of a club and it would be surrounded by cops and paparazzi, all of them looking—hoping— for problems. A problem is a story. That's their currency. People have fun, and their pleasure causes a problem for those in charge, for those without access. So they seek out problems, ways to slow down the pace and subdue the provocateurs.

They started to target the clubs, through drugs, and taxes, and slimy tabloid outrage, because they wanted New York to be like it is now. Cleaned up, in their eyes. Under control. Much of the energy of the pop-culture celebrity music world as it is now evolved during those few years inside a very small area of Manhattan, but just as the pleasure-seeking wildness of Studio 54 was gutted, the energy that exploded out of the counterculture, and a belief in progressive change, has been domesticated.

It was the essence of dramatic transformation for performer and watcher. Fantasy made real. Really, it was a kind of showcase for the idea of disco—you'd go and do drugs, drink, mix with the famous, be the famous, and there would be people dancing, but in a much more planned way than in the clubs where disco was born, and in spots like the Mudd Club, Danceteria, and later the Saint, where the more curious music lovers would go.

Those clubs were the music connoisseur's revenge after the excess of 54—more creative places where new hybrids of sound became new genres. Max's was erased as a central place to hang out once the disco scene emerged, at least for the discriminating followers of fashion, or those more interested in the instant hit of a great night out. Punk and then new wave, disco, early electro—they were all in different rooms and places back then; the dots weren't yet joined up, the tunnels between rooms and scenes not yet dug.

The dancers at 54 were increasingly hired to do the dancing, for free drinks and whatever, rather than the club being a place where people danced for real. Naked musclemen painted silver on horses covered with glitter seagulls dusted with white powder became more important than mere music. Studio 54 was an illusion, really, a very smart setup, the disco night out exaggerated into this absurd sensationalism—it was where the reality of disco was treated and distorted in the way Andy and company treated fame, art, shopping, and media. Disco as disco was destined to have fifteen minutes, which seemed to go by a lot quicker because the cocaine there was always the best; the vodka and quaaludes were the icing on the coke, and then next there was the hangover: You'd be in a really bad mood, flagging from your sins, and sometimes you'd feel like death.

I invited Nile Rodgers of Chic there for New Year's Eve in 1977. The original 54 was only open for about three years, so there were actually only two New Year's Eve parties held there. This was the first one. He came along with Bernard Edwards, Chic's guitar player. I wanted them to produce my next album—as always, I wanted to work with the best. It was very cold, and snowing; they were both dressed up in their most expensive dress suits, proud disco princes with their finger on the pleasure pulse heading into the center of the disco universe. What could possibly go wrong?

They hadn't yet totally broken into the mainstream, but they were already very popular. Their names weren't on the guest list. Apparently that was my fault. I'm certain I put their names on the list, but I think at that point it was so full they weren't letting anyone else in, not even around the back, where the celebrities got in. Whoever you were, even the ghost of Elvis, you wouldn't have been let in. Standing in the freezing cold, they said that I had invited them, but still the doorman wouldn't let them in. He told them to fuck off. That "fuck off" rang in their ears. Their music would be playing inside but they couldn't get in.

They went home, fancy dancing shoes ruined by the snow. They were so angry that inside half an hour they had jammed up a new song on guitar and bass about their experience, with this groove that was as hot as it was cold outside, which they called "Fuck Off" in honor of the doorman who had barred their entry.

The chorus went, "Aaaah, fuck off." It sounded like a hit song but obviously needed a different chorus, so they changed it to, "Aaaah, freak out." They called the song "Le Freak," which was about a brilliant new dance craze that they couldn't even see because they couldn't get into the club, and it was number one in America for weeks. A year later it was the first track on a Studio 54 compilation album that Casablanca released, and it became the biggest-selling Atlantic Records single of all time. Without the "fuck off," without me forgetting to put their names on the guest list, there would never have been "Le Freak."

Norma Kamali designed my costume for the performance Nile and Bernard never got to see. She was going out with Ian Schrager at the time, and he asked her to make something for me. There was always this fascination with what on earth people were going to wear next; eventually what Bianca Jagger or Liza Minnelli was going to wear next became more important than what song was going to be played next. Norma had learned a lot from visits to London in the 1960s and was known for turning ordinary clothes into something else completely—taking fleece sweatshirts and turning them into flamboyant dresses. She had designed that red bathing suit Farrah Fawcett wore in what became a very famous poster.

Norma had me wear a very revealing and clingy, shiny gold unitard over a sticky, shimmering bodysuit. It wasn't my usual stark but vivacious Miyake look, the fantastic turned into costume, but I went along with it. She wouldn't have been my choice, but she was with Ian, and Studio 54 was the capital of disco, so it made sense. It wasn't a Disney princess look, but a glitter-coated Studio 54 superhero princess look, all sparkle and feathers, from shaved head to silvery knee-high boots. Later, for my birthday party in 1978, I dressed up as Nefertiti, Egypt's most beautiful royal queen. (Picasso had described Josephine Baker as "the Nefertiti of now.") I rode onstage on a Harley motorcycle with Divine and various naked musclemen as part of my entourage. This was a frenzied fantasy world I felt very at home in.

I met Marianne Faithfull that New Year's Eve. She once said she never hung out at Studio 54, that she didn't have the clothes or the desire. She was definitely there, though, unless I'm making it up. Maybe it was the only time she went. I remember it well, because that was the moment she introduced me to Cocoa Puffs: marijuana cigarettes laced with cocaine. I would call them Mariannes, because she was the first person I smoked them with.

I was in my dressing room, which was actually an office, with drab filing cabinets and a little, stained toilet next to it, nothing painted. They hadn't worked that part out. They'd worked out the music and the lights and the mix of people, but backstage was very basic, like a soiled hospital waiting room.

There was something going on with the payment of my fee. I didn't want to go on until I had been paid. First rule: cash, then I will do the show. No cash, no show. Sy and Eileen weren't allowed upstairs. They were banned from coming up to tell me there was no money. It was a chaotic night in all sorts of ways. There was a snowstorm, and people were pissed off that they couldn't get in, but . . . once we got the cash, it was a success, as far as the show-business illusion went! Then it was back to earth. It ended pretty badly in the real world.

I got all the shit. I felt used—they hadn't let my friends in; my managers were trying to reach me to say they hadn't been paid all the money; I never got to meet Nile and record with him at the exact moment Chic were hitting their stride—in fact, I didn't work with him for nearly ten years. But then, he did get a big hit song out of it.

I was still living mostly in Paris, regularly going back and forth. The Concorde made life a lot easier, and I was the symbol of a Concorde crowd that had replaced the jet set. I flew on the Concorde so many times I knew the pilots. I knew their families. I could have flown the plane, except I would have wanted to do it naked, sprayed silver, in roller skates. I could split my time between Paris and New York without much trouble. The five-hour time difference gave me the chance to do a lot more in a day. It was like there were two of me spinning between cities.

Fabrice, the French king of the night, had come over to New York and seen what was going on at Studio 54, witnessed a world being created by the new, powerful, competitive young, obsessed by celebrity, experiencing reality through the mutating fantasy of fashion. He opened a new club in Paris, Le Palace, which was bigger, had more space for performance. He might have learned a little from what he saw at Studio 54, but really, it was in the spirit of his own Club Sept. Club Sept had been a tiny, more stylish anticipation of the fame-drenched, debauched grandness of Studio 54. He didn't need to be told how to achieve the celebratory alchemy of Studio 54—he merely needed a bigger venue.

Fabrice removed the seats from an old music hall and installed a monstrous, spaceship-size strobe lighting rig that would swirl above the dancers and descend so low it was almost among them. I performed on the opening night of Le Palace. They were very late finishing the place; they were still banging, sawing, and hammering with hours to go before the opening. The place was absolutely packed, as if all of Paris had squeezed inside. It could hold thousands of people, but that still wasn't enough. It was quite an occasion. The coke laid on was tinted pink.

I wore the costume I had worn at the New Year's Eve party at Studio 54, not the complete works, only the body stocking, so I looked nude. It was so crowded that when I went onstage, the whole crowd was moving, but in different directions from row to row. It was like watching a field of corn being swirled around in a strong wind. They were hammered; they had taken whatever they could get their hands on.

I liked to break free of the stage sometimes, if I felt claustrophobic. There was a ladder I used to climb on, up to the boxes at the side of the stalls, so that I was a few feet above the audience. I loved to clamber about and didn't think there would be a problem climbing over them on the ladder. I didn't think about bodyguards or anything.

As soon as I got on the ladder, someone sprayed Mace into my eyes, and as I crawled up the ladder, my unitard was torn off me. It was mayhem. I had no clothes on, I couldn't see anything, and I was supposed to sing "La Vie en Rose" as the last song. It was a song that belonged to Paris, and now it belonged to disco. To some extent I had been adopted by the Parisians, and it was a sign of Paris making it in the new New York, the one where Studio 54 was like a new nation, with Andy Warhol the minister of propaganda and Bill Cunningham like a shadow minister. No one was going to leave before they heard that! They were in such a state they would have burned the house down if they didn't hear me sing it.

I stood next to the stage totally naked, eyes stinging, and watching from the side was Yves Saint Laurent, the center of the fashion universe, give or take his rival Lagerfeld, with his muse, Loulou de la Falaise, a very original dresser, a regular at Club Sept. Some say he might have been her muse, that she was the designing brains behind Yves Saint Laurent.

He had launched his Opium perfume the year before with an ad campaign featuring Jerry Hall in purple harem pants photographed by

Helmut Newton; Opium seems quaint now, and smells pink-powdery, but it was pretty avant-garde and provocatively erotic at the time, like Yves was not only celebrating drug use but selling drugs, taking abandonment out of the writhing dark rooms of an elite club into the everyday department stores. It smelled like it should really have been called Cocaine, or Cum, which is what it smelled like when it smelled like the 1970s of Thin White Duke David Bowie and "I Feel Love," or the warm musky breath of lovers in a blissful postcoital sleep with a fragrant hint of the pissoir and the dark, heavy smoke of a Gauloise.

I was an absolute shivering wretch, sticky with fury, not sure what to do next. The audience were beyond mad with frustrated energy. They were screaming for me to come back. Yves calmly took off his cummerbund and wrapped it around my bare breasts. Lou was wearing this gypsy scarf full of tassels, very typical of the flowing, colorful things she liked to wear, and he took that from her and bound it around my waist. Voilà. He gave me a very gentle shove, and there I was back on the stage, styled by Yves Saint Laurent, singing "La Vie en Rose" to an audience who didn't want anything else to happen at that moment but complete and utter make-believe. I was dressed in make-believe, and sang a song about casting a magic spell, about being in a world apart. Later, Yves gave me a little drawing of me in the outfit he had spontaneously created.

In their own way, Sy and Eileen were smart and shrewd. Music wasn't their area, but they had enough energy and commitment to get things going. For a while, we were each as energetic and committed as the other, but they couldn't see beyond disco, whereas even when I was known as the queen of disco, my restlessness kicked in, and I would wonder: *What will I be next?*

In a way, I outgrew them, or at least, I wanted to go in a very different direction from the one they had in mind for me. I had a battle with them, because I thought more radically, and they were safe to the point of cozy. They kept saying, "No, you need the long, satin gown—it will be perfect for you." I wanted to run naked onstage! *I'm a nudist! You've got to be kidding me, darling.* I wanted more skin than clothes. I wasn't sure exactly what direction I wanted to go in, because the more exciting things were in a constant state of flux, not yet named. Creative people were investigating further what could be done by playing a certain sequence of records in a club, how to make them fit together, and deliver new kinds of sensation.

I was still excited by the DJs in the smaller clubs who were breaking away from disco and generating other forms of dance music, because disco was becoming such a corporate monster. The ones who had helped invent disco were rebelling against disco, as much as any punks or rock 'n' rollers.

Imagine that the club music of New York didn't get labeled disco, and carried on as these DJs experimented with embellishing the ritual of playing records and creating and breaking communal tension. That was what interested me. I definitely had one foot in the 54 world, but not really for the music—more for the theater of the place, the combination of people craving spontaneous excitement. Musically, I was going with the flow along with the DJs who were resisting disco as a trend, as a headline, a dead end.

My shows were getting attention; "Trouble" was my second dance hit, and I was refining my stage show so that it was more than exciting and a long way from what Gloria or Donna or Sister Sledge would be doing. I was determined not to perform like other singers. This was one of the reasons I originally didn't want to go into the music business. There seemed to be a lot of bad taste in the way the female singers were expected to perform. It seemed fabricated. It was not connected to the fast-forward vitality of fashion. I don't know why. Singers seemed as removed from what was happening in fashion as sports stars. There was no coordination between the two worlds, no individuality—certainly not in America. It was either bad taste in fashion, a tackiness in how pop singers looked, or a looking down on the fashion world, as though it was not important, and never could be. Moving between the two worlds meant that I could see how progressive Issey and Kenzo were, and how that could make dramatic music presentation something surprising and new.

I wanted to combine what was happening in new fashion with new music. I thought that was what it was meant to be about, to make the music presentation seem more magical. It was more apparent in Britain—Twiggy did actually look like a pop star, and treated modeling as a type of performance. But America didn't have that; they were always behind the Brits when it came to trends and looks. A female entertainer was expected to look very square and wear blandly glittery clothes that could have come from the 1950s, or to not care at all, and be very punk. I thought more like a punk than a disco queen, but I didn't want to dress like a punk. Ultimately, I didn't want to walk in anyone's shadow.

Sy and Eileen created the momentum for what happened next by signing their Beam Junction label to a licensing deal with Island Records. Island was owned and run by Chris Blackwell, and he had made it one of the great independent labels. He was raised in Jamaica, and his mother, Blanche, descended from Portuguese Sephardic Jews, dates 1765 as their arrival on the island, where they began working as merchants. He came from colonial aristocracy, but he always felt that the British "had fucked up everything."

Jamaica is why Chris's label, formed in 1959, was called Island, and he had his first international hit in 1963 with a tremendous Jamaican record, "My Boy Lollipop" by Millie Small. It still has enough cockeyed modern—and very female—energy to sound great today. The guitarist and arranger was Ernest Ranglin, who had played on the first album Island released in 1959, *Lance Haywood at the Half Moon Hotel, Montego Bay*. (Chris taught water-skiing at the hotel.) It was an album of jazz played by the blind Lance Haywood from Bermuda, and one of only two Island releases recorded, at the Federal Record Studios in Kingston, and released only in Jamaica.

In the early '70s, Chris had worked hard in tricky circumstances to help Bob Marley and the Wailers take reggae, catchy but political and abrasive, to soft-rock ears, off the island, and establish it globally. He'd had huge success with Cat Stevens, Free, and Traffic. (It's interesting to note that perhaps his three biggest signings, Cat, U2, and Bob Marley, all had a very religious dynamic, and there's a tempestuous religious dimension hidden, or right out there, in much of my music.) I knew very little about him, and for a while, as I had the disco hits and made my first three albums, I never got to meet him. He was somewhere in the background, which is where he likes to be, making an impact by moving things around from afar.

I came from the fashion world, and Chris was not involved in that. He knew nothing about it and didn't really care. Beam Junction was simply one label among many that Island distributed, and he had no direct contact with it. He wasn't a disco kind of guy, and when it came to yet another actress/model who wanted to break into the music business, he said he would have had his fashion blinkers on.

People around him at the label were saying, *She's Jamaican, she's different, you have to meet her!* He'd seen a photograph of me in *New York* magazine accompanying an article about me by Nik Cohn, the writer of the story that became the film *Saturday Night Fever,* and he loved the look of it. The photograph was actually the first thing that I did with Jean-Paul Goude. Nik had seen me do my three songs at a small club, freaked out at the sweat, flesh, and fearlessness, and he gave an amazing description of what I did. It was my first appearance in a serious magazine, profiled by one of the greatest ever writers about pop music.

He was friendly with Jean-Paul and asked him to do the illustration for the article. That was where the photo of me naked and shining with one leg in the air came from—Jean-Paul wanting to reflect in his way what it was I was doing, and what Nik had seen: this brutal, animalistic energy that was part disco, part theater of cruelty, two lucid ways of representing an appetite for life. It was a visual description of an impossible original beast, only possibly from this planet, a voracious she-centaur emerging from an unknown abyss and confronting people's fears. Perhaps in this image you can see Jean-Paul falling for me, and turning it into a visual love letter.

I thought it was beautiful and, of course, I would eventually realize that as much as it was about me, it was also about Jean-Paul. He had trained as a ballet dancer, and it's a ballet stance in a challenging, Africanesque way, so he tangled us both up, edited between us, collaged our desires and dreams together. There was an erotic mingling of the two of us, one life penetrating the other. From this very first image, this was going on. No building up to it. Suddenly, there it was. A blueprint for our relationship. Something impossible made possible.

I was thrilled. It looked right to me and how I felt: athletic, artistic, and alien. It obscured and revealed my origins. It was like no other image I had ever seen. Often with photographers and the way you are styled, you could really be anybody. This image could only be me. It was a long, long way from where Sy and Eileen saw me; this was Vegas on acid. This was show business and performance as a super trip. It also represented me outside time, outside my age. It didn't tie me to a period, the '70s, or the '60s, or a vision of the '80s. It belonged in all those decades, because it was telling my story—where I had come from, where I was then, and where I was going, in one image at the same time. I loved that, because that was how I thought about age and time. I didn't want you to look at me and think of an age, whether I was young or old for my age. I wanted you to simply see energy.

I saw in it the shedding of skin, flimsy disco sheen being ripped back to reveal something poised on the verge of striking, like a snake, with the upper-body strength of a galley slave. It was the opening up of a brand-new me, totally secure in my darkness, which was merely an abstract shade, not political, and it was me almost with my savage insides on show. It was hard to work out what I was thinking, but I was obviously thinking something.

I didn't like wearing clothes in the house; I liked to walk around naked. Jean-Paul had gotten that. This was where I was the most comfortable. I didn't need to wrap myself up. All of me on show, and that all of me on show then boosted to the max. It wasn't nudity to shock, or titillate, or sell something—or maybe obliquely all that; it was nudity as something natural but placed inside a danger zone.

Jean-Paul's photo-elaboration of me put me inside my very own fantasy, connected to Jamaica, and New York, and Paris, and performance, and worship, and hallucination, but ultimately in a world of my own. The picture became like the ground zero of how every solo female singer since wants to be when she tries to be a little edgy, potentially a bundle of headline-making trouble. Once Jean-Paul had created that image, it became more and more apparent that the music I made should reflect it, be the soundtrack to that suggestive, analytical perversion of me.

When I realized what Jean-Paul wanted to do—strip me back to take me forward, bend me out of shape—I said to Nik and Jean-Paul, "I am not going to show this to my managers, but please go ahead and do it. Just don't tell them, whatever you do." I had to perform all sorts of maneuvers to get that butt-naked picture published. There was no way I wanted the sweet, trusting Berlins to know, or they would have asked for it to be scrapped. That was not their image of me.

For me, it was a real sighting of how I saw myself: unreal, untamed, utterly dramatic. I managed to get it into the magazine without them knowing what it was going to look like—I was used to keeping things from my parents, and this was the same thing. I had to make sure they didn't know that I was up to something fabulously naughty.

The article was very powerful and unforgiving—Nik lovingly talked about me farting and drinking from the bottle, and I was thinking, *Yes, yes, yes, I don't want to be anyone's example, this is who I am. I do not want to be the girl you feel safe taking home to meet your mother. Anything but Sy and Eileen's Virgin at Vegas in a nice pretty dress! How boring is that. I would rather sing in church with my mother than go down that road.*

Nik described me as the ultimate beast—a troublemaker out to disrupt harmony. He tore down all the soft, shiny glamour they were trying to drape around me. He ripped it apart and portrayed me as this hungry, horny, mannish animal, warts and all. Thoughts and all. I loved it. This to me was glamour—not the maintenance of ordinary glamour, but something that was unknown, even occult, examining the idea of glamour based on its original meaning. Witchcraft.

When the magazine came out and Sy and Eileen saw it they were totally furious. I suppose I knew the picture, and the article that went with it, would really shock them. It was my way of taking control, which some would say was not nice, considering all they had done for me. "It is so disgusting," they said. "You broke wind, you drank wine from the bottle, how could you!" They felt they had treated me like family. I had stayed at their place. They had advanced me rent. Their son had a crush on me, and we might even have gotten up to something if they didn't think of me so much as a daughter. They were lovely to me, and they worked hard on my behalf.

The problem was I was not a Vegas act. I remember seeing Diahann Carroll and Diana Ross in the old lady wigs and high heels doing Vegas, and it's really hard—no one listens, you might as well have a robot on-stage. No one pays attention, and I need the attention.

We fought. We really fought. I got so frustrated being pushed in their direction. I was drinking a milk shake at some rehearsal and I was getting so angry with their cabaret vision that I poured it all over Sy's head. It was so childish, but I was like a child. I wanted things to be the way I wanted them to be. I felt I was being forced, and then I ended up sneaking behind their backs.

It was the start of the parting of the ways between me and the Berlins. We were fighting so much. I loved them and we had a great relationship, but I could see the divorce coming. They were not going to be flexible. And I needed to be with people who understood where I wanted to be. I always need to be excited with what it is I am doing. As soon as I am not excited, I pull back, I give up. I will even sabotage it! To this day, if there is something I do not want to do and it is not excit-ing me, I will not do it.

Chris didn't know me from the modeling, or from the Studio 54 world, and in fact, those things didn't interest him. Chris was not someone you necessarily got to meet even if you were signed to his label. I think in the end, he thought, *Well, she is from Jamaica, and she's making some noise; maybe I should check her out.* He loved the picture in *New York* magazine because, he said, I didn't look like just another model, I looked like a creature. Sy and Eileen were happy to sell their contract with me to Island. Chris had called them Ma and Pa Kettle, and they were very different from the kind of rock managers and in-dustry manipulators Island usually worked with. The Berlins recovered their investment and then some. And the sale meant that Chris and I could start working together.

Chris and I finally met at the opulent Russian Tea Room in New York on Fifty-Seventh Street. You pay the rent as soon as you walk in there. I don't remember much about the meeting. I was living at the Wellington Hotel around the corner, and he had his offices inside the nearby Carnegie Hall alongside the dancers' rehearsal rooms.

I don't remember what we talked about. I only know that I don't talk about what I don't know, and I don't ask questions, and Chris doesn't give a lot away. I suppose we talked about Jamaica, and living in Paris, and what I wanted to do next. The Russian Tea Room is very loud, so I guess we carefully circled each other.

I remember that he never seemed to wear shoes—he's in sandals all year round even when it is cold. But despite wearing little but shapeless T-shirts and faded shorts, he is one of the most truly glamorous people I have ever known. You can tell he used to hang out with Noël Coward and Errol Flynn when he was young in Jamaica—the most glamorous thing he said he ever saw was Flynn dressed for cocktails, clutching a long, slender cigarette holder and carrying a groomed dachshund under his arm—and he spent a few months hanging out with the notoriously intimidating Miles Davis in New York. They would swim together at a health club near Central Park. Because of his experiences in Jamaica, Chris was completely comfortable in the company of blacks, but for Miles it was something very unusual coming across a young white boy so at ease with him.

Chris and I got along really great, and he seemed impressed that I knew what I wanted to do with my music and image. I think he could tell that, like him, I was absolutely committed to being in control of my own destiny. Such ambition and determination surprised him, coming from someone he thought was going to be a pushy, superficial Jamaican model.

I was definitely determined. If I still lacked focus, I didn't lack self-belief. I didn't want to be babysat. I wanted to be in control, and I certainly didn't agree with Sy and Eileen's vision of me in Vegas, a kind of cut-price Diana Ross. I need that to be clear, right away. I was definitely a reigning disco queen, one of the glitter-ball dynasty alongside the likes of Sylvester and Donna Summer, but I wanted to progress, not get stuck being part of something that was becoming a laughingstock. I knew that Chris could help me change. He likes to build things, make things happen, put people together who he thinks will fit and see what unfolds. He stays in the background, watching how things play out.

I was very demure that day. I made sure it wasn't one of my crazy days. I didn't want Chris to think that the rumors he might have heard of my wildness were anything more than show-business hype. I wanted him to see the determined, professional side, and not the unruly disco barbarian.

I know that I was the wildest party animal ever. I pushed myself to the limit and started from there. I had no limits. If you asked me to do something, I would do it. Dare me. There was nothing I wouldn't try. "Whatever it takes" was my catchphrase. Experiencing life itself was the point: to propel myself out of my comfort zone, to feel alive, to take revenge on reality. I was the ultimate specialist in pursuing insatiable appetites and shameless lusts, even at the risk of disaster.

I was always in control, though. I might have lost control a couple of times, but if I had been totally out of control I would have died. I wasn't going to do anything that threatened my life, even though I came close. I didn't want to die, but if you take risks, you can come close. I took risks, I had no fear, I drove as fast as I could, but not because I was being self-destructive. In a way, it was the opposite. Speeding to the limit was a form of self-preservation.

I was all over the place, taking naughtiness to a whole new level, in the press, on TV, in jail, at the most explosive parties, with friends, lovers, and fellow fantasists who ended up dying all around me. But still, built into me was this button—when pressed, the button would save me. I don't know if I was in charge of this button, or if someone somewhere praying for me was in charge of it. I would abandon myself, like when I took the super pill. I would return, though, I would recover. Others stayed out there, in a lovely but remote place. Because of the church thing there were a lot of prayers keeping me alive, however underground I went, however far out I went.

I was split between Beverly of Church Jamaica and Grace of Club

America. Getting rid of Bev was the most important thing. I landed in America as Bev, and then set about becoming Grace. With a vengeance. But Bev has not totally gone, even now. That's why I still say that prayers protected me. There is still Bev the believer, and there always was, whatever I got up to, however much I chased experience, however much I lavished myself with pleasure and adventure. In the middle of this, Beverly still believed that whatever I did, I would be saved. Grace relied on Bev to protect her from destruction. It was sex, drugs, and the Holy Ghost.

I received the Holy Ghost when I was baptized at eight as Beverly, and it penetrated so deep into my being it never disappeared. I don't know if that was discipline or faith, but subconsciously I thought, *Whatever happens to me, whatever I do, I will be safe.* I was desperate to escape the church, to escape the punishment, this most uncomfortable of upbringings, but even as I fled, there were still inside me the remains of faith. They're still there. I know where I am going. I know what my goal is. And how I get there is God's grace.

Faith, however perverted, was hammered into me with such force that nothing could eradicate it, not even being the sybaritic Grace Jones bare-skinned in Studio 54 lathered in foam and coke, tongued and flailed by drag queens, total strangers and horny hedonists, entertaining the creeps, weirdos, strays, and lionized, living the un-American dream. Deep down, Bev believed. And either because Bev believed or because the church and my family believed in Bev, no harm came to me. Nothing could stop me. There was always something happening next. There was always love, sex, food, beauty, fame, work, bliss, money, success, identity, art, parties, common things, and gossip.

5

Andy

Richard Bernstein used to take me to the Factory building on Union Square because he would do the *Interview* covers every month. This was when it had just moved from the Decker building at Union Square West to its third location at 860 Broadway at the north end of the Square. The Factory was the center of Andy Warhol's empire, a few blocks from the Empire State Building, which he thought was a star and filmed as though it was. New York was the center of the artistic universe, and the Factory was at the center of the center, and at the center of that was Andy Warhol, who had New York and art at his center. As soon as you walked into the building you could tell that something extraordinary was going on.

The Factory was his Hollywood, his TV channel, his publishing house, from where he created stars, instantly labeling them superstars; made his movies; and measured out time, fame, scandal, disaster, repetition, talk, his form of a high society. He helped promote artists who would never have been heard of if he hadn't given them a platform. From his lair, ultimately more famous than just about anyone alive, he would lure people in from that high society for chats, portraits, and interviews.

Andy had encouraged Richard to stop painting his multicolored pop-art pills and to start painting people. Richard was given the task of creating the covers for *Interview*, which people naturally thought were by Andy. They were portraits of the rich and famous, done in a way that looked to the casual viewer like they might be Warhol, but they were all Richard's own work. Like Andy, because of Andy, he moved from face to face, and I became one of those faces.

Richard was very insecure and always concerned the *Interview* team wouldn't like his covers. There were people—colleagues, assistants, hangers-on, court jesters, groupies, nutcases, foreign receptionists who intentionally couldn't understand what you were saying—that you had to go through to get to Andy. But Andy would ask to see you; you wouldn't ask to see Andy. So Richard would have to show his covers to someone who would then show them to Andy, and the response would come back: *Shave that, trim that, cut that, add more color, bend that, alter that nose*—Andy was like a plastic surgeon in a way, adjusting appearance, but only in a fantasy—or, now and then, *Leave it as it is.* There was a pecking order, though. Peck, peck, peck, power would pass back and forth, back and forth through various levels of ego, tension, and hysteria. The covers also had to cross the desk of editor Bob Colacello. Richard always felt that it was Bob who amplified Andy's indecisions. Andy was sort of in the distance, where he liked to be . . . watching, but hard to see and hear.

Oh, Grace, Richard would say, *I have to take a cover in today, I am nervous about it. There was this one bitch who will tell me to make changes.* He didn't have the sharp tongue of many of those who occupied the Factory, and there were plenty trying to take advantage of him. I would go along with him to give him confidence. His high-ceilinged studio was on the ground floor of the Chelsea Hotel, a short walk around the corner from Andy's studio. I would go to the Factory a lot.

I can't remember if I met Andy at the Factory or in a club on one of those nights you can't help but forget, even if during the evening you were given a joint laced with angel dust by Divine, who sat between Truman Capote and Woody Allen. Something like meeting Andy Warhol for the first time is one of those moments in your life that are so unique, you can't remember the details. One minute you don't know him, and then you do. He'd been Catholic Andrew Warhola, like I had been Pentecostal Beverly Jones, and there was definitely a religious intensity in the way he operated that I could recognize.

Once we met, he would invite me all the time to the Factory. It wasn't the easiest place to get into, so it helped to be asked by Andy himself. You had to have the right qualities, and I must have passed the test. That's the kind of test I like. You don't even know what the questions are, but all your answers are correct.

He would call me and say, "I am interviewing so-and-so for the magazine at the Factory—why don't you come by?" I met André Leon Talley there; that's where he was working, answering the phones—with a very hearty *bonjour*—and starting to write the Small Talk column for *Interview.*

He was brought up very strictly by his grandmother in North Carolina, and the pride she took in her appearance rubbed off on him. He moved to Manhattan in 1974, and then burst into life. Together when we were out, sharing mad moments amid the swishy fashion commotion in the club scene, we would explode, urging each other on. He felt like an outcast at the time; he was looking to work out who he was and where he belonged. Very smart about design and the history of personal style, he developed a grand, insightful sense of luxuriousness. I insisted when *Vogue* wanted an interview with me that he do it. It was the first print interview he did for *Vogue,* and then he worked there for thirty years, starting as news editor and ending up an editor-at-large.

Andy always had these sorts of people in close proximity, working on their own lives and on their own ways of recording and announcing them. A lot of people were competing for attention, jealous of each other, fighting for space, and somehow he commanded their attention. Some of them were afraid of him, though, and hung around because they felt they had to. If they left him, they would be in a kind of exile.

He surrounded himself with action, and it all made it seem as though he was more active than he actually was. Andy didn't like to go to the clubs, really. It was a social obligation, part of his schedule, meticulously worked out by his entourage, but he liked to keep his

distance. When he did go to a club, he barely moved. He would melt
into the background, pretty static, observing all the me's making out
and making themselves up. I was one of the few people he would dance
with on a dance floor. "Oh," he'd say, "nobody gets me on the dance
floor but you, Grace," as we danced to Michael Jackson. He loved Michael. They made a nice couple. I was also one of the few who could get
Michael Jackson on a club dance floor dancing for the sake of it. I would
have been best man for both of them if they had married, which in
some universe was their destiny.

I met Michael a few times, whenever we happened to find ourselves
in the same club, or studio, the same artificial zone, as entertainment
associates sharing some of the same highs and lows. He was somewhere
between being a total stranger to everyone and a friend to everyone. He
was a really nice, hopeful young man who started to become too dangerously aware of himself, and how life changes, and how big and awful
and complicated the world could be. He lacked Andy's wary ultimately
quite tough ability to keep everything at a distance. Andy was better at
camouflaging himself.

Andy preferred to watch while everyone else cavorted. He would
usually be against a wall, the Warhol wallflower. After he got shot in
1968 at the original "Silver" Factory on East Forty-Seventh Street, a
few days before the assassination of Robert Kennedy, when he went
out, he liked to stay in one place with his back to the wall. You wouldn't
know if he was in a club or at a party unless you were called for. He
had someone scouting for him. You would tell the scout some news,
and if Andy was interested, he would ask for you to come and tell him
yourself. He would be in the dark somewhere, hiding, almost merging
into the wall. Ever since he had been shot, he had changed his style to
protect himself. He wasn't being a diva; it was a necessity. He could still
go out and get information, but he had to do it more discreetly, so that
he could never be circled by people and trapped. He had a fear of being
in a crowd, though he would never admit it.

When we were together, we would chat about nothing much. *Where
have you been, what have you done, who did you meet, what was it like?* He was

so curious. He wanted the gossip, however trivial-seeming. He wanted to hear confessions, however lurid. He had his tape recorder inside his pocket, whirring constantly, which not many people knew at the time. He'd show me. He'd have it hidden close to his heart. It was a part of him. Whispering to itself. Stirring up the gossip he thrived on. He called it his wife. When he went out, his pockets would be filled with tapes and batteries, and he would be frustrated when someone didn't want him to have the tape running at a dinner party or in a meeting. It didn't matter to me that he was taping all the conversations he was having. That was his business. I'd tell him the same things whether the tape recorder was on or not. Maybe I exaggerated a little knowing the tape was on, performed more—but then, everything I did was like a performance, so I was his ideal subject.

He'd watch life pass as quickly as the tape. He said that when people told him their problems, once he started taping, it was no longer a problem—it was an interesting tape. It was a kind of show. We were all part of an extended conversation Andy was having with the rest of the world. As long as the batteries lasted.

I didn't think he was a vicious person, so I never thought that he would use what I said against me. He didn't judge. There were a lot of preachy, bossy people about at the time, but he was perhaps the least judgmental person I had ever come across. Perhaps he didn't want to upset anyone in case they came after him again with a gun. There was simply a flow of chat that passed through him. It was his way of getting a feel of what was happening around him. The tapes were exploited after Andy died by those who had an agenda, who didn't use the material as Andy would have. I didn't have an agenda. I wasn't in the club or at the Factory to get something out of him. I didn't suck up like a lot of the others. I spoke to him like he was my brother.

He liked to encourage others to do things that he never wanted to do, but that he wanted to experience through you. Like when I appeared in the Bond movie *A View to a Kill*. Andy loved that. It was as though he could then experience what it was like to be a Bond villain without actually having to do it. He put me on the cover of *Interview*—

he never had before, but once I was in the Bond film, he put me on the cover. In his eyes, the movie role officially made me star Grace, more than the music.

He definitely saw the future. When he took a photograph of himself with a Polaroid camera, he was taking a picture of the future, when it seemed like everyone started taking their own photograph. Everyone wanting to be on a stage, on a screen, in a photograph, on the cover of a gossip magazine, communicating their thoughts, everyone thinking about themselves—the wide embrace of everyday chatter. Andy knew what was coming. He shaped what was coming.

The photographer Christopher Makos, who had apprenticed with Man Ray, had given Andy his first camera and taught him how to use it. Chris had taken some fabulous photos of Andy in women's wigs and full makeup referencing Marcel Duchamp's female alter-ego Rrose Sélavy. Makos chronicled the choppy, supercharged New York mid-'70s period when disco and punk, uptown and downtown, art and fame, sex and money all blurred together. If you were photographed by him, as I first was in 1974, fresh faced, short haired, and a shade cocky around and through the eyes, at the 860 Broadway Factory, wearing a Le Jardin T-shirt, it meant you were put into a world where there were also Andy, Patti Smith, Anthony Perkins, Tennessee Williams, Richard Hell, Elizabeth Taylor, Quentin Crisp, John Paul Getty III, and Alice Cooper. A special community. You were someone, marked out for attention, in this exciting new somewhere between New York City and the future.

Andy's Factory and the ambitious people who gravitated there and worked for and with him was where the craziness of the '60s was transformed into something the whole world would start to experience. He saw that this whole celebrity thing was where everything was happening. He was a voyeur, and he saw which direction the energy was heading. He saw the art in everything, in what was happening around him.

Andy was obsessed with celebrity, and because he was a watcher, it sort of echoed out from him. So he became an example of a celebrity, without really acting like one, and he anticipated that the curiosity he had about it, and how that impacted his own status, would infect the whole world. No one really got to know him, though. He was the blank canvas everything got projected onto. He himself was very, very private—I only went to his home once, filled with art but none of his own. I never saw him get high. He preferred to watch other people get high. The ultimate high.

Andy would often ask me to go places with him—events, clubs. If I did a show, he would be there. We would have dinners together, and Richard would join us. We went to a restaurant called Holbrook's on Seventy-Fifth Street and Third Avenue, which was filled with celebrities—John and Yoko, Tom Wolfe, Princess Grace of Monaco, Robert Redford, all the Kennedy kids—all the time, because even in a fantasy, you have to eat. It was there one night that Andy suddenly said, "Stand up against that wall." They'd shut down the restaurant. He put me next to a long table, took out his Polaroid camera, and the next thing I knew, he had done four silk-screened portraits of me. He said, "I want to give you one"—mostly, you had to buy from him.

The most famous thing that happened with me and Andy was when I was his date at Arnold Schwarzenegger's wedding to Maria Shriver. They got married in April 1986 in Hyannis, Massachusetts. Theirs was a big storybook wedding, modest but moneyed, with almost the entire Kennedy clan there, and thousands of photographers. It might have been relatively low-key, but it was all perfectly set up for a very greedy media. We had to fly on this little private jet to get there, and the weather was terrible. Andy was saying, like a delicate version of Alice's White Rabbit, "We can't be late, Grace, we can't be late," because of course I had the reputation even then of being late. "Can't be late, Grace, it's a wedding." I was on time, but only because I hadn't put on my makeup or gotten properly dressed.

I got ready in the bathroom at the airport when we landed. All the time, he was taking photos, taking Polaroids. He was like a kid, Andy, so enthusiastic about every single thing. I wonder sometimes if that had something to do with him being shot. Once you have had five bullets pumped into your chest, it changes everything. You become more conscious of life, of the smallest detail; you become more astounded by how people behave, and by what happens when they become so famous they change. In a way, fame is a kind of death of the person you were before. If you are really famous—Marilyn Monroe famous, Liz Taylor famous—you are never the person you once were again. He started to see through to the temporary, fragile heart of things very quickly and forensically.

He would be taking photographs all the time, the tape recorder whirring in his pocket, helping him remember. He'd ask me about my sex life. He would send spies out as well. I remember when I started going out with Dolph Lundgren. The grapevine hummed very quickly. Andy got the news before anyone else.

Andy would ring up wanting to know how big Dolph's dick was. It was that kind of world. Everyone was curious. He wanted to get more information about my new boyfriend, so he set up a photo session with Helmut Newton.

Dolph and I ended up naked in our session together, me riding him skin on skin like he was some mythical, muscular Swedish beast. It was our baptism as a couple. Apparently getting us naked was the intention all along, cooked up between Andy and Helmut. When I arrived at the session, late, naturally, Dolph was already down to his underpants. *Grace has a new boyfriend. Let's see how he's hanging.* Andy wanted to know that I was in good . . . hands. He wanted to make sure I was going to enjoy myself. It was his way of showing he cared.

Because of the weather, and the traffic, we were late for Arnie's wedding. I swear it wasn't my fault. It was an Irish wedding, and I wore a very tight, full-length, fishtail, forest-green Azzedine Alaïa dress; Kenzo Takada had made me a bright green fur hat; I had a high-collared green coat; I even had green contact lenses. I was doing the Irish celebration thing to the hilt.

I had put all that on at the little airport—I was in the bathroom getting dressed, and one of the young Kennedy sons saw me and decided he wanted to wear one of the green contact lenses. He couldn't get it in, so I wore them both. Andy and I got into this jeep that had come to get us, no limo, and we arrived at the church, a charming little white wooden building, and everyone is cheering and screaming outside, and we enter the church. Late.

At the exact moment that Arnold and Maria are on their knees finishing off their special, intimate ceremony, we arrive. The doors noisily creak open and they turn around to see what the commotion is, and it is, guess who, Grace and Andy. Late. They didn't say anything, but you could see from the looks on their faces that they were not at all impressed. Green, grinning, furry me and Andy being the usual pale deadpan Andy in his uniform, always the same, wherever he was, whatever he was doing—black turtleneck, leather jacket, jeans, silver wig, and glasses, little black rucksack over his shoulder—very slight and insignificant looking amid all this top-hatted celebrity wedding fuss. I don't know the reason for the wig. I never asked. Maybe it was like my hoods. To keep the neck warm.

He was shy, even after all those years dealing with the rich and famous, running his studio, organizing his art, monitoring the center of attention. He would push me when I got shy—because I can be shy too. And all the Kennedys from age fourteen up wanted to dance with me at the party afterward. And I was saying, "No, Andy, I can't—my dress is too tight." I wouldn't take off my coat, and he was the one telling me to go and dance: "Go on, go on, dance with the Kennedys!" I was going, "Darling, no, my ass is sticking out." He would say, "Don't be silly, get on the dance floor." He didn't want to dance with me; he wanted me to dance with them. I got scared, but Andy made me.

He pushed me to do a few things I didn't want to do. He would say, "Oh you are making a big deal out of nothing. Do it. I want to watch! I want to see what happens." Living through others. So I had a couple more drinks and danced with the Kennedys—including Ted—and Andy got to see what it was like. He had fun and remembered everything. It would be great if Andy was still around to bounce ideas off of and get his knowing response to the instant, self-generating world he helped spawn.

I remember I was always difficult about signing autographs. I hated it. We would be out together and there would be all these autograph

hounds. They didn't have phone cameras like now. They wanted sig-
natures, to prove they had met the famous. I didn't want to do them.
I said, "No. I don't do that." Andy turned that around. After all, he trea-
sured a signed photograph he had received from Shirley Temple when
he was thirteen—"to Andrew Warhola."

After I refused to sign autographs all night, Andy asked, "Why do
you say no?"

I said, "It is trivial, a waste of time. It's not fun."

He changed my mind. He said, "When you do that, these people
go away feeling really bad. They will go, 'That spoiled bitch, doesn't
she know who put her where she is? I am not going to buy her record.'
With the energy you take to say no, instead you say yes, using the same
energy, and they will go home happy."

I said, "But Andy, if I start signing, we'll end up the whole night
signing autographs."

He said, "It doesn't matter. Having the positive energy you get back
is worth signing the autographs even if you don't want to. Smile and
sign. No one gets upset. And," he added, "the most important thing . . .
they will buy your records!" I was thinking of the moment; he was
thinking of the bigger picture. I never thought about record sales!
I don't say no anymore. I got it. And you realize people stand around
for hours waiting for you. They will fly to other countries. "Everybody
must have a fantasy," he said. "For some people, you are the fantasy. You
must not spoil that." To this day, when I am chased and surrounded by
paparazzi, hunted at all times of the night and day, I remember what
Andy said to me, and I make sure however tired or private I might be
feeling I try to put on a little show for them. After all, we were once
photographed jogging in Central Park, him in jeans and jacket, me in
little "batty rider" shorts. That was a performance.

I am aware of the fact that what is being photographed is the fantasy
of fame, and for that moment, that is what I am representing. At that
moment, I am at the center of fame. Andy would want me to look and
act famous, because I have been given that power, and with it comes a
certain amount of responsibility. It's to be taken seriously. Even if that

sometimes involves scaring the pants off someone, wrestling Kate Moss to the ground, or posing at an awards ceremony as if it's the best place in the world to be even if it's boring and you hate who you've been sat with and don't actually know who they are, although you're told they are the hottest thing on the planet right now.

Andy would never make you feel guilty about selling yourself. That's what he changed—that artists don't have to die before they make a lot of money. He would probably have said, "Why wouldn't you sing 'Boogie Wonderland'? It's only entertainment. Don't take it so seriously." But he had a line over which he would not go; there was definite quality control, which was why Richard was so nervous showing him the covers. Andy would look at everything before he issued the final touch, the final approval, and nothing less than perfect in his eyes would get through.

It was awful, how he died, ten months after the Arnie-Maria wedding. It was a simple operation, but he would always talk about it. He didn't want the operation. He put it off and put it off. Like he knew something was going to happen. In the last photograph taken of him, as he sat in the back seat of the car driving him to the hospital for his surgery, you can see from his expression that he believed he was heading into the unknown, his final appointment. His near-death experience had made him a little psychic. It is so strange he should die when he did, and how he did. It makes you wonder. When the pieces don't add up, and they don't fit—and they didn't—then you wonder. It's too bizarre.

He passed so suddenly; it was quite shocking. It was as though he had been erased. He found life so interesting. Death itself, being inside it, not seeing it happen, wasn't so interesting. No more images. He once said he didn't believe in death, because he wouldn't be around when it happened. He said he couldn't say anything about it because he wasn't prepared for it. Death happened to other people. He knew, though, that there was a close relationship between celebrity and death. Death could make the obscure famous. The true celebrity would have a life—many lives—after death. She would be immortal, posing forever, hiding the truth, and revealing it.

6

Discovery

When we left Jamaica, all the Jones children scarred by the force of Mas P and Bishop Walters swore we would never go back. We wanted to get as far away from Jamaica as we could. The church had ruined Jamaica for us. Burned it down. I was the first one to go back, after about seven or eight years never going near it. I crept back in, feeling more Paris than Jamaica, with a French accent that was American, a model and singer, not a teacher or a preacher's wife. I thought I had put enough distance and trips and enough experience between me and the Bible to deal with the church, but I still thought the followers of Bishop Walters were going to burn me at the stake when I came back.

I did feel that the island tried to kill me. I had near-death experiences. I put that down to the fact that my religious family didn't want me back, and strange things would happen, like they wanted to keep me away because I had brought such shame. There were three very close shaves with death in Jamaica. A boat almost struck me while I was swimming in the ocean, and a car nearly hit me while I was filming in Ferngully, a few miles outside where I now live part-time in Ocho Rios. Ferngully is on the way to Kingston, where the road slowly curls upward, deeper into the green world, and is named for the different varieties of giant fern there reaching to the sky, competing with each other for light and almost joining in the middle, blocking out the sun and cooling the air.

On the two-lane roads that wind around and through Jamaica, a lot of drivers will try to make what we call a third lane. They will overtake on a corner at sixty miles an hour without caring that a car might be coming the other way. I got out of a car; nothing seemed to be coming, and then suddenly, a car sped out of nowhere and grazed along the side of me, metal scraping along my skin.

Thirdly, at some point, I swear someone planned to murder me. Certain forces on the island seemed very interested in wiping me out of existence because, they figured, I had gotten above myself. There's a whole other book in that story, and there were a few other minor near-death experiences as well. There was a definite sense that took a long time to fade away that certain people wanted me taken off the island in a wooden box, either because they thought I was the devil, or because they though I didn't belong there. I thought, *I'm going to be killed here.* If I had a choice, yes, sure I would like to die on the island, but not yet, and not suddenly, out of the blue, chased into the grave by fate or hate.

It wasn't the island threatening my life. It wasn't the church, really. It was my own anxiety. I went back feeling I was now armored because of those teachers I had found across the water—Sam, Tom, Andre, Antonio, Richard, Issey, Helmut, Hans—but I still felt as though I was entering a haunting. I needed to come back and not be scared by the ghosts. Not dead people ghosts but memory ghosts.

To deal with the ghosts, I visited a psychic, the one used by the Reagans, and she was very keen that I keep crossing the water and visiting the island. The more I did, she said, the more the island would want me. The island was more important than the church. I had to keep going back to Jamaica to overcome this feeling that I wasn't wanted there.

My main teacher in Spanish Town, certainly in the matter of basic, inspiring common sense, had been my aunt Sybil. "Nothing beats common sense," she would say. She always tells me how she trusted me to deal with whatever happened in my life because I could always read situations well and find a way through. I might get lost, but I would always find myself again.

You can see how organized she is by how tidy her garden is at her Kingston bungalow. Like me, she grew up among lots of brothers and had to develop a lot of strength to deal with all that male energy. "You had to fight to keep your place."

Sybil loved her brother, my dad, very much, and however far out and over the top I was—running around naked in New York, dressing up and stripping off in Paris—she saw through the wild escapism to her young niece making up for lost time. She thought that I was breaking away from a world where it was always *You can't,* never *You can.* She always kept watching over me.

When I went back to Jamaica the first time after being away living some new lives, Sybil told me that she wanted me to take a drive and see the island as it really was. She said, "You are now so international, but you don't know Jamaica at all. And you should! It is where you are from; it is what made you strong and powerful."

I drove with my French then boyfriend Jeanyves. We did what Aunt Sybil said, followed a route she had mapped out for us, and I saw Jamaica for the first time. I had grown up there, and I knew nothing about it. I didn't know how close the beauty was to me. I only knew the dark religious stuff, and very little about what was over the border of Spanish Town, whether it was glorious or dangerous. We found Jamaica, not the Jamaica of religious freaks. I flew out of the cage.

There was darkness and danger out beyond my community, places that were like the American Wild West. I knew nothing about an edgy, volatile Jamaica where you had to fight to survive, the knowledge of which would have given me a better sense of life. I knew nothing about the island's colonial history, and nothing about the third-world parts of Jamaica; the glory and the squalor. There is the Jamaican paradise, where the cruise ships land and the air seems painted blue and the bold, outspoken people have the widest smiles in the world, the reggae plays, and no one seems sad; and then there is the smell of the slums and decay in Kingston and you wonder where all the money is. There is this tension between a special place that is always growing and a ruined place where growth is stunted, the gap between a beautiful beach with a rapidly arriving sunset and a trip into the corrugated roofs of Trench Town. The history of poverty, slavery, and industrial pollution scars the landscape, and there are the sun and sea, doing their thing.

Looking at the island from outer space, it's tiny, but inside, it's crammed with enough life and variety to fill a planet. There are the obvious tourist things to experience in Jamaica—the spectacular views, the coach tours to craft villages, the changing vistas within a few hundred feet, the warm, soft air. The tourists come and they stay in the swish all-inclusive resorts, and maybe visit the coffee-growing areas in the Blue Mountains. There's a different Jamaica beyond the usual holiday centers: remote, drowsy back water villages where life is mostly lived outdoors; dirt-floored beach shacks; the pulsating, chaotic and exhausting Kingston, seen stretched from the hills like a cockeyed cousin of Los Angeles, bursting at the seams with energy, all that inhaled rhythm, the shock and recoil of the traffic; the blown dust; the constant tropic din; intoxicating rums; luxuriant molasses; trees felled by hurricanes and left to fend for themselves; treacherous mountain roads with hairpin turns surrounded by thick vegetation, where you ride along walls of green above a steep drop to the ravine below; roads that lead nowhere but the end of the road; places with names like Treasure Beach, Buff Bay, Silver Hill Gap, Frenchman's Cove, Pum Pum Rock (shaped like a woman's genitals), and Hellshire, which is actually a fine sandy beach outside Kingston loved by the locals, and fizzing with open-air, fish-frying life. Fleeing slaves discovered the therapeutic Bath Fountain in the seventeenth century, and it seems to have stayed exactly the same since then. Cockpit Country is an inland forest preserve, where there are native plants with names like Madame Fate, horse poison, spirit weed, and dog's tongue.

There are glowing phosphorescent waters, hot springs, bubbling streams, healing waters, white-water rafting, tropical fruit you've never come across before, the most beautiful sights, very spiritual and restorative, and a frenzied, swelling lushness. Even the cemeteries are flush with green, as though death doesn't put a dent in the life of the place. You can see one place, the grass and trees and vines; visit a few weeks later, and there is so much new growth you would not recognize it. It made me think that everything growing excites me.

On the northeast coast, at the very edge of things, there's Port Antonio, denser, rougher, hard to get to, where paradise is wonderful, but weird. It's like a fucked-up heaven, which suits me. It takes a couple of hours from Kingston deftly navigating a spiral of twisting and turning roads that cut into what becomes more and more a jungle. The gigantic ragged vegetation thriving either side of the road makes Jurassic Park seem like a window box. The trees and grass that threaten to conquer the roads have to be constantly cut back. Eventually, you reach Port Antonio, arranged around a spectacular bay, simmering with freestyle frontier action, typifying how Jamaica can be for both the dropouts and the globetrotters, the bums and the billionaires. Watch the people milling about, and you get a real sense of how the Jamaican sensibility can be an exuberant hybrid of pirate, gadabout, British Empire orderliness, enigmatic, indigenous swagger, slave resistance, all roughly tossed together in the heat, rolling mists, and local history. Gossip is perpetually in the air, and grown men speed around the streets chasing deals or just feeling the air racing past their face on battered small kids bikes, because they're cheap, and within reach.

Outside the no-nonsense town center, where the population thins out and there are either a few warped shacks or a few smart well-tended villas, it can feel like you're at the mouth of the Amazon, over the border from the heart of darkness. The mountains foaming with foliage crash into the sea, which is always putting on a performance, serenely or a little aggressively, under clouds that change shape and color by the minute.

There are names, places, initiative, history, energy, enterprise, music that shows how inventive Jamaicans are. I needed to see some of that. Aunt Sybil was encouraging me to get out and see all of the island, even if it meant starting out as a tourist. I needed to reacquaint myself with a place that had become so corrupted in my mind.

On this road trip, it was all new to me. The generally toothless roadside vendors with their shacks propped up on breeze blocks, selling acai and salt fish, fresh coconuts, jerk chicken, jackfruit, strips of mango, and yams. Leaves on trees so big they would hang over you like umbrellas. It was like going on some unknown journey. Sybil didn't tell me what was going to happen, but she planned it brilliantly. I had no idea what I was going to see or encounter. It was like being born, seeing the island for the first time, outside of the bubble, outside of the religion. I could feel my own spirit awaken. She wanted me to see it and then come back and tell her what I thought.

I have been coming back ever since. And I changed the minds of my brothers and sisters. "My God," I said, "it is not that fearful, awful place that we fled." And whenever I came I would get a bus and put everyone on it, get some music blasting, a bit of rum, some ganja, some coconuts, *Let's party*. We would stop at the side of the road and get some jerk chicken. It was good, because we started forgetting that other Jamaica, and we got used to this Jamaica, the real Jamaica, where the most extraordinary things have happened, and where it was all about beauty and energy, not Bible-black ugliness. That was the most astonishing thing about what the church did to us. In the middle of this island that is surely one of the great examples of creation—as crazed, crooked, and derelict as it can be—they blotted it out and replaced it with all this cruelty.

Jamaican culture is very strong and resilient. The place has survived so many hurricanes; there are deep caves that thread through the land that hid escaping slaves and pirates on the run. There are glittering treasures, secret coves, and listening hills. The language bends into itself, resisting the indifferent imposition of the Queen's English; the music booms and booms and booms and cracks and slaps. It's laid-back and lively, gentle and menacing. There's a continual sense of motion, and time seems larger and looser than it does anywhere else.

On that trip, I was in awe. Sybil wanted me to love this place. She'd tried to show me a different world when I was younger, and she tried to save me. She waited until I was old enough to see for myself, and she set me straight.

The time away added other geography to my personality. It threw a foreign aura around the tenacious Jamaican center. I've got something fluid and precarious in addition to the Jamaican. I'd gone through sensible Syracuse, hippie Philly, helter-skelter New York, and into the stinky, sensual depths of Paris. By the time I came back from my travels, I was prepared to take on the island. In Paris I was worried that I would not be understood, not because of the language but because of who I was as a person. I didn't really understand myself, and I realized that if I didn't understand myself, how could anyone else?

The main reason I didn't understand myself was because of what happened in Jamaica. I knew I had Jamaicanness in me, but I didn't know what it was. Finding the Jamaica that I was running away from helped me understand myself. I needed to recognize myself in order to gain the confidence I needed.

The moment my music came together as something that came from me was when there was the introduction of my Jamaican roots. That was me. That suited me. Previously, I had been more of a mimic, a sponge, absorbing and learning other styles, mastering experiences, putting them on like a costume, wearing them like a wig. I was a transplanted transatlantic creature with one foot in an airport and one foot in a nightclub. I was making my presence felt by posing for photographs and dancing on tables. I needed to come down to earth a little.

Once Jamaica became part of the music it was so much more natural, because that reflected who I actually was. The voice matched the music. That's me. I can do all the other stuff, but at the heart of it is the Jamaican experience. It's unprocessed; it's me, naked. It's where my soul was, so if I wanted to make soul music, however mutant, I needed to be in touch with my soul.

In Jamaica, I don't need lipstick; I don't need to dress up like I did in Paris and look perfect. There is a Jamaican side that few get to see. I don't wear any makeup, and basically I just wear loose cloth. I stay in a bathing suit and a sarong. In and out of the sea all day. I can spend hours in the sea, like I'm floating in space. You lose any sense of time. There is no time. You drift into another dimension. The sea is doing a million things at once, but it's also only doing one thing. It's very natural. My music needed the natural me that was resurrected, or there for the first time, during that trip to Jamaica that Sybil organized. The mirrored, costumed, bombed me didn't disappear but became a part of what I did. The natural, native me could take the lead. Once I got that base right, found my roots, which I had been afraid of, everything started to fit.

Jamaica has an attitude you can feel. It's hard to explain until you go there, but it has had an enormous influence on the rest of the world. It is very organic and magnetic; it has a real, definite aura that is in the air, the sea, the earth, the history, and it is like nowhere else, although in many ways its closest comparisons are other stray, enigmatic pieces of land surrounded by water, like Iceland, Sri Lanka, and Venice. Jamaica has this powerful life force, and it can take hold of you, like its reggae does. Sometimes people don't want to leave the island; sometimes it's like the island doesn't want you to leave. You can get trapped, and you can't leave, and you don't know why. And you're not too worried about it, actually, but it's not what you expected.

It sometimes feels like an animal with a consciousness all of its own. It's a lion place. There's lot of pride and fierceness. If you're not fierce, you're going to get eaten up. I grew up with it. I had it from being a little girl going to school in my uniform. You see it now on the schoolgirls making their way to school like I did, as if nothing has changed, except there are more things to remember. Every pleat, every detail, every braid, on the girls, however willful they feel, is held in place. It is a source of such pride. You have to be a lunatic to fall apart on the island, a total rum head. Struck by the moon. Let down by the land.

The bus filled with tourists would pass me when I was six on my way to school looking so immaculate—perfectly pressed uniform, everything matching, not a hair out of place, immaculately positioned beret—and I would stick my tongue out at it. My appearance resulted from a discipline that came from stiff, domineering British formality fed through the Jamaican sense of pride and resistance. The Jamaicans took discipline to another level.

It's like me. No matter how much I rebel, I have that discipline: I press the button and I take control, however wild I might be. My pride takes over. And my vanity. Jamaicans are very vain. The guys want to look good, and they have this show-off thing, and they go as far as they can in terms of looking strong, sometimes to the point of ridiculousness. They are very sure of themselves—sometimes with very little. There is a tendency with the men that the lionesses go out and do all the work, while the men want to look good, sleep, eat, charm the pants off every woman, and have sex. Men know it and the women know it, and they've worked out how to get along knowing this is how it works.

There's a thing a lot of Jamaicans do when they first meet people, which is that they look them up and down to check them out. Their figure, what they're wearing, their general demeanor. They'll give you a quick once-over, discreetly and yet pretty obviously, weighing you up to make sure you're worthy of a little attention, of their time.

Jamaica smells like nowhere else. It smells of the stars, of sweat, skin, freshly washed and filthy, fresh fish and clogged drains, vegetation and sin. Some smells you cannot describe because they change all the time. The sun pounds down, and then suddenly there is a rain shower and a new kind of smell comes up out of the earth. The rain beats down, but the sun is still shining, and the smell scrambles your senses. It's a smell that takes you on a journey into a dream, that almost causes hallucinations. It doesn't cost anything. I like Jamaica because of how you can have the most intense, sudden experiences, due to the land, the weather, the combination of heat and dirt, sea and forest, and they don't cost anything.

It's always growing and exploding into life. The people are perhaps so proud and vain and confident in order to tame all of this exuberance. It was always a place of comings and goings and staying put. It feels like it could be the center of the universe, but it doesn't make much of it.

It's all coast, tightly holding in mountains, flavors, plants, music, dancing, growth, enterprise, spice, movement, creatures, violence, bitter history, the Caribbean lilt and cockiness, and a way of stretching and displaying the body that started here and traveled the world. It's a constantly creative place. Its genius is in its music. There are more producers of music than consumers, something that is happening around the world now, but which happened in Jamaica first. The creative entrepreneur, doing a bit of this and a bit of that, realizing their potential in any number of ways. A new dance comes along all the time, channeling all the raw, funny, sexy energy, and spreads around the world, because it's irresistible. There is an amazing humor on this island; even when people are being edgy or provocative and challenging, you want to laugh with them.

Their attitude is contagious. The fun they have having fun, finding ways of having fun, and poking fun has infected a lot of modern music. Jamaicans are super-athletic as well. Fast, long, high, powerful. They have a kind of elemental determination to make their presence felt. When they're good at something, it goes without saying that they want to take it to another level. Sure, there's Usain Bolt, shining fast, but at another extreme, you ain't seen nothing until you've seen a flexible Jamaican lady pole dance. It all takes a kind of physical genius.

A lot of my attitude about money comes from the fact that I know I can come to Jamaica and enjoy the place itself without having any money. If making money becomes too stressful—the need for luxury or maintaining a lifestyle or just to pay the rent —I can go, "See you. I'm going to Jamaica. Leave me alone. I'm going to plant a tree and watch it grow. Build a house and pass the time. Sell the shells and ice-cold jelly from a shack. Look out to sea. Look out over the mountains. Disappear into the woods." I can find happiness in Jamaica even though my childhood was so scary and brutal. There was still enough of the power of the island that kept me happy and positive.

When I go back, I often spend some time with Chris Blackwell. He's been a constant in a life filled with so many changes, in my music, my management, my personal life, and he remains a fixed point. Since I first met him, he has always been involved in my music and my life whether I was signed to Island Records or not. Chris is my first best male friend. We totally bonded. He understood me and always wanted the best for me. He pushed me in every way, tested me musically and creatively, making me stretch and demanding the best. He always wanted me to learn and develop. He taught me also how to do things for myself in this crazy business. He never wanted to keep me ignorant. A lot of people in the music business like to keep you ignorant, but he likes me to learn for myself.

There's no agenda with Chris; he's simply interested in the best for me. He tells me how he feels, I tell him how I feel. He thinks he's right, I think I'm right—in a way, we're both right. Ultimately, we're after the same thing. We sometimes go about it in different ways. We both go against the grain, but sometimes we battle each other.

When I was at his house many miles inland, surrounded by many shades of wild green, sensing the constant pulse of the island, hearing the wind in the coconut trees, talking about this book, he said to me, "Make sure there is Jamaica in there. Don't forget the Jamaican you."

He always says that my image, throughout all the changes and countries and manipulation, is totally Jamaican. "From outer space, but very Jamaican, strong and grounded, like your mom and dad. I think people thought you were American because of the accent, but you are totally Jamaican. What makes you so determined and powerful comes from Jamaica. The island is somehow blessed. There is something about it that is unique."

My home is here, but I have traveled a lot, and I love traveling, but there is something about Jamaica, the energy, the soil itself, and mostly the people. They have a sense of identity, a strong sense of humor. It is an incredibly stimulating place. And since 1960 Jamaica started creating its own popular music, and it is still relevant now. It's one of the few places that did that. After America and Britain, no other country has managed to do that with such distinctive style. To invent a popular music that could only come from one place that has traveled worldwide and that constantly changes. Such a tiny island has done this.

Jamaica has been important for five hundred years. Since America was discovered. Jamaica was discovered at the same time. In a way, it was more important, because a large country wasn't so easy to handle back then. There were no cars, no way of covering the land easily. So the coastlines held the value. Islands were really precious, and if you were going to go inland you had to find something of value very quickly. That's why South America became important. Kingston was the seventeenth-biggest natural port in the world. The Dutch, the Spanish, the British all squabbled with each other over ownership, and in its own way it was a kind of gold rush. Since the beginning of time people will go to where the action is, and Jamaica for five hundred years has been attracting all different kinds of nationalities. It's full of all kinds of people from all kinds of countries—Chinese, Lebanese, Syrian, Jews, many races living next to each other with definite ease, adapting all the time, more than people really understand: out of many, one people.

That action from early on, all those different people, it has never been a sleepy place where little is happening. It can seem really sleepy, but the truth is it is never asleep. That's my theory: It has had action since the 1500s, and you cannot curtail that buildup of energy. It's like when the West was being opened up, Jamaica was playing a starring role. It was like being at the beginning of Silicon Valley. Jamaica was the Silicon Valley of its day.

7

Change

I had no idea that there was already a problem between Jean-Paul and Toukie. When we were all together in New York I'd hang out with the pair of them. They were still together, but after Toukie's time in Paris, they were talking about splitting up. I didn't know that. Me and Jean-Paul would talk and talk and talk until dawn while Toukie read or slept next door, and then I would go back to my apartment. There was nothing going on; we would talk about art and ideas and life. How he saw his work, what he was interested in.

Some people I loved to get to know because they'd take me to new places I would never have gone on my own. With Jean-Paul, I would dress up as a boy—which was easy to do with my flat chest, big jacket, no makeup, thicker eyebrows, maybe a pencil-thin mustache drawn on—and go to peep shows. Peep shows were everywhere around Times Square in the 1970s, dirty, sleazy places on the edge of legality, where you'd drop a quarter in a slot and see crackling film loops of lewd strip-teases or real topless girls gyrating, stroking themselves, moaning, licking their lips, dancing with dildos. It was masturbation central, dripping with sticky desire.

Forty-Second Street was lined with giant porn movie theaters, each boasting that it had the filthiest show in town. Inside, there would be all sorts of people—junkies, drunks, businessmen, hookers, loners, underage curiosity seekers, and Jean-Paul and I would blend in. It was a way of going on a date without it seeming like we were going on a date. Two guys looking for some furtive fun, a stimulating change of environment.

Times Square was very different in the 1970s from how it is now. It was almost a no-go area, where the all-things-are-possible American dream had turned rotten and was leaking something foul into the city. Manhattan was separated into zones, and they all existed apart from each other, and yet they also intersected. Parts of downtown were run-down, even derelict, so there was a rough zone. There was also a money zone, a tourist zone, a drug zone, a park zone, and a club zone, and there was a sex zone. Prostitutes were on the street in broad daylight. For a couple of blocks, New York seemed paved with hypodermic syringes.

The mood changed as the lights went down and the neon glowed grimy as if the colors were powered by sweat and desperation. That's when neon meant little but sleaze. Steam randomly spumed up out of the ground as though it would eventually cover the streets. There was real racy theater on the streets. It was very kinky. There was a blatant sense of danger, and violence never seemed far away. This was the world Travis Bickle cruised in *Taxi Driver,* wanting to clear the scum off the streets, the "whores, skunk pussies, buggers, queens, fairies, dopers, junkies."

Back then, the center of the city was adults only. Eventually the deviant XXX energy was annihilated by the corporate world, and Times Square became somewhere you could take your kids. It went from Travis Bickle to Hannah Montana. The naughty bits were chopped off. The scum was cleared from the streets. The area was refreshed, offering a different brand of consumer satisfaction. If it hadn't been pulled back from the brink of something postapocalyptic, you imagine it would have dragged the rest of the city, and the world, down with it. They've taken the smell out of it, though. It's not the Big Apple to me anymore. It's turning into one big shopping mall, one big Apple store.

It was easier to love then, somehow. Truer, if sicker. Jean-Paul and I used to go for curious, creepily romantic kicks, crossing over into a shabby, sex-filled reality, and we started to bond in the steamy, dark recesses of Peep-O-Rama and Show World.

We'd talk and talk into the night, until the sun came up, and even though he wasn't my type physically, I fell in love with his mind, with how he saw the world. I loved how he saw me—he saw me in ways that I had felt instinctively but never been able to articulate.

He was an amazing dancer, and had come to America on a ballet scholarship. I'd get him on the dance floor sometimes, and he'd drop in a few ballet steps. He was always exercising and keeping fit. His mother was a dancer with the Ziegfeld Follies, and she would tell him a lot of stories about the exotic dancers.

I loved boxing—my dad was an amateur boxer—and so did Jean-Paul. He was obsessed with it. Warhol was fascinated as well, with tough, driven characters literally fighting to make a name for themselves and escape their poor backgrounds. Jean-Paul and Andy had a project they developed together, *The Main Event*, with the boxer and actor Chu Chu Malave. They took it to a big Hollywood producer, and he took it from them. It went to Barbra Streisand, when it became something else altogether, with Ryan O'Neal. Streisand was at her Hollywood peak—there was no competition, even with Warhol involved.

The dancing, the boxing, it all fed into Jean-Paul's thoughts about the body, how it moved, how it dealt with danger and changed shape when it was stimulated or threatened. He was interested in representing the body not as it is but as it feels, as it dreams, as it could be if the imagination was in charge. He was a choreographer and coach and analyst and he wanted to take revenge on reality as much as I did, for his own reasons.

Esquire was where he obtained the training for the techniques he would use when he worked with me—how he would illustrate and conceptualize ideas, marking a fluid border between the blatantly avant-garde and the unashamedly commercial, and how he would somehow treat product as human, and people as product, giving glamour depth and the profound something glittery. It was astounding how precise he could be, and at the same time so extravagant—simultaneously unrestrained and composed. He also had that French thing, that insolent, provocative humor, where the clown and the existentialist are as funny and as serious as each other.

I admired his work so much that I would have done anything he asked me. We met at a time when we each needed someone—someone who could deepen us, who we could change with, who we could become. That was how it was. And each of us was the one the other one wanted. I was, after all, an art groupie, because I loved being with painters, writers, photographers, illustrators, designers, and often because that turned me on I would want to get closer. I wasn't interested if there was no vision. There had to be something that kept me interested. He wanted a living person to whom he could apply his ideas, about desire, blackness, primitive cultures, image, control, someone who was prepared to make their body available. He needed a volunteer.

It is very difficult to say what came first—the two of us starting a romantic relationship or us starting a creative relationship. I think the two things happened simultaneously. As soon as he started to photograph and draw me, we were together. As soon as we kissed, we were together. As soon as we started talking—Toukie would be in the next room, and we would be talking—we brain-fucked each other, but we didn't have sex.

It was all very innocent, and then it wasn't. When we would secretly hang out together around Times Square we were sublimating sexual tension behind so-called research trips into the sleazy. Eventually, we became our own peep show.

Some people think we were collaborating from the beginning, but there were three disco albums before Jean-Paul Goude and I started working together. And "La Vie en Rose" had already been a big hit by the time he appeared.

The first three albums were with Richard, who treated photos by Antonio Lopez and a photographer, Francis Ing, who would take photos of me in New York that were the perfect background for Richard's freely scrawled pencil strokes. That was a different style of enchantment, reflecting the world as it was at the time in New York and Paris, in the clubs, in the night, in the world and Factory of Warhol, the un-raveling of a very specific form of surface energy.

Richard wanted me to be his muse, no one else's. I didn't like the idea of a Svengali/muse thing. I wasn't a muse. That seemed so passive and uninvolved. It was Richard who named my third album *Muse*. I was amused to be a muse, and that was something else to try on, but it wasn't important for me to be one. I wanted to collaborate with artists on an equal footing. I was interested in being a part of the process, not simply a decoration to be manipulated.

Jean-Paul's method of enchantment went deeper and was more aggressive. Richard softened and sweetened me. For a while, looking at the disco sleeves, and the way Richard colored me green, navy blue, charcoal, you wouldn't have known what color I was. Jean-Paul dug into me, bit into me, scratched and stretched me, and made very clear what the color of my skin was. His work with me was more a contin-uation of where Issey Miyake and Eiko Ishioka had been, exploring bodies, faces, settings, material, theater in the search for the sublime point—working in imaginary places, in cities not yet invented, with clothing not yet dreamed up, for impossible bodies, for a time that was neither daylight nor night, dream nor real, a twilight zone.

That was where I saw myself. Always in between, on the way some-where else. My head in the moment, but other parts of myself strewn across centuries and countries. I had always left myself open to move-ment and change. I didn't want to go the way of Sy and Eileen, into a glitter-ball land more Liza and Bette. I didn't want to boogie on down for the rest of my life.

Disco was squeezing me into a room that was looking tackier and tackier, and I was worried I was going to be trapped. Meeting Jean-Paul and Chris Blackwell helped me follow my own route, into an elsewhere I felt more at home in. I knew I was hurting Sy and Eileen, but what they offered was not what I wanted. I had my own purpose and wanted to try other doors, other roads, other recipes.

Disco had been an accident, but within a couple of years I had re-leased my three disco albums—*Portfolio, Fame,* and *Muse*—produced by Tom Moulton. They were becoming his vision more than mine. They all followed the same formula—the thumping dance, the showboating Broadway, some inevitable French spice, the glossy, tightly arranged Philly frills. There were songs and medleys that were souvenirs of the Studio 54 era, and they had titles that referred to my modeling career and to my association with artists and photographers. I was becoming the decoration, and I was getting bored with that.

They were the soundtrack to the party I was having, the clubs I was singing at, and they formed an informal trilogy. There was nowhere else to go, though, and disco was now the most loathed form of music—the essential racism, sexism, and homophobia of the white rock audience had forced it out of the way, which was easier to do when it became so crass and commercial.

I had done my Studio 54 time. There were other clubs where the music was still about change and forward movement, which was actually about putting dancers deep into the moment. The Paradise Garage opened in SoHo in 1977 on the second floor of an old concrete parking garage, when disco was bending toward campness and stupidity. It was built on the utopian blueprint of the Loft. The kind of music that followed, best known as house, started at the Garage, and so it was also known as garage.

At first, Paradise Garage was only a space with a great, towering sound system and those loyal nomads looking for a place where the experiments that had led to disco were still evolving. By 1980, it became more of an experience, possessing the atmosphere people remember, with Zen chill-out rooms, intimate lounge areas, and a movie theater, but without the dressing up and the celebrity-saturated, cocaine 54 thing. I was partial to that—I could take it all on—but the purity of the Garage connected me more to my mind-expanding acid trips. There were still parties, but on a different planet from the ones at Studio 54.

The Garage was members only, and you had to be interviewed to become a member. That was a bit strange, having to pass a test to prove how free-spirited you were, but it seemed to work. There would be a thousand, two thousand people in there—by the 1980s even more—and for a while most of them knew each other's names.

There was no alcohol, so no need for a license, and the club could stay open as long as it wanted—its best hours were four in the morning until midday. They'd shut the doors at about 6 A.M., when there'd be a shift in the sound of the music. You'd go to bed around ten at night, get up at four in the morning, go to the Garage, and leave at noon, refreshed to the soul.

In my case, after I'd been going for a few years, I would call Keith Haring and turn up with him. Andy had introduced us. We were always the last to leave. The Garage was heaven for Keith. It changed his life. He went every Saturday night for three or four years. He always said he was open to everything and spent his life "gathering information," which is something I identified with. He gathered a lot of information, about himself and others, at the Garage. He developed the dancing outlines he became famous for by watching the dancers, hands up in the air, banging up against each other, life bursting around them, dancing until they dropped. Outside, his aliens, babies, penises, televisions, and barking dogs were sprawled on the walls, Dumpsters, and subway ads throughout the East Village.

We'd go to Fire Island for tea parties in the afternoon. We were very easy together. Some people can be very draining. Like bloodsuckers. Keith was very relaxed and positive. He had this childlike innocence, which suited me. We were all individuals with similar sensibilities who were connected in various ways, as though it was always meant to be.

If I had any personal appearances to do I would call Keith and tell him, *I'm doing something tomorrow*, and we would prepare something for the show really, really fast. He liked to try things out. I always liked each show to be visually different. I didn't like to repeat myself. It got around that what I was doing was a one-off, which made it special. And it kept me interested. It's boring to do the same thing over and over, especially because these club shows were very short. People would come to the shows dressing like me from an earlier show, so you would look out and see lots of me.

He would paint my naked body like it was a canvas, and always differently. Keith always said that as soon as he saw me, he knew my body would be the ultimate body to paint. What Jean-Paul would do to me in a photograph, externalizing my spirit, Keith did to my actual skin and body. They both understood that the truly beautiful is always bizarre.

I remember once when he painted me for a photograph, I went where I was going next with the paint still on. If I could, I would go out wearing nothing but his paint. Covered with Haring—his light and joy, his swoops and strokes, his handwriting—I would be dressed perfectly. As he painted me, I could feel myself change, become someone else, like my body, not my mind, was on an acid trip.

The Garage was a cult, like the church, but unrestricted and non-judgmental. It became a cliché to say so, but you felt it at the time. You'd be hit with the Holy Spirit. And if you go there and you are not going to dance, get the fuck out. You had to be ready to sweat your ass off. Then you'd get close to God.

It was dark. There was no distracting light show. It was all about the music. It wasn't a place you went to be seen or to search out the famous. If Mick Jagger or Diana Ross turned up, they were one of the crowd. You went to experience this brilliant new music. Music was the thing, the funk, soul, R & B, and edgy rock that had become disco, the best disco, and where disco was heading, into hip-hop, and the first foundations of house. The love and peace that were in the air, both in a lot of the songs they played, and the togetherness in the room, were a continuation of those anti-Vietnam protest songs people like Curtis Mayfield would sing and Roland Kirk would blow in the early '70s, before there was disco.

You entered by walking along an extended ramp, like a fashion-show walkway, and that was such a thrill, your heart would be pounding like you were about to enter a fantasy. You were about to become surreal—it made you realize how great music played in the right surroundings is in itself a surreal act.

I had my baby shower at the Garage when I was pregnant with Paulo. Debbie Harry of Blondie and Andy Warhol threw it for me. That's showing you normal. (Paulo and Keith Haring would also become very close; to Paulo, he was Uncle Keith. They would draw together, like it was the most fun you could have in the world.) The papers called it the first disco baby shower, and Paulo was being talked about as "the first disco baby." I did an interview with a magazine, *Jet:* "I want a boy—family tradition, boys first. It should be surrounded by music." The magazine said I was hoping for natural childbirth and breast-feeding "if I don't chicken out first." I was dressed up as a deviant toy soldier, carried onto the stage by my troops on a pedestal, with the audience of lusty Garage boys screaming, "Show us the stomach, honey." I then sang "Get Down on Your Knees." The Garage was the kind of place where this kind of drama could happen—a world unto itself embedded in but separate from the surrounding city, where the party was more important than business, and the vibe reached higher than the skyscrapers.

The DJ booth at the Garage was very difficult to get to, and it was guarded. That was the pulpit, ten feet off the ground. It was the one place where you could get a drink. There was spiked punch in a couple of bowls in the early days, to give you a lift, but officially no alcohol. I liked hanging out in the DJ booths. Among a writhing, dedicated sea of people blissed out on beat, it was the only place where you could get away for a while. It was like an island of calm in the middle of a stormy sea. Not many people were allowed in the booths. Frankie Crocker was allowed in, on one of his visits to check out new sounds for his radio show.

I would sit on a stool in the booth and have a glass of champagne and watch main Garage DJ and club conceptualist Larry Levan at work, dropping the needle onto the wax with such precision, playing with the volume, bass, treble, measuring the silence between certain tracks to the millionth of a second. There was no time to say hello. You didn't want to mess with his concentration. He wouldn't let you anyway. It was as though he were on a high wire as he structured his set and wrote his history of music. Drop in, take it all in, feel his power and mastery. It was such a privilege. Watching him was like being right next to Hendrix as he played the guitar on stage.

After a night there, it was like you had been worshipping, but there was no preaching. They called it the Church because a great Saturday night would end on Sunday. People would be going home from the

Garage as people went to church, and the two audiences would cross over. I remember once on a Sunday around midday, downtown, no one really around, and there was someone walking down Hudson Street totally naked. Not drunk, but nude. Very erect and proud looking. And you just knew he had been to the Garage. He had that look on his face. No clothes. A sense of peace after a night of the best kind of noise. He was thinking, *Nothing bad will ever happen to me.* He would never need protecting.

I wanted my music to be played in these places. I wanted to perform in front of that crowd like I had in front of the Studio 54 and Le Palace people. For that to happen there had to be an incredible change in how the music sounded.

At his house high up in Jamaica, as the light drifts off into a radiant gloom and the crickets perform all around us, sounding like they're on quite a trip, Chris Blackwell remembers how we went about making the change.

I loved "La Vie en Rose." The intro went on forever, it used a drum machine, a gentle groove, building the drama, and it was brilliantly produced. It still sounds great today, nearly forty years later. That was an early sign of the movement into technology.

He didn't want you in the studio until the track was done, and that was the only problem, really, in how Tom Moulton worked. It was a new way of making records where the artist had minimal contribution to how the track was built; in fact, the singer was low down on the priority [list] of the producer, just something to add at the last minute to give the track some identity. He distanced you from being involved in your own music, and I think by [his] not involving you and your personality, the tracks had less and less impact. There was no sense of your own identity on your own records, because you were not allowed to be a part of the creative process, even if in terms of the music reacting to your presence and your energy.

This was the problem with disco ultimately, that it became more and more anonymous despite it being all about performance and visuals. Those three disco albums represented that— how a very strong character is somehow ignored by the music. Your music needed to be all about Grace Jones, but it was ultimately more about the producer, who used Grace Jones as the face, the person who [would] promote the music, but not the spirit. The first one was so strong, and it put you in a great position, but the next ones tended to copy that. I decided I wanted to produce the next album, because I thought it was an interesting problem to work out.

I thought we were in a bit of trouble after the third album. It didn't sell very well, and I thought that you were very strong, but the music was getting weaker, and it wasn't who you were. I thought, *Well, part of the trip is that you are scary.* When people thought about you, as a performer, in your photographs, the whole image they had of you, there is a shock feeling. I thought, *My God, you're Jamaican, whether people know it or not, so let's give you a rock-steady Jamaican bass and drum.* I didn't want to lose what Tom Moulton had done on "La Vie en Rose," but I wanted it to move on into what was happening to music because of the development of electronics and now that punk and disco had become more sophisticated and knowing.

At that time we had Black Uhuru on Island, and first of all, the name is great, and it has bloody, mysterious connotations— the Mau Mau tribe used to daub the word *uhuru* in blood on the house of those they murdered, and the fighting insignia of the Mau Mau terrorists is long braids smeared with blood. The name Black Uhuru was very scary because of that, the *black* reinforces the *uhuru,* and you get a very powerful feeling of what they are going to sound like. Then you'd see Sly [Dunbar], Robbie [Shakespeare], Mikey Rose, and Duckie Simpson walk into a room, and my God, you'd run for the hills.

Their music sounded like their name, and I thought it would

be great to get Sly and Robbie to give that kind of edge to you. There was something about you that was more from that world than from disco. More a member of the Uhuru tribe than the disco tribe. We'd recently made a record with Marianne Faithfull, *Broken English,* with this great, screaming guitar; I thought that was something to get into the new mix, a solid sense of the midrange, because reggae never had an interesting midrange. It was still the early days of computer music, but I wanted to find someone to boost the midrange.

Wally Badarou was recommended to me as doing something interesting in that area, and it was exactly what we needed in terms of creating a Grace Jones sound. His DNA, his Parisian/ African roots, were perfect. When he was young in West Africa, he listened to James Brown, Ray Charles, Otis Redding, Stevie Wonder, Congolese rumba, Afro-Cuban cha-cha, early salsa, but also Hendrix and [Carlos] Santana, and he was experimenting with electronics. He'd played on M's "Pop Music" and later on Robert Palmer's "Addicted to Love"; he'd played on a few anonymous disco records, which he saw as funk for the masses. He didn't look down on them. He was deeply passionate about the new studio toys that were emerging at the time. He was a multi-instrumentalist who saw the synthesizer as a way of opening up the number of instruments he could play. It was new territory; there were no scripts to follow, bringing synth music into other styles, but Wally had the right musical instincts.

I was after a mix of the very Jamaican, a very organic groove, with something technologically brand-new. I reached out to Wally, and he was a genius to have in what became a group known as Compass Point All Stars, because we recorded at Compass Point Studios, which I had opened in Nassau in the Bahamas, with a core of Sly and Robbie, Wally, Mikey, and Sticky Thompson. Then there was Barry Reynolds, the guitarist from Marianne Faithfull's record, which gave the group a rock dimension. There were different histories and styles—the reggae rhythm, the rock energy, and the new electronic element coming from someone with an African background and yet a Euro touch. Wally had worked on disco records in Paris, so there was something coming from that Parisian side—you had a continuity, a link with those disco records and the French chanteuse element. Later, as part of the All Stars, there was Tyrone Downie, who'd played keyboards with Bob Marley and the Wailers and Burning Spear.

I wrote "My Jamaican Guy" about Tyrone, because when we were in the Bahamas recording I remember him in the swimming pool, and he came out of the water with his dreadlocks flashing in the sun. As he came out of the water, he shook his dreadlocks like a dog would to dry off, and the water sprayed around him like sparks flying, and I thought of the idea, my Jamaican guy. We were not having an affair; it was an impression of something around me. I was watching things as a voyeur, being excited by something unexpected. It doesn't mean it was about something real that I was involved in. I was using my imagination.

The Compass Point All Stars were an experiment in finding a Grace Jones sound. They were all working on various projects for Chris elsewhere, and he brought them together. Chris took all my different worlds and stuck them all together to create the Compass Point All Stars—the erotic French side, the acid-tripping rock 'n' roller, the Jamaican drum and bass, the androgynous, android electronics—it was magical, this assembly of pieces that fitted together. We would try out the mixes at the Garage, which had the best sound and most sophisticated system in the city, and therefore the world, at the time.

Lots of labels would use it as a testing ground. Once a mix sounded great through Larry's speakers, you knew you were onto something. He treated the speakers like they were his orchestra and he was the conductor. He put a lot of work and time into making sure the speakers/orchestra were perfect for the room, his ears, that they could deliver awesomely loud volume without distortion, and that they lost nothing of the detail when a complex, exciting multitrack studio mix was played in club conditions. There was an art to all of this, as well as a science, and also something that is about magic. It's voodoo. Once those Compass Point mixes sounded right coming out of the Garage speakers, we knew we'd cracked it.

I eventually got to play at the Garage, carried above the crowd to the stage, cracking my whip, at five thirty in the morning, which for me is really late enough at night to feel most alive. The last time I played there, in 1985, two years before it closed down, Keith Haring painted my naked body with white tribal patterns, and I was covered with space-age red wire tubing spiraling out from two cones covering my breasts. An Egyptian empress as astronaut. Flesh turned into graffiti, skin into a canvas, Africa into space.

The Compass Point sessions were important for me because I was still experimenting with my voice, and realizing that there was no point in trying to sing in the generic radio key. Chris wanted me to have hits, but knew I was not comfortable singing how other singers sang. He didn't care that I sounded like a man or an entity; he simply wanted my voice to sound strong.

After the disco albums, I had decided that I was going to sing in my way, not try and become a conventional pop singer. I had found my voice, and once I started singing along with the heavy bass and machine-gun drum of Sly and Robbie, it was actually an advantage that I had the voice that I did. There was no place for a standard soul or funk voice in that sound. My voice was perfect for it, somewhere between half-speaking and half-singing, between expressing emotion and not expressing anything, between telling a story and remembering a dream.

It would be better for me to have a voice that suited my appearance, and once Chris had put together these musicians, I found my place. I realized that those Jamaican elements suited my Jamaican voice, but there was also rock, and funk, and something not yet determined. Now that I had lowered my voice I didn't need anything sweet around me. I could move into other spaces, like I had moved into other spaces via the mind and manipulation of Jean-Paul. I had made a decision not to try to be like the gospel-inspired female singers I admired. There were male singers I loved that perhaps made more sense: James Brown, Bobby

Womack, and, of course, Barry White. Hearing Anita Baker sing "I Just Wanna Be Your Girl" in the late '70s with Chapter 8 was a revelation. She wasn't afraid to go low and proud, and gutsy too, and it made me think I didn't have to pretend to be pretty.

The Compass Point All Stars first all played together on my records, which made those records very unique. I had no idea Chris was putting them together. He could imagine what it could be like, and the more he understood me, the more he realized what kind of band would be good for me. He never asked me what I thought about it; he just went ahead and did it. He read me and my multifarious, international attitude, and he saw I had a rock 'n' roll side, even though I was never rock. He interpreted my wildness as a rock energy, and that I could bring it as a character into the music. There was the French, Euro, synth part, and the deep, menacing Jamaican drum and bass. That was his vision. Chris, being a prophet, can hear something before it is actually played. He went out of his way to create a sound that suited my personality.

It also had a little bit of the naughtiness he knew I had—he would go to bed at Nassau, and me and his girlfriend at the time, Natalie, would sneak upstairs, tiptoe into his room and say, "We've come to play, Chris, let's have some fun." We tried to attack Chris in bed. He was never interested; he would always kick us out. "You girls get out of here. What are you up to? Leave me alone." But that mischievous, high-spirited side of me went into the music.

I never saw the All Stars play before I was actually singing with them. I was hearing the group from within, immediately a part of what they were doing. I could sense from inside that it was perfect for me, the groove they hit instantly, the mix of the organic and the electronic. It fit me like a bloody glove. We did all those *Warm Leatherette* and *Nightclubbing* tracks live in the studio. We fell into a pure, instinctive groove that didn't need hours and hours of preparation. They set up the groove and worked out the beats, and I got in the chariot—but I was out front, leading the procession, behind when I needed to be, sometimes ahead, sometimes right on the moment.

———

The work Jean-Paul and I were doing was originally separate from the music. I kept saying to Jean-Paul, *This image would make a great cover.* Jean-Paul had never done that kind of thing, but I could see clearly his images would make great record sleeves. At first, once we were going out together, there was a sense at Island Records of *Oh, he's the boyfriend. She only wants him to do the artwork because she's pushing his career.* It took a bit of time to persuade Island that Jean-Paul was the way to go. He had done a lot before we worked together, and proved himself in the world he was in, but not to a record company. Their attitude was very much, *Well, who are you, and what have you really done?*

They wouldn't pay him much, because in a music context he was inexperienced. Then Jean-Paul wanted to take control of producing the music, which alienated Chris, who said, "Okay, if you want to produce, then you do it," and he walked out of the studio. Jean-Paul soon realized he was out of his depth. He did find the "Libertango" track for me later, and over time he did begin to understand my voice and music and figured out how to contribute musically, but it was too early for him to be involved in the music.

I insisted to Chris that I wanted Jean-Paul to look after the visual side of everything I now did. Having learned from Issey, Eiko, Antonio, Helmut, Andy, Richard, the absolute masters of astounding commercial art, there was no way I was going to go further into the music business without being in control of the artwork. That meant having someone like Jean-Paul. It had to be someone as brilliant as Jean-Paul because of who I had been working with, the ones before who had presented me to the world, Grace as their Grace, which came out of who I was, and then who I would become. Eventually, Jean-Paul won Island's respect, and Chris loved what he did. He turned them around so much they would hire him for projects that didn't involve me.

We did some photographs, and I showed them to Chris. Chris would say, *Blow up that image*—something Jean-Paul and I had worked on, for the sake of it, with no end in mind—*and take it to the studio.*

We blew up this photo that was eventually used for the cover of *Warm Leatherette,* me as an ominous, hard-eyed samurai filtered through something occult and African, the killer clown interrupting some mysterious ceremony. It was huge and covered the whole wall of the studio. Chris said to the band, *Make a record that sounds like that looks.* So we started playing with that photograph in front of us. Then we made sure the music suited the photo, what Jean-Paul described as the erotic menace, where he took me as the fighter out of the ring into a new theatrical space, me as the beast out of the wild into a geometrically minimalist setting, me as the shadowless warrior out of the battlefield into a kind of empty, polished museum. Skin like no other skin, Baudelaire's brown deity: Jean-Paul exaggerated my differences to the point of exorbitance, and the music had to follow.

In that picture, actually, I am pregnant with Paulo. You could see my tummy sticking out a little, but if you didn't know, you wouldn't be able to tell. We found a way to cover it up. When I was seven months pregnant, it hardly showed. You couldn't tell, looking at me, that I was expecting. My breasts got bigger, almost up to my chin, which I loved, as I always felt a little inadequate in that department. I had no morning sickness, none of the classic symptoms of pregnancy. I felt very normal. I swam, I toured. I had a lot of energy.

The first thing I did when I was pregnant was give up quaaludes. Your body immediately tells you what to do, and I obeyed. Jean-Paul was much more concerned than me about what having a baby would do to my body. I instinctively felt it would be a powerful, positive thing. The baby started to move inside me, and that was very alien.

Mostly, it was the most natural thing in the world. Now and then I would panic, wondering how it was going to come out of that hole. When I first saw a cock, I wondered how that was going to get into the hole. Now I wondered how a baby could get out of the hole. I thought about it, and then I forgot about it. It had to work. Life itself is a sign that it does.

I was living on Fifty-Fourth Street, and Jean-Paul lived on the top floor of a commercial building on Union Square, some forty blocks south. We were together but maintaining our independence. You could look from Jean-Paul's apartment into Antonio's window. They could wave at each other. The artists were all downtown. Nothing above Chelsea; maybe Thirtieth Street was as high as the artists went. There was no real gentrification at that point; the farther you slipped downtown, the more basic and sprawling it became, and the artistic communities were not yet being pushed out by money and those looking for interesting creative areas they would then spoil by moving there.

I would be at my apartment sometimes, and other times I'd spend a few days with Jean-Paul. One weekend, I was staying with him. His Sixteenth Street penthouse apartment opened out onto a terrace—you can see it in the video for "Libertango," where all of New York becomes the backdrop. All the doors of his flat opened onto the terrace, which was filled with big plants. There was a stairway coming from below leading to the terrace on the outside, which should have been locked. Jean-Paul's was the only residence on the block, and it was the weekend, so everything underneath was shut.

It was one of those ordinary mornings—well, probably early afternoon, because it was the weekend. I was walking from the bathroom. This tall black guy suddenly appeared out of nowhere on the terrace, quiet as a panther. He was wearing a beautiful Italian-style suit and had the most perfectly shaped Afro. He didn't look like a New Yorker. He had a bag slung over his shoulder, very casual. My eyes scanned him very quickly. I said, a little shocked, but there seemed nothing else to say, "Hello, can I help you?" Then I noticed that he was holding a gun. A very small gun, which somehow made it even more threatening.

Butterflies tore through my stomach. I could see through to the far end of the apartment where Jean-Paul was working hunched over his desk, wearing glasses, cutting up small pictures of me into small pieces and moving them around. He was totally oblivious, concentrating on solving some puzzle about how I might be turned into a new shape. I ran to the bathroom and closed the door. The tall guy followed me and kicked down the bathroom door. He thought I was running and getting a gun, so he was on high alert. There was fear in his eyes. I was on the floor quietly freaking out.

This was when it became serious and Jean-Paul heard the commotion. He came to see what was going on. He saw the surreal glint of the small gun.

The guy wanted cash, and Jean-Paul only had deutsche marks. The guy didn't know what they were, that they were at that time the stron-gest currency in the world. Jean-Paul was offering him camera equip-ment. He didn't want to carry that. He really just wanted cash.

Jean-Paul's work was always scattered over the floor. He never hung anything up. There were pictures of me strewn across the floor. The guy recognized me from the photos. I had done a talk show the week before. "Didn't I see you on *The Merv Griffin Show* last week?" he asked, a little softer than he was before, intrigued that I might be someone.

I thought, *Oh no, now I really am dead. There's no one in the building and now he has recognized me: I am dead.* I became oddly calm. He tied us both up. Jean-Paul started giggling from nerves, like he was in a movie. There was a small mirror next to the bed to make the room look big-ger, nothing kinky, and he was being tied up on the bed and seeing it happen and he laughed. I was thinking, *Please don't do that—here we are, a mixed couple, and you are laughing at him. There's a black guy in the house with a perfect Afro and a gun, and you are giggling.*

I hissed at him, "Stop it, this is serious," giving him a really stern ex-pression. I started to use my mother's technique and tried to charm the guy and get a grip on the situation. "Yeah, I was on *Merv Griffin.*"

"Oh, yeah, you're that girl?"

I got us to chatting so that it was almost as if we were having a cup of coffee. I said, "You can change that money at any Thomas Cook agency; you don't need ID." There were about two thousand deutsche marks, so he was going to get a lot of dollars.

He could have easily killed us, and no one would have found us until Monday. We started to communicate. He eventually said okay. The eleva-tor door opened into the loft. He untied me but not Jean-Paul. I told him where to go to change the marks. I gave him our keys so he could get out, because you needed to open the lock to make the lift work. I said, "Leave the keys on the fourth floor, and we will give you time to get away."

After he had gone, Jean-Paul asked me to untie him. I said, "I can't, I promised him that I wouldn't untie you for a certain amount of time," like he was still watching us somehow. It was like an episode of *Kojak,* "Die Before They Wake." After about twenty minutes I untied Jean-Paul, much to his anger and relief. It ended so much better than it looked like it was going to when we were tied up, but it is something that has stayed with me ever since.

We were recording in Nassau at the time, and it was going very quickly. I was due back in the Bahamas for the session, and I went to see my doctor before I got on the plane and he said, "There is no way you can travel." He said, "You have to go straight to bed." The holdup had accelerated the pregnancy, and I was close to being due weeks before the baby had fully developed. I had to spend weeks resting to slow down the progress of the pregnancy.

I moved in with Jean-Paul because his place was nearer to the hospital on Seventeenth Street, Beth Israel. I was taking classes to have a natural birth. Jean-Paul said to me that he didn't want to see me give birth, because he thought that if he did he wouldn't be able to have sex with me again. I said, "Don't come, then!"

Jean-Paul worked at home, so he was there if I needed anything. He was wonderful, considering he had been freaked out about me having a child. I think he thought my body was going to get out of shape and get fat. I said, "That's not me. That will not happen. I am a jungle mother." I believe that was his biggest fear; that I would give up work like his mother did and become a housewife. After she had him she gave up her career. A lot of women do. He was worried I would do that, and become reliant on him.

I stayed in bed for two weeks on doctor's orders. I woke up one morning feeling a certain pressure and I thought I was constipated. I sat on the toilet and I started to push. I had no labor pains. I sent Jean-Paul off to get some laxatives. I pushed and pushed. It turned out it was the baby. Another half an hour and I would have given birth in the bathroom at home.

I was only feeling a pressure, no pain. It didn't seem to be the baby. Finally Jean-Paul said, "Let's get a taxi and go to the hospital," which was just three minutes away. As we arrived I felt a little cramp, but

I still told my doctor I am badly constipated. He told me that I am giving birth. I didn't believe it because I felt no pain. I was screaming for a laxative and then when I thought the baby is coming, I worried that I was going to do a number two at the same time. This was now my biggest fear. My doctor tried to explain to me that this was physically impossible. One hole closes as another gets bigger. Mother nature has elegantly sorted that problem out. I had no clue. It felt like it was all going to pour out.

Within half an hour Paulo was born. It turned out Jean-Paul had been in the delivery room the whole time. He saw everything. He had on a doctor's coat, mask, and hat, and I thought he was one of the medical team. I was looking at him the whole time, not knowing it was him. He was there, a very proud father—his curiosity took over and he couldn't help himself. He saw me give birth and still wanted to have sex with me.

I think that was when he fell in love with me in a more organic way. Years later, he would use my expression as I gave my final push before our son appeared, my mouth stretched as wide as it could, for the cover of *Slave to the Rhythm,* one of his most amazing images—he extended the last, big scream, the final push, the birth moment, made my mouth impossibly open, made a still picture appear to be in motion, capturing an extraordinary part of our lives and turning it into art. It was another extreme example of how he told our story, transforming the normal often underestimated edges of everyday life into the truly astonishing.

I still stayed in my apartment. I have too much stuff. And I love stuff. I never seriously thought of having any more children, with Jean-Paul, or anyone after. I knew Paulo wouldn't hinder the very strong career drive I had, but I never felt an urge to have any more children. My career was like having a lot of babies to look after.

As Chris recalled:

We were supposed to start in November 1979, but you gave birth to Paulo, so we started a few weeks later. I didn't turn up for the first few days because I knew it was going to be difficult as the musicians all settled in. They didn't know each other, and they didn't necessarily all get on at first. Different worlds. It worked itself out by the time I had arrived. The personalities got themselves orchestrated. Wally and Sly were of the same complexion, but God, they were very far apart. It's what made it work in the end—there was a tension between each faction in the group that gave the music both its tightness and its looseness.

We recorded from scratch, as live as possible. It was very exciting, because I had had the wisdom to get Alex Sadkin as the engineer at the Compass Point Studios. He was beyond compare for his talent, his taste, and his ear. He was the final part of the puzzle. [The record] needed someone fantastically fluent at mixing on the go, to capture the groove as it was happening, mostly played live, to give the process a certain balance and coherence. I would sit in there and sort of nudge it in the right direction. I would support and encourage you singing with a band.

This became the Grace Jones band. You'd never been exposed to that kind of thing before, but it suited your personality, and that in turn influenced the direction of the music. When you weren't involved in your music, it could really have been made for anyone. This was music that sounded like you really were— all that international input, the different energies, but at the heart of it, very Jamaican.

When they recorded "Private Life," I couldn't believe it, it was so smooth and cool. It all worked out better than I could have hoped. There was a punk influence as well in a way, because that was still raging, as an energy, an approach to making records, not so worried about any gloss. Instead of there being a lot of overdubs, and a precise layering of the music, I would get them to play together live. They would start playing, and then when they were locked into the groove, I would tell Alex to turn on the tape. We were so lucky to have Alex; he was responsible for the sound, and he got a sound that is respected to this day, in any form of music. It was a classic sound, and that was down to Alex.

I loved that sound. It was to me coming out of the same balance of sounds as Bob Marley, where I had performed a similar role. I don't like a crowded sound, I want clarity, but it was a whole different approach. It was rooted in a minimalist sound, but with new, almost abstract details pulling and pushing inside. You could hear everything really clear in the space it occupied, but it was all completely together.

Your strong constituency then was definitely the gay community, coming from disco. I thought I would do some research and see if there were any songs that were doing well in that underground, in the gay clubs but not disco, and I heard "Warm Leatherette" by the Normal. I contacted Daniel Miller, who was both the Normal and also the owner of the label it was released on, Mute. It wasn't a huge hit, it was very underground, but I was looking for something that you could introduce to a wider audience. It was a calling card; it said there was a new, upgraded Grace Jones. This one was something else.

Chris and his team brought in songs that were unusual pop, or relatively unheard of, or plain unexpected, to suit our new approach. Nothing that was as obvious as the show tunes, perhaps, but in many ways, new forms of show tunes. New-wave show tunes, Iggy Pop as the new Frank Sinatra, ones emerging out of the new kind of songwriting that there was because of glam, punk, new wave, electro, reggae, postpunk. Songs that sounded like the kind of thing that creature lurking in those Jean-Paul fantasies would sing. A creature that was based on me, that was all me, but made more, made bigger. A creature from another land, where the standards are not quite what they are in this world, where the highs and lows, spaces and surfaces are all different. I treated the songs as though they were already classics.

Some of the songs they brought me I didn't feel comfortable doing—the Stones' "Brown Sugar" and "Concrete Jungle" by Bob Marley didn't work. "Warm Leatherette" sounded really interesting, and I could immediately get into character on that one, sex as a car crash, bodies embedded in metal, metal penetrating flesh, broken glass scattered everywhere, blood staining shiny silver. Been there, done that; it was like Sondheim on the other side of acid, of Studio 54 and the Garage, of performing in semi-naked splendor for ecstatic gays, and watching bony girls in plastic miniskirts masturbate on the other side of a Plexiglas screen in sweaty booths off Forty-Second Street.

When I sing a song I need to get into character, because it is all theater for me. I have to believe in them and see them in my world, where I am, and where I'm going. I could bring all my theater experience into those kinds of songs and that kind of music. I never listened more than once to those tracks we chose. I know as soon as I hear it if it is going to work and reflect my own particular philosophy, and then I leave the original behind. You can feel insecure that you are not doing it the right way if you are too aware of the original. I wanted to drag it off into my territory without worrying I was not being faithful. I don't want to feel I have to do it like it was done before. That was their voice. I have to find my voice. Make it my song. Take it from Chrissie Hynde, Bryan Ferry, Smokey Robinson into *my* place, where the view is completely different.

On "She's Lost Control" by Joy Division, I took it literally. I lost control. I can't listen to that track now. I lost control to such an extent I scared myself. I let everything build, build, build, and I let the words take me over. I decided, *Oh, that's not written for me, but I think it might have been written about me.* It's hard to listen to myself going insane. I had no idea who Joy Division were. I just loved the song. I heard "lost control," and that was enough for me. As far as I was concerned it was a self-portrait.

I was breast-feeding Paulo in the studio during the making of the first Compass Point album, *Warm Leatherette*. I was doing sit-ups as soon as he was born; six weeks later, I was back in the studio. Paulo was always with me. I guarded him ferociously. He was such a personality. He would bounce to the music, really get into it. He would sing "Burning Down the House" in his high chair. He traveled with me everywhere until he was six and started going to school. I had him in an international school moving between Paris, New York, Los Angeles—wherever I moved, he relocated to the local branch of the same school. He moved around a lot because I moved around a lot, and sometimes that meant staying with friends or relatives when I was too busy. It was a mixed-up, on-the-road childhood. Only he can say what impact it all had on him, but I like to think he's come through without too much emotional scarring. He's a lot quieter than me, but probably more stable, and grown-up.

Once, when we were in the studio, Paulo was sleeping to the music peacefully, and I suddenly decided I wanted to water-ski. I'd never done it before. Chris used to give water-skiing lessons when he was a teenager in Jamaica. Here was a way to show Jean-Paul I was still up for action—less than two months after giving birth, I was going to learn to water-ski. I didn't want Jean-Paul to think that after having the baby I was going to be the fat mom staying at home.

As I tried to water-ski, I fell over so many times and the water rushed into me so much it was like I was being given an enema. The water was racing through every orifice. Chris, driving the boat and shouting instructions, would not accept that I couldn't do it. He refused to stop until I got up on those damn skis. That's our relationship. I'm stubborn, but he's more stubborn.

Chrissie Hynde's "Private Life" was easy for me to relate to. It was as much about my own history coming into being as hers. I could take that intense perception of emotion right into my world. I could make the timing all mine, and timing is often more important than content. Lovers, relationships, you get angry, you break up, someone's mad at you because you didn't have dinner with their mom—singing a love song during the time of Jean-Paul was very easy, because our relationship was so intense almost from the start. I got right inside his head, and I don't think he'd ever had a woman in there apart from his mother. It was the most intense relationship I had been in, so perhaps it was inevitable that within months I would become pregnant. His ideas alarmed most people, and they ran away. I couldn't get enough of them, but it also meant that each of us was as driven as the other, and as much as we were very attracted to each other, arguments would ignite all the time.

Minutes before we shot the "Private Life" video we had a fight. Not a serious one, relatively mundane, but I would talk a lot with Jean-Paul about his ideas and give my opinion, and he wasn't used to that. He still isn't. We would agree on most things, and if I didn't agree with him about something, he would try to change my mind. There was a clash of wills. I had strong ideas and he had strong ideas, and this would often lead to a confrontation, because he would always consider his ideas to be better. We were both fighting for dominance in our relationship. We made amazing things because we were so together and at the same time so competitive. We'd have a fight; I'd write a song. I wrote "Nipple to the Bottle," after a row—*You're never satisfied*—and he responded by making a storyboard for a video where I was shooting myself. The worst of us brought out the best of us. ("Nipple to the Bottle" was banned on American radio at the same time as Diana Ross's "Muscles" and Marvin Gaye's "Sexual Healing." They eventually played Diana and Marvin, but "Nipple" stayed banned. The nipple was too much for them. The nipple blew the mind of conservatives.)

I remember "Private Life" was the first time I had done a video that didn't have me jumping all over the place, like you were supposed to. In those days there were so many cuts in videos—everything was shredded, dazzling, empty. Then the rapid cuts went into the movies and then eventually even into the news.

For all my excesses, I was more of a minimalist, taught by Miyake. I preferred stillness, which I thought had greater impact. My expressions didn't need such fast edits; they relied on being held over time for their effect. Jean-Paul did the video for "Private Life" where I was totally still, and he moved his hands to create shadows—there were no edits, and people thought we were crazy. The music and what was going on with my face made up for the lack of edits—I looked scary, channeling Mas P again, because we'd had a row. We were creative sparring partners, and the fights made the work fresh, giving the encounters with otherness this note of the real, so that there would be something synthetic and analytical, but also emotional and aching about both the music and the image.

I had the track for "Pull Up to the Bumper" from something Sly and Robbie had written called "Pour Yourself over Me like Peanut Butter." My friend Dana Mano came up with the idea of "pull up to the bumper, baby," which sounded nicely naughty, and we started to write some silly stuff that sounded good to go with it. There was a double meaning to it, and I liked to write lyrics that had double meanings, but I wasn't conscious at the time that you could interpret these lyrics as being about— perhaps, if this was how you wanted to take it—anal sex. If you want to take it that way, please do. Take it any way you want. They were some words that sounded good to sing, and sometimes that is more important than the meaning.

Later I would mature more and tell the truth about how I was feeling, but when I wrote that, I was still hiding away from what I really felt. There was nothing personal about it; it wasn't about anyone. It was a way of having fun with some words that suited a track that sounded like you were having fun. So we have a car, and it's long, because it's a limousine, speeding down a Manhattan avenue, all the lights on green, through the steam pouring into the night, and you want to keep it clean, so you wax it and rub it, giving it a shine, and it's hard to park, because we're in the city, and it's so big, so you have to squeeze it into tight spaces, between certain obstacles, and nudge up against the car in front of you or behind you or both. You make it fit, and it is such a great feeling. Obviously, this could sound like you were talking about something else. If you wanted, you could imagine that I am not singing about a car at all. But that's up to you. If you think the song is not about parking a car, shame on you.

The Compass Point collaboration yielded another informal trilogy; *Warm Leatherette, Nightclubbing,* and *Living My Life.* By the cover of the third album, Jean-Paul was still slicing and dicing me, manning me up, changing my shape, worrying about my humanity, savoring what you can do to a face without hurting it. I wasn't aging, according to Jean-Paul, who was more concerned with collage and assemblage than with my real age. I was mutating.

I was, abstractly, sweating on the front cover of *Living My Life,* either because I had been in a fight after some kind of argument—there is a plaster over my eyebrow, and I look like I've just delivered a killer blow—or because I had just had sex with someone, somewhere. Or perhaps I was thinking about the world around me, and what was happening after all those parties, and all that togetherness. The sweat of the 1980s, of anxiety and threat, was very different from the no-holds-barred 1970s disco sweat.

My relationship with Jean-Paul was the most 360-degree relationship I had ever had. It felt unlimited until I started to feel claustrophobic. I had the collaboration with him, and also with the two Toms, Richard, Antonio, and then Chris Blackwell, but I also had romance with Jean-Paul. We worked together, we had sex together. Friends and lovers, art and intimacy.

There would be jealousies—Richard became jealous of Jean-Paul, Jean-Paul became jealous of my publicist, and I had to be the peacemaker. Richard still had my attention, but he thought I had rejected him. He was godfather—and art father—to Paulo. But they felt I was leaving them behind. My attitude was *Let's all work together,* but I suppose some people thought I was being isolated by Jean-Paul. It was through how Jean-Paul rendered me, imagined me as a realistic fantasy, that I first really entered many people's consciousness as an original being, an original beast. To some of my old collaborators, it was as though I could not exist without Jean-Paul piecing me together. I was in an ivory tower and he was making it harder for me to work with other people. I didn't care. He gave me everything I needed.

Jean-Paul would say, later, in a book he wrote, when he was angry and frustrated with me, that he had created me. I knew that wasn't the case, that I was creating myself before I met him, and that I was still creating myself during our time together and continued creating myself after we parted. I wasn't that put out by what he said. "People are only going to look at the photos," I said. "They're not going to read what you have to say!"

He knew it would hurt me, and he tried to take it back later, but it was too late. It was in the book. It's okay—I never had a problem with it, even though a lot of people around me got upset because their part in the creation of me got erased. And it was definitely not all Jean-Paul, even if his was the most illuminating expression of the creature creation. But the input of so many others was needed to get me to the place where Jean-Paul could focus his creativity, and the project definitely needed my active input. Not just physically, but also mentally, because from the moment I left Jamaica, my body was an extension of my mind and of my needing to achieve difference after years of being forced to conform.

I fell for Jean-Paul in a big way. I fell for him like a teenager. To some extent, I *was* a teenager. The first twelve years or so of my life didn't exist in a normal sense. I was never allowed to be daring, as a child should be for their personality to develop normally. If you say my life started to become less confined when I was twelve or thirteen, then it's true that by the time I met Jean-Paul I was behaviorally somewhere in my teens. I was still testing boundaries, making trouble, like a rebellious teenager. When he first came across me, he liked that I caused trouble. He liked the daredevil in me.

I was crazy about him. My legs would go weak when I visited him at his studio. It turned out he was born on the same day as Mas P, and it turned out that that, like the church, he wanted me to be perfect. He could make me perfect by turning me into an illustration, a sculpture, a video, a special effect, a record sleeve, a stage show, a car commercial. He could create, and constantly modify, an illusion, plant me in a flawless phase of glamour midway between machine-ness and she-ness. He wanted me to be perfect. He wanted me to represent An Ideal.

As with the church, it was an awful lot for me to live up to. Prick me, and I bleed.

8

Fight

I was in Britain on a promotional tour for what was becoming a hit single, "Private Life," with the new Compass Point sound. I had never been to Britain; all my modeling friends went to England during the '70s, but I never went, even when I was close by living in Paris. I don't think I realized how close London was—this was before the Channel Tunnel and the Eurostar linked the island with the continent.

The Irish bombings in the 1970s made me feel it was like the country was a war zone. Back then, in my blinkered naïveté, I thought I might accidentally kick something in the road, and it would turn out to be a bomb. When I started coming to London, I would just pop in and out; I never spent any amount of time there. When you visit places only as a part of a promotional tour, you don't really get to know them. You're always on the move, and only get a slight, biased view of where you are from the windows of cars and trains, from hotel rooms— mostly brick walls, shop fronts, and endless fields. You're never actually able to spend any time getting to know the details.

Britain was more another country on my itinerary than a central location in my world, a place I only knew very superficially. I didn't know the culture, and didn't specifically realize how much of a forced influence it had been on Jamaica. It should have been a place where I felt very at home straightaway, especially considering the close ties between Jamaica and Britain, but for some reason it was very much an alien place to me, and it felt very alien when I visited it.

Years later, I did a gala concert marking the anniversary of the HMT *Empire Windrush* sailing from Jamaica and Trinidad in 1948, bringing the first shipload of Caribbean immigrants. In the early 1980s, I was oblivious to the fact that Jamaican servicemen and women were brought back to England—the "mother country"—from Jamaica after they served in the war. While I was in London for that *Windrush* show, I went to my friend Philip Treacy's hat shop looking for something to wear. I didn't know him then, but my friend Tara Tyson told me I had to go to his shop. She loved hats, I loved hats. It's a church thing. We all had to wear hats going to church. When you go to my brother Noel's church in Los Angeles, you see the most amazing array of hats. Philip loves to go to Noel's church to see the hats.

Women cover their heads in Jamaica—perhaps it goes all the way back to Africa, to make sure you don't burn your head. It's common sense, first of all, and then it comes from dressing up. Each hat tells a story, about the person wearing it and what they are doing as they wear it. It is always with me: a hat, or a hood, or a hat and a hood.

Philip wasn't at his shop the first time I visited. There was a hat on display that was a ship, a ship that was a hat. The shopgirls were told by Philip that this hat was never, ever to leave the shop. But as soon as I walked in and did a quick scan of the place, I set my heart on the ship. *That one!*

I loved the hat even before I knew how appropriate it was—the *Windrush,* after all, was a ship. The two or three girls in the shop said, "We are sorry, Miss Jones, but we cannot let that leave the shop. Philip has forbidden it." In the end I said, "Why don't you shut the shop and come along with me and look after the hat, which I will wear at the show." So they came with me, and I wore it. After that, I always went to Philip for my hats.

I stayed in England for a while when I did the Bond movie in the mid-1980s. That's when I really started to get the feeling for London and Britain, and it started to fill out in my imagination as a place I could get to know and live in. Even then, though, England was simply a gray, cold, nondescript place, where I stayed in a low-grade generic hotel, and really only passed through, working on set from four in the morning to past midnight.

It was strange, because Britain definitely liked my music more than America, especially the music I started to make after the three disco albums. Britain was where the positive critical response started to happen. They definitely got the Compass Point music. It made a lot of sense to the British, this stylized border crossing blending of reggae, electronics, pop, and disco, the way I was gazing out from an abstract Jean-Paul designed environment. They had the fashion and the style and a brilliant history of making new forms of pop in the underground and on the charts. They liked it when the underground made it onto the charts. Their magazines were very strong, and new ones being published were connecting fashion and music in the same way I had done with Jean-Paul and the Compass Point All Stars.

I think people thought I was closer to Britain than I was at the time, because I was signed to a label that was based in London and a lot of the music on the Compass Point albums was very British. But I didn't really move to Britain to live until the middle of the first decade of the twenty-first century, which I did because of the record producer Ivor Guest. He had asked me to work on a song for a group he was producing, and I liked the way we worked together.

I had vowed never to make an album again after some bad experiences in the 1990s. The idea of music had been destroyed for me after some flavor-of-the-month producers had ruined an album I was making. They thought that I was old-fashioned and needed to move into sampling. I fought this, as I didn't want a whole album of samples. I was being bullied because I still wanted to work organically, like I had at Compass Point. They were more interested in staring at screens, tapping and clicking their lives away.

I still wrote and thought about music, but I wanted nothing to do with the business once they wanted to produce me like they would produce a new young singer, as merely an ingredient in an electronic process. It was like disco all over again, without the excitement of emerging from something so recently radical. They didn't want me to sing like me, but like a version of me, one I didn't even recognize.

They weren't interested in the performance, in the theater of it, in me doing different characters, to tell stories. They only wanted me to pronounce words, and then they would feed my voice into the other ingredients. They cared nothing about live performance, and therefore, nothing about life. They might as well have turned me into a machine— perhaps they chose to work with me because they thought I was a machine, because of how I had presented myself. They wanted to work with simulations, not with the human me. They wanted to work with the product, not the designer of that product—and I was the designer, as much as anyone I had collaborated with.

After working with Chris Blackwell, the All Stars, Trevor Horn, Nile Rodgers, the whole situation was very counterproductive for me. It was definitely a big part of why there were no albums by me between *Bulletproof Heart* at the end of the 1980s and 2008's *Hurricane*. I wasn't happy. It was not my method of working. They gave me no advice; they treated me like I wasn't there, excluding me from the making of my own record. I might have taken it from them if they were Nile, and had been in Chic and produced David Bowie, or Trevor, who had been in Art of Noise and produced Frankie Goes to Hollywood. They weren't.

I don't like being bullied into doing something that I don't agree with. I started to misbehave then, I admit. I was depressed by doing the vocals and then watching producers who couldn't play instruments make up these sampled collages of beats with my voice roughly chopped into them. To me, they were crushing the performance into powder. I didn't think I was being old-fashioned. I thought I was being right.

One night I started to cry. I was so frustrated, I shouted at them and walked out. It wasn't professional, but it was a horrid situation. They made an album that could not be mixed. It was like a bag of broken bits that didn't fit together. My songs, containing thoughts and feelings that were very precious to me, had been minced. It felt like all my babies had died. It put me off making music, and I decided to stop. There were plenty of other things for me to do.

I enjoyed working with Ivor and I still had some material from fifteen years earlier for the album that I'd walked out on, and other songs I was thinking about. I remember the first time we met, after being introduced to him by Philip Treacy. I said to Philip when he told me about Ivor, "I will meet him, but tell him that I will talk about anything, but please don't talk to me about music." The first time we met, at a dinner party, Ivor tried really hard not to talk about music. He said later that all the way through the meal, he was absolutely dying to ask why I hadn't made an album for so long.

By the second meeting, Ivor had gingerly brought up the idea of me making some new music. It started to seem like something I could do again after more than a decade of not wanting to record. I'd written some songs, guested vocally on records, and still toured, but I got by quite happily not going through what had become an ordeal.

Ivor and I fell in love, and I moved to England to be with him and make the *Hurricane* album. It was released eighteen years after my previous one. No time at all, in my mind. And after the sampling debacle, working with Ivor reminded me of how it should and could be. I felt calmer being with him, both personally and professionally. I liked his attitude toward making music. It was fresh and inspiring, and that meant recording the album was as much a pleasure as any I'd made before.

There seemed to be more happening in London than in New York, more interesting artistic people to collaborate with. I had vowed to leave America if George Bush became president, and the day after he was voted in I left. I had a friend in Italy, and I went there. From there, I moved to London to live. That was about twenty-five years after I'd first visited Britain, a stranger in a strange land, because I was promoting a record, and got into a fight.

In each country you visit, the record label has a list of things they want you to do: favorite photographers they want to use, favorite publications in which they want you to be featured. You move about so much on these tours that everything becomes a blur. Essentially, you do what you are told, and you go wherever you are taken without really absorbing where you are. I do what I usually do to get by and start operating on autopilot. On that promotional trip for "Private Life" I was taken somewhere in the northwest of England, I think, a derelict dockland area to shoot a short film. I think it was Liverpool. It might have been Manchester. The towns all looked the same to me. The only thing I remember for sure is that it wasn't London.

The place where we went to make the film was something of a ruin, filled with crusty pigeon shit, a beautiful, rusty shell, unused for years. I am sure it has been modernized by now, but then it was beaten up, with a hint of the end of the world about it. Old crumbling brick buildings filled with broken windows, ghostly cranes, dirty water, piles and piles of bird shit dried up over patches of decaying wasteland. Somebody was no doubt very pleased with it as a backdrop, but it didn't work out for me.

My sinuses got infected, and I became unwell. The next day, I had this TV show to do, and after the scuzzy dockland shoot, I was in a bad way and not thinking very clearly. To top it all off, somebody gave me some really bad coke to keep me going, because I was clearly wilting. That's how it was.

"No," I said, "I am not taking that!" That's not really my thing. I am happy to take something that I think will do me some good, but I was not so sure about sticking this powder up my nose without knowing if it was a weak coke substitute. I was a connoisseur, and it looked suspicious to me. It looked like it had been through a few distribution centers, diluted at each stop, cut down until it had lost its authentic kick. Bad coke was the last thing I wanted before I went on a live television show. The purest form, maybe, but anything else was not going into my body. I am not a big fan of taking something that is meant to give you pleasure but actually causes pain, or even worse. And in my basic state, I am already a little bit perky. Even a coffee can cause me to speed up beyond normal parameters. I'd rather take a Valium tablet, really, to slow me down a bit. I need slowing down, not speeding up.

After all the traveling I had done in the days before I did this television show, I was basically running on adrenaline. You can end up getting so tired that you enter another zone. You are so sleepy but you can't sleep. You start hallucinating naturally.

We had a rehearsal for the television show, which had a theme, I was told. They were going to talk to me about modeling and photography, because one of the other guests on the show was the royal photographer and the Queen's cousin, Patrick Lichfield. After having become established in music, I was going to be kicked back to talking about modeling, which in my mind I hadn't done for a few years. But that was okay, I didn't mind.

There were other guests on the show as well. I can't remember them at all—they were completely obliterated from my mind after what happened next. Looking back at it now, they all seem weirder than me, and I seem better dressed for action in a powerful long leather coat. I'd made an effort, even though I was feeling rough. I'd made myself up and looked good. They all looked like they were in a dusty gentlemen's club about to fall asleep after a big dinner and possibly never wake up again.

The day started out fairly innocuously, as though it was all going to be very ordinary. The host of the show introduced himself to me. I didn't properly hear his name. I must have been told it a few times, but it meant nothing to me. My television world was very much American, where I'd had experience on talk shows with people like Merv Griffin.

He was quite an awkward man—very English, in my mind, very eccentric, probably quite kindly. He explained that he was going to ask me questions about what it was like to be in front of a camera, and ask Lord Lichfield what it was like to be behind the camera. Very nice, an intelligent theme, and it was put to me in a very straightforward manner. I asked someone what his name was, because I couldn't remember it. Russell, I was told, Russell Harty. Very English. A little odd around the edges.

We rehearsed the show in some detail; the three of us politely sat all facing each other in a semicircle. There didn't seem to be anything to worry about, as tired as I was. Just another show where the people working on the show treat it as though it is the most important thing imaginable, whereas for me it was simply another obligation on a tightly packed schedule. Turn up, make conversation, try not to come across as an idiot, sing your song, smile if you can, be polite, and then on to the next engagement. Nothing memorable, and you would probably never think about it again.

On the live show, the real thing, it was all very different. There was a live audience, which immediately changed the atmosphere. Things moved very fast, and I wasn't feeling any better. I still felt infected by pigeon shit, rust, and stagnant water. It made me feel sluggish, which I hate. I like to feel the world is crackling around me.

The seating plan seemed different, and I quickly felt that, as the musical guest, I was not part of the main discussion. A couple of perfunctory questions, and then my time was up, and Russell Harty didn't seem to be particularly interested in what I was saying. For some reason, he spent a lot of time with his back to me—once he had finished with me, he turned away completely to talk to Patrick. This totally infuriated me. I was not having any of it. I'm thinking, *How many miles did I fly to do this show, and I end up sitting with a back turned to me?* Where I was brought up, you don't turn your back on someone who is your guest. If I have to turn my back on anyone for whatever I reason, I will always say, *Excuse me.* Turning your back on someone, to me, is an absolute insult.

I knew I was going to be on the show for the duration. I sang at the beginning and the end, and for the rest of the show I was meant to sit next to Russell Harty and keep still and quiet. I was all dressed up like an Amazonian seductress, and treated like the hired help. I thought, *This is no way to treat a guest.* This wasn't at all what we'd rehearsed. Being stuck there while he ignored me made me feel very uncomfortable. He started sucking up to Patrick big-time, and I was effectively dumped, or so it seemed to me. Also, I had no idea who Russell Harty was. I had no understanding of British TV. I didn't even know much about the BBC, that this show was on BBC 2, or that it was, I was told, very important. It was all very new to me. I didn't care. I was doing what I was told, and quite prepared to be fairly docile and do my job.

I knew nothing of Russell Harty's history—that he actually had a reputation for making slightly quirky, fairly silly programs and had quite an ego himself. I knew nothing about his camp reputation. He was simply some snooty-seeming plummy-voiced English guy hosting a show, and he was being rude to me. Apparently that was part of his provocative technique, but I didn't know anything about that.

He had probably worked out that I was highly strung and easy to tease. When I was teased by my brothers as a kid, I would fight back. That was my default position, to defend myself. I felt I was provoked. I was feeling exhausted, had no idea where I was, and was coated in pigeon shit; now it seemed I was hallucinating that I was on a live chat show and the host was ignoring me.

Pissed off, I poked him in the back. He made a slightly irritated move like I had interrupted him mid-flow, and looked at me like I was dirty: *Oh, what do* you *want?* He turned away and then acted like he was going to carry on ignoring me. That made it worse. I started pouting like a little girl. I was rolling my eyes. *How dare you!* I was thinking. *I've come all this way to be treated like garbage!* He said something like, "Just sit there and behave yourself." Like he was a schoolteacher putting a pupil in her place.

I said, "If you turn your back on me one more time I am going to walk out." He scolded me some more. I thought, *He's using me as the butt of some joke I don't really understand.* It all kept escalating. I kept hitting him more and throwing his script at him. Slapping, not to hurt him, but to get his attention. I really thought about tipping his chair over, because I could see it was teetering on the edge of the small stage where we were sat. That was very tempting, but I remember thinking, *Well, he might break his neck, and then I will really get into hot water.* I didn't want to hurt him, not really.

When you are on a tour like that, you are not expecting people to act unprofessionally. In the end, I think it was he, not me, who was overwhelmed by the situation. Not so much having me on the show, but having Patrick Lichfield. He seemed damp with excitement about that, and I was getting in the way of his time with the Queen's cousin. Afterward, I heard he tended to treat artists and singers a little perversely. He could be very impatient with them, and verbally beat them up. Well, if this was his routine—it stops with me!

I wasn't attacking him because I was drunk or stoned. I was lashing out because I felt he was not being proper. You can see if you watch it. I am being very sensitive rather than unruly. In fact, because I was tired and disoriented, everything was heightened. I never wanted to do these kinds of shows high. If anything, I get high afterward. Everyone who knows me will say I have to be in control of myself—and everyone else around me! That's where the problem started. More than anything, I behaved like a very tired child trying to get his attention. I was being naughty. But I would have done anything to get his attention, and he wasn't paying me any.

I started to entertain the studio audience while he was talking. That was a way of getting some attention! He didn't know why they were laughing during some parts of the conversation he was having. He didn't understand what was happening behind his back. The audience were giggling, and he was trying to take control. I started slipping off my chair like a very agitated child who has to sit still in church. I was bored out of my mind. I was also wearing this metal breastplate that was very awkward, and I was in no mood to be left behind while he got on with his show. When he did turn around and look at me, I started to see Mas P in his face, and an irritable expression that seemed to say, women are the root of all evil. I was looking right at Mas P and he was looking at me like he was about to lash out. I needed to defend myself.

I kept lunging at Harty, hitting and hitting him, in an almost girly burst of defiance, more to humiliate him than to hurt him. That was it. I don't remember what happened next. The show ended, and both of us were in a state of shock and walked off in different directions.

I was ignored by everyone. Afterward, I was sat in the green room all on my own. No one wanted to talk to me. I was totally shunned, like I'd done something really terrible and unprofessional. I could feel waves of contempt. It was like people would be cursed if they talked to me. I thought, *I am in the shit now, but I don't need this shit.* I was in a foreign country, feeling like a foreigner. I didn't know anyone outside the publicists looking after me, except someone I was seeing in London, who I don't want to name. Or can't name, after all these years. I felt so alone. I didn't know England at all, and this had happened. I felt totally adrift.

A lot of people assumed that I was at home in England. It was completely foreign. I had a lot of trouble understanding people's accents, and to this day have to turn the TV up to really understand English-speaking British people who speak fast. I need them to speak slowly. This also added to my sense of dislocation, these men talking in a way I didn't quite understand, very comfortable with each other, treating me as a temporary impediment, actually as a kind of freak.

The people at my record company, Island, were so mad at me. They were embarrassed and hostile. They thought they would never book an act on the show again, or even on all of the BBC. They thought I had blown it for the whole label. I wanted to get out of the country immediately, but it was late so I couldn't even get out of the city. I skulked back to my hotel, put my head under the covers, and started sobbing. I felt very alone.

Naturally, the next day, the incident got blown up by the media. There were pictures of me in the tabloids, wearing boxing gloves. *Grace was a disgrace. Bonkers. Drunk.* Some of the press was in my favor, and there was an enormous amount of coverage. Island thought it would go against me, that I would be more or less kicked out of the country. Faced with the amount of coverage, they started to see it as an unexpected promotional opportunity.

They said, "Everyone wants to interview you." I was in no mood to see anyone. I wanted to escape, to get the hell out of the country.

I said, "If you send any journalists around to my hotel, I will throw chairs at them." They didn't mind that—it was what people were expecting now! I had to sneak out of the country. The boyfriend whose name I don't want to say, even now, helped to smuggle me out of Britain.

I said, "I need to get on a flight. I want no press anywhere near me." I didn't want it to look like a stunt. I made my plans to fly back to New York.

Everyone at the label was calling Chris Blackwell, the Island boss, to complain about my behavior. They were moaning about what I had done on the show and how awful and unforgivable it was. Then, after all the attention and front pages, they were moaning that I didn't want to do any interviews and exploit the situation. First, I'd messed up by acting so bratty, and then I acted up by not playing along.

I was screaming, "Keep everyone away from me! I am going to re-sign! I am going to marry somebody, anybody, and have a whole bunch of babies and plant trees. No more of this. This is not what I wanted." I got a flight back to New York. Sanity, in all its insanity. A New York insanity I could understand. A New York insanity I thrived on.

Chris was bombarded by calls, but luckily I had a number where I could get straight through to him. I said, "I want you to hear this from me first. I am leaving London, and they are pissed off that I have snuck off when everyone and his mother wants to talk to me. This is what happened, and I don't want people to think it was a cheap PR stunt. I am not well. I have been infected by bird shit!"

He said, "You're right, you don't want it to look like it was all set up and planned." I didn't like the way all the PR people flipped on me either—one minute treating me like a leper, and then suddenly all jumping on it and seeing how they could make it work. It was a spontaneous act, for better or worse, and I think it has probably lingered as an event because it wasn't contrived. My instinct afterward was to not laugh it off and make it seem contrived.

Chris didn't see it when it happened, but he has seen it over the years. He saw the bigger picture. He once said it was like when the Stones peed on some petrol pumps. It becomes one of those career-defining moments, and however badly you think you were treated, however much the press made a meal of it, there is always a grain of truth in what happened in terms of reflecting some part of what you are.

Harty was rude. I wasn't going to put up with it. I lashed out on live television. It takes balls to do that, which could be seen as a little crazy. I didn't give a damn that it was on live TV. The man was rude. Fuck him.

And then they tried to get me back on the show! The ratings soared. I had done him a favor. They wanted a rematch. It was all so tacky. I suppose it was me being ahead of my time, the idea of the event, the stunt, the scandal, amplified by social media, which is now very much what goes on. It was always bubbling under back then, but now it is the whole thing. Entertainment has become pure self-promotion, a

sequence of mere "look at me" stunts. I wanted what I did to be entertainment, but the entertainment that is really art that likes to party.

Russell Harty never got so much press in his life. For all the things
he did do in television—and I've now discovered he was very original
and even influential, if a little strange—this incident was the one thing
he would really be remembered for. He must have known what a fuss
I would cause very soon after it had happened. Maybe he even contrived to produce this kind of response from me, or at least once it was
obvious I was angry with him, made sure it got worse. If you Google his
name, what comes up immediately is "Barmy Diva Grace Jones." If you
Google me it's pretty near the top of the most popular searches. We
were married in some fraudulent media ceremony, manacled together
whether we liked it or not.

Afterward, I was doing a lot of talk shows in America, like *Joan
Rivers, David Letterman,* and *Johnny Carson,* and I became notorious for
beating up the English talk show host live on TV. Those kinds of hosts
relished it—*We heard what you did over there.We promise to treat you with respect!* Joan and I became very good friends; she respected me for standing up for myself when faced with boorish condescension. I became a
great booking because of it, and they would act scared, like they didn't
want it to happen to them, the unleashing of the hot-tempered virago.
Of course, that's exactly what they did want.

It's the first thing many people think of when they think of me. It
gets voted as the top moment in TV talk show history. I don't mind at
all that, despite whatever else I might have done, that's what they remember. I am glad I had a hit record. "Private Life," that's what I was
promoting—private life, drama, baby: it all fit. That's why I was on the
show, and I followed it up with a hit album. In the end, that is what it is
all about—to be noticed, to be remembered. Had I not had a hit record
afterward, it would be my only claim to fame, but at least I would have
done something for people to talk about.

It's funny that such a spur-of-the-moment thing as the Russell Harty
incident is remembered after all these years, but my attitude is that
when these things happen, then clearly they are meant to happen. If you
can't think of me without thinking of me slapping Russell Harty, then

that is because it was always meant to be. It's part of my story, and it's a part of me—I like to think I did it because I was standing up for myself, and that's very much an important part of who I am. I had a hit record, but because of the incident, I also had a hit life.

When he died, my phone never stopped. It rang off the hook. *What do you think about Russell Harty dying?* Well, I am very sorry, but what do you want me to say? I didn't know him at all. I didn't kill him. I had nothing to do with it. I wasn't there at all. I had an alibi.

I would give people something more to talk about at the Queen's Diamond Jubilee celebrations in 2012. When the invite came through to perform in the show, I kept saying no, because I didn't think I would fit. The request came through the BBC, and they seemed to think I might not fit as well, as the show featured more light entertainment that I thought very tacky. I didn't see where I would fit among Sir Paul McCartney, Sir Tom Jones, and Sir Elton John, and many people I had never really heard of, junior British pop stars. It was very British, and it wasn't like there was a Commonwealth feel to the show so that I was representing Jamaica.

The BBC didn't seem put out when I said no. But they kept asking me. I kept saying no for a month, and they kept coming back. Eventually, they had to tell me that I had been asked by royal request. I was never officially told who actually asked for me, but I guess that it was Prince Charles. He had a sense of humor, which was something the BBC didn't see, and must have thought that I would bring something seriously lighthearted among a lot of earnestness.

I had met him before, at the premiere of *A View to a Kill*. We were all standing in a line waiting to be introduced, as is the ritual, and when he got to me, he leaned in close to my ear and said something, winking knowingly, about one of the blond actresses in the film, along the lines of, *I wonder how she got the part.* As he said this, Diana was right behind him. We both laughed out loud, and the picture of us laughing made the papers. Everyone was asking me afterward, *What did he say that was so funny?* I didn't tell anyone.

A similar thing happened after the Diamond Jubilee performance. I performed "Slave to the Rhythm," which some might have considered a discreet commentary on the slave trade of the British Empire, wearing a barely there Eiko Ishioka costume that let my bare legs do a lot of the talking and gave me plenty of space to show off my hula-hooping and challenge people to wonder about my age. There was no one else on the show—or elsewhere in pop, of whatever age—who could have done that, or even thought of it. That was my gift to the Queen! I thought, *You shouldn't take all this too seriously,* not as seriously as some of the others took it. I decided to have some fun with it.

Everyone was worried before the performance, and couldn't believe my nerve that I wasn't wearing more formal clothes and was revealing so much flesh, but afterward, once it all worked out, the BBC were desperately trying to interview me. They hadn't allowed a backstage pass for my mom or for Paulo so they could come to my dressing room, so I said, "Well, I will give you an interview next time if you give my mom a backstage pass."

It was cold, naturally, so after the show I put on a long coat to keep warm while I was waiting to be introduced to the Queen. When she got to me in the lineup she did seem a little disappointed that I had changed, and said to me that it was a shame I was wearing something else. I think she might have hoped I was still hula-hooping. I said I didn't think it was appropriate to be introduced to the Queen with my legs all on show and my ass hanging out! We both laughed and everyone afterward was asking, *What did she say to you?* I didn't tell anyone. Perhaps I should have said she was congratulating me on how I had dealt with the rudeness of Russell Harty.

9

One Man

I had been on tour while Jean-Paul stayed in New York, working. After it was over, I tried to take him with me on vacation. He couldn't understand why I needed a vacation, because as he saw it, when I had been touring, I had been in this exciting place, and then this exciting place. He thought being on the road was a holiday. He'd say, "That's not work." He didn't get it.

To show him what it was really like, I took him on tour with me— I was on my own, without a band, still using playback. It was all my responsibility, the performance, and I wanted him to see how much work it was, even if I was traveling to exotic places. The show was full of set pieces we had designed together. It was not only me standing there singing the songs to the backing music. It was like a minimal musical starring me, and I carried the whole show. He had a nervous breakdown on the third day on a rooftop in Saint-Tropez. I said, "Now do you see how much hard work it is? Now do you understand? This is no holiday." He couldn't take the pace, and he wasn't even performing. He had to go back to New York.

Another time he came with me for some American shows and I got a knee infection during a show in Florida, from crawling onstage. I would throw my body about during a performance. Someone had dog shit on their shoes, and some of it was left on the stage. It got into a cut on my knee, which became infected and extremely inflamed. They had to put my leg in a cast—I almost lost the knee.

I was on a lot of painkillers, but I still went out and performed. The pain was so bad for me that Jean-Paul decided to go back home—he couldn't bear to see me suffer so he couldn't just stay with me and help me. I was pregnant at the time as well—before Paulo—and because of the knee, I had to abort. They said that because of the antibiotics I was taking the baby would be born without limbs. I think Jean-Paul had trouble dealing with these practical problems. I became very disillusioned, concerned that he preferred the illusion he had created, not the actual me.

That scared me. It made me feel very insecure. It made me think that if I wasn't this perfect human being, it would not satisfy him. I couldn't count on him to be there for me when I really needed him, because if I needed him, he saw that as weakness. The Grace Jones he had designed with me was not weak. She would not need a holiday, or get sick with fever. He didn't want to see that I could be vulnerable.

I wanted to get pregnant again, having lost the first one. There was no doubt in my mind that Jean-Paul was going to be the father of my child. There might have been doubt in his mind, but he didn't use condoms, so I figured he wanted a child with me. I'm not sure he really thought about it. We carried on, and we had Paulo. When I told him I was pregnant, there didn't seem to be any joy in his response, not like the first time. I think he thought it was going to interfere with everything going on between us. That was *his* fear; I didn't think it would.

The pressure to be perfect for him started to get to me. He said I had a problem with authority, that I don't like to be told what to do. He wanted to be the authority in our relationship, and I wouldn't lie down. I was never mute, like the image he invented based on me that said nothing. I had plenty to say. I was not a bed warmer. He was used to bed warmers—your basic housewife types. *Go to the spa, keep yourself busy, do your nails, come home, fuck, go to sleep.* I was too manly. I always kept my own apartment. I felt that was necessary. *God bless the child that's got his own.* I could say, "This is my house, you get out."

I could always feel when a fight was coming. I was never

diplomatic—I would put my foot in it and we would end up in a big fight. I would say, "Okay, I'm going home." But if he really wanted to let it out, then I would have to wait and have it out. My mouth was cutting. I would never mince words, always saying exactly what was on my mind. Jean-Paul and I would get pretty personal. Now and then our fights would get quite physical. There would be blows. He whacked me once, took me by surprise, retaliating for something I had said or done. Then I would write a song about it and he would turn it into an image.

I laughed when he said, "In this picture I am going to have you shoot yourself." It made perfect sense as a metaphor. He was angry with me in an argument and it turned into an image where he had me hold a gun to my head. As an idea, fabulous; as a way of getting things out of your system, great; but you don't want that to leak into real life.

Whatever was going on in my private life I would channel into my performances. Jean-Paul knew that; sometimes he would upset me so much I would be in tears before a show. I began to wonder if he was doing it on purpose. It's like that movie *All About Eve,* when someone says to Anne Baxter as Eve Harrington, once she has gone through something torrid: "After this, you will give the performance of your life." I had a couple of moments like that with Jean-Paul, because he was provoking me. Why else do what he did before I went onstage? Either that or he was nervous for me. Sy and Eileen used to be so nervous for me. It was as if they were going onstage. They would be shaking, and they would touch me before I went onstage. I would say, "No, don't do that," because it would change my state of mind and make me feel something I hadn't been aware of. I tended never to be nervous before I went onstage; if I was, it would go the other way and I would have yawning fits. Early on, I would clear the dressing room and meditate. I would isolate myself from whatever chaos was going on around me.

My vocal coach told me there is no such thing as nervous. You are excited, not nervous! I liked that—nervous is negative, excited is positive. It's a different way of looking at the same thing.

————

Jean-Paul was using me. And I was using him. I thought what he did to me as an object was beautiful. He loved my lines, my shape, my color, and he loved manipulating those things to reproduce me and remake me. The universe to him is visual. It is a fantasy he wants to control.

I was so in love, and I realized that he didn't love me as I loved him. The way he loved me was not how I wanted. He showed his love through the work, but he couldn't do it any other way. At that time, I didn't understand that.

I would tell him about being a nudist. I realized that I preferred to cover my head, not my pussy, and that would become an image. He would put my head on my brother Chris's body, knowing the tangled nature of our relationship, the mix of me and him, her and me. He transformed the story of my life into a series of visions and fantasies. Talk would lead to him thinking, *I will do you like this.* There was a lot of talking, and then the idea. It was collaborative, never him only doing me. I was not a model. I was a partner in design.

An idea is worth so much. It's beyond money. Jean-Paul has a store of ideas that could last a thousand years. He'd talk about the war, when he was growing up, seeing the Nazis walk into his village when he was a kid, monsters in stylish uniforms, evil dressed up to the nines.

I had a thing about uniforms at school. I had to make sure that every pleat on my skirt was still in place after a day at school, even after all that moving around and sitting down. My beret had to be absolutely just so after a whole day of it being crushed into my pocket. I never want to have to go through that kind of thing again, wearing a uniform to be so obviously obedient to a repressive force. The uniform represented how there was no escape from having to be perfect.

This combination of his memory and mine led to me goose-stepping in a video. We would talk about real stuff—horror, cruelty, fear, pain— and it would become an image, a way of dealing with the horrible, truly a kind of fairy tale in the tradition of the Brothers Grimm, where nastiness is cast aside through storytelling and imagination.

That would become my role: to suggest to him an image that he would turn into a visual moment, part of a story that contained darkness but was heading toward a happy ending, or that contained beauty and was heading toward disaster. I would say his work was based on the experiments I performed on myself. The images were reflections of my past, my memories turned into visual expressions. I loved how artistic he could be in a commercial world, how funny, perceptive, strange, surprising. He was the best at being an artist in a commercial world. Those kinds of people come along once in a lifetime.

A lot of his work is very sexual, and I loved that he was so kinky. But when we started to have trouble in our relationship, it led to me putting my foot in it. One of the reasons I kept my own place for a long time when we were together, apart from the need to maintain my independence, was because he had these statues of Toukie in his house—it was his work, but it was other women, their bodies. I was jealous and silly because of that. I did not want to see his creation of another woman right in front of me all the time.

It made me think of what Helmut Newton had said—I didn't have big tits. Toukie did! I knew I had something else. But now and then I would think, in my insecurity, *Maybe I need to bring him a girl like the sculpture. Maybe that's what he wants.* So I did: I brought home a girl shaped like Toukie, so that we could all go to bed. I was so pleased with myself. I thought, *Have I got a surprise for you!* Boy, did I blow that.

He went through the motions with the two of us to be kind of hip, but the next day he was not a happy bunny. He said, "Don't you ever do anything like that again! What on earth were you thinking?" That shows you how my mind works. That was my attempt to enter his fantasy world, by bringing in my fantasy world. He was kinky in the pictures, but he didn't want it in our life.

I remember I had a beautiful girlfriend called Nina, and we would pretend to make love in the other room to see if we could take him away from his work. *Help me out, Nina, I can't get him away from his desk.* We'd make these sex noises. I didn't think about his deadlines, or about how long it took him to complete a piece; I was being selfish. *I want attention! Now!*

Jean-Paul thought it was simply me being crazy. He loved it at first, when he was looking at me from the outside, causing mayhem on small club stages, attacking a gay audience with pure relish. The reality was less amusing to him.

It was always me he was working on. It wasn't like he was paying attention to another woman, but I became jealous of me. That, in the end, is what broke us up. He was paying attention to me. He was looking at nothing but me. He was inserting his imagination right inside me, and he has a very big imagination, believe me. But that meant he was ignoring me. He was a perfectionist, and he was always obsessed with making his work flawless. In a relationship, this can be difficult. He was always turning me into an ideal being, the perfect specimen, and meanwhile, I was living in the real world.

This was the battle—him creating the perfect Grace through the manipulation of image versus the flesh-and-blood Grace in the real world. I was so scared of appearing less than perfect that I would pose even on the toilet. The toilet door didn't have a lock, and I would be like a statue on a throne in case he came in while I was there. I so wanted to please him, but had I known better I would have just kicked him around a bit. If I had to do it all over again, I would say, "This is silly, stop making me feel silly." I was looking up to him too much. We were putting each other on these pedestals, whereas where we needed to be was more down-to-earth. We needed to be realistic with each other.

Jean-Paul became well known after working with me, but from the outside, he was as much relegated behind the image of me he designed as he was promoted to a new level of success. He would be called Mr. Jones when we checked into hotels, and he did not like that. If you have an ego—and he does, and I liked that—it's difficult to be seen as a supporting act. It wasn't my fault, though, and I hoped he could forget it.

He was in my shadow, as much as he had emerged from the shadows of the underground, where he had been before. This did bruise his ego, and in the realm where he was inventing himself as much as he was me, this disconcerted him. His best creation was an obstacle in front of what he ultimately wanted to be his greatest creation—himself.

He would be working, working, working on me, but I needed the physical comfort. He thought my work was enough to keep me company, in the way his was. But I was not with him when I worked on the road in the way he was with me as he worked on my appearance in the studio, at his desk. Perhaps if he had been using computers it would have been different. He could have moved around with me; but then, you had to work at your desk, in your studio. Jean-Paul was wrapped up in me, carving me up, remaking me, putting me together, paying very close attention to me on paper, but ignoring me for real.

As Janis Joplin said, when you sing you are being adored by thousands of people, but you go home alone. The kinds of people who want to come back to your room with you are not the kind of people you want to have in your room. I could have had groupies, two dozen in line, next, next, next, but that's not what I wanted. There were hundreds of people after me, guys and girls, but if people are chasing me, I back off.

I like a quiet, slow build, rather than being accosted. People could come back with me, to the hotel, to my room, but at the end of the day, I go to bed alone, and everyone has to leave. I like to be quiet, and sometimes that can attract people even more. You want to be alone, and this intrigues people. They want to conquer you.

He was alone with his work, and I was surrounded by a ton of people, most of them wanting something from me. I was dealing with madness on the road, and in the end all you want to do is get high, because of the anonymous crush of people around you, and yet the loneliness.

Being onstage is a high, but I never wanted to get high to get onstage. I could never do that. I would see singers get high before they went out, and I would go, "How on earth do you do that?!" I was almost jealous in a way. My voice could not take me being out of control. Probably a good thing, because I might have OD'd by now if I needed to be high to get out and perform. I have to be completely straight.

When I sing I have to be aware from second to second—of the breathing, the note that has just gone, the note that is coming. I need it all in my head, plus I am thinking of the lighting and of everything that is happening around me. Getting high wrecks my concentration. That's where I am very disciplined.

I tried a joint once in a show during "My Jamaican Guy," but it totally dried my voice out, and I got very paranoid. I thought I would use it as a prop—the song is all about the spliff—and I lost control of my whole body, of my whole senses. I lost the flow. You get so high from singing beyond anything you could take. Holding notes, breathing very quickly, you get high after doing that for an hour and a half. It's like sex, if you do it right.

I met Dolph Lundgren while I was on tour. Jean-Paul was at home— with me, but not with me. Dolph was Hans Lundgren then. Jean-Paul and I were looking for a place in New York to move in together. Paulo was two, it was 1981, and I met Dolph on tour in Australia. This is a time and date I can be relatively precise about.

I was saying to Jean-Paul, "I really need you with me," not for needy reasons but because I loved him, and missed him when I was away. He was editing *A One Man Show*, our masterpiece, a live show he was turn- ing into a film, so he was probably feeling that I was in the room with him. But I felt very distant from him. He said, "I cannot come; you have to control yourself—I am working on the film."

I said, "Get over here!" I remember saying, "I don't cheat, but I am giving you a first warning: if you don't come, I might start thinking of cheating. Three warnings, and you're out." I couldn't control my hor- mones; they were all over the place.

I find it very difficult to masturbate, so I couldn't get it out of my system that way. Any other woman might have dealt with it all by mas- turbating, but I thought the whole thing was absurd. I imagined myself doing it, and it was so ridiculous—I project myself doing it, and I just want to laugh at myself. If I was a guy, it'd be easier. A guy masturbating is very sexy. A woman masturbating is preposterous. That is my Oscar Wilde statement about the whole rigmarole.

I couldn't relieve the tension and loneliness that way. I knew if I ever did cheat on him, it would be all over. We were so connected, in every way, that there could be no frivolous escape through a trivial one-night stand. I started to get high when I could to such an extent it was dan- gerous because I was hurting so much.

It's easy to get high when you are on the road. Everyone is throwing shit at you. They throw it on the stage. I didn't smoke because it spoiled my vocal cords. It was the coke period, and coke doesn't really agree with me. I never really got it.

It makes you want to talk, but I can do that anyway. It makes you chatty, but I didn't get the high. Pills were more my thing—the quaalude, Mandrax, Valium—they make you relax. I far preferred downers, and was always wishing that instead of giving me bad cocaine, the last thing I wanted, people would give me quaaludes. Just half a quaalude was perfect for me. They were so sexy, as long as you could stay awake more than fifteen minutes after you took one. They were like downers with an edge. Whatever it was the scientists did with the ingredients in that pill so that the psychotic people they were designed for would love everyone, when you took it for fun there was a very unique sensation.

In the end, all drugs, legal or illegal, are bad for you if you take them in the wrong way, or you take too many, or they simply don't agree with your personality or basic DNA. I believe in drug use, not drug abuse. Coke was never my drug, although there are some who might be surprised by that. By being so closely associated with Studio 54, the assumption is that I was a complete cocaine fiend. There are rumors that my rider can include a demand for $30,000 worth of cocaine. This is from that part of Google that is pure fantasy, the part of Google that is itself high on something. If I had taken as much as cocaine as it is rumored, I wouldn't have a nose. If I was such a coke monster, I wouldn't have a life.

Actually, I preferred to put a rock up my ass rather than snort it. Sometimes it might get blown up there, one way or another. Then you get a very wonderful sexual feeling in your lower half. Stick a tiny little rock up your butt and it feels fantastic. The coke must be clean, of course. Very clean—that's the word, more than "pure." Or you put it in a bit of lotion and rub it on your skin. Tried that with a couple of girlfriends in Paris—nice. And the Cocoa Puffs. That way of taking it, rather than putting it up my nose.

The coke created this babble. Ideas, ideas, ideas, fabulous, fabulous,

fabulous, and the next day none of it makes sense. You feel on top of the world, but a world made of powder.

Coke you had to keep taking to keep the buzz. The pill buzz lasted.

Coke was a constant thing that you had to keep topping up. It can take over your day. I figured out later it was because the coke was always cut, diluted. Eventually, I would want to know everything that I was putting in my body. I became a scientist, a doctor of medicine. I wanted to know what was okay, what might kill me. I could break down the ingredients of everything I was taking. I wanted to make sure that if I took coke, most of what was in there was coke. By taste, by smell, by look.

Sometimes in clubs, at parties, they would put down coke on a big table, loads of lines, and most of what was in there was heroin. That could have killed me without me knowing what I had taken. I quickly learned to come really prepared. To know what I was doing. I didn't want an accident, which would be so stupid. I would sample every pill I was given before I swallowed it, even aspirin, and I could tell on my tongue if something was up, if there was some strange ingredient that did not belong. I became such an expert.

I had my very first ecstasy pill in the company of Timothy Leary, which is a bit like flying to the moon with Neil Armstrong, and I learned the taste of what was good, and what was bad. I developed my taste buds to tell when something was wrong. On very good ecstasy, I was okay. I would only take half a tablet, because my body is not good on excess. I know my body. I like to be in control of being out of control. Extreme, but in moderation. Crazy out there, but within reason. Take nothing in your body without being completely fussy. Be very aware. Make rare visits to certain drugs, so that it is a treat rather than a necessity—so many people, once they start taking drugs, binge on them, and that ruins the point for me. I don't want drugs to wreck me, I want them to give me power, and strength, maybe warp me for a while, but not permanently.

I'm not an excessive person, except on tequila, perhaps. I don't take acid anymore because it can make me lose control, and that is not a feeling I like to have now. It was right at the time when I took it under controlled circumstances, and it opened my mind, but it got about as open as it could. Now people take stuff without knowing what they are taking and what the consequences are. It was all very chic at the beginning, when it was open, and then shit turns to shit, and it becomes secretive, and the whole thing changes. Instead of having a line like a cup of coffee, very normal and everyday, it becomes dark and dirty, and then dangerous and life-threatening. When it becomes something to hide, you binge on it as quick as you can while you can.

I was getting in a spin. I said, "Jean-Paul, I need you, I'm losing it, please come." He didn't want to come; he was only interested in the film. The film me, not the real me. I could see it coming, that something was about to happen.

I was playing this huge theater in Sydney. Australia really liked me; I had a massive gay following there. I had a big dressing room filled with goodies, loads of food and drink, and it was my birthday. Mel Gibson and Sigourney Weaver were in town filming *The Year of Living Dangerously,* and we were going to be taken out to meet them. Dolph—Hans then—was at the University of Sydney studying chemical engineering. He was from a long line of chemical engineers. He had been hired for two weeks to do security at the theater, to make some pocket money. He was standing in front of my dressing room door, keeping people away. My friend Mary Vinson, who would later marry Chris Blackwell, was there with me, keeping me company.

I invited Hans in. We changed his name much later, when he started acting. I was in the mood to start flirting. I said, "Oh, you look like you are hungry. I have all this food." He and his colleague were in the dressing room with Mary and me. Mary naughtily said to them, "Well, why don't you take us somewhere, so we can go dancing." They were both very quiet and proper. Very nice, unassuming. From college, straight, and they were still treating it as a bodyguard job. Well, that soon stopped.

I remember saying to Mary, "Ooh, I don't know which one I want. You choose for me!" We were high after the show, and buzzing, being a little silly. We ended up in a club, dancing, and we were two girls thinking it over, for fun, and she said, "Well why don't you dance with them both and see which one you like. See how they dance!"

I was feeling very vulnerable. It was my birthday, and I was feeling I couldn't count on Jean-Paul, that his work was more important than me. All these insecurities were raining down on me like a fucking storm. I was feeling very depressed and trying to deal with that by getting high and forgetting. I still had the whole tour ahead of me— everything was conspiring. I thought, *Well, I'm going to sleep with one of them* . . . and I decided to go with Dolph.

When I came back to New York, I told Jean-Paul. I figured, *He has to know, because I would want to know.* I was always straightforward and honest. There were too many secrets growing up. I didn't want that in my life, so from the beginning of a relationship, I was always very up-front.

It was all I could think about when I flew back to America. There was Jean-Paul, and I had a small child, and I had warned him that if he didn't come and help me, things would change. I wasn't married, I hadn't made that commitment, and so there was still this place for something to happen. Once Jean-Paul had recoiled from the physical me, the one that existed off the page, outside of his carving and modifying, changed very fast.

I said to Jean-Paul, "If you can forgive me, I still love you. Why don't you take some time to think about it?" He said, "No, I will give you my answer now. And it's no." So that was it.

It was very difficult, splitting up. I was childishly in love with him—I had so much love for him, and I never felt that he loved me in the same way. Later he told me that he was trying to show me how much he loved me through the work. I was too young to understand that. I was in my late twenties, but emotionally I was like a teenager.

Hans and I wrote to each other for a few months. Then he came over to see me. Jean-Paul and I carried on working together—a romantic breakup couldn't break that up, not immediately. We were too intertwined. We'd had Paulo. It took time for the inspiration to fade away. We still inspired each other creatively, and there was still a sense that we might get back together again.

Jean-Paul was still editing *A One Man Show* in New York, which came out of the idea that Jean-Paul thought I was sexier dressed as a guy than as a Christmas tree disco star. He liked me more in disguise as a savage or a surreal superhero than obviously dolled up and stripping off to impress.

With Richard, I had played with the Marlene Dietrich imagery, my head on her body in the sailor suit. Jean-Paul saw me as the black Dietrich. There was something about the idea of her that he wanted to update. The French saw me as the new Josephine Baker, even before the music, and he updated that as well, an imaginary Africa dislocated even more than it was, a distorted reincarnation of the *danse sauvage,* an uproar of the senses.

I met Josephine Baker once at her last show in Paris. It was very brief; she passed away shortly after. We didn't really have time to talk, but I remember she wore a lovely turban, and she was very sweet to me.

I had a friend, Patrice Calmettes, who managed at Le Palace after Fabrice died. Patrice and I are very close, and he was close friends with Marlene Dietrich. When I was with him one night he put me on the phone. I said, "Hello," in my usual deep voice. And she said, "Well, you sound just like me." It was close to the end of her life, and she had become a recluse—she didn't leave her apartment or speak to many people. Patrice was one of those she still spoke to. Our conversation was very brief: "We have the same voice," she purred. She wished me all the best.

I remember meeting Lauren Bacall at a party for Giorgio Armani. She was also taken with my deep voice, because she had one as well. She said, "We have the deep throats!" It was like being in this community of deep voices. Lauren loved my lips. She started kissing me. It was like we were in a little club of deep, manly speakers.

It was interesting, though, that a lot of the time it was others who wanted me to be the new this, the new that. Others said I was the new Dietrich, the new Josephine Baker, even the black Monroe after an Italian *Vogue* shoot for which they made me up like Marilyn. A lot of the acts I was compared to were white, and it struck me as being a way for critics to take the me out of me. The me I had worked so hard to be.

There was also a job I did that forced me to explore my male side in pictures. After a few months in Paris, I was hired for a shoot for La Perla in Côte d'Ivoire. I had turned down an important shoot with Yves Saint Laurent because although it had incredible prestige, it didn't pay much, and the La Perla shoot paid well and I had bills and rent to pay. Also, it was a chance to go to Africa, and I had never done that before.

I got held up at the airport after the flight because, they said, my papers weren't in order. They wouldn't let me into the country after a long flight from Paris. I was frustrated and scared, as the rest of the party were allowed in with no trouble, and suddenly, in the middle of the night, I was on my own, surrounded by threatening security guards. I think they were after a bribe, but I had no money on me. They decided to deport me.

I was very tired and had taken a Valium for the flight. Three guards lifted me up like a sack of potatoes and threw me onto the plane, ready for the flight back to Paris. I pretended that I was ill and kept my eyes shut and let a little foam form at the side of my mouth. They were speaking in French and didn't think I could understand them. They were talking about how Americans thought they were comedians, taking the piss out of them.

The pilot refused to take off with me on board, because he thought I was seriously ill. This was good news for me, because I wanted to get into the country. They carried me off the plane and put me in a cold, dirty cell—not much of an improvement on my circumstances. I was still playing ill, and started to cry. One guard definitely seemed in the mood to try something, and I was worried that I was going to be raped. Basically, I fought this by making it seem as though if they messed with me, they would catch a disease. Foaming at the mouth and being incoherent because of the Valium put a barrier around me. *Do you want to catch what I've got?* He didn't. Eventually I was allowed into the country, although they took my passport, which made getting out of the country another adventure.

Because I was late, and the male models got sunburned in the boiling hot sun, I ended up having to play the male part in the shoot, and my openness in agreeing to this kind of thing, when a lot of the models wouldn't, became part of my thinking. I was comfortable playing the man. Because of the trouble I'd had getting into the country, in all the photos I was in a bad mood, pouting hard, staring at the camera with a lot of aggression. I look at those early pictures, often taken in beautiful parts of the world by fantastic photographers, and it makes me laugh that it often looks like I was in a really foul mood. It made for a good photo, but also told the story of what was happening—the trouble I was in, the hangover I had, or the annoyance with some of the people I was on the shoot with.

Jean-Paul loved the man/woman idea, because he wanted to mix and split everything up in the pictures, so that they were tough but soft, manly but female, ancient but modern, mystical, everyday photos but hyperreal and painterly. It was all part of the puzzle that became the androgynous thing—it became the obvious direction for me to go in. The images also were made up of a series of lies, and here was the classic deceit—the woman dressed up as a man, or the man as a woman, or which was it? Masked and unmasked. I remember once when I was shopping at Bloomingdale's in New York and I was trying some clothes on in a changing room. A woman saw me and complained that there was a man in the dressing room. I swiveled around, naked to the waist, and casually announced: "Can a man be pregnant?" Paulo was on the way at the time.

A One Man Show was my first world tour. I'd been seen in crowded discos, with the kind of cheap, improvised theatrics suited to the club scene, but never on such a grand level. It was everything I had always been, but made new. I would make the whole theater my space. I borrowed ideas from church—this formalized interpretation of desire, and yearning, and charisma. I was preaching pleasure as a certain sort of threat, getting the audience to get down on their knees, bringing them onto the stage, blessing them in my own way.

A One Man Show was the distillation of this process where I was as much a performance artist as a pop singer or actress. Or at least, I was interested in presenting myself as a singer in a way that broke away from what had quickly become a very narrow set of traditions. Most pop performance didn't take into account pop art, or Warhol's films, or a European catwalk, or Japanese theater. There seemed to be many different ways of doing a concert where you would be influenced not by a rock 'n' roll show or a soul revue but by minimalist art, expressionism, and avant-garde film.

It was Jean-Paul inventing a new context for me to inhabit, as though Marlene Dietrich, Bertolt Brecht, and Piet Mondrian were as important an influence on pop as Elvis, as though music could be connected to art and theater. It was like the invention of a new genre, related to the musical, to opera, to circus, to cinema, to documentary, to the art gallery. To magic as well, because Jean-Paul was like an illusionist, creating magic tricks that somehow philosophically dislocated reality, and my image, and even my soul.

It was also about stripping back prejudice. It was about rejecting normal, often quite sentimental and conventionally crowd-pleasing ways of projecting myself as a black singer and a female entertainer, because those ways had turned into clichés, which kept me pent up in a cage. I wanted to jolt the adult world that is traditionally led by bland white men, to shatter certain kinds of smugness through performance and theater.

I never really thought of myself as black, so it wasn't as though I consciously decided that I would behave in a way that black people didn't usually behave. In America they tried to force me to be, in their eyes, a traditional black person, to limit myself to the limitations imposed from outside on a black American, but I didn't want to go there. It seemed that would make me act like a victim, like the inferior person they wanted me to be by dismissing me as black—ruled by the language of the prejudiced—and I wanted to be ruled by my own language, my own way of putting and seeing things.

The unmoored power that people recognize in the *One Man Show* is possibly because I was simply being me, not thinking about the color of my skin, or my sex—I was outside race and gender: I considered myself an energy that had not been classified. Jean-Paul amplified my own exaggeration and perversion of how the female path to survival has often been through seduction.

I never wanted to limit myself to being A Black Woman, because that immediately puts a person on their back foot—beginning from a kind of negative space in order to prove the positive—and I never wanted to think of who I was as anything less than positive. If there was any woman in there, she was abstracted, hidden behind a mass of disorienting contradictions. I didn't want to act black, or white, or green.

This was immediately shocking. I was behaving in a way that was certainly not perceived to be African, or Jamaican, not least because the show was clearly interested in things Africans and Caribbean people apparently had no interest in because it wasn't part of their history—things like minimalism, cubism, musical theater, absurdism, Happenings. (This attitude completely underestimates and misunderstands the African and Caribbean openness to experimentation and renewal that is essential to how they deal with radically challenging circumstances.) And I was dressed as a man, or an animal, or an alien. I didn't invite the audience into a familiar set of spaces, so there was no safety there.

There was also a robotic quality to my performance, a mix of the human, the android, and the humanoid, and that was also disorienting to those expecting to see a black woman essentially act either like a passive black woman playing along with the rules, or a strong, defiant black woman blasting through the rules with what were still essentially compliant black "soul" elements.

I was being entirely natural, given that the whole thing was deliberately heightened. I was never coached in how I moved, or regarding my facial expressions. I picked all that up from various places. From Issey and Japan, from my acting coach, Warren Robertson, who made me realize I was being my abuser, Mas P. This was why I was being so scary; this was what I was channeling.

Theatrically, I was not thinking, *This is a way of finding a different way to be black, lesbian, male, female, animal.* I didn't want my body language to betray my origins. I wanted to use my body to express how I had liberated myself from my background, ignored obstacles, and created something original, based on my own desires, fears, and appetites. I was using my body as a language. A language that comes from a dark continent. And dark is dangerous.

We never discussed its being about blackness, or femininity, or masculinity, about the breaking of certain taboos and traditions. The power of a black female entertainer being so confrontational in a world where that meant you didn't challenge or provoke was not something we set out to do, and maybe that's why it was seen as so challenging and provocative. We were not limited by thinking there were barriers to break down. We didn't even consider the barriers. As far as we were concerned, we were so far on the other side of any barriers that we never even thought of them. We were after a kind of freedom to experiment with performance, and we could do that more by not limiting ourselves to any categories. I was a human being, and more than anything we were seeing how far you could stretch being human before it became something else altogether.

Jean-Paul, perversely, as the creator/master of a show about freedom, might have considered some of these themes and processed them through me. The black woman as a weapon—the black woman who felt she could exist anywhere, who could change what it is to be black at will, who didn't want to be fixed so that she couldn't move through and into different worlds. Maybe he was scared of me, and this was his way of explaining it to himself. Perhaps he was exoticizing me, and these were his fantasies about me taken to the limits. Perhaps he wanted to reconfigure my celebrity status in a way that turned him on. He wanted to invent a brand-new sort of diva—Marlene Dietrich, the other side of Kraftwerk; Eartha Kitt, the other side of David Bowie and Klaus Nomi. We didn't talk about it, but I know there were certain things he liked me to do, poses to adopt and expressions to use, as though moving through a dream about which he was making a documentary.

I was playing a character—a number of characters, masculine and feminine—but not feminine with big tits and a big butt, feminine in the brain, through mental discipline and flamboyance. And human, as an energy, a force, a creative act that did what creative acts are meant to do: to break outside of categorizing us sexually and racially, which causes problems.

The show came out of the minimalism, the cubism, and of creating a great effect without much money. It was also show business bent out of shape. It helped that I was fearless. I was prepared to take on whatever challenge Jean-Paul set for me, or I set for myself. A gorilla wearing lipstick? Absolutely. Bring it on. I loved it all—I loved his perfectionism and the madness that sometimes startled me that I could then turn into my own madness and startle him back with.

You don't necessarily realize that you are onto something as you are doing it. It blossoms as you do it, and it turns into something that happens to be unique. At first, when we performed it live, people didn't clap. They didn't understand what the fuck was going on. And then jaws dropped. There was a slight state of shock. I could feel it coming off them, but of course I couldn't react, as I was acting as if in a play. I was in another reality. It wasn't Grace Jones onstage: it was Grace Jones playing Grace Jones, with the help of other people playing Grace Jones. I couldn't come out of character.

My immediate reaction as I was doing the show was that it was a complete flop, except no one left the theater. They stayed. They watched. They wanted to work it out.

We used a catwalk, to refer back to the modeling part of me, that I would walk down into the audience. One night a fan handcuffed himself to my leg so that I couldn't move. The audience rose up as one to demand that this person who had done it set me free so that I could finish the show. The bodyguards threatened to break his fingers if he didn't let me go. I was shaken, and no one was sure I was going to continue after he let me go, and the whole theater stood up to urge me on. Then I realized it was working. They were quiet because they were seeing something new, not because they didn't like it, but because they were concentrating on what on earth was going to happen next. It was a show that created a series of incidents, and you wanted to see how it ended.

Once you're onstage, if they are not applauding . . . well, as long as they are not leaving, it is not a complete disaster. I concentrated on doing my part, making sure my voice was strong, that I hit my marks. It was a very new kind of show, even down to the fact the lights were shone on the audience. That was new in pop, that challenging of the audience, that bringing them into the show by making them a part of it. Big lights would come out at them, searching their faces, putting them on show. A huge fan blew confetti all over them. They weren't used to that, to being abused. They were forced to keep their wits about them.

They weren't sure how to react, not because they didn't like it but because it had never been done before. The idea was that there was a story, or a series of stories, that was new. The idea that I was playing different characters, all based on me, or connected to me, but not really me, was also new. There was a lot to take in.

I was not being passive in the slightest, in the way most singers are. I whacked the cymbals. I dominated the audience. It was what I was always like, but much more so. I used to drag people onstage and pretend to sodomize them and pretend to whip them. It was total confrontation. I would beat the audience up. Bang them over the head.

Orson Welles once told me on a talk show, *The Dinah Shore Show,* that I raped the audience. I had just performed a song, and to be honest, in the confines of the TV studio, I was not particularly extreme. For me, fairly reserved. There was still enough of the drama for him to see something. He said, "Certain people seduce an audience, flatter an audience, beseech an audience. Grace, you rape an audience—your show is a sexual assault." He meant it in a good way. . . .

I had bought a house in the Bahamas as part of my deal with Island, and I went there to write. I lived there with Paulo, and my family would come. After a while, Dolph came to visit for a holiday. Jean-Paul was working on me, but he knew I was with Dolph. We did try after Dolph left the Bahamas. Jean-Paul said he had changed his mind. He came over and we talked it through.

I think he realized he loved me when it was too late. He loved me as an object during our relationship, and he explained that to me. Later, he realized he loved me as me, but by then I was too aware of being loved as an idealized object, and I didn't want to be loved like that. I don't think I was selfish to say, "I am on tour, working hard; please come and help." He might have understood if he had been a professional dancer and experienced what it was like, but he hadn't.

One day, in the Bahamas, trying to fix everything, Jean-Paul suddenly said, "Well, let's get married." I was driving, leaving our apartment, and I panicked so much I slammed the car into reverse. I put my foot on the gas and went backward fast and almost crashed into a wall.

He thought that was what I wanted, but what I wanted was to get back together, not to get married. "No," I said, "you don't get it. That's not what I want. Marriage is not going to solve anything."

I knew he wasn't going to change. The relationship wasn't working because he was more intense than ever in trying to make it work. Which wasn't natural. And I could not adapt to the pressure of being perfect. I had grown up with that and did not want to repeat it, even with Jean-Paul. I didn't want to lose him as a friend. I didn't want to lose him as an inspiration, as what made us work—I couldn't lose that. I panicked. I could see the future. I knew Jean-Paul. That was it.

I didn't want to change him. I couldn't change myself. I knew deep down in my heart that if I had gone back with Jean-Paul, he would never have forgiven me for going with Dolph. For the rest of our lives he would always bring it up. I would have to pay for it for the rest of my life if we stayed together. I always made sure Dolph was never around when Jean-Paul came to visit Paulo.

Jean-Paul still brings it up—that I cheated on him. But I was always trying to tell him it was going to happen. He was always a little jealous—of John Carmen, of Chris Blackwell, of others who were part of presenting me to the world. He wanted to keep me to himself. Jean-Paul would be jealous of my press agent, even though he was gay. John could be sleazy, but he was very good at his job. Chris would say, "Your PR guy is the best."

He would get me in the press all the time without it becoming too much. John was naughty—he'd say, "When you get out of the limo, scratch the car, jump on it, make noise." Basic stuff, but it did the job. Pictures of me went in the papers. We would always be a bit high. Living the dream of the nightlife and the music, laughing and having a ball.

Jean-Paul didn't like to go out. He was a workaholic. I was the mistress; the work was his wife. By the time he realized that was the problem, it was too late. He would see me frolicking with John, laughing pictures of me on the town making the newspapers, and he thought there was something going on.

Dolph could see that I was unhappy, that I needed some reality, and to be cared for—not in the way that would turn me into this impossible, anomalous African queen, this battling elongated beauty encased in reflections of perfection, but as a person, in the real world, where I breathed, and cried, and bled. Dolph, being gentle and disciplined, a European and Australian karate champion, and also a Fulbright scholar, was exactly what I needed. I'd raced away from discipline after I left Jamaica, and Dolph brought it back. He understood the performance side; from the kickboxing, he appreciated the strain on mind and body of performing in a way that Jean-Paul didn't. The way that, after you have performed and given so much, you can feel naked and exposed, horribly vulnerable and sensitive, and you need rebuilding. It's as if you have been skinned alive. You open up a fantasy, and then you instantly revert to normalcy.

You can see why singers like Janis Joplin couldn't cope. One way is to take someone to bed with you after a show, but I could see with Janis how that can make a person feel lonelier, more estranged. I didn't want to go that way, but the physical distance between Jean-Paul and me, and his inability to understand what it meant to actually perform for real, not on paper or film, was putting mental and emotional distance between us. It was pushing me closer and closer to believing that taking someone to bed with me every time I felt alone was a solution and not adding to the problem.

Dolph could have been the beginning of that, of me taking the next available good-looking man to my bed. Luckily, Dolph didn't take advantage of the situation, or quickly disappear after it was over. He wanted to get to know me, and he took me seriously as a person, not just a famous person.

He knew how to deal with my extremes in a way Jean-Paul didn't.

Dolph could see I was getting high a little too much, I was getting too wild, and Jean-Paul didn't know how to ground me, or didn't want to. At the top you are alone, and it was an intense cycle of records, shows, promotion—and I am not in a band. Sometimes I think it might be better to be in a band and share the pressure. Mostly, I think, *You're born alone, you die alone—handle it,* but sometimes, especially during that period of the international hits and the growing fame, and Jean-Paul being in a band with me in a way, but always elsewhere, I would have liked the company. To be with the only other three or four people who understand what you are going through because they are as well.

Being with Dolph had nothing to do with him being big and beefy. He really took care of me when if he hadn't done that, I would have died. I was so adrift because of how Jean-Paul refined the image of me but neglected the actual me. I would say that Dolph saved my life. I was touring so much. I felt super mature, but I was still very young in the sense that I was only really born when I moved to America—my childhood wiped out, devoured by my upbringing. So when I was twenty it was like I was eight; at thirty I was eighteen.

I think Dolph understood that. He didn't accuse me of being immature and childish. He looked at my situation and he thought, *I am going to help you. Instead of you waking up and feeling self-destructive, taking something as a barrier to the stress, you should do something healthy.* He said, "You will find a different, better sort of high, a sports high. You will get addicted to an oxygen high." My regimen changed, during that one world tour, which would have destroyed me if I had carried on indulging.

I was automatically drawn to Dolph because he was a gentle giant—very intimidating, being so big and fierce looking, but he was the opposite. He didn't bully me, didn't tease me when I was feeling fragile, and he turned me back on to sports. I had loved sports as a child; it was the one way I could play without getting into trouble. He renewed that enthusiasm I had, and he made me realize it could be a positive way of coming down after a performance, of dealing with the pressure of having to perform so regularly. He trained me to realize that exercise and discipline would save me.

Another problem was that I was becoming a big pop star, and yet

I still considered myself an underground act, almost an amateur in a way. I'd never really banked on having to deal with all the pressures of stardom when I set out—the decisions you have to make, and the way it both opens up your world but also shrinks it. You travel the world, but the walls close in.

I knew that I was limited, but I understood how to make the most of those limitations. But I wasn't really a singer or a dancer—a Jagger or a Tina—so I took things in unusual directions. In a way, I must always do that, because that is what works for me. If I got rid of that, it would be the end of me. I am not here to sing like Aretha and dance like James Brown. My goal was still in a way to do theater, and I was passing through. I knew that no one could match me in terms of theater; that's where I was less limited.

Jean-Paul and I were nominated for a Grammy for the full-length video of *A One Man Show*. Jean-Paul missed his Concorde flight from Paris and couldn't make it to L.A. for the ceremony. The Grammy publicists were trying to find me a date. They nominated a number of people to accompany me, and in the end settled on O. J. Simpson. Well, there was no way I was having that. I must have seen what was coming. So I asked my friend the actress Sarah Douglas, and we went together. I wore this massive Karl Lagerfeld hat shaped like victory, because I was fairly sure we would win. We didn't.

Following the event, I lost my invite to the after-party. I had presented an award, and I had been nominated, but I didn't have the right pass to get into the party afterward. I got incredibly upset—we were in this huge line, and they would not let me in. When they turned me away, I tried to hold it in, but I was so upset. There was a lady in the queue, and she said, "Don't mess with Grace!"

I had had enough, especially because I didn't even win the award. Duran Duran won, and they said to me, "Oh, Grace, you deserve the award, not us. You should have it." I said, "Well, give it to me, then." They kept it. They admitted that they had copied the staircase in their winning video from me and Jean-Paul in *A One Man Show*. To me, being beaten by Duran Duran reminded me of the Oscars a year or two before, when Martin Scorsese's *Raging Bull* and David Lynch's *The Elephant Man* were beaten by *Ordinary People* and Robert Redford.

There was a really long hallway in this big building where the party was. I let out a huge scream that lasted as long as I could make it as we left the building. The police were called, and they were going to arrest me for disturbing the peace. Sarah tried to calm things down: "It's okay, she's okay, she's feeling very upset, she didn't win her award, we're leaving now, it's okay."

We had a limo pick us up. My hat was so big I couldn't get it through the door. I ripped it off. I was in a really bad mood. The limo driver recognized Sarah from her appearance in *Superman II,* as one of the villains, and even though he had the glass partition up between us and him, he was eavesdropping on our conversation in the back of the car. He started to talk to her. I was livid and started screaming at him, "This is private!" And he said, "Well, this is my limo. Why don't you get out?" He kicked us out of his car. I took my lipstick out and wrote all over the back of his car: ASSHOLE!

We ended up catching a cab, with this awful leopard-print pattern on the seats. I sat with my Lagerfeld hat on my knee, miserable because it had all gone wrong. *A One Man Show* lost to Duran Duran, enough to make me scream and scream.

Jean-Paul and I are still friends, more than thirty years later. We have our son, Paulo, a musician who often plays on stage with me, another of our masterpieces. We carried on collaborating. We still talk for ages on the phone. We exchange a lot of information about each other, which is true friendship. When we start talking we don't stop . . . as long as I take time to listen. He always said, "You talk, but you don't listen." It's because I get excited! He has to say, "It's my turn now." His ideas still thrill me and make me see things in a new way. He also still does things that annoy me. When he took a photograph of Kim Kardashian with a champagne glass perched on her ass in an impossible pose like the ones he did with me over thirty-five years ago, I asked him why he was giving her—as a basic commercial product—his ideas? This seemed to contradict his spirit of integrity, which he has protected for so long. Why was he repeating himself, just to give her a little flare of publicity, quickly absorbed by the next puff of self-promotion? Well, he replied, "I got the feeling that if I didn't do the photograph, she would simply have the idea copied anyway. I might as well copy myself." His ideas are so powerful that repeating them decades later still causes a hell of a fuss, however temporary. I also think he wanted to get a little respect from America for what he had done as an artist and in a way as a creative prophet. He might have done it to wind me up a little as well. Which he did.

I think I know him better than anyone, certainly after his current wife, Karen. He knows me and I know him because we did spend a lot of time talking very freely. Even when we argued, we would end up laughing.

Because we were working on *A One Man Show* before, during, and after our separation, it became pretty intense. Plenty of that positive and negative sexual, creative, and romantic energy went into the performing and making of it. It was entertainment, and the analysis of entertainment, and it was the story of a relationship. It's what helps make it so fantastic. Ultimately, it is a love story, taken beyond belief.

10

Octopus

I was numbed by love and, at the time, I believed everything Jean-Paul said. Love weakens you. It makes you blind. It's definitely an alien feeling, like you've been abducted. I turned down a role in *Blade Runner* because I was weak in the knees in love. It wasn't because I didn't like the script. I had so much respect for Jean-Paul, and I listened to him about what I should be doing and always asked for his advice.

Jean-Paul wanted me only to work with him. Especially if I was going to do a film. He wanted me to do a film only with him, before anyone else. He always wanted to direct, and it was me who pushed him. We pushed each other, because we were artistic sparring partners. Jean-Paul didn't believe in himself as a director at first, and I pushed him to try. He gained his confidence, and once he had it, he didn't want me to work with another director.

I knew he would be adamant that it was a bad move to appear in *Blade Runner*. I immediately said no, before I had even read the script and before I had even asked him. Jean-Paul was always in my head as I made decisions. When he heard about the film, he said what I thought he would say—it would be too commercial, and I would become too Hollywood. I would become a sellout.

That was the worst thing to say to me. I was moving with artists who really were underground—known, even successful, but rooted in the avant-garde, experimental, and definitely not commercial—and you felt that you were all in it together and that to accept mainstream work was an unforgivable betrayal of some essential nourishing, progressive spirit. You felt part of a club, even if you didn't get together every night, and there was an understanding of what that meant, and what you didn't do in terms of accepting degraded commercial work.

When I told Jean-Paul, even though I had already said no, he couldn't resist going on about why it was such a bad thing to do. He told me that I would be exploited—my biggest fear. It was like joining another cult where you are told what to do, even as you pretend what you do is all about not being told what to do.

One of those things you didn't do at the time was a big budget Hollywood movie, even one based on an acid-tripping, time-bending 1960s science-fiction book by paranoid psychedelic activist Philip K. Dick. Turning down such jobs was definitely the spirit of that time, and it's a spirit I have found difficult to shake off even as the world has gotten less discerning and discriminating.

I still had the script, though, and the night after I had passed on the part, I was flying to Paris. I decided to read it on the plane. I absolutely loved it. It was set in a universe I visited a lot in my work and play. As soon as I landed I decided I would call them back and reverse my decision. I was too late. Overnight they had cast someone else.

The director, Ridley Scott, must have really wanted me, because the part they offered me was bigger when he was thinking of me than how it appeared in the film. The character of Zohra, the Snake Lady they wanted me to play, had shrunk in the finished film. I think there would have been more of that character if I had accepted. Of course, everyone in that film, which was so much more cult and cool than commercial, went on to be really successful, their integrity enhanced by being in such a movie. The film's reputation only increases with time.

I should have made that decision myself, rather than being caught up in Jean-Paul's rivalry with Ridley Scott in the world of commercials. At the time, they were both at about the same level, moving from art direction and TV ads into film. Ridley was slightly ahead, and I got tangled up in Jean-Paul's jealousy. If I had seen the film Ridley had made a couple of years before, *The Duellists,* which was fabulous, I wouldn't have thought for a moment about accepting. I said no without reading the script, which was very stupid of me.

I found out years later when I hung out with Ridley's brother, Tony, that Tony had fought so hard for me to be in one of his movies, *The Last Boy Scout* with Bruce Willis, but he just didn't have the power. It was for a character called Cory. A small part, because she dies quickly, so she has to be memorable, so that people remember her. Her death sets everything up in the rest of the story. He wanted me; the producers wanted Halle Berry. They won. In a fight between the director and the producer, usually the producer wins.

Ridley never asked me to work with him again. We saw each other a few times at functions and events, and I never bought it up. Tony said that Ridley fell in love with Joanna Cassidy, the actress they ended up choosing to play Snake Lady in *Blade Runner.* Later, they split up. He associated me with the heartbreak, so he never considered me again for any of his films. Tony said, "That's why he hasn't called you."

Later, I made the conscious decision after passing on *Blade Runner* that I would try the kind of movie I had turned down, the kind Jean-Paul had warned me against. I would get my feet wet. I don't like re-grets, but I did regret that I had not taken that role, and was struck by how quickly things had moved after I had said no. Within a day, some-one else had been given the role. I had no chance to say, *I've changed my mind.* I reminded myself of my motto—try everything once. Because Jean-Paul's influence was so great when we were together, I had not followed my own credo.

I was intrigued by what it was like in that supposedly forbidden and corrupt Hollywood world. I felt I was made of stern enough stuff not to lose my head and be won over by false promises and fake charm. I wanted the experience, at least once, in the same way I had wanted to be a Playboy Bunny.

The James Bond producers had really wanted me to be in a Bond movie, because in the 1980s, with the franchise threatened by changing times, they were chasing fashion and looking to reach a wider audience by involving more pop and rock. They had wanted me to be in *Octopussy*, in the title role, played by Maud Adams, but there was some anxiety about having a black woman as a villain. A Bond movie is, for all the appearance of sex and violence, a fundamentally very conservative franchise.

They came back and offered me a part in the next one, *A View to a Kill*, the fourteenth Bond film. This time I was ready, and I followed my own instincts. I battled with memories of what Jean-Paul had said about *Blade Runner: They are just going to exploit you*. I wanted to prove to Jean-Paul that I could be in a movie without losing my integrity.

It was what I always believed would happen when I went from modeling into music, that the musical door would open out onto the acting doors. Music was going to take me to theater and film. Acting was always where I felt I was going to end up. Here was my chance.

That's why I studied with Warren Robertson, on the recommendation of Jessica Lange. She'd gone to his classes, and people like James Earl Jones, Diane Keaton, Christopher Walken, and Viggo Mortensen studied under him. He made me realize that it was about having absolute confidence in your own ability. He said, "I am going to teach you how you hold your own regardless of what everyone else is doing. How to find that one thing that can anchor you and your performance. Concentrate on yourself, and everything else will work around you with its own momentum."

He encouraged me to find an inner story. A memory that was all mine. May Day, my character in *A View to a Kill*, was very much of the attitude that if you messed with her, she was going to kill you. And to get to that point I did think of my step-grandfather. In the Bond film, playing the ruthless dominatrix in catsuits, mad hats, and flamboyant capes, taming a wild horse with a sneer, parachuting from the Eiffel Tower, I began to emulate Mas P, to copy his intense scowl. It's there in the stare of May Day.

I didn't really think of it at the time, but I can see it now. I can be as scary as he was to me because I had him as a kind of role model, or at least as an adult showing me how a person got his own way. He taught me something about how to demand attention, but I could turn it into a cartoon, which takes the sting out of it for me. I can see it now in old pictures of him, this force in the eyes that I use in various ways as a performer. I realize now why that look has been second nature for me—I saw it all the time; it was part of how he controlled us. He tried to intimidate me, a vulnerable little girl, keeping me in check. That was my way of dealing with this monster—turn it into something he would have been horrified by. I threw it back into his face even if he never knew it.

Roger Moore said to me, "Please stop looking at me like that, with such venom." It made him really uncomfortable. I was a killer. I was willing to kill. In my real life, I would only do that for my son. More for blood than for a lover. Generally I would hurt myself before killing anyone. Roger Moore was such a softie, although he did have incredibly hard legs and the stiffest hair, and he was so relaxed about the whole thing—some would say too relaxed—that he didn't like me glaring at him off set like I really was a henchwoman and he really was the spy I was determined to kill.

I was on such a strict schedule, and it could become quite taxing. I had to be in the car by four forty-five in the morning. When I was doing James Bond in Britain, I met Danny Huston, the son of legendary film director John Huston. He was directing the "making of" film for the Santa Claus movie where Dudley Moore played Patch, one of Santa's elves. It was his first professional job, and he was editing at Pinewood near the set where we were filming. He was only about twenty-three. We had a very secret affair. I was very good at secrets. It was good to have some privacy. It was nice to get up to something that no one knew anything about. Danny and I didn't really get involved at first; we just started hanging out. I would go to his editing room and have a little joint. It was a little bit of wild time outside the discipline of making the film.

They didn't know who was going to be my lover and boss, the film's main villain—at first it was going to be David Bowie. He declined, because he said he didn't want to be in a film where for most of it his character would be played by a stand-in doing the stunts. He also wanted to see the script, and for a long time they weren't ready. They then asked Mick Jagger, because they definitely wanted this to be a rock 'n' roll MTV Bond. He didn't want to do it either, and they were struggling with getting a male rock star for the villain.

The role was eventually taken by Christopher Walken, styled in the film to be very Thin White Duke Bowie—lean, mean, blond, and suavely narcissistic. Chris was very cool and friendly on set, but it took a little bit of time to get close to him. I had a crush on Chris in real life, but for the sake of the role I wanted to keep my distance. I was totally committed to him as my boss, but I decided to play it that when we had a love scene it would feel intense to me, that I would really feel the moment. Plus, I was really very shy in this world.

At our first meeting the director, John Glen, had said, "You are the actors. You do the acting, and anything you do wrong, I will fix it in the editing room." He was very much an action director and not really interested in the mechanics of acting. The actors were left to it.

I interpreted his speech about the editing room as meaning: *If you are no good, you will be cut. Most of you will disappear onto the cutting-room floor.* I remember being incredibly scared. *Fuck, what do I do now?* I didn't like the thought that I would be left to my own devices.

I said to my teacher, Warren Robertson, that the director was not going to help me much as an actor. I was on my own, and I didn't think I was experienced enough to deal with that, especially as part of what was such a brand, and such an industrial process. I wanted to be super-professional without taking it too seriously. I just wanted to get on set and push a button and be in character. I had wanted Warren to teach me this, to help me work out how to do it.

Warren told me to go to Chris for help. He had taught Chris. And Chris was very helpful. We would slowly get to know each other. In the script, we had a sex scene together, and that becomes an important part of the dynamic. You know the sex scene is coming. Everyone on the set knows the sex scene is coming. The tension builds up. I didn't want

Dolph there. He is very Scandinavian about sex—he wasn't the jealous type. He was very open, and that openness bound us together, and was never the direct cause of any problems we might have had. But I didn't want him there while I filmed the love scene with Chris. There was another reason, really. Dolph was beginning to try acting, fairly informally at first, and there was a little friction because it seemed he might be hanging on to my coattails. I felt, for the sake of my Bond character and her single-mindedness, that I needed to be on my own. I was feeling nervous about the scene. It would have been too distracting having Dolph around, as if this was about him as much as me.

The sex scene with Chris involved nothing more than some passionate kissing, but it ended up so intense that it was edited out when the film was shown on certain South American airlines. Chris and I managed to generate some genuine sexual tension—his wife said to me, "If I didn't know you were in love with Dolph, I would have been jealous."

I was the first Bond girl to help create her own costume. Usually it was Cubby Broccoli's wife, Barbara, who was in control of the clothing, but I thought that a part of why they asked me was because of my own style. I knew what I wanted, how I was going to look as a Bond girl. I was way ahead of the game. I looked at Disney colors, because I figured being a Bond girl was like being in a cartoon. I picked out every piece of fabric. I took in tips I had learned from Issey and Kenzo, and had direct input from one of my other favorite designers who became a friend, Azzedine Alaïa, but Bowie and Jagger were right in thinking that you have trouble operating with any kind of soul, or intimate energy, inside such an industrial production. You are a small cog, as huge pieces of machinery are dropped in around you. Your main job is to try to make sure you are not crushed by all this falling machinery.

The Bond team was amazing. There were bits I was afraid of, but I did the best I could to make sure I looked in control. I watched all the previous movies. I developed the character so that you would know her even if she was miles away, hidden in the shadows. I took in all my experience of being me, wearing certain clothes, pulling certain faces. It's a Bond film, but the way I looked at it, I wanted it to be the best cartoon I had ever seen. Take it extremely seriously up to a point, and then stop.

Take the film for what it was, and try to have a great time. I also wanted to make sure that people didn't look at me in the film and say, "Well, that's just Grace Jones." I wanted people to think of me as May Day.

I got on great with Roger Moore. He was very funny and easygoing. He helped me a lot, because I wanted so much to be good. I was a worrier. I worried that I didn't know what I was doing. When I got stuck he would humor me.

I remember I had to walk in on Roger as Bond in a scene, and I was meant to look surprised to see him alive. It is very difficult to be surprised to see someone who shouldn't be there when you know he is going to be there. We had done three takes already, and I wasn't experienced enough to work out how to look surprised when I knew exactly what was about to happen. *I know he's there! I read it in the script, and we have rehearsed it and done some takes. He's there in bed; how can I be surprised?* That kind of pretending I found a little troubling. I couldn't look surprised! Eventually Roger stuck something stupid on his head, and I was really surprised to see it, so I looked surprised, and that was the take they used.

It seemed appropriate that I appear in a James Bond film, because of the connection between Bond; his maker, Ian Fleming; Jamaica; and Chris Blackwell. Chris's mother, Blanche, was for many years the mistress of Ian Fleming, author of the James Bond books. He visited Jamaica during the war, attending a naval conference exploring the potential presence of Nazi U-boats in the Caribbean Sea, and he fell in love with the island's peace and silence and what he described as its "cut-offness" from the world. He was determined to come back after the war, and in 1946, he built a holiday home in Jamaica on the north coast near the quiet banana port of Oracabessa. The twisting, tree-lined roads hugging the coast alongside the sea would have reminded him of English country lanes, but with the addition from paradise of the glittering, sometimes choppy, purposeful sea, the soft white sand, and the neon-blue sky. He found fifteen acres of land, an old donkey racecourse on a secret coral beach protected by a reef. He called the modest, minimal bungalow he built Goldeneye. It was where he wrote all fourteen of the Bond books—without Jamaica, a universe away from the low-sky postwar grayness of London, there would be no Bond. He loved birds, and one of his favorite books was a reference book, *Birds of the West Indies,* by James Bond.

Chris worked as a location scout on the first Bond film, *Dr. No,* when some scenes were shot in Jamaica, including the classic scene where Ursula Andress's Honey Rider, wearing a belted white bikini, walks out of the sea—a private beach called Laughing Water—suggestively carrying her conch shell. May Day was a descendent of Honey Rider. We all belonged to the same family.

Chris bought the Goldeneye estate in 1976 after trying to get Bob Marley to buy it, and turned it into a resort that protected and showcased the Fleming history. Fleming's writing desk, where he would write the Bond books, is still there. Elizabeth Taylor, Charlie Chaplin, and Sophia Loren used to holiday with Ian Fleming; now it is Jay Z, Johnny Depp, and Bono who come to stay, and in between there was Mick and Bianca.

Ian Fleming loved to snorkel, and one day he was snorkeling in the water of his private beach at the foot of the cliff where his house was built. He swam out to a small rock that poked out of the warm blue sea like something human frozen in time, and spotted an octopus just under the water's surface. This became the setting for a short story he wrote, "Octopussy."

I have visited Goldeneye many times, and spent some time there working on this book, because of the way the place clears the head and revives the soul. I have taken my mom and dad there, who agree with Chris that the place has a magical atmosphere. Many who visit plant a tree there, labeled with their name, helped by Ian Fleming's original gardener, Ramsey Dacosta. I have planted a tree there, alongside those planted by the Clintons, Princess Margaret, Bono, and Pierce Brosnan, and I love to see how quickly and confidently it has grown over the years. One or two others nearby have not fared as well.

Noël Coward was one of the first visitors to Goldeneye after it was built. Coward was once described as fourteen men in one; I often feel I am fourteen in one as well. He adored the location, although not so much the modest house Fleming had built—with no hot water or glass windows. He first built a home called Blue Harbour, five miles along the coast from Goldeneye, but that became such a social whirlpool he felt the need for a quieter, less accessible place. He had a simpler house built farther up the hill, in the local, spartan tradition, on the site of an old pirate lookout that was originally called, unsurprisingly, Look Out. You can see the Blue Mountains in the distance across Port Maria Bay, one of the longest beaches on the island, where Europeans first came ashore. His new house was kept apart from the rest of the island by rugged narrow lanes tightly winding upward under sparkling canopies of trees and bushes, each leaf laid sleekly in place, a true, divine hideaway.

Noël Coward renamed his island home Firefly, because of the lightning bugs that covered the ground. This was my nickname when I was a child. One of Chris Blackwell's companies now maintains Firefly as a museum. The place is still as hard to find as it once was, close to what it was like when stars, royalty, and politicians would visit. Chris talks of having tea with Noël Coward once—another of his early mentors— with Burt Bacharach and Marlene Dietrich. It all seems to be part of what I called the Giant Octopus, where huge tentacles stretch out around the world—and my life—generating a tangle of coincidences, associations, and connections that spring up and multiply as fast as anything growing on Jamaica.

11

Delay

I remember this one time when Keith and Andy were waiting for me because Keith was going to paint my body, and Andy was going to watch and take photographs. I was late. They waited two hours. They waited patiently, because they expected it to happen. When I did arrive, on the back of a motorcycle, Keith was fine, because, he said, as soon as the task at hand was under way, I was totally committed. I was in the moment.

It was as though that's why I was late—because where I was before, I was totally committed to that task, and wouldn't leave until it was completed. Whatever it was, something important or something trivial, I concentrated on it to such an extent that the next thing I was meant to do was forgotten. Even something as special as having my body painted by Keith Haring, while Andy Warhol recorded it all.

Was I always late, for everything, all my life? As a child, no. I always had to be on time. There was definitely a punishment for lateness hanging on the wall. Slowly, as I left my childhood, I would be later and later for things. I didn't think of it as being rude or lazy. I am always busy doing something, even if that is simply getting ready, or getting ready to get ready. Sometimes I am a bit late for the first thing I do in a day, and then a bit later for the next appointment, and then the lateness will multiply. By the end of the day, I am very late. Then I will stay up late, which means I begin the next day later than I should. Even if I think I am early, I am a little late.

Sometimes I might be in one time zone but feeling I am in another. I will be in London or Paris on New York/Jamaican time. Locally—when I am at my home in London—it is three in the afternoon. In my head it is ten in the morning. It takes me some doing to catch up with European time when I am feeling more New York, or more Jamaican. In London, I'll reach peak wakefulness at four in the morning, because in Jamaica it is eleven at night. A lot of the time I am on L.A. time, which is eight hours behind London. As dawn rises, I am having what in Los Angeles are end of the evening conversations with my brother Noel, my mother when she's staying out there, or Marjorie Grant, my business manager. I'm in three or four time zones at the same time.

The lateness also became more apparent, and notorious, once I started to perform. Half of the time I was late arriving onstage. I was asked to be late. That's a big secret about my lateness. It has to do with money. A lot of the time when people are waiting for me to appear, I am waiting myself backstage. The clubs want to make money on the booze, and because people leave as soon as I finish, they make me wait so they can sell more booze. They pay me the door money, so they need the money from the bar. That was in my contract. They wouldn't let me go onstage even if I wanted to. In that case, I might as well turn up late, rather than hang around. And then people started to expect me to be late. It became a Grace Jones thing. There would be disappointment if everything ran smoothly.

I admit, sometimes it will be my fault, the lateness, but never in vital circumstances. I might be a week late sometimes, say, for a chat show appearance in Australia. But I turn up and give everything I have, and, secretly, I think the late Grace is preferred in those circumstances to the Grace that politely turns up on time. It is not as though being late has ruined a whole performance. When I need to be on time, because something relies on total punctuality, I am on time.

It became part of my reputation. Part of my image. I should not spoil the mystery concerning my lateness. And I do help the mystery along. If people expect me to be late, I arrive late. *How boring, she has not arrived. She's two hours late. What on earth is she doing?* The audience would boo and jeer—*Burn the witch! Burn the witch!*—and then I would go out there and say, "Okay, bring it on!" Or I would sing one line of a song, and they would forget how long they had waited. It was worth the wait—that was the point. Keep the audience waiting, and then make sure it was worth the wait.

You can't be late when you are filming. You couldn't be late for the Concorde. (Well, actually you could be—I once arrived just as the plane was about to take off, and they stopped the flight and came and got me.) You can't be late for the theater. You can't be late for a court appearance. You can't be late for live television. You can't be late for Pavarotti. You can't be late for the Queen of England. There are some things you can be late for, and I'm very good at being late. But there are some things you cannot be late for, and then I can be amazing at turning up on time.

When I am filming, I am never late. There were many productions I was involved in where they worried about me being late, because there were always rumors about how long people were waiting for me at photo sessions and live shows. It became part of the legend. But for films, I had to be there at four in the morning, and I could not possibly be late, because it would cost so much money. On the Bond film, Barbara Broccoli was put in charge of coming to get me because I was known to be late. But I was never late. It's a different animal, filming. It is not the night, it is not about anticipation, and it is not about the kind of glamour that lateness can accentuate.

I remember when I was recording "Slave to the Rhythm" with Trevor Horn. Trevor produced records in the tradition of the disco producer. He didn't expect a collaboration, but in his case, if you inspired him, he would give everything, whatever the time and cost, to produce a very special piece of music.

He spent most of the time with his team in the studio building the track like the extreme perfectionist he is. I was very happy to let him make the blueprint to his exact design—order the material, build the foundations, start to construct the rooms. It took time, but when he had a vision, there was no one better to trust.

I had never worked with anyone like Trevor. He allowed me to experiment with my voice in a way no one had before. He let me be free to try things out in every part of the song. To attack, to be sweet, to be operatic, and then he pieced all these fragments together. The voice led to the tone and texture of the track, and the arrangement and dynamic of the music were devoted to how I had sung each word and phrase. The music was built up around my vocals.

I felt that Trevor totally understood the scope of my voice, the theatrical extremes. He totally got it.

He reminded me of my German singing teacher in New York, allowing me to try whatever came to mind. I don't have to sound like Aretha, or whoever the producers had finished working with, or whatever song was the last big hit. He wasn't thinking about whether a song would sound good on the radio, or in Madison Square Garden. He wanted to get the best possible performance out of me within the limits of me being me. That was his template. He had a way of motivating me without putting pressure on me. Working with him reminded me of when I used to sing before it became a responsibility, when it was like a hobby, but he also made me realize that my singing is my responsibility, and I like it like that.

Trevor really tapped into me and understood that I was going through something, and that this meant the record would sound better, and more intense. He never said no to any of my ideas. He always wanted to see what I would come up with, so that he could see how it would be of use in how he was building the song. He allowed accidents to happen, and intended moments of great intensity.

This was very exciting for someone like me, who wanted to learn about the voice. About my voice. I was a student of my own voice, and a part of that learning was to get to like my voice. I never liked that people thought I was a man, how they thought my voice sounded too low and monotonous. I learned that this was my voice. Trevor played a big part in helping me reach that point of acceptance, and also of appreciation. No one else could sound like Grace Jones. A lot of pop singers sound the same. If you shut your eyes they all blend into one. It's the pop music equivalent of the Chinese binding of the feet of young girls so their feet don't grow but stay dainty and apparently more feminine.

I decided I would learn to go even lower. There was no point in going for the high notes. I knew also that as I grew older it would go lower, so I might as well make a virtue of it. And I would sing my old songs not as I originally sang them but as I was, and as who I was becoming. That made sense to me.

I was happy that Trevor spent so much time making the record. You never mind when a person is that talented. I want to work with someone that good all the time. He takes his time, but that was perfect for me, because I was occupied, making films. He was working closely with Jean-Paul—two geniuses working together—and I totally trusted him. Trevor did to my voice what Jean-Paul did to my face and body. Like me, they took their time. Trevor was months late delivering "Slave to the Rhythm," but the time it ended up taking contributed to its brilliance.

I would be called to studios in London or New York to make my contribution, one day at a time, spread over many months. With Trevor bringing the best out of my voice and giving me the freedom to experiment with how I sang, "Slave to the Rhythm" turned out to be like an autobiography of my voice, and what I had been through to become the singer I wanted to be. When you make a record, as a solo singer, the producer is a kind of ghost, selecting, compiling, and organizing your thoughts and memories into a structured musical narrative; "Slave to the Rhythm" was a definitive example of this form of production ghosting that is the essence of much popular music. (The person you can hear interviewing me on the record as part of the autobiography is my collaborator on this book, Paul Morley, who was then part of Trevor Horn's team. Without knowing it, we were starting to write my story.)

Trevor called me once in the late evening in New York, where he was recording. He had been having problems with the rhythm of the track, which was based on a music coming out of Washington, DC, called go-go that Chris Blackwell was obsessed with. It was the sound of that city, like Detroit had Motown and Chicago had house, but much more underground. Go-go was like disco funk slowed right down to half speed and turned inside out. It was hip-hop out of an alternative collection of influences. Go-go never took off like Chris imagined it would, and "Slave" is one of the few signs that it ever existed.

There was a drum pattern on this record, "We Need Some Money" by Chuck Brown, the Stevie Wonder of go-go, the Duke Ellington, and Trevor really got excited by it and based his arrangement of "Slave" on it. An old colleague of Trevor's, Bruce Woolley had come up with the idea of the song, which was originally intended to be the follow-up to Frankie Goes to Hollywood's "Relax." The group had turned it down, preferring to do their own material.

When Trevor called me at my apartment, I was having an argument with Dolph. The relationship had reached a turbulent period. Trevor had called because he really needed me to get down to the studio a few blocks away and add some vocals so he could check that he had cracked the rhythm problem—he called just when I was setting fire to Dolph's trousers. I was in a very bad mood. Trevor said, "I need you now, please get down here." The studio was only fifteen minutes away from my apartment. It wasn't like I had to cross the Atlantic

I made it three days later. I had some things I needed to clear up. A few more items of clothing to cut up and burn. When I got to the studio, though, I was in a very good mood. Did he want me on time and in a bad mood, and therefore of no use, or late and in a good mood, and ready for action?

Sometimes being late has nothing to do with me. One time I was asked to do a promotional event for a new Absolut product, White Vodka. There was a huge press conference to launch it in Spain. Press from all over the world were invited. I asked Jean Paul Gaultier to lend me a sumptuous white dress to go with this big white wig. I took their theme to the extreme. Doing this sort of work is a little like being a prostitute, but I still want to make it as original as I can.

I arrive at the hotel on a Saturday and everyone involved in the promotion is there, and there is no money. They can't get the money, because the banks are shut. They say they will send me the check. My mantra remains, No cash, no show. You learn over time that if you don't get the money immediately, you will never get the money. Once you have paraded on behalf of their product, they forget all about you. You lose your value instantly. The instant depreciation on being a luxury guest is huge.

They come to get me in my hotel room and I am all dressed up, ready to go. I look the part. That's my job. That makes me a little late, but only enough to build up the tension. A little of my lateness comes from knowing how much time it takes to get people excited. That's my job as well. Being Grace Jones. Well, becoming Grace Jones.

The press are all in place, waiting for my entrance. There is, though, no money. So I won't do it. I have had plenty of experience of not ever getting the money once I have done the presentation, and I don't want that to happen again. I lock myself into my hotel room bathroom—becoming Grace Jones—and grandly announce, "I am not coming out until you pay me."

I am sitting in there, and I can hear the executives and party planners talking in the room. One of the guys organizing the event is on his knees to my people. They've got two gorgeous blondes in white fur to accompany me. Everything is all sorted. The journalists hear that I am there, but I am not coming out. Rumors circulate. They assume I am playing the diva—demanding drugs, men, oysters, champagne, some of which might be true.

We say to the Absolut people, "Well, get the money from all your friends." In the end, that's what they do—they manage to round up the money and pay me, and I make my entrance, all in white. I never say anything, I suddenly pop out of a cake, a giant model elephant, a scrum of shiny musclemen.

I am something like six hours late, and no one really knows why, or what was going on behind the scenes. Nothing gets explained—I am simply late, and that adds to my reputation. If the journalists ask why, I say, *No comment*. If you are a proper journalist, you will work it out. I don't spoil the mystique. It would be more of a disappointment if I turned up on time. It would be boring. The wait is a part of the occasion.

I survived on corporate parties for quite a few years when I wasn't making albums, fed up with what was expected of me, fed up with being treated as though my best years were behind me. Making personal appearances helped me carry on being my own sugar daddy without having to engage with a music industry that really didn't suit me in the 1990s. The mix of fashion and music is perfect for the luxury brands. You can live well on five or six events a year.

They spend an absolute fortune on these parties. The money they spend on the flowers alone is staggering. I find out what they pay for flowers, and I make sure I am getting paid a little more than that. You find that they have paid $200,000 to fly flowers in from some exotic country, but they only want to pay the artist $50,000. I say, "I don't think the flowers should be more than me. I should be the big flower, the big, unusual flower. The flower that costs the most. The people are not there waiting for the flowers to appear." That's one way of putting value on what you do.

And the more they spend on the artist, the worse they treat them. They think they have bought you and can treat you as badly as they want. They think they own you. To the extent of not paying you, at least the money they owe you, the second half of the fee. They will often pay half your fee up front, pay for five first-class fares, and they will book you into the presidential suite—I tell them I am the president . . . of my own corporation. Sometimes they try to renege on paying the final amount, as if the second half is not a real part of the fee. I have been ripped off twice in those circumstances, and I decided it was not going to happen thrice. They try to skimp once I have arrived. I don't think they realize I will call their bluff and really not appear if they do not give me my money.

There was one event I was asked to do when LG were launching their first flat-screen television. It happened in London, and I was booked into a royal suite at the Mandarin Oriental. There was a real royal family booked at the time from some Arab country, so there was a lot of commotion on the same floor as me. It was difficult to see where the royal family ended and my show-business family began.

We are in the suite, and I am ready for action. The champagne is flowing, the oysters slipping down nicely. Again, though, no money, and it is a Saturday. They are begging me. *We will have the money on Monday.* No, I am not moving until I am paid. I won't even leave the hotel and go to the venue, because there is too much pressure once you arrive.

We say, "Well, give us all your jewelry and watches, your Rolexes, as a deposit. We'll keep them in the safe until I get paid." They do not want to do that. They get increasingly desperate. Finally, after a couple of hours with me not budging and everyone trying to come up with a solution, they call with an idea for a deposit for the weekend until they can get the cash on Monday. They say, "We have an employee who has a baby she is prepared to offer as security. We have a baby! You can keep the baby until we bring you the money." Brendan Coyle, my new manager, could not believe it. This is the kind of thing that happens to me, but when I tell people, no one believes it. I say, "Now do you see how crazy it can get?!" The baby is the most outrageous story of them all. I am glad Brendan took the call. The look on his face!

I didn't take the baby. They couldn't get the money. I didn't do the show. Everyone waiting for me to burst out of a giant glittering TV screen at the launch party thought I had simply not turned up, that I had flounced off in a diva sulk or not even gotten out of bed or drunk too much champagne or taken too much coke or was busy slapping someone in the face for ignoring me. What else do you expect from Grace Jones?

12

Hollywood

Dolph and I toured America on a motorcycle, which was great for me, because I had not seen much of the country outside touring either with the church or as a performer. We traveled all over the country, and I would wear this full-length Issey Miyake leather outfit with a helmet that covered my entire head. You would not know what color I was, which was important in Middle America. I was covered and masked, so no one could see me. You wouldn't have even known I was a woman.

It helped that Dolph was as much a gypsy as me. He loved discovering new places. He liked to move around and study, and earned a number of academic scholarships. He had a Fulbright scholarship to a college in Los Angeles, but that was too far away from me living in New York so he decided to go to MIT in Cambridge, Massachusetts, one of the world's great engineering schools.

We traveled to Boston to see where he would be living. I moved some plants from my apartment to make him feel at home. We had a look around and liked what we saw; then we traveled back to New York. On the way back he suddenly said, "I don't want to do this. I am only going to school for engineering because it was what my brother did, and it is not what I want." Dolph decided he was not doing it for himself—he was doing it for his family, because it was what they did.

I said, "If you don't want to do engineering, try something else."

I understood the whole family thing and knew how important it was to break out of the box. I encouraged him to find something else to do, and he listened. It's horrible to be doing something you don't want to do.

We moved back to New York, and I cut off his hair—worried I was taking away his power, like he was Samson. He came everywhere with me. We were inseparable. He became familiar to the people I was working with and for. Kenzo put him in a fashion show, but he did it in a loving way, because Dolph was very shy and very sweet. He was briefly in the Bond film I did, *A View to a Kill,* playing a bodyguard, because he was hanging out with me and looked the part. He loved the atmosphere on set, and he loved studying, so he started studying with my acting coach, Warren Robertson. I told him if he wanted to take it seriously he needed to study. He relished that, as he loved to learn.

This part came up in *Rocky IV,* as the mighty Russian heavyweight fighter Drago. There was a long search for someone to play Drago. Warren had once roomed with Sly Stallone, so it all fell into place. Before I knew it, boom, Dolph had a career.

It quickly took a toll on our relationship. It was Hollywood that tore me and Dolph apart: the place, the industry, the bullshit. Offers for film parts would come along for him, but they often wanted me to be attached. This caused problems. *We want you, Dolph, but we want Grace too.* We ended up fighting about it, even though it wasn't really our fault. We were plunged together whether we liked it or not, and that led to us falling apart.

There was ego. Out of nowhere, the ego Dolph didn't have before, he now had. You need it as an actor, as both a form of protection and a way of projecting yourself, but it can harm you as a person. Necessary self-confidence erupts into arrogance. Ego can get in the way of growth, because it makes you think you know it all. People started to fill his head with stuff because they saw a chance of making money through him, and he believed it.

Dolph and I ended up living in Los Angeles after all, because he wanted to be where he figured the action was. We went through bad

Video shoot for "Living My Life," where
a passionate argument between me and
Jean-Paul Goude becomes a song becomes
an image. *(Adrian Boot / www.urbanimage.TV)*

With Iman and friends.
(John Carmen)

LEFT: Model Naomi Campbell and Sven (my biggest boyfriend) celebrating my birthday at Stringfellows Nightclub, NYC. *(John Carmen)*

BELOW: Me with Paulo and his dad, Jean-Paul Goude, at Paulo's birthday party, November 2014 in Paris. *(Sophie Christophe)*

Standing with Angelo, my film double for many years, and Sara Douglas. *(Grace Jones Private Life Collection)*

Performing in 2009 at the Island Records 50th anniversary show in London. A Philip Treacy hat that could lift me into outer space, and a Jean Paul Gaultier corset. I still wore Gaultier even after Madonna stole him from me years before!
(Adrian Boot / www.urbanimage.TV)

Backstage with comedienne Sandra Bernhard at a gay benefit in New York.
(John Carmen)

A quiet drink at the Studio 54 bar,
a little overdressed. *(Adrian Boot / www.
urbanimage.TV)*

Using a New York rooftop as a stage, totally believing in myself, in 1981.
(Adrian Boot / www.urbanimage.TV)

With photographer Greg Gorman and crew at the photoshoot for the cover of this book. Alligator Head, Jamaica, April 2015. *(Greg Gorman)*

Hugging genius—Polaroid of me loving Issey Miyake at some point in time in my Paris apartment. *(Grace Jones Private Life Collection)*

ABOVE: Backstage at the Heaven nightclub in London, 1985. *(Adrian Boot / www.urbanimage.TV)*

Wearing Jean-Paul's clothes, getting a little mixed-up, ready for the New York night. *(Adrian Boot / www.urbanimage.TV)*

At my first Fashion Rocks appearance with Annie Lennox and a friend. *(Grace Jones Private Life Collection)*

Christmas 2014 at Goldeneye, Jamaica. Four generations are pictured: Me, my mom, Paulo, and his daughter, Athena. *(Grace Jones Private Life Collection)*

Performing in London, 1984, giving great shape to the 1980s. *(Adrian Boot / www.urbanimage.TV)*

patches. The relationship failed a few times, and we would try and resuscitate it. There was a magnetic attraction that would draw us together, but then the real world would intrude. We would be wrapped up in each other, and then we would be apart for two weeks.

When we first met, Dolph had brought me and the reality around me down to earth, from a very dangerous place that was beginning to swallow me. Once we were living in Hollywood, our relationship had left planet Earth, because Hollywood is not on planet Earth. Despite the magnet that pulled us together, it didn't work. The ending to it dragged on, really. There was too much interference, too many people were giving advice, it became very complicated. We weren't left alone to work it out for ourselves.

After Dolph did the *Rocky* movie and we moved to L.A., the New York restaurateur Tom Holbrook took over his management. He had never managed anything before, other than his restaurant. He wanted to represent me, but I didn't want that.

I never felt Tom was good for Dolph. I definitely think he took advantage of his innocence. They went on tour together to promote *Rocky IV,* and when they came back to Los Angeles, Dolph didn't come back to our house. Holbrook decided he would move into the Sunset Marquis Hotel with Dolph. He said to me, "Well, you are filming during the night, and Dolph is working during the day. You never see each other anyway, so Dolph might as well stay in a hotel and be looked after." He said it was a practical decision, that we both needed space. This was where other people began taking over the management of our lives, not only of our careers. I always felt that Holbrook was trying to control me and Dolph, and I was having none of it.

I was filming a camp sex horror vampire comedy, *Vamp,* and we ended up shooting later and later into the night, which worked for me, and also worked because I was playing a vampire, Katrina, the leader of a nest of vampires running amok in the night. I ripped hearts out of chests, wore a wire bikini, and was an erotically fucked-up stripper taking her clothes off like she was in a kinky avant-garde Japanese ballet, and had a stare as creepy and evil as any cult overlord. For me none of this was weird. All in a day's—or night's—work.

I had no dialogue. I said everything I needed to say through how I moved, used my eyes, and feasted on the necks of my victims—silent-movie stuff, really. To prepare for the role I watched a few times F. W. Murnau's gloriously sinister and brilliantly designed 1922 silent film *Nosferatu*. Playing a vampire, I had to honor the screen original. Max Schreck played the supernatural vampire—in this case, the hideous Count Orlock—for the first time in film. I loved how he portrayed the creature, and how the film established much of the Dracula mythology, including the idea that sunlight kills vampires. That detail wasn't in Bram Stoker's 1897 novel, which *Nosferatu* was closely, if unofficially, based on. Stoker added some elements to the traditional myths and legends he based his story on, such as the inability to see vampires in mirrors, but many other now accepted details came once the movie versions started. In the novel, vampires can walk around in daylight, although they lose some of their power. Really, they're merely nocturnal. Night is their time, as it is for me. *Nosferatu* creates for the first time the notion that daylight is deadly to vampires.

I was enthralled by the shadow on the wall as Schreck glides upstairs, his elongated fingers and nails, the bald head, bat ears, and sunken eyes, the mental makeup—all of it was my kind of weird. The way Schreck rises abruptly from his coffin onboard a ship made a huge impact on me. The fact that the film was silent made it much more ominous.

In *Vamp* they wanted to give me words, and I said, "No, I am too powerful to speak!" Too many words and you can get tangled up, trying to coordinate the words and the expressions. When I saw *The Artist*, I thought, *Well, I wasn't that far off the mark.* For me, a silent movie and the atmosphere it creates are the pure essence of cinema, and if I had been alive during their heyday I would have been in my element.

Maybe Tom Holbrook took Dolph away from our house because I was getting a little Katrina-ish in real life. It's hard to tell in Hollywood. If New York is a tragic, comic, stupendous, absorbing, sexy, enchanting opera with huge sets, Hollywood is a bright, corny advertising jingle that doesn't even rhyme. In New York, you know when you are going mad, and you can enjoy it, or deal with it, or make art out of it. In Los Angeles, you cannot tell that you are going mad, because everyone around you is consumed by their own madness, hoping to make a movie about it.

I was so angry that Dolph was not coming home after being away for a week that my sister-friends Sarah, Tara, and I descended on the Sunset Marquis like we were Charlie's Angels on a dangerous mission. I actually had a gun. It seemed very natural that I would go and fetch Dolph holding a gun. I did so out of desperation—we had been together for years and had made this move to L.A., a place I absolutely loathed, against my better judgment, and then he comes back from being away and Tom seems to want to block me from even seeing him. What is going on?

We three girls got ourselves worked up and then decided, *Let's go and get him!* Sarah asked me where I'd gotten the gun. I said, "Well, it came with the house." In L.A., everything came with the house, including a gun. We turned up at the hotel, not to shoot anyone, but to make sure he came with us. We banged on the door of his room. *Bang, bang, bang! I've got a gun!* Elsewhere, Los Angeles carried on being Los Angeles, expecting such behavior, a similar scenario being played out elsewhere across the synthetic city; it's what they base their myths on—violence and despair and money. I'm screaming, "Let him out, you bastard!" It was as though Tom was holding him hostage and we had come to rescue him, hair flying, legs flailing, breasts heaving, guns flashing, music pumping. This was the kind of hysteria that took place in Los Angeles.

In one of the many lives I never got to live, another Grace (one who never came true) shot Dolph there and then. Or rather, the bloodsucking Katrina wired for sex shot the titanic Drago bound for glory, one savage beast pulled down by another, in a city teeming with savage beasts tearing each other's hearts out for the sake of a part, a hit, a job, a high, a fuck, an award. And that was the end of the ballad of Grace and Dolph. Dolph lived to see another action movie, and another, until the end of time, and I got to move the hell out of Hollywood.

Jessica Lange went to Hollywood for similar reasons as Dolph after she modeled and then became an actress. I once bumped into her on the street in New York. I was pregnant with Paulo at the time and was going to the Carnegie Deli for a sandwich. It was raining, and I hate umbrellas. I wear a hooded coat by Issey Miyake, so I don't have to carry an umbrella. And there she was, passing me on the street. We hadn't seen each other for years, not since Paris. We were standing in the rain talking about what we were going to do with our lives. I said, "Come up to my apartment on Fifty-Seventh and Seventh."

We were so cozy in my warm and dry little flat. She was telling me all about her film career after she had made *King Kong*. She had signed a big Hollywood contract, and I could see that the heartbreak had already started. No matter what you sign, they never pay attention to it. That's why I don't sign anything anymore. What's the point? You sign something, and they still do what they want to do. You have big hopes, and that inevitably means big disappointments. She said, "I was supposed to get this role, but someone else got it. Nothing is going like they said." You could see the frustration and despair written on her face—on the verge of becoming destructive. That kind of deal with Hollywood as the devil can be totally dangerous.

I remember saying to her, as if I were exorcising a demon, "GET OUT OF THAT PLACE!" It was like a monster movie: *The bogeyman is going to get you unless you run! Don't even collect your stuff, get the hell out of there!* I said to her, "If they want you, they know where you are. If they really want you, they will go to the ends of the earth to get you."

Jessica listened to me! Shortly after that, she did a movie with Bob Fosse, *All That Jazz*. And she never moved back to L.A.

Hollywood always maintains the illusion that in order to get a job there, you have to live there. That's the most ridiculous thing ever—when you have jet planes, it's a hop, skip, and a jump from New York. It's not the other side of the world. My attitude was: *If you want me, you know where I am. I don't have to live among you.* As free as L.A. is supposed to make you feel, that is where I feel the most in prison.

That's why I hate it there—I'll go for a couple of weeks if I have to now, but it is a very destructive and dangerous place. It was easy to see how horribly phony the place was after a couple of visits. It was like a little birdie told me: *Here's a message. A strong message. This place is not for you. This place is going to be the death of you. It's a place that is cursed and that perhaps goes all the way to the early fallout of the big bang that created every- thing. It is dead earth, dry earth, a desert never meant to be built on. It is such a destructive place, and if you have to go there, go only for a short while, and make sure you protect yourself. Otherwise, they will suck you dry.*

Some people only see the sunshine. But that disguises the disaster. They call it the City of Angels? Jesus Christ—it's the opposite, it's a demon city. That place can convince you to wreck your integrity just like that. It's built on making people sell their souls for the smallest chance of a part. Perhaps I felt it through meeting Jessica on Fifty- Seventh Street, how trapped she was, how much pain she was going through. *Get out now! Are you waiting for them to beat you up and bury you?*

I had another girlfriend, Sarah Douglas, with whom I'd worked on *Conan the Destroyer.* She was the Bad Queen, and then she was in *Super- man* with Terence Stamp. And then she went to Hollywood. I told her to get out of Hollywood as well. She didn't leave. Years later, she said to me, "I wish I had listened to you." She was made to feel that she had to stay in L.A. in order to get work . . . even though she wasn't living there when she was cast in *Superman II.* The whole casting system makes it all seem so urgent. They act like it is all such a hurry: If you are not around, you blow your chance. It's best to keep a kind of mystery. Maintain a kind of deception.

The whole Hollywood world loves the organized chaos of the pro- cess. Especially the casting process. They will write a role for you and then make you jump through hoops to get it, almost make you beg— even though they have already decided it's for you.

I landed a part in an Eddie Murphy film, *Boomerang.* Jean-Paul and I had hired him early in his career as the support on the American shows for *A One Man Show.* We needed someone who wouldn't get in the way of the show itself or the set—a stand-up comedian was perfect. And Eddie Murphy was the perfect comedian to hire. Years later he started to make movies that were essentially one-man shows, and he invited me to do the film as a thank-you for hiring him early in his career.

In *Boomerang* Eddie plays a debonair stud, naturally, and I, naturally, was hired to play someone raucously silly from the fashion world with a silly name—Strange, pronounced *Strawn-j*. My role involved taking my knickers off in public, rubbing them in people's faces, chasing the pants off Eddie, and saying the word *pussy* a lot with an accent that is from nowhere on Earth. Styled like an Egyptian sex doll, I was launching a new fragrance, which I was thinking about calling Love Puss or Pig Puke or Steel Vagina. . . . I have no idea why they thought of me for the role.

They were apparently amassing information about me when they were writing the role, because they wanted the character to reflect who I was. They were asking people who had worked with me to tell them funny stories about me, so they could use them in the writing. Stories about my behavior to build up a cameo from real life, even though what they ended up with is as far removed from real life as you can imagine. They did the same with Eartha Kitt, and she ends up playing a nymphomaniac.

They asked the director of *Vamp* for stories about what I was like. How I behaved when I did certain things, what I did when I had to turn into a vampire, how extroverted I would be on set. There was one incident on *A View to a Kill* when I was recording some dialogue for the film in a vocal booth, and my clothes were rustling. So I took them off. I did my lines nude.

That became a kind of legend that was passed on to *Boomerang*. They built that into the film: I go through a metal detector wearing a metal dress, which sets off the alarm, so I take the dress off and walk through the machine naked. You find yourself acting out chewed-up versions of your life as you pass through something that has absolutely nothing to do with you. And a Hollywood movie doesn't really belong to anyone; it is not really the result of a great, single vision. It is a peculiar misshapen collaboration between hundreds of people who only know what they need to know in order to make their contribution. No one is really in charge, just the momentum that is generated by the fact it is being made, and costs millions and millions of dollars. That movies end up looking in any way coherent is either a fluke, or because they have been so fastidiously designed. The standard kind of Hollywood movies are as empty and unreal, as strange and unnecessary, as the town itself.

You realize that you are easily replaceable as well, even if you are the only person on the planet who seems qualified to play the horny, eerie, vampiric, stripping, singing, alien, semi-naked, bloodthirsty character with funny hair. They will find someone else, and you find that you can replace someone else too easily as well. I later found out that Bianca Jagger was the first choice to play Katrina in *Vamp,* and during the pre-production of *Boomerang* I bumped into Iman at a fitting at Alaïa's. She had been promised the role of Strange and had no idea that I had been given it. That was embarrassing, as we are really good friends.

In music, only I sing like I do; only I can make Grace Jones records. I star as myself in a setting and story I can control, and there can be no substitute, at least not one with my name, face, attitude, voice, and songs.

I really thought that acting was where I wanted to go. After making the kinds of films I ended up making I realized that this was not actually what I wanted. I had to have the experience to realize that it is not really for me. In the kinds of films I was hired for, I was moved around like a pawn; I was effectively a cartoon character. That is okay in theory, but not when I think of all the effort I put into it.

I always play a character clearly based on the public version of me. I wanted people to see through me to Strange, and it always pleases me when people see me in the streets and mention Strange, or May Day from *View to a Kill,* more than Grace Jones. These characters so obviously looked and sounded like me, and I was chosen more because of my scary, wayward pop image than for my ability to become someone else, so it is great that people see the characters, and not me. There were elements of the characters that I managed to make stronger than me, and that was very satisfying. To some people I did more than merely play myself, and even though I never got a chance to play a character who was not essentially me in a cartoon setting, I took the characters outside myself.

In the end, there are only so many times I can play the demented diva based on the zanier parts of my reputation. Maybe if I had accepted being the Snake Lady in *Blade Runner* I would now be acting in things a little more serious, in *Game of Thrones,* or the *X-Men* series, cartoons, still with semi-naked girls and far-fetched monsters, but with something realer and deeper added.

I saw that the film business was a motherfucking beast, and one that would have killed me if I had kept going. If I had taken more control, had attempted to become a more serious part of a project, not simply a loopy, sex-mad caricature, even directed, I would not have lasted. If I had gone into film full-time and become more creatively involved, I would have killed myself by now. It is next to impossible to get in a situation where all the people involved in the project are moving in the same direction at the same time with the same purpose. Even making a record with a few people, it is hard to get that, but more likely.

Making a movie is about climbing the highest mountain, flying through the sky, landing on your feet, swimming across oceans, surviving avalanches, walking in space—it all keeps coming. I have total respect for whoever can come through all of that without losing their mind, or being treated as though they have.

13

She

Nile Rodgers had wanted to work with me for a long time, and I had obviously wanted to work with him, since the disco days with Sy and Eileen and the Studio 54 fiasco. The opportunity finally came years after the Studio 54 doorman had told him to fuck off, and when it did, he was more or less the number one producer in the world.

My contract with Island Records had run out. I had promised to re-sign, but Capitol was chasing me like crazy. They had courted me for a year, sending me baskets of fruit and cheese. It was one of those million-dollars-an-album-for-five-albums deals. Very tempting. In the end I felt really bad that I didn't stay with Island, but Capitol was offering so much money. I was in tears at the thought of leaving Island, but Chris Blackwell said there was just no way he was able to top their offer. I was unsure. Chris and I talked about it at length. I felt like I was breaking my word.

I had a feeling I was going to regret it. I said to Chris, "This might not be the best move."

He said, "Oh, go on and take the money. We can't compete."

It was a heartbreaking moment for both of us. I was in tears. I took the money, but I should have resisted the temptation. It was emotional turmoil, and I learned my lesson: Don't always go for the money.

None of the people who were keen on me, though, was the head of the company. To some extent the head of the company would always change, and eventually the person in charge didn't really like me. The people who were chasing me to sign with Capitol were reactivating the great Blue Note jazz label, which made the move seem human, and about music . . . but they were replaced. I ended up dealing with a whole different set of people who never wanted me in the first place and didn't really like what I did. They decided I was a disco queen whose crown had slipped, if not totally fallen off. Fashions moved quickly in the 1980s, and within a few years you could go from being totally today to just someone else half-forgotten from yesterday. Keeping up was hard, and the fact that the record industry itself was going through all sorts of changes and panic didn't help. I was stuck with them and they were stuck with me, and after the creative, family closeness of Island, the corporate nature of Capitol was quite a shock.

In the end, the heads of companies like Capitol in the '80s and '90s had more in common with Sy and Eileen than with Chris Blackwell in terms of where they wanted to position me—as a cabaret-style cash cow, not as an artist-creature-object reacting to and creating atmosphere. Their idea of my wildness and creative ambition was that it was nothing but a pose, not something rooted in my entire being. At Island, I had been allowed to fuse the visual and the musical, and I took it for granted that would happen at Capitol. It was very different, though, much more brutal, and very basic.

Chris said, "Let's end this with one last record for Island," and that became *Slave to the Rhythm*. That was like the transfer fee: It was a Capitol release, but Island got a percentage. Manhattan Island was a label formed only for the release of *Slave to the Rhythm,* a one-off joint venture between Capitol's Manhattan and Island Records. It was an in-between moment between one label and the other.

Trevor Horn had spent so much time and money producing the one track that he and Chris suggested making a whole album from the one song, a sort of musical documentary in record form of my life. The budget for the record would make more sense for an album than for a single, although even then it was gigantic. It was certainly one of the most expensive singles ever produced, if not *the* most expensive single.

I nearly fainted when I saw the final bill, which ultimately was what I was paying, even though I never sanctioned that amount. It would take until the end of time to have paid it back even if it was a number one single all over the world; it was a relative success but not a complete smash hit. But once Trevor was in the zone, there was no stopping him. It was as though he was directing a movie, and he was Steven Spielberg, with a limitless budget.

Also, even though we were no longer together, Jean-Paul was working in close collaboration with Trevor on the artwork for the record, so the perfectionism of Trevor was further complicated by the perfectionism of Jean-Paul. The result was art, art fascinated with the whole legend that pop music, entertainment, and fashion had become by then, dedicated to rearranging and enhancing it, opening up new directions, but Capitol was more interested in an efficient piece of dance product, practically packaged, that would do the job.

Chris and I sat in a room with the executives at Capitol to play the album for them—they were anxious because they had thought it was a single and now it was an album. They were bickering away, worried about what to call it, and I was kicking Chris under the table. It wasn't a single, it wasn't an album. Trevor had delivered this selection of tracks that derived from the original song, not a collection of remixes, but the same song variously extended and rewritten so that it became a number of songs. It was ingenious, but not an instant commercial hit—playfully controversial like a Madonna album, or slickly frenetic like a Janet Jackson record—that Capitol had been expecting.

Chris came into the office, put it on, told them it would take about thirty-three minutes, and then walked out of the room. He knew it would be okay. He loved what Trevor had done, and thought it was the perfect, elegant way to say goodbye to Island and hello to Capitol. He saw it was a way of taking in the disco me and the Compass Point me, and then introducing the next me, extending the brand, deepening the myth. He said to me, "Don't worry, they're all going to want a piece of this. It's one song, but it's a hell of a show. No one will care when they hear it—it's not the same thing repeated over and over again."

He was right. After they heard it, the Capitol people stopped bickering. Of course, what I didn't anticipate when I signed to Capitol, especially after having been on Island, was that even though I'd been granted creative control in the contract, they didn't ask for my approval of the record sleeve and went ahead and printed what they wanted. I wanted Keith Haring to design the artwork on the first official album I recorded for them after the Trevor Horn project, but when the album was released, the cover was a very commercial photograph by Greg Gorman—a photo I originally shot for a drink commercial, a total contrast to an album containing specific, personal emotions and confessions. I loved shooting with Greg. He had built his entire studio purely for the light, and would always use me to test a new piece of equipment, but it wasn't what I wanted for the album. A nice photo, but not what I expected, and not what I had worked on with Keith—a very moving, very avant-primitive image, totally from inside his world, and therefore completely, brilliantly unique. Capitol should have been so lucky as to have one of their record sleeves done by an artist as respected and successful as Keith Haring. Their image was attractive but sanitized. Keith's would have been more cutting, more comical, and more energetic—more me. It would have been me telling my own story, which consistently involved being interpreted and reimagined by a great artist, and not them telling their story of me, which was very perfunctory.

After Island, this was quite a shock, that something so important to who I was and what I did would be treated so flippantly and without me being consulted. It was an early sign that they misunderstood me. They saw me as representing the world of fashion, still the celebrity model/ singer, the haywire Studio 54 chanteuse, not someone who was always experimenting with herself and taking responsibility for every detail of her work.

I had some demos from working with Bruce Woolley, one of the writers of "Slave to the Rhythm," that could almost have been released as they were. Nile was very in demand at the time, though, and Bruce wasn't known to Capitol as a producer. The record company wanted the profile. They wanted big hits, with no messing about. And Nile had the profile. He was known to deliver quickly and have success. Bruce or I should have asserted ourselves, maybe coproduced the album with

Nile, but Capitol bulldozed us a little. Nothing against Nile, of course, he loved the material, but we already had momentum and knew what we wanted. I wasn't in a position to push them. I could write with whomever I wanted, but they wanted to choose the producer, and at that point in my new situation, I didn't have the power to get what I wanted.

Nile was great, but he was working very hard at that point. He was burning out, working on a lot of records. That year alone he produced records by Laurie Anderson, Duran Duran, Bryan Ferry, Al Jarreau. The year before he had worked with Mick Jagger, the Thompson Twins, Jeff Beck, and Sheena Easton. It was as if I was next on the conveyor belt. He did the album so fast, inside a month—Trevor had taken twelve times that amount to produce *Slave to the Rhythm*—and a lot of the material never felt finished. You could feel the rush. He was in a hurry. He had a schedule. Bits of his mind were elsewhere.

When I listen to *Inside Story,* I can hear the energy of what was going on the moment it was made. It is different from *Nightclubbing,* different from *Slave to the Rhythm,* but I listen to that record, and I love it. It's where I was at the time. Nile's ear was different from mine, and he was responding to his idea of me, and it was an American Nile production, with all that entails, but I think it is beautiful. There were other ways of doing that material, but I like how it ended up.

I don't listen to all my records, but I play that one a lot, because it is interesting to hear what Nile was thinking. I will do some homework, if I am performing and need to remember the lyrics, but I don't play my albums when I am alone. I listen to them with friends, when I am on tour, but mostly, I know those records, and I don't need to keep hearing them.

We got Fela Kuti involved. I had been obsessed with his music since I had gone to Paris, where you would hear it a lot. Years later I went to Monte Carlo. I used to go there with Keith Haring and Helmut Newton. I was there with a boyfriend, and he knew someone who knew how to get to Fela Kuti. I said, "I want to work with him, can you get him?" And I got Fela! I introduced him to Nile, who didn't really know who he was. But I wanted to take Nile out of his usual American patterns.

Fela didn't do much—I don't think he quite understood what I wanted. He just tried to marry me and my sister Pam. Pam had decided to move in with me at the time. She has a brilliant mind. She had quit Harvard because she got bored and didn't want to turn out like all the other students. She had a kind of eight-year itch, was a little restless with her life in general, and asked if she could work with me. She effectively started co-managing me. I was managing myself, with Chris Blackwell on the side, and various business advisers. After Sy and Eileen as ma-and-pa managers, I started to manage myself, because I felt that if I was going to have to argue with my management then it would become a tug-of-war and wouldn't make sense. It would just have been one more annoying layer of people not understanding where I wanted to go or why.

You get a lot of things thrown at you—do jerk sauce commercials, advertise cigars—and I would call Chris and he would always say, "Stick to what you know. Otherwise, as soon as you reach the top, everyone wants you to do something, and they can pull you down. There is a lot of money there, but in the end it is always a distraction from the music." And over time, I had become addicted to the music even though that hadn't been my original intention. Even with film there was a point where I had to decide between that and music. The Capitol contract I signed was so intense it was hard to do both. If I did a film, I wouldn't have time to properly promote a music project.

Fela was in the studio while we worked on *Inside Story,* but all he wanted to do was seduce Pam and me. Nile didn't then realize who he was—it wasn't his area—so as far as he could see, there was this strange guy trying to pick me up, not an absolute musical living legend. Fela didn't do a bit of work. He would put his arm around me. We wined and dined at Mr. Chow in New York, to no avail. It's such a missed opportunity, but I tried my best. He just didn't want to play along.

Eventually I got to work with his drummer, Tony Allen, on the *Hurricane* album, when I was in a better place—so it did work out, because what I loved most about Fela was always that rhythm. It was more fitting for *Hurricane,* because that was an album that was as much about drumming up the voices of my ancestors as anything. My mother sang on that record, one of the reasons it was so important to me. It came out of Jamaica, and how that was out of Africa, and how that was out of this world, rather than being out of disco.

A video directed by Nick Hooker for "Corporate Cannibal" from this album showed how far out from disco, and even post-disco, and fashion, I had gone. It was why I enjoyed making the album with Ivor, and having a free-form group of musicians that included Tricky, Brian Eno, and Tony Allen from their own free-form studio ensembles producing a music that slipped through and around obvious genres. No one had caught up with what I had done at Compass Point and with Jean-Paul, and in this video I am stretching myself further, beyond the reach of those thinking they are being inspired by me. I am not decoration; I am pure signal. I transmit. The video says, yes, it is about entertainment, art, performance, advertising, controversy, the transferring of extreme imaginative energy, about maintaining creative freedom by living at the very edge of uncertainty, but above all, it is about pure consciousness.

Capitol had wanted me to be set in stone; the fluidity of *Hurricane* is more reflective of my temperament and how far I was along the road and yet still beginning. It is about existing in a world where images are the most vivid of realities, a world where any point can be connected to any other point. It was something I started to learn with Issey, Andy, and Jean-Paul.

My presence, my body, in the "Cannibal" video is distorted, and elongated, and cloned, so there is a connection to how I was broken apart and transformed over twenty-five years before. I have moved on, though, even though I am still no age at all, pure force spreading out into the world as technologies grow. I am keeping up with whatever I need to keep up with without it looking like I am trying to merely stay up-to-date.

I am still a monster, still a rare, troubling beauty, still beyond body, still naked; there seems to be nothing in the world outside me, I am still in my very own space and time. I am still moving as an energy, and perhaps that is what I have become, an energy that belongs in ancient Egypt as much as it belongs inside a limitless machine.

The album with Niles was more fixed in the time it was made, and is, if anything, about glossiness, and consumerism, and fame, and what happened to the spirit of disco at the height of '80s glamour in a world that had sweetened it and eaten it up like cake. When it came out, *Inside Story* wasn't behind the times, it was ahead of them, peering forward to Daft Punk, not looking back to Studio 54. If we'd had more time, I think the concept would have been clearer. We had a hit in America with one track from the record, "I'm Not Perfect (But I'm Perfect for You.)" It wasn't an international hit, so it didn't make Capitol as happy as they wanted to be, considering the size of the contract.

I'd gotten the idea while Mick Jagger and I were playing off each other, which was something we often did when we met. Our flirting was often done through games and wordplay, and frolicking about like brother and sister behind our parents' backs. I had been filming *Conan* in Mexico, and the Stones were there making a video. We were thrown together one day in the same studio complex. I ran into the Stones a lot—we were often in the same place at the same time.

Mick and I started talking about the idea of being in a relationship when you are famous, and having to be as perfect for your partner as you are as a performer. We had an idea for a song. He said, "You do one line, I'll do one line." In the end, we only got two lines: *I'm not perfect, but I'm perfect for you.* That's as far as we got! I said, "I'll take it on and finish it off." He never asked for credit or anything. I completed it by imagining what me and Mick would have done.

Because the track was so personal, I decided I would direct the video for the song, having learned so much, especially from Jean-Paul. It was a retort, in a way, to not being able to live up to the image that my lover had literally created for me, so it seemed important that I be in control of the video, rather than act as the subject. It ended up being completely out of my control.

It was so hard to do. Not the directing itself but working with Capitol. They were a corporate company, so there were all these people breathing down my neck at the time, unconvinced that I knew what I was doing. They were very music industry, and I was trying to do something ambitious and conceptual, using all of my contacts, who were delighted to help me.

I had to struggle to get respect from the Capitol people. I was in every shot, so I would always have my makeup touched up in a room away from the studio. And when I came back they would be shooting something, or having the cast change clothes. I would say, "What's going on? I am the director. I know what I am doing." I got very paranoid. The Capitol people were all whispering behind my back, undermining me. It was deeply ironic considering what the video is about, but I don't think they had the first idea I was actually making any kind of comment in the video.

I had to be a bitch to maintain any kind of authority. Well, if I were a man, I wouldn't have been considered a bitch. If I were a man, I would simply have been in charge, however aggressive and demanding I was. I wouldn't have had other people running about filming things behind my back. A man putting his foot down is in control. It's strong. A woman putting her foot down is out of control. She's weak.

In the video, I am the ultimate primal diva under pressure to stay youthful, going through all the painful, intrusive processes of self-healing and beautification—mud baths, waxing of body hair, acupuncture to repel aging around the eyes, violent massage, near drowning in a milk bath, and a nightmare psychotherapy session. Many of those treating me are sinister, Mas P sort of characters, witnesses for the defense, so to speak, testifying to my actual perfection. I submit to all the treatments in a state of desperation because I know I must stay on the path to perfection, because that is my job. I go through all the tasks you need to go through to be ready for a performance.

It's all a metaphor for how Jean-Paul rearranged me, as a combination of advert and art, because to look like one of his impossible Graces, these are the processes I would have to go through in real life. I would be pummeled, invaded, electrocuted, suffocated, bleached, blackened, dissected, and skinned in order to become such a fantasy, wild- or blank-eyed and ready for action.

I had gotten Richard Bernstein to storyboard the video on my living room wall in New York. I had learned the importance of a storyboard in working on my videos, and I would always learn from whomever the director of photography was when I was acting. I remember there was one famous DP on *Conan the Destroyer,* Jack Cardiff; he'd worked on *Black Narcissus, The Red Shoes, Girl on a Motorcycle*—so many great movies. He loved that I wanted to learn and was always showing me things. He was very funny. I think he liked my strong perfume, which he could smell as I leaned over him to look through his lens. I think he also liked the very skimpy suede bikini they had given me to wear as Zula.

The character was a fierce, no-nonsense warrior and bandit, with a hint of vulnerability, so I had the necessary qualifications for the role. As strong and powerful as Zula was meant to be, the wardrobe department had made a costume for me where you could see the whole crack of my ass. I thought that was pushing it a bit, but once you have signed on, you have little say in what you wear. Hollywood sees a dynamic, murderous female outlaw as being obviously dressed like an irate stripper. I found this furry rabbit's tail, and I stuck that over the top of my bikini bottom, so that covered me up a little. You could only see anything if I swung my tail, which at least gave me a little control over how and when you got an eyeful.

I had hired Keith Haring as my assistant director, to help make a more dramatic, and dignified, outfit for the "Perfect" video. He was in Paris. We sent him the storyboard, and he filmed his part separately there. It was beautiful. He rented a huge space and painted the whole floor. The floor became part of my skirt, white, sixty feet wide, because I am so manipulated and extended, and so diva aloof, covered in Keith's playful abstract symbols. I go up in a lift and all these therapists, cosmetologists, and stylists, all my admirers and worshippers, those that celebrate me and those that manipulate me, go underneath my skirt, so that I devour them inside of me.

He did his piece and sent it, and we connected it to my part. His part was amazing, and we sped him up painting the floor. Eventually he is stuck in the middle of his own painting. He was so fast and so spontaneous when he painted. They would appear in real time, these amazing shapes and lines and patterns. When he was not available for a small reshoot of the paint appearing, we hired someone who was also meant to be an expert, and she took fourteen hours to paint what Keith had painted in a few minutes. His hand-eye coordination was absolutely extraordinary.

We had a lot of guest stars in the video. Andy was in it—it was the last filming he participated in before he died. He was always so enthusiastic: *What are you guys up to? What are you doing?* One day I said, "Well, I am doing a video for 'I'm Not Perfect (But I'm Perfect for You).' I'm directing it, Keith is helping, come down." Andy played Andy, turning up to say, "Grace is perfect." He is, of course, the perfect person to say such a thing, in such a video, all about the corruption, commercialization, and delusions, of perfection. Speaking of perfect, I had Timothy Leary play my psychiatrist. I'm rolling on the floor freaking out in panic as he calms me down.

Tina Chow gives me acupuncture. She was my "aesthetician." I wanted Divine to be my masseuse, but he passed away a little while before we filmed the video.

It was a complicated shoot. I had been apprenticed to Jean-Paul, after all. I knew that preproduction was important. I had asked for two weeks to do the whole thing, and they chopped the production down first to three days and then two. It was so much pressure. After I finished, I vowed that I would never direct anything again. I know that I should never say never, and that with the right people in the right circumstances it is something I might want to do, but they made it such a nightmare. Instead of having a week in which to edit, I had two days. I was never really given a chance. They treated me as though I was a temperamental, unstable mess, and were so impatient and intolerant it did start to seem to those close to me that I was genuinely going mad.

There was a plot to put me away in a facility, because people thought I was on the edge of insanity. There was an actual conspiracy to have me sectioned. It wasn't in my head, although, naturally, it was made to seem as though it was. I was being worn down. The circumstances were making me crazy, not mad. I was simply frustrated to such an extent about how the video was going, people thought I was in mental trouble.

My sister, my mom, my dad, Capitol Records—a weird alliance, whose members cared about me from different corners—could easily have convinced people that I had lost all sense of logic, that I was losing touch with reality. My family felt I was being paranoid, but I wasn't going mad. In truth, I was deeply upset that Capitol was interfering with my vision. I was not being a prima donna: I was just trying to concentrate on a technically difficult task while I was being talked to like I was a silly pop singer who'd gotten carried away with her own ego.

I was female, and they decided that I was rock 'n' roll insane. Had I been a man, they would have considered I was merely retaining control, or professionally fretting about the details. Once they start treating you as though you are losing your grip, it becomes kind of true—in reacting to accusations that you are paranoid and incapable of acting responsibly, you end up seeming to confirm that you are paranoid and reckless. When you try and explain to people who have decided you have lost the plot that you haven't lost the plot, and try to demonstrate your emotional balance, often by shouting about how absurd they are being, they think you are being hysterical. If you try and calmly deal with their fears, they think you are not being yourself, and that you are on the verge of collapse. They wore me down. They sabotaged me.

You can tell why there are so few female film directors. It's the same with any job that society has decided can only be done by a man: They find ways to undermine and undervalue a woman doing that job. And the fact that you end up saying "they" makes you sound paranoid. But there is no doubt that a particular job is usually for the boys: If a woman tries to do it, she is treated as though she is doing something wrong, even perverse.

What are the chances of a female president being elected? The men-only corporate reaction is: *What about the tampons? Will she bleed everywhere? What if she gets pregnant? What if she is going through menopause? What if she's been through menopause and is therefore old and used up?* It's the same old caveman shit, a power thing. It's why I want to fuck every man in the ass at least once. Every guy needs to be penetrated at least once.

Do it yourself if you want. But that's the vision—a woman lies there and the man goes in, takes control, whoosh. It's all about power. The woman is always in the vulnerable position, and the man takes control. Come on. Everybody can be penetrated—mentally, too.

Slowly, slowly, it changes. Too slowly.

Signing to Capitol was like signing a contract where they give you something on the first page, and on the final page they take it all away. They wooed me with treats and pleasantries, and then they wanted to dress me in a little leather bikini and have me submit to being fucked in the ass.

The other album I made for Capitol, *Bulletproof Heart,* was also tricky to make, because my personal life was becoming a psychodrama, and the record didn't recapture the creative and commercial momentum I had in the first part of the 1980s. The Capitol years were, to put it mildly, not as exciting or inspiring as the Island years, or the Trevor Horn collaboration. The music business—which I had now settled into after making the decision that it would allow me to be more me than the film world, where you could not be in control of your appearance, art, psyche—was letting me down. I felt that everyone was expecting me to be much bigger commercially than I was, because of Madonna's driven '80s success with what the label bosses simplistically thought I did—that exhibitionistic disco-pop with videos unashamedly borrowing from art history and underground pop culture. That was not really what I was about. Even if it was, I had been there, done that. I am very stubborn, and I was always looking for the new, even if it makes life difficult for me. The new, or nothing.

I would rather do nothing than do something that doesn't satisfy me. If I am not enjoying what I am doing, I will beg to be fired. If I think, *This is not making me feel motivated,* if I am disappointed in a project because it has not gone in the right direction, I will stop. I stood there in a sixty-foot-wide skirt, painted by Keith Haring, who understood me, who knew that I belonged at all points in time, not only in Studio 54 or an MTV video, and the Capitol executives walked underneath my skirt, and I floated off into the sky.

14

Crash

There is a picture from the '80s taken of me, Andy, Antonio Lopez, Keith Haring, Richard Bernstein, and the producer of *Vamp*. Yoko is in there as well. Looking at it now, it's almost like The Last Supper. It's spooky, because as you look from the edges, all the men started to die. One by one. All still young, and this one's dead, this one's dead, this one. Lovely Richard didn't die in the 1980s, but his death in 2002 at sixty-two was still years too early.

Because of Yoko you can't help but think of John Lennon, who died at the very beginning of the decade. I would look at the picture and think, *It's creeping in toward me.* There was a lot of death going on. You feel guilty for being alive. You don't want to be around without them.

People started to die very quickly, too. You heard they were ill, and then they were dead. It would hit strong, and it was horribly crafty, whatever it was. You seemed fine until you weren't. It was that kind of thing. You'd see some lesions and think, *Uh-oh, that's a bad thing.* Keith and I were dancing at the Garage a few weeks before he died. When Antonio passed away in 1987, no one knew what the cause was, or they wouldn't say. It was still something that would be hidden. They said it was pneumonia. I thought, *You don't die from that.* He was forty-four.

Antonio was one of the first people I was close to who died from what they called complications from AIDS. There was a viral cause for the cancer he died from, Kaposi's sarcoma, but that link wasn't discovered until 1994. The 1980s were the dark ages, even though AIDS was first recognized in 1981, and several thousand men in New York and San Francisco were estimated to have been infected by HIV by 1978.

Then it all came like a hurricane. It was before the drugs, before they learned how to control it. It wasn't only AIDS. Death was swooping down in all sorts of ways. Andy died in surgery in 1987; Alex Sadkin from Compass Point died in a car crash the same year at thirty-eight; and in 1988, Jean-Michel Basquiat died from a heroin overdose at just twenty-seven. I wrote a song with Barry Reynolds called "Well Well Well," really about Alex Sadkin, but it could have been for any of my friends who died. *I'm on a tightrope / I think I'm falling / I can't tell right from wrong / And I feel I'm alone again.*

There was this world where friends and friends close enough to be family were disappearing around you, leaving you feeling very vulnerable. AIDS was a dreadful, chaotic amplification of the deathless facts of mortality that we evaded while we partied in the '70s. After the years of hard partying and sweating because of pleasure, it was becoming more and more a case of sticking around. Hanging on as people very close to you suddenly dropped out of sight.

Keith worked until the end. He couldn't stop. He had so much to say. He should still be saying it. It's a world he helped to create. He should still be watching it, reacting to it, drawing it, brightening it.

He was doing exhibitions all over the place up until two weeks before he died. He wasn't even in bed for those two weeks. We all knew. It wasn't talked about much. We didn't have the words. I didn't have the words.

The attitude among many of those who were diagnosed was, *Well, I am going to work as much as I can.* There was also a feeling that they would find a cure, that a cure was right around the corner. *If I can just hang in there, a pill will arrive, a cure will be found. Someone will sort it out.* No one saw it coming, but once it was everywhere, a visible, terrible problem, it was surely going to be dealt with. Keith was only thirty-one when he died.

At first there was a lot of paranoia, when people thought it was like a cold, that you could catch it by touch, or by being in the same room. People thought it was something you could breathe in and catch. A sneeze would give it you. The sweat of someone else. A kiss, the swapping of saliva. It was like we all needed to wear protective clothing.

Any little scratch, feeling under the weather—vague symptoms, rashes, infections, marks on the skin, it was surely coming to get you. It was not a good time. You think you are next. Everyone in your circle, your crowd, might be next, the ones you had been hanging around since the days when you would have quick, glancing encounters with people as you passed through a city, a club, a party, a scene. The world seemed to accuse a certain section of people as though they had brought it on themselves through their careless, deviant behavior. Those were dangerous days, but we didn't know it at the time. We thought we were unstoppable.

Tina Chow was one of the first women to be infected. She was diagnosed in 1989, having contracted it in the mid-'80s after an affair with Kim d'Estainville. He was quite a notorious bisexual playboy, and she knew at the time she was being a little naughty. Naughtiness was not meant to lead to such devastation.

She was such a contemporary of mine, our lives almost running parallel—except she moved from America to Japan in the mid-'60s, but that move set her life in the kind of motion mine had, close to the same orbit, close to what turned out to be the same edge. She was photographed by Helmut, drawn by Antonio, painted by Andy—on the other end of the phone with Andy, him living through you, asking what you were up to today—muse of Miyake, feminine and masculine, androgynous haircut, the dressed object, the uncluttered look, blending cultural nuances from very different places, the imposed standards of perfection from her husband, the constant struggle to define herself.

Even dying in 1992 meant the tabloid headlines shrieked that she had died of "the gay plague." Tina's death made it seem closer than ever. You couldn't help but think of the people you had slept with or, even more so, of the people who had slept with the people you had slept with. It had been so easy to sleep around. In the places I was, everyone was so sexual. In Paris, it was food and sex. Wine, food, and sex. You can't leave out the wine. Sex was a vital part of individual freedom. It was meant to lead to more life, not death.

It was a catastrophic return to the days before syphilis, before antibiotics. I had always been so intrigued by sex because it was such a blank space and such a no-no growing up. For me, discovering it, savoring it, understanding it, were a part of escaping an emotional prison. The church made it seem like you would be punished in the most appalling manner imaginable if you indulged. I had made my mind up that they couldn't be more wrong. Now, it started to seem as though maybe they had a point. Sex without love, without the protection of God, led to horror.

Tina's was one of the strangest of those deaths. It was very shocking, and it still throws me even now. I'd never thought of her having an affair, and getting into a position where she would be vulnerable. It was only one night, I think, and it made me realize how easily transmission can happen. A chance meeting, a spur-of-the-moment decision, and everything changed.

Even by the time Tina died, no one really knew how you got it. People were guessing, and even when it became clearer what was involved you didn't immediately trust the information. I thought, *Well, if Tina can catch it, and sleeping around is definitely something she did not do, then anyone can catch it. It can't be difficult to get. She was very private and very careful.*

An actor and model named Angelo Colon was my double in films, and he passed away because of AIDS at twenty-eight. He would sleep over at my place and sometimes sleep in my bed, when I wasn't there. I thought, *Well, that puts me at risk.* There was a time when I believed, *It's bound to happen. My double died. Me next.* It seemed a definite sign from above, or below. The random bullets were flying all around, and some of them were grazing my skin. I was never as careful as Tina.

I remember saying to my mom, "I think I have it, I think it have caught it. I think I am next."

She was so positive. She kept telling me, "You are okay."

I got tested because my mom pushed me. I could feel it breathe down my neck. Angelo had bleeding gums, and I used to say to him, "Go and take care of your teeth." He was so gorgeous and perfect looking, with flawless skin, very careful about his appearance, but he had little things happening to him beyond his control that I now realize were serious signs.

We were in Ibiza once in the late '80s—an inevitable next stop on my trail, just as the sunshine Balearic beat was being dreamed up. I was—casually, which was becoming increasingly lethal—seeing someone on the island, a roguish, very appealing Australian, Tony Pike, who had opened the Pikes Hotel in the late '70s. One of his first guests was Stevie Wonder, who loved the place. Tony was very Hugh Hefner, and the hotel was notorious for hedonistic excess and attracting celebrities. They filmed Wham's "Tropicana" video there, with a brief cameo for Tony, and Freddie Mercury's monster-size forty-seventh birthday party was held in the hotel. Freddie knew by then that he had contracted AIDS, but very few at the party knew. The party was Studio 54/New Year's Eve in Paradise–level; the end of an era, and therefore the beginning of another.

Tony likes to tell stories about me that I am sure are quite true, or not true at all. The kind of stories that you wouldn't remember too well if they actually happened. So you will never know for sure what's real or not. I can make a few educated guesses.

Tony made up a whole lot of stuff. He went off the deep end. He was totally obsessed. He fantasized quite a bit, made up his own version of Grace Jones, and then talked about her as though she existed. I became his project, except he didn't turn me into a work of art; he turned me into a movie, or perhaps a soap opera with a hint of porn.

Men would often fantasize about me, create this very out-there creature. I am out there anyway, and I am quite happy to play their out-there version of me, to go to their extremes, but when I get home, it's over. Out there, I am onstage. At home, I am offstage. Some men couldn't understand the difference, and that caused problems. They wanted the onstage Grace Jones at all times and didn't understand how at home, behind closed doors, I am less prone to excess.

That happens a lot with me in relationships; it is not so much my personality, but everything going on around me, and how people perceive me, that creates tension. There is always a point in any relationship I have where it becomes a case of that other Grace, the Grace that has been created around me through my reputation and image—she is the one that the other person begins to respond to.

I have tried to simplify this as I've grown older, but maybe it has gotten more complicated for men. I think that when a man comes into my life, he believes he is going to get the public Grace, and not who I really am, which is much more of a house cat. I stopped going to parties (unless I am working) a long time ago. It takes a lot to get me to a party because it is so much work. After all the parties I went to, and gave, there's nothing that can really surprise me. I tend to wait until most people have gone before I turn up.

Men often have a preconceived idea of me thanks to the press. But the press me is never the real me. I work hard at never showing the press the real me. I jump on tables—that's my trademark—I scream and shout, I play the diva according to their expectations, but this is not who I am at home. I jump on tables on talk shows, I release energy and wildness during a show, but essentially I am having fun with the idea of the performance, with me as a performance. I turn myself into a kind of party, but after you've been to a party, you don't come home and have the same party.

If I go out, I go out to do something different. When I go home, I like to watch tennis on the TV. I like the pace of it all, the characters and the inventiveness, the construction of a kind of argument. I have gotten to know many of the players. This is my private passion, and it's not what a boyfriend expects, one who is expecting party Grace all the time. I used to watch with my dad. It was something we used to love doing together. He particularly loved watching the Williams sisters, Venus and Serena, either apart or together.

Now, I will watch with one of my close sister-friends, Suzette Newman, who has worked with Chris Blackwell as long as I have known him, and before that. We get so inside the matches that nothing else matters. Sometimes we go to live matches, and we often make our presence felt at Wimbledon. On the day of the Wimbledon final in 2012, between Rafael Nadal and Roger Federer, I was in the audience, but I was also due to perform in front of forty thousand at the outdoor Wireless Festival at Hyde Park across London. I had neglected to tell my management where I was in the afternoon, having decided I could fit both things in. I knew that I would be told it was impossible, but I knew I could make it work.

The final was still being played long after I was due at Hyde Park. In the end, I got changed and made up in the car on the way to Hyde Park, and eventually told my manager I was on my way—after much freaking out—arriving just in time to walk onstage and do my set. I considered this perfect timing, but Brendan Coyle, my manager, still feels the cold sweat to this day. It's a Grace Jones performance. The band is all ready. The audience is all ready. Everything is ready. The curtain is about to go up. The intro is about to be played—the actor Ian McShane intoning the words, "Ladies and gentlemen, Miss Grace Jones," as Trevor Horn got him to do during the "Slave" recording session. (How Ian got paid for supplying his voice cannot be revealed for legal reasons, alas.) But no Grace Jones. I had to see Rafael win before I did the show. I did, and still made the show, lipstick perfectly applied in a moving vehicle. I've got that down to an art, speeding through a city and getting ready for a show in the backseat of a car.

I am known for being a huge Rafael Nadal fan. Even Andy Murray knows I am in Rafael Nadal's camp. When Suzette and I were in the players' lounge during the Wimbledon 2014 tournament, we happened to bump into Andy, and Suzette asked if we could have a photograph of us together. "Oh," he drily remarked, remembering the last time I had met him, when I'd admitted my true preference. "I thought you were a Rafael fan." He genuinely did not look that impressed. He was the defending champion that year and lost the very next day. Suzette was convinced we had jinxed him, and that he thought we had purposefully put him off his game by asking for a photo. Suzette and I totally live through the matches together, whether we're watching them on television or at the venue, and from the outside our passion must look fearsome, but not in the expected Grace Jones way.

Another obsession that alienates some new boyfriends is making jigsaw puzzles. I will sometimes stay up all night doing them, usually when I need to clear my head and get some inspiration about something I am working on. In a brand-new relationship where the man is looking for the screaming idol to hit the heights, this is often not tolerated. I love the big 1,000- to 3,000-piece puzzles that Ravensburger makes, and by the end of a project I will have a finished one. I always pick up a couple at Galeries Lafayette when I am in Paris, and in Piazza San Marco in Venice, or at Times Square in New York.

I think of Kane's wife in *Citizen Kane,* Susan Alexander, alone in his big mansion, clothed in diamonds and chiffon, surrounded by majestic statues, completing puzzle after puzzle, her actions representing the passage of time, fractured personalities, and unsolved mysteries. The couple's voices echo in the vast emptiness of the hall. "It makes a whole lot more sense than collecting statues." *Why do you do it?* "I do it because I like it."

I like to cook, especially those meals and marinades that I feel have been handed down from my ancestors like bone structure and deep memories. In the end, I am quite normal. I don't have odd habits. I might dramatize things a bit, but only because I take things seriously, or sometimes not seriously enough.

I need a man who is not blinded by the temporary-performance Grace, the working Grace, the Grace that works at play. That Grace, the one people want to hang out with, the ones who want to photograph me, go wild with me—it is all very temporary, and it's a Grace that will not exist once I become a nobody in the eyes of everybody.

Tony talks of cocaine binges and intoxicated lust. Well, he might be on to something there. He remembers parties I threw in the dark on the waterfront in New York that smelled of semen and marijuana. Orgies I hosted. If a party I was at turned into an orgy, well, I always let people do what they want to do. I can't think of any warehouses where there were the kind of orgies he describes, but there would be parties

I hosted where I would wake up and there would be bodies every-where, in the bath, spread around, some who I hadn't even invited, gate-crashers. They weren't called orgies in the '60s. They were called "love-ins." Hell, I'm a hippie—like Jesus, who probably enjoyed a good love-in himself.

When I reluctantly lived for a year in L.A. with Dolph, when he was seriously pursuing an acting career, I got the nickname "the Errol Flynn of the '80s" because of my parties. It was the only way I could cope with the evil of Hollywood while I was living there. I couldn't stand it. I couldn't go anywhere, because I wouldn't drive, not into this paved-over empti-ness. I would be sent home by the police if I walked anywhere. I had the worst claustrophobia, and at the same time, I didn't want to go out into this creepy artificial paradise. I thought I was going mad, trying to scratch out some sort of personal space where I felt myself.

Getting high was how I got through, and giving special weekend parties that I would design to perfection. I would give the very best party. I would have the best coke, and let it breathe like a fine wine, pile it up and put it under a gold dome on a silver platter, with a gold spoon. I really did prefer to get the coke for others, to look after them. Then I would have the Quaalude room, the marijuana room, the Marianne Cocoa Puff room, with music in each room to match the high or the low. I would make sure everyone was well catered to, whatever their interests and tastes. No one would go wanting.

If there were ever an orgy—or love-in—in my vicinity, I wouldn't be hosting it. I would be at the center. I'd be the queen bee, darling. I wouldn't want everyone else having all the fun. And if it was in a pe-riod where I was with no one in particular, well, there would be plenty of men around who had been wanting me, waiting for me, and who were waiting to jump in. I would move around, never stay too long with one person, be very friendly with them all. None of this seemed to be taking any sort of life-threatening risk.

Venice was a great place for these kinds of parties. The ornate masks, the billowing water lapping against the walls, the sexual dreaminess. But I would always be at the center. Never anything as dreary as the host. I didn't want to run things. I wanted to perform.

At my parties, I would let people do what they wanted as long as they didn't die. That was the number one rule. People could have all the fun they wanted, but no one should die. No overdoses, no drinking too much, no collapsing, no falling out of the window, no drowning in the bathtub. No accidents. Don't spoil the party. If you wanted to kill yourself you had to leave the house and walk across the highway.

Tony says that I asked him to pick up the ugliest girls he could find so that I could watch them have sex. An ugly girl? Absolutely not! He is making that up. That is his fantasy, or his crooked memory. I experimented with a certain openness with Dolph, and he had a very open, Scandinavian approach to sex, but that was a very private thing, and not what Tony is talking about. I admit I occasionally like window dressing, if you know what I'm saying. I don't know what he means by ugly, but I was very particular about my choices. I wouldn't even want someone who had a funny voice. If their voice was odd, I would want them to keep their mouth shut, so that it didn't spoil the fantasy.

Tony says that he became my road manager and would have sex with me minutes before I went onstage because I needed the power that he was there to provide because of his colossal organ and his eternal erection. He did have an enormous penis, and I was happy to take care of it. I am not saying we didn't have sex. A few times. We weren't together for very long—and he was not my road manager. We never spent a lot of time together; I would hook up with him when I was in Ibiza, but no more than that.

He was a cool guy. I like those kinds of ebullient, charming characters, and I meet a lot of them when I travel. They help pass the time easily. Tony was another man with a full-time girlfriend I knew nothing about who tried to kill me when she found out about us. I had no idea. He started to have a huge portrait of me more or less naked painted to hang above his bed, and she was not pleased with this idea. I can understand that. She came after me with a knife. I was often the target of a spurned girlfriend with a lethal weapon.

I don't remember being at the Freddie Mercury party, like he has said I was. I was only in Ibiza when I was working. I genuinely don't think I was there. I don't think I would have forgotten that. I don't get that carried away. I think Tony made up the guest list after the event, an ideal guest list that didn't take into account who was actually there. You would think that Grace Jones should have been at such a party, so the legend becomes that I was. Perhaps it was my double, one of my clones, my shadows, the one with the epic coke problem, not me at all.

Perhaps these tall tales helped promote his hotel and his own legend. I have nothing against that, but I have my own story to protect, and I want the details to be right, or, if they are wrong, to be wrong in a way that works for me!

There was even a story that we were getting married. We made the papers on the island, around the world. It was news to me. He helped make Ibiza the clubbing capital it became. He became a mascot of it, and even though the world was slowing down, if not growing up, because of AIDS, it still wanted to party. Actually, it wanted to party even more.

I guess we would have been the royal family of rave if we had gotten married—ruling the island where people went to get stoned out of their minds, get off with each other, and see the best new DJs. But the whole point of that world was transience. It happens, it happened. If you stick around after you have your moments, it gets sad. There's a time to arrive, and a time to move on.

This is an example of another Grace Jones that gets released into the world, and then people think that is as much me as the real me. You find that your identity is being assembled by others, by the gossip and repetition of the Internet. I absorb it, I can deal with it, but sometimes the made-up Grace is so inaccurate, and she is beyond my control. There are numerous fantasy Grace Jones out there, especially now that there is the Internet, and some of them are closer to being me than others. One day we might all meet. Maybe some of us are meeting in this book. Maybe one of them didn't make it through the drug-fueled sex orgies Tony talks about. In one universe, in that Last Supper photo, I am one of those who died.

I must have come very close. There were the thousands of women whom Tony slept with—so he says, but there must have been a few. And there must have been many men that Angelo slept with. He had appetites. We talked about it. We swapped stories. This surely meant we would catch the same diseases.

One night after another crazy party at the hotel with too much drink, I saw Tony coming out of Angelo's room holding a bottle of champagne. I don't know what was going on, but in my mind I thought, *Oh, me and Angelo are sharing the same man.* Can you tell when someone is coming out of somebody's room whether they have done something naughty? Maybe, maybe not, but after that, when Angelo passed away, I put the worst-case scenario together, and imagined that I would be next. Naughtiness had become toxic, especially in a paranoid mind. You would get tested, but at that time, they said there was still a chance over the next year or two that it could emerge. The science of it was all very rough.

It was like surviving a plane crash when everyone else died. Why did I survive? My double dies, Tina Chow dies—it was getting closer and closer. My mom helped me through that period. It was such a cloud, and it was over New York, and Paris, and the whole world. She encouraged me to stop beating myself up. I made sure I stayed busy. At some point you figure, What are you going to do anyway? You have to keep going. The "enjoy life" spirit of the '70s had become "enjoy life while you can."

I was in the hospital with Angelo when he was very ill, shrinking in front of my eyes, and the closer you were to it in the flesh, so to speak, the more you began to understand about the reality. Some people would run away from visiting those dying in the hospital, but for many, seeing their friends ill cleared up of some of the preconceptions and prejudices that were circulating at the time. It cleared away the mud and misreading surrounding the epidemic. It made it more real, and somehow, even as it was awful, less vague and horrible. It was something that could be dealt with, and what was important was to face up to it, not turn away from it and keep it amorphous. Keeping it a puzzle was helping no one.

I still feel there was a conspiracy. If you hang out long enough with Timothy Leary you realize how the government is always asking for new lethal poisons to be invented. For security reasons, for defense reasons, to control populations, they would synthesize a substance that was not meant to exist in nature.

Spies need to be killed, terrorists executed. Usually the government has the antidote. This might have been something that they started to develop, and then it got away from them before they were able to discover an antidote. The way AIDS appeared out of nowhere, it makes you wonder. They blamed it on fucking monkeys. *Oh, yeah, of course. Makes perfect sense.* I think someone high up took a look at what was happening in the New York sex rooms in the mid-'70s, in the secret Studio 54 chambers, the straights that swung, the colors that mixed, and the gays exploring everything, and thought, *We need to sort this out.* They spiked the punch.

I remember when I did my shows during the '90s, I started to change some lyrics to acknowledge those who had gone. I imagined all my friends who had died were watching me and I was keeping some sort of flame going. For me to shed the depression and guilt I felt, that I had survived the parties, it was as though when I was onstage it was my job to keep them alive. I would do a riff about seeing them in the light; I would stare into the spotlight on me to the point of blindness, which is why I often wore sunglasses onstage, and talk about them being in the light, still alive. I would completely believe that my friends who had died were all around me, and that we were still together. Doing so helped me balance a little better on the tightrope.

15

The Shepherd

My dad was faced with many problems because I was his daughter. He felt that his role as a pastor and a committed Christian was undermined by my volatile reputation, and it was difficult for him to acknowledge me as his child, at least in a public setting. A number of the church hierarchy were uncomfortable with me, and it stopped him from becoming a bishop until late in life.

Appearances counted for a great deal, and as far as he could he would avoid any publicity that associated him with me. He built his parish assiduously, sold real estate for two decades, and worked hard for years in Syracuse, working closely with the local General Motors factory to find work for members of his community. He was a member of the board of directors for the Americanization League, assisting immigrants from the Caribbean. He was living a very generous, caring life, and I was essentially indulging myself in various fantasies, and selling an image of myself based around sex, drugs, and stark raving craziness.

My world was very removed from his, and although he never made me feel awkward about how I lived my life, and never told me directly that I was an obstacle to his progress, we never talked about what I did in any great detail. He would stay very much in the background, while my mother would sing on my records, and be fine if she was mentioned in interviews. She took a more active interest in what I was doing.

In the end, it was a visit to South Africa in 1993 that changed things. I went there to be a judge for the Miss World competition in the gambling resort of Sun City, eighty miles north of Johannesburg. South Africa had been barred from the competition for twenty years because of apartheid, and had only been readmitted the year before. The cultural boycott that had stopped outside artists and celebrities from visiting South Africa had been lifted, and the country was determined to show off to the rest of the world that there had been significant change. The ceremony was broadcast around the globe. The girl representing South Africa in the competition was black, the first time that had happened.

The organizers said I could bring whomever I wanted with me; they would pay for first-class tickets. My mom wanted to go so badly, and she wanted her husband to come with her. My mom loved being on the move, my dad less so, especially by then. My mom was the greatest housewife. So much of what she did got taken for granted. She was obedient, self-sacrificing, to the point of being invisible. Even if she wasn't cooking and cleaning—if someone from the church, one of the sisters, was doing it—she was the one responsible for making sure there was always dinner on the table and clean clothes for my dad according to his schedule.

She could never go away on her own terms. If he didn't want to travel anywhere, then she didn't go. Finally, I pushed her, and she started to travel on her own. These days, she's always traveling from Syracuse to Jamaica to Los Angeles and round again. She loves moving about, but back then she rarely went far on her own. I said, "Go, he will be there when you get back. Someone from the church will stay in the basement and look after Dad. Don't worry about him!"

It took decades for that to happen, but ultimately she would travel while he stayed in Syracuse. Eventually he said to me, "I will come to South Africa if you introduce me to Nelson Mandela." This was perhaps how powerful he thought I must be in the world. I had become famous, apparently; surely I knew everyone, including the man who by then was one of the most famous people in the world. Perhaps he thought it was such a ridiculous request I would never be able to make it happen, but

I swore to him I would even though I didn't have a clue how to do it. I had never met Nelson Mandela, did not know him, and had no idea how to get to him. I could have introduced my dad to Giorgio Armani, to Gianni Versace, to Mick Jagger, all of whom had become my friends, but these names meant nothing to my dad.

I promised him, though, because I really wanted him to come with my mom, and a promise is a promise. At the time, Mandela was campaigning to be president in the first multiracial elections to be held in South Africa, in April 1994, a few months after the Miss World show. He was on the road campaigning for what would be a highly historical moment, and that made arranging a meeting between him and my dad seem even more impossible.

When the Miss World jury got together, I had Dali Tambo on my right and Twiggy on my left. The other judges included Jackie Chan, Lou Gossett Jr., and Vanessa Williams. It was like being at a really bizarre wedding. Dali was a celebrity, a television personality who happened to be the son of Oliver Tambo, one of the founders, with Mandela, of the African National Congress Youth League. Dali called Nelson "Uncle," he was that close. When I mentioned my dad's dream of meeting Mandela, he said, with great confidence, "I'll arrange it." He had a TV show, so I said I would go on his show. He never said, "I'll arrange the meeting if you appear on my show." He said, "Leave it to me," but because Nelson was traveling around the country and we were in Johannesburg, it still didn't seem likely.

I mentioned to my dad that there was a small chance that he might get to meet his idol. My mom and I went on a safari, but my dad sensibly refused to leave Johannesburg. He said, "I'm not leaving, just in case he comes to the city." My dad stayed in the hotel, and then the message came through that although Mandela was tired, he would take time to see one person. He wasn't told who it was or why he was there, simply that a Reverend Robert Jones, who had founded an apostolic church in Syracuse, New York, very much wanted to see him.

My father proudly went into the meeting with Nelson Mandela, and I'm not sure how it came up, but Mandela said to my father, "Well, and where is your daughter?" It came back to me from his advisers that he would have been happy to see me as well, but if it had been between me or my dad, I would have made sure it was my dad who met Mandela. He had set his heart on meeting him.

My dad was known as the Shepherd, and there was a Mandela quote that summed up his work in Syracuse and Jamaica; "A leader is like a shepherd. He stays behind the flock, letting the most nimble go out ahead, whereupon the others follow, not realizing that all along they are being directed from behind." Months later, Mandela was elected president of a democratic South Africa.

They talked for about fifteen minutes. My father was very discreet about what they discussed, but he said that he prayed with Mandela for the future success of South Africa. They had some photos taken together shaking hands that made the Syracuse newspapers. They look like old friends meeting for a catch-up. My dad fell in love with the country. He said something about it reminding him of Jamaica, and a short while after meeting Nelson he met a young local minister whose ambition was to set up a church in Johannesburg, in the way my dad had done in Syracuse. My father loved a big crusade, and always wanted to reach out to as many people has he could.

He embarked on a new mission, and he helped this young minister to start a church, advising him on how the church could support itself, become self-sufficient, including by opening a bakery to raise funds. They named it after me, because I was the one who had helped make it all happen by bringing my dad to South Africa.

My dad used to say, "Well, God really does move in mysterious ways. You might be a sinner and a backslider," he said, not entirely joking, "but none of this would have happened without you getting me a meeting with Nelson Mandela." I must have had some considerable local influence—the winner of Miss World that we chose that year was actually Miss Jamaica, beating Miss South Africa, who took second place. My dad always said she came second because, when it was my turn to ask her a question, I asked her something so difficult to answer she didn't know what to say.

My dad returned to South Africa twice every year with my mom. The man who didn't want to travel anymore would happily make the eight-thousand-mile journey. They would sometimes bring Syracuse parishioners with them and bring clothing and goods over with them. By 2001, eight years after my father had met Mandela and fallen in love with South Africa, there were twenty churches in the area that he was responsible for founding—he became a diocesan bishop for the South African Forty-Ninth Episcopal District of the Pentecostal Assemblies of the World. My mom said sometimes it was like he wanted to move there.

He came on Dali's television show with me, and of course, once they found out my dad was a bishop, with me being such a notorious character, we helped the ratings. Behind the scenes, my dad had a sense of humor about my reputation. I think he sneaked a peek at me on the television sometimes, when no one was looking. I think he realized I was putting on a show, that it was like a circus.

When we were on TV together, he was very sensible, and answered questions very calmly. Very cool and in control, not shy at all. He had spent his life in the pulpit, after all. They asked him what they thought of what his daughter did, and he said, "Well, it's a job like any other. She does it very well. Nothing she does embarrasses me." A very simple, unflustered answer.

Years later, as an ardent fan of the tennis-playing Williams sisters, he did the same thing—made me promise that I would arrange for him to meet them, probably once more thinking that as a famous person I existed inside a world where all the famous people intermingled and met each other. I did not know Serena and Venus then, but again I managed to arrange a meeting, and he had them sign a tennis ball each. He was so proud. The tennis balls were placed in his coffin when he was buried.

I think in his own way my dad was intrigued by what I had achieved, and he enjoyed the stories I would bring back from my travels. He appreciated what I was doing, and could easily separate the apparent scandals from the truth of who I was. I think he understood that Mas P had shaken me to the core, but not obliterated my spirit or, in my own way, my faith.

In his religion you have to have your own family in order to tell other people what to do, so if you cannot get members of your family picture-perfect, you have to kick them out. He didn't do that with me, and suffered in silence, having to wait to become a bishop because of my behavior and how it was covered in the press—it set off alarm bells. In the end, he was ordained a bishop the same time as my brother, his son. He had to wait that long, and that was really down to me. He never seemed to resent it, though; he accepted me for who I was, despite it interfering with his lifetime role as a religious man.

My father died suddenly when he was eighty-three. He had gone into the hospital for some blood tests, and there didn't seem to be anything dramatically wrong with him. I was always very suspicious about what happened, because he wasn't sick when he went into the hospital, and he fell ill while he was there. I became convinced that they used an infected needle when they took his blood, and they poisoned him. But there was no way of proving it.

I was at the hospital when he died. I wasn't sure whether or not I should be there. Some people said it would not be a good thing, because the experience can be so traumatic. I decided to stay with him as he died, as he took his last breaths, and I am glad that I did. I found it the most beautiful, transcendent moment. It was very peaceful, and the look in his eyes as he approached death was something I had never seen before. It was astonishing.

As he died, the expression in his eyes was as though he was seeing something so extraordinary it took away any fear and panic he might have been feeling. He opened his eyes wider and wider, as if he wanted to see more of what he was seeing. The light never went out in his face as he died. Life seemed to enter into him. His eyes lit up.

The nurses went to close his eyes after he had passed on, and I said, "No, please don't close them, he is seeing something so important and wonderful. Keep them open a while, so that he can still see." He was seeing something that made sense of everything he had believed in for so long. I was so happy that I was there at that moment. He was not suffering or scared; he seemed to be passing into something glorious.

After he died, I found out that he always kept a photograph of me inside his wallet. He didn't think I had let him down, and he never turned his back on me. I thought he was ashamed of me, but he carried a photo of me around with him. However far apart we might have traveled at times, I think he was always praying for me and protecting me. After he died, my mom carried on where he left off. As my brother Noel says in a sermon he often gives in church, "Other people often pray for you more powerfully than you can pray for yourself."

16

Reason

According to the Internet—which is in many ways the population of the world having an acid trip—it seems as though I married or was engaged to all of the men I spent more than a few months with. Certainly Jean-Paul, Dolph, Sven-Ole Thorsen, a few others along the way, and the record producer Chris Stanley, my relationship with whom, to cut a long story short, almost led to my death in Jamaica.

It was another work-and-love, sex-and-image, together-in-art-and-life relationship. He produced my second album for Capitol, *Bulletproof Heart*. He had a studio in Kingston, Music Mountain, and he released records by Marcia Griffiths, Big Youth, and himself on his own Mountain Sound label. He said he had once worked with Billy Paul.

At some point, *Bulletproof Heart* looked like it would be my final album. The critic Robert Christgau, who once wished I had sung "Pretty Vacant" rather than "Send in the Clowns," called it "incongruous"—one of my favorite reviews ever. He was very perceptive. If I had always liked to be on top, here I was slipping a little underneath something or other. Once, you couldn't work out if I was man or woman, rock or disco, robot or animal, plant or insect, fuck you or fuck me, shriek or laughter; now I was mixing up alive and dead. It was a disorienting record, because these were disorienting times for me. Chris lived life with such force, and we were swept up together . . . and then into something very dark and traumatic.

Chris felt we had been together in some other life, where we knew each other inside out, but had to keep our love secret because together we were dangerous. He was definitely someone who liked to dramatize life, to set things going by building up tension. He was not interested in any kind of peaceful life, which suited me at the time. I like men who make me think, who make me laugh, and in Chris's case, I like men who bring the best and the worst out of me, who seem to know secret things. He had visions that we had been alive in Egypt together thousands of years ago, and that something was going to happen to us. He had forebodings about his future, and liked to be a recluse. He had a very powerful aura, a very strong presence. He had a very unusual eye color, like a dark, inky red; he was like half Rasta, half something else completely. Charming like the devil. Very talented—I am always attracted to turbulent artistic temperament, like a moth to a flame. I find creativity in anyone who feels passion for something. Because he felt we had known each other in another time, and that our relationship was forbidden, he thought our time together would end badly. Which it did. It was epic. I would need to write another book to tell that story. Or it could be an opera. Definitely a film.

I once sat next to David Lynch at a party and said, "There is a film I would like to write," and it was this story—a Jamaican ganja-gothic freak show murder mystery. "Where do I begin?" I said to him when he asked to hear what happened.

I kept warning Chris that this woman who worked for him at his studio and at his house was dangerous. He had a daughter by his ex-wife, Bernice, and we became friends because their daughter would play with Paulo. Bernice warned me that this girl, let's call her Maya, had broken them up and that she was very erratic. Chris couldn't see it. She had a big family in Jamaica, and she became very jealous when Chris and I got together.

Chris became very ill, suffering a stroke that left him with significant brain damage. I thought he was poisoned by this girl, although there was no proof. My mom said to me, "Make sure you don't eat anything she gives you." Chris got so ill he slipped into a coma, and when he woke up he had short-term memory loss, this problem where he couldn't remember more than a minute before. He had to keep writing notes to remember where he was and what was happening.

One night when we were staying in his big mansion in Stony Hill, an affluent suburb in the hills above Kingston, the police, acting on what they said was an anonymous tip-off, came in during the early hours and arrested me for possession of cocaine. That night Maya had had her cousins move Chris into a room other than the one where we usually slept. I joined him, to look after him. I was convinced she had her cousin go into our now empty room in the house and plant this cocaine, and that this was part of her campaign to get rid of me and have Chris all to herself... I had no proof but I remember once picking up the phone in the house and she was already on the line, talking to someone. This other person asked her, "Have you got that bitch inside a box yet and moved her off the island?" They were talking about me. I have never felt as chilled.

The police took me to the local station, and I spent three nights in a cold, concrete jail cell with nothing but a thin, filthy blanket and a filthier toilet. It was a weekend. I thought they were going to get rid of me, kill me in my cell and smuggle my body away. I was left totally isolated. There was a change of shift, and the next policeman on duty let me make a phone call. I managed to get hold of my press agent, John Carmen, in New York. I screamed, "I've been arrested, I've been set up! If you don't get it out there where I am, I don't think I am going to survive this weekend."

He blasted over the news to every media outlet he could. You'd have thought I'd died—the news about my arrest was everywhere. Once it hit the press, nothing could be done to me. I had to be treated according to the law; there was too much international attention being paid. John, as always, did a great job, and here was a brilliant, unusual example of the power of publicity—it saved my life, or at least saved me from being jailed for years.

I spent a year in court on and off after being released on bail, because of all the publicity. No one wanted to try the case. It was postponed seven times. I flew back and forth; there was always a lot of press, describing what I was wearing, reporting with a bias toward it being obviously true that I would have cocaine. It was front-page news in Jamaica. They had actually only found a tiny, tiny amount of cocaine in my handbag, and when I was tested, there was no trace of any drug in my blood or urine. I was looking after Chris, who was in a terrible way. I was not going to get high.

I had to keep my distance from Maya during the trial. I got my stuff from the house, and I was forced to leave Chris with her in the house. I was not allowed any more contact with him because of the court case. I pleaded innocent. The case took a month to hear, because of more delays, and finally I was found innocent. I walked out of the court and told the press, "That is a big weight lifted off me." While it was happening, Maya had taken Chris over, and after the case I had to back away and leave him with her. He didn't know what was going on, and it was horrible to see.

Chris got worse, and essentially suffered from dementia. I think she had some horrible plan, and put him under her spell under the guise of being his health caregiver. As far as I was concerned she weakened him, and he never recovered. He died a few years later, and then she started to battle with his ex-wife and his children for his estate—cars, houses. Chris was rich enough to have the kind of house on the hill that they joke in Jamaica are the kind that are only ever owned by drug dealers. (Some of these ornate mansions in the mountains never get finished because their owners are jailed during construction. They become ruins before they're even lived in.) The case was still being heard in 2004, after years of appeals and counterappeals. I think the money was what Maya was after all along.

I was never married to Chris. If I had have been, I would never have allowed this girl anywhere near him. He didn't see how dangerous she really was until it was too late.

The truth is, I only ever married one of my boyfriends, Atila Altaunbay, a Muslim from Turkey. I didn't release any albums in the 1990s, but I did introduce my father to Nelson Mandela, and I did get married. The tabloid view is that I did it absentmindedly, in jest, and then tried to ignore it and pretend it never happened, but I was very serious about it. I thought it would last forever. I always said I would never get married because I don't believe in divorce. If I'm going to get married, I don't see the point of getting divorced. On the other hand, I also always say that I want to try everything once.

I kept it as private as I could because relationships when you are famous become the target of people out there who do not want to see you happy. It is as though everything you do if you are well known is fair game, and you have to fight this energy . . . which takes an awful lot of energy that you should be saving for the relationship. There can be so much negative energy, and so I kept it as private as I could with Atila.

He didn't really know about me as a famous person and he was certainly not interested in me as a raging party monster. You get very wary of those who only want to know you because you are famous. He didn't care about fame. That impressed me a lot, that he was not bothered at all about me being famous. He was interested in the me I held back from the press, from the publicity world that was beginning to make up the hallucination of the Internet. He liked staying in the background.

Atila was quite young—it turned out he was even younger than I first thought. I met him in Belgium, but his family still lived in Turkey. He was a student, like Dolph, but he also sang at weddings. I only found that out later, that he had a wonderful voice. He was very good-looking, of course. I'm a bee looking for sustenance, craving nectar to lap up, attracted to the most eye-catching petals. We hit it off chemically, instantly, and fell in love very quickly.

Within a few months of us meeting and hitting it off, I was flying to Brazil for work, and he wanted to come with me. In a way, it became an elopement. In the Muslim family, the males must marry in order of age, and he was the youngest brother, so he wasn't allowed to get married until his older brothers did. Maybe the idea of upsetting religious rules, of rejecting family expectations, appealed to me. It was, after all, me who did the proposing—it was a leap year, and on the plane, I thought, *Well, women can propose*. I said, "Will you marry me when we get to Brazil?" He said, "Don't joke with me." I said, "I'm not!" I was being impulsive, but some of my best decisions have been made that way.

When we did the paperwork, I found out that he was a few years younger than I thought he was. He was six foot four with a receding hairline. He was very mature and responsible; his family ran pizza restaurants around Belgium; and he didn't seem boyish at all. Believe me, he looked about thirty-seven.

It turned out my husband was twenty-four. The family was soon looking to kill me! Because he was not meant to get married, not yet, and I was, shall we say roughly speaking, twice his age, or very close to it. Certainly a lot older. Naturally, when people in the media found out, his age was made even younger, and mine was made even older, so that he became twenty, and I became fifty. My age has always been very elastic, and now his was as well. I think the idea was that they wanted him to be younger than my son, which he wasn't.

He couldn't go back home, because he had disobeyed the family and their religion. He became paranoid that his brothers were hunting him down. I had met his father, but not his mother. She had a voice like me, very deep. We tried to keep the marriage out of the press, but it got leaked from Brazil. It was a very modest, rushed ceremony. We couldn't find a priest, and someone actually said the priest we used was gay, so our marriage was invalid.

But my father remarried us at our family home in Syracuse. That's how seriously I was taking it. We were married twice. My mom and dad loved him; they never thought of our marriage as a whim, or a mistake. I suppose they saw this as a part of real life, not the fantasy life I was living elsewhere. Getting married was probably the most grown-up, down-to-earth, and responsible thing I had done, in their eyes.

It was a very simple, relaxed relationship, really, connected to that part of me that enjoys being based in one place, cooking, eating, sleeping, talking. I had been on the move for so long, and to an extent still was, that being a little cozy was very inviting. We would cook for each other, talk about our families. He loved music, and in my apartment in New York, I had lots of instruments from around the world. We would sit together, banging drums and singing together. It was a long way from Tony Pike in Ibiza. It was a form of settling down, for me, and I was very happy with our lives. It was hard for him, though, being separated from his family, from his friends. His friends started to come over, but it was very difficult.

We loved each other, and he was very tender and very shy. He would come to gigs and events, but no one really knew who he was. He would make sure I was okay and then let me get on with it. He didn't want any of the attention. He would stay well in the background.

Atila was not jealous, but he could be territorial. There is a difference. He would get angry and accuse me of doing things behind his back. These things usually involved work, or dealing with old friends, or, yes, having fun, but never the sort of fun that would threaten our relationship. I was committed, and as playful as I could get with other people, I would never have let that disrupt our togetherness.

It turned out he had an aggressive streak. Jean-Paul said I had a way of bringing violence out in men because I tell the truth, because I fight back in any argument like a man. The truth hurts and I would never hold back for the sake of a peaceful but dishonest life. I have marks on my thigh to prove it.

The frustration Atila was feeling, regarding not only his worries about me, but being estranged from his friends and family, eventually erupted in our kitchen. He was holding two sharp knives, and it looked as though he was going to attack me. It seemed serious enough for me to imagine he would cause genuine harm. Physically, I was totally freaked. Mentally, I took control of the situation and gently talked him down and calmed his temper. The menace instantly disintegrated and we both started crying. Things were very different now.

There is a point in a relationship where you have to make your mind up what you can live with, and what you can live without. Violence is something I can absolutely live without. That's when I walk away. I have thrown things that could decapitate people. I would be aiming right at you. You would have to know when to duck. Once there is that kind of aggression, it is time to go before someone gets really hurt, or worse. I never wanted to be like my mother and my grandmother when it came to relationships. They were always following, always submissive.

Atila and I sat down and had a quiet talk about what had happened. He said, "I was only trying to frighten you." He thought that was a way of keeping control over me, of making sure I didn't stray too far away from him. I was all that he had, which wasn't what either of us wanted. I said, "Well, you have done a very good job, and I am now very scared of you." We couldn't be together anymore. He didn't hurt me, but there was this vivid vision of what could happen, a vision that was shaking next to the veins on my neck.

That was it. We're not divorced. We are still married. I can't find him to get the divorce sorted. He disappeared back into his family. And anyway, I don't believe in divorce.

Since Syracuse, since Sam, I have gone from relationship to relationship. If I wasn't in love with someone, someone was in love with me. People would be in my life for a long time before we became a couple. I had an Italian driver, Massimo, who was like my friend. I had known him since he was seventeen.

When I was touring in Italy and I was with Jean-Paul, Massimo would be my driver. People said, "Oh, he is in love with you," and I said, "No, never, he's a family friend, I have known him since he was a teenager." But he was always around, and anytime I split with someone, with Jean-Paul, with Dolph, there he would be, concerned, and slowly, our relationship became more intimate, and suddenly, we are together.

He waited all these years for a gap, and we got along very well because I had known him for so long. We ended up together because I am a creature of habit. It is rare that I meet someone and there is an instant connection. I prefer the slow build-up, and I am a gypsy, I am on the road. Those who are often along for the ride with me become familiar to me, and something can change.

There was a strong connection with Massimo and it did eventually spill over into a relationship. He was there all along, but not like that, not *in bed* there—*friend* there, *family friend* there. Our relationship went from the North Pole to the South Pole, but he was obviously waiting and waiting for the moment when he could move closer. Watching from afar, biding his time.

Perhaps because I was in the habit of always being with someone, it was an easy transition. I'm used to that feeling of hugging. Maybe that happens when you are not all in one piece, when you are feeling bad, after a breakup. If you are in one piece, you might be able to postpone the moment. *Don't stay with me now, I will see you tomorrow, I'm not feeling so good.* Instead, not being whole makes me open to approach. I'm vulnerable enough to feel that I want to be alone, but vulnerable enough to need some comfort. I guess Massimo, after being near me for so many years, seeing my boyfriends come and go, had worked this out.

He turned out to be the most jealous boyfriend I ever had. The sweet, sensitive friend becomes a lover and then immediately becomes extremely jealous. It felt like I couldn't go to the bathroom in a club by myself because he might think I was going to meet someone. He seemed to resent me going to a club with a girlfriend because I might be up to something with her. That became too intense. A nightmare. You would think that after knowing me for all those years, in a rock 'n' roll world, after seeing me getting high, dancing on tables all night, he would have accepted how I lived my life. But no. After waiting for years, once he finally had me all to himself, after watching me with others and being patient, he was determined not to let me go. But he had to let me go, because I let him go.

I met Sven-Ole Thorsen through *Conan*. He trained Arnie for the Mr. Universe competitions, and they were best friends. He's Danish, so I was becoming a Scandinavian connoisseur. I always stayed in touch with Arnold after making *Conan*. He would always invite me to his birthday party. I would fly in, turn up, look fabulous, dance on the tables, sing "Happy Birthday," be that Grace. Me and my sister Pam, whom Arnold and Maria liked, would be invited to various fund-raising events. I became close to Maria, and like a buddy to Arnie. I was the only female in Arnie's cigar club. I would wear a suit and be one of the guys.

One year there was an earthquake in Mexico when we were there for an AIDS foundation event for Mexican children who had been infected. I had known Sven for eight years, and I wasn't with anyone at the time, so Arnie suggested Sven bring me to the party. He was a friend, and we had this mischievous relationship as friends, and then suddenly, after being friends for so long, we got together. After all those years when nothing happened, abruptly, inside a few minutes, our relationship became something else. I wonder whether us coming together caused the Mexican earthquake.

Dolph would come down to the *Conan* set, and Sven would be there hanging out with Arnie. I was a little uncomfortable with Dolph being around, because they had dressed me in that rag of a bikini and I was almost butt-naked. I wouldn't leave my trailer for weeks, because I felt so exposed. I am at my most comfortable being naked, but I prefer to choose my own time and place when I am. I don't want to be pushed into taking my clothes off by Hollywood executives treating me as nothing but a body they've bought and think they own.

I spent a lot of time with Arnie, Sven, and Dolph. One Austrian, one Swede, and one Dane. They were very funny. When the three of them hung out on set, they would tease me via pretend, but also sometimes quite serious, fighting—expressing affection through little tussles and provocations. It was like being with my three brothers all over again. We would all be in the gym working out together, the three big men and me. I became one of the guys.

Sven, Arnie, and Dolph: very European, giant, and gentle, and fond of silly practical jokes. I understood that, and I understood their accents a lot more than many Americans because I had spent so much time in Europe. You can still hear a trace of their accents in how I speak now. I live in four or five time zones simultaneously, and I have four or five accents blended into one, a kind of French-Scandi-Latin-Jamerican.

When we were together, Sven kept me very healthy, continuing the regimen Dolph had started, but sometimes it was too much. He liked to be in the gym by seven in the morning, and if I wasn't ready, he would gently lift me out of bed and put me in the shower. It became too strict for me after a while. A little too church.

With Sven, after four years of a long-distance but close relationship, what broke us up was the Tequila Incident. There would be lots of tequila parties, and I liked tequila back when I was young and never thought about liver damage, or that it was a pleasure but also a pressure on your mind and body. Tequila was guaranteed to send me to extremes, as well, so I always know to be very careful with it.

I had a birthday in L.A., and I was with Sven. There was a surprise party at one of those drag clubs where one of the drag queens does me very well. Before I knew it, I wanted to party all night, and I was pissed off because we are in L.A. and everyone thinks that 2 A.M. is really late.

I am used to Paris, to New York, where you go until morning. I was drinking tequila and demanding that the party continue. I do remember saying to Sven, "Please take care of me tonight, because I will need you if I am going to drink tequila."

I was in such a state that Sven and my friends Sarah and Steve Newman, my publicist, had to lift me into the limo. Apparently I wouldn't shut up, going on about wanting to party more as we drove home. Sven opened the car door and jokingly told me to get out of the car. He loved his practical jokes, even when no one thought they were funny except him.

Well, I did get out of the car. Sven drove off, and his idea was to circle the block and come back and get me, probably to teach me a lesson. When he came back to get me, I had disappeared. Sven couldn't find me, so he drove off. Sarah and Steve were looking for me in the Beverly Hills bushes with a flashlight.

They didn't find me. Somehow, wearing knee-high boots, Bulgari jewelry, a Claude Montana fur stole, and dressed in the style of '50s Hollywood, I had crawled off and found an apartment complex near the highway. I woke up the next morning crumpled on the hard concrete stairs in a stairwell, clothes all wrinkled as though I had been molested. Apparently I had curled up on the stairs and taken off my boots as if I was at home in bed.

I woke up in complete confusion. *Where is everyone? Why am I in a stairwell? One minute I am at my birthday party, the next minute I am abandoned in a strange building.* I was in complete meltdown, banging on doors, crying for help. Where was Sven?

The people living there, faced with a crazy lady screaming nonsense, sensibly didn't let me in, and they called the police. A couple of young cops came. They said, "You're lucky it's us." They hadn't yet turned into some of those older, more publicity-hungry cops who like to tell the press about celebrities in distress. They said, "Where do you live? We will call you a cab."

Apparently, I was crying, "No, no, no, please take me home!" They saw that I was in such distress that they agreed to take me home.

When I got there, Sven was fast asleep, snoring like an earthquake, not a care in the world. He loved to sleep. I shook him awake and shouted, "Why didn't you take care of me? I could have died out there!" I couldn't really blame him. I shouldn't have drunk so much. I am responsible for myself, but I was so angry with him, and that was really the end of our relationship. The Tequila Incident. It wasn't the same after that night. My relationship with tequila changed a little, too.

We've stayed friends to this day, and I remember before we finally broke up, I went out, met this beautiful black girl I thought he would like, and took her home for him. I said to him, "Sven, darling, I want to introduce you to someone. . . ."

The only time I went to a psychotherapist was not for me but because my partner at the time, Ivor, asked me to go and see one with him. We'd had a very intense love affair, and worked together on my first album for many years, *Hurricane,* which I think only Ivor could have persuaded me to make. (And I could only have released it with the help of Alison Pearson, who I borrowed from Philip Treacy where she was a PA. She organized the whole project and the tour that followed as much more than simply an assistant. In my post-Island life, I need committed, loyal, incredibly energetic personalities like Alison to help me deliver my new projects.) Ivor made making music—the whole process of writing, recording, and conceiving an album—exciting again. He had a different way of working from Tom, Chris, Trevor, and Niles, but it was exactly what I needed—something different but that flowed out of the songs I had done before. I loved knowing Ivor, and being with him, and things got very serious between us. Early on in our relationship I was determined to impress him, especially because of my notorious reputation for uninhibitedness. He was a good influence on me and I didn't want to put him off. I took him to my apartment in the Meatpacking District neighborhood of New York overlooking the Hudson River—all the places I live in look over water. I hadn't been there for some time, and while he was looking around I went into the room where I kept all my old costumes. It was unbelievable—a host of flapping, squawking pigeons had found their way through the air conditioning and were happily nesting in there. Having not been used in months, it was chaos—old nests that had been used by previous occupants, new nests filled with eggs, pigeons treating it as their place. The room was packed with pigeons and shit. I was so worried that this would confirm to Ivor I was out of control that I tried to keep him out of the room. Eventually I gave in, and said, "You won't believe what's happened in there . . ." It didn't put him off. This wasn't the kind of animal behavior that was going to alienate him! We both had very traditional and old-fashioned backgrounds to deal with—mine very Jamaican, his very British—and negotiating that brought us together. After a while, we had to start thinking seriously about the future.

It reached a point where he was, and therefore we were, having certain problems, and I wanted to help him through them. So I went with him to see a therapist. He was more open to the idea. I could tell the psychotherapist was uptight as soon as we walked into the room. It was unbelievable. I needed to help her.

I had mastered therapy in my own way for my own ends. And when I went to see a therapist after many years, decades, and relationships during which I did not see one—I thought, perhaps too quickly, *What a waste of time and money.*

I studied her as she was studying us. Her shoes, her stockings, her tight, cool posture—very Nurse Ratched, the nurse in the film version of *One Flew Over the Cuckoo's Nest.* She got so overwhelmed by my background and Ivor's background. She couldn't see very deeply, and her solutions were very basic and straight out of a textbook: *On certain days of the week, make sure you do something for each other—three days you do something for him, three days you do something for her.* She had charlatan written all over her. Only the gullible and desperate could take this satanic nonsense seriously.

I have always been my own psychotherapist since I was very young. I would stand outside myself and talk to myself, talk through whatever was bothering me. There's a schizophrenic element to it, but I have accepted that part of me since an early age. I analyze myself completely, so I have never needed to go to therapy. A lot of people I knew went to therapy, and I never thought it did them any good. In fact, lots of friends come to me and I say, "You need to cry now, you need to let it out." A lot of people come up to a wall and then they cannot break through barriers. They don't know how to cry and let it all out without wanting to kill themselves.

I find that mostly in men. They won't cry. I am like that—very male. I won't cry. I am very male emotionally. Tough, with a very strong male side that I developed to protect my female side. As my own therapist, I have told myself that, and worked with it.

When I analyzed myself, I never thought of it being a way of mending myself. I saw it as a process of calming myself, or releasing tension, of making space to think, of understanding when I need to be alone. *Get to know yourself, have fun, by yourself.* That was often my decision.

Funnily enough, often the next thing that happens, after I come to the conclusion that I need to be on my own, I want to be on my own, is that I meet some guy and he moves in with me. It often takes me by surprise. *How did that happen?* I'd go away for a bit, do some work, and when I came home, there would be more clothes in my apartment, more shoes, unfamiliar furniture.

It always happens. It's never the right time, but you go along with it, see what happens. In the end, you realize the decision to be on your own was the correct one. They complain about my habits. They moan about the fact I want to watch tennis. But I don't think there's a problem with me that needs to be repaired. The solution is for me to live on my own.

Warren Robertson was a kind of therapist. As my acting teacher, he made me think about my emotional state. I could take it from him. He didn't make me feel like he was fixing something that was wrong; he was just digging into me to get me to use parts of myself to become another person. I didn't think he was saying there was something wrong with me, and I really don't like it when someone implies there is something wrong with me. Perhaps I think the next thing that will happen is that they will select a whip. Warren was simply looking at all the emotional textures that made me who I was, and suggesting ways of using these parts of me when I performed. That worked, because it is a positive action

This woman me and Ivor saw took it for granted that there was a horrible problem that needed to be resolved. She transmitted nothing positive or negative. She was blank. At the same time, there was an air of superiority about her that tilted into negativity. She made me want to kill myself. I'm not kidding. In the end, she split us up. We were closer before we went to see her.

She was blocked, and I really wanted to turn the tables and ask her questions. She was so guarded—the way she sat, the way she held her arms tight across her chest. She was only interested in our backgrounds, in talking about constructs she had invented based on a little research, not the real human beings we were, tangled up inside a relationship that was reaching a crucial moment. Our reputations went in front of us and she could not see beyond them. You could tell by the questions she asked, gathering basic information. She hit a wall, and because she hit a wall, we hit a wall.

Although she didn't impress me as a therapist that could make a difference, something tipped the scale, and she set us back. Her negativity had reached Ivor. He felt it. Everything changed. I remember thinking, *There is nothing I can do.* I wasn't there for me, I was there for him. And it wasn't working. She wasn't helping Ivor, I could see that. These things are good to talk about, but not in this way.

So I went through it, and it made me realize I'd been right all along not to do this sort of thing. I got out of there. I ran out after the session so quickly my knees buckled. I ran out so blindly into the street outside I could have been squashed like an ant under a bus.

I left, and Ivor sat where he was. He stayed behind with her. I think he was in shock. She watched as I staggered out, stunned by what had happened, and returned to this blanket blankness. There seemed to be no life in her. We gave her our life; she reacted for a moment, enough to disorient Ivor, and then me, and then withdrew behind her mask.

Ivor and I would eventually have separated anyway, but I wish it could have happened without her being involved. She was the third party. We looked for help and found Satan. I'm not sure what the end result was meant to be. I think Ivor's family felt that he was reaching a certain age and that he needed to have children and settle down more conventionally. That was somewhere I couldn't go. But that wasn't the main issue. I knew we would have to face that discussion, but it was something we needed to do on our own. She was perhaps meant to help us make a decision, but the whole situation was far too complicated for her.

I have to be particularly choosy about who I enter a relationship with. I always was, but I am even more so now. Because I feel as though I am many ages all at once, it becomes increasingly difficult to set out on a relationship with someone of a certain age who perhaps feels more fixed. I am an energy in search of energy. There aren't many places you can go where the energy you want hangs out.

It doesn't make any difference to my life in the end. People ask if I will be so choosy that I end up alone. Well, we are all alone, ultimately. If I compromise too much in a relationship, then I am hiding so much of who I am that I am still on my own. It is better to truly be on my own than to pretend that I am with someone and go through the motions, but in the end be so compromised I am even more alone. Jerry Hall will sometimes say to me, "Grace honey, you really need to settle down and find yourself a man." I am okay without a man. I have my brothers, so I am less likely to need to have a man; for Jerry, it was all girls growing up, her mom and sisters. Her dad died when she was young. She thinks I need a man, but what I need is more complex.

A relationship is always a work in progress. Both sides need to understand that's what it is. I have made a big effort in my life to enjoy being alone, so that I don't enter a relationship only because I am afraid of being on my own. I enjoy my own company because there is no guarantee even if you are in a couple that the match will last all your life. And I like myself. I'm the best form of entertainment I have! Look at my mom—her husband has died and she does not want anyone else; she enjoys life on her own. The key is to make friends with yourself. Children make imaginary friends. If I have to do that, I will do that.

They will say I'm crazy, but I will be happy. Sometimes it is better to find ways to be happy alone than to have a relationship in which you are miserable for the sake of not being alone.

Being alone is not a bad thing, unless I make it a bad thing. Being alone doesn't mean that I am waiting for something to happen, that I think being alone is second best. I am writing a song about it, about how I am alone, but I am not lonely. If you are lonely when you are alone, you're in bad company. I have plenty of friends I can call, friends I can go and see, who come and see me. So far, I have no need for the imaginary friend. I have no reason to complain. I am an energy, confident that I will find exactly the energy I am looking for. Sometimes being alone is the energy. Sometimes that energy is positive, and sometimes it is negative. It's the empty space between the stars, and it never scares me. It excites me.

17

Climax

One of the musical projects I worked on in the years between *Bullet-proof Heart* and *Hurricane* was the Pavarotti and Friends benefit for Angola in 2002, at which I was a guest. The show was one of Pavarotti's annual series of concerts in his hometown of Modena, Italy. Other guests included Lou Reed, Andrea Bocelli, Sting, and James Brown.

I am going to call the boyfriend I was with at the time Casanova. That's what he was like: very charming, exotic, Italian, a great cook, a wonderful lover. Women fell in love with him very easily. He made everything seem beautiful. He could make everyday life seem so dreamy. He would materialize on a gondola on the canal in Venice, where he lived, and I sometimes did, with a bottle of expensive champagne, wearing a black and red cape. He would have a surprise for me, and I hate surprises, but I trusted him. Before I knew it I would be looking up at fireworks that he had set off above the Venetian skyline. Even when he was in pain from a break up or even a divorce, he was positive.

He was the sort of treacherous character who if he felt emotionally hurt would cause you hurt, as if he could get rid of the pain by transmitting it to someone else. Dangerous, but alluring.

I had always wanted to sing opera. It would be the ultimate proof that I had finally found my voice and that, after the difficulties I'd had in the early years, I was truly a singer. It was especially uplifting to sing with such a demanding, knowledgeable personality as Pavarotti. He was not going to indulge me if I could not do it.

I was working on songs with Bruce Woolley at the time, after our experience on "Slave to the Rhythm." We were attempting to find an aria, because Pavarotti had asked his guests to pick a song to sing as a duet with him. People were saying that I should choose one of my old songs, the way that Lou Reed was doing "Perfect Day," for instance. Just do "La Vie en Rose," they said—a song that had become identified with me, but was still someone else's song.

I wanted, as usual, to stretch myself completely, and do something from an actual opera. My German singing teacher Madame Monbot always used to say to me, when she wanted to compliment me and give me confidence, "Grace, you have the voice of [Maria] Callas!" I approached the project as a sporting event, something I needed to train myself for, and get myself into absolute peak condition. I hired a singing coach, and Bruce and I brought in a tenor to test out the songs we were thinking of doing.

We found something from the Camille Saint-Saëns opera *Samson and Delilah* to be sung by a tenor and a mezzo-soprano: "My Heart Opens Itself to Your Voice," which Delilah sings to Samson to get him to reveal his the secret of his strength. We thought it could be sung together. We suggest it to Pavarotti. He says no. We are working at two hundred percent strength trying to crack the problem. We send him a couple of other suggestions. He is still not happy.

We think of a duet between two men, where I could sing one of the men's parts. Another refusal. I am beginning to despair at all the rejections, and start to think I should not do it. I am in a great amount of distress, and I go to stay with Casanova in Venice, a couple of hours' drive from Modena. While I am with him, I get more and more stressed about the Pavarotti problem. I cannot sleep at night, I am pacing around like a tiger. I eventually decide that I am going to say I cannot perform. Enough is enough. I am going to pull out.

Casanova's father is a music lover with a deep knowledge of music history. He suggests a sublime aria from Jules Massenet's *Werther*, "Pourquoi me réveiller"—*why do you wake me up, you breath of spring.* As someone who likes to sleep late, I love the title. Also, I am in such a state that I feel that being woken up will remind me of the dilemma I am in. The opera is about how the love that burns with the brightest flame is often the one that is fated to fail—been there, done that—and it has a classic melodramatic plot, about a poet who would rather die than lose the woman he loves. The aria leads to a suicide.

We send it to Pavarotti. He says yes. It is such a relief.

And then, more stress, because the duet is now on. The pressure starts to build up. I train like an athlete. I give up all vices. One night, to relieve the tension, I succumb to some strong, sticky Italian liqueur, and I completely panic and have a meltdown, thinking it will mess up my voice. I am scared. I have betrayed myself, broken my vows. I break down in tears in front of my singing coach, who explains that it will have an effect, shaving off a little fraction of my range from both sides of the three octaves I can sing, from both the high and the low end, but that my voice will come back in time for the show.

Casanova is being very supportive and feels very involved, because his father recommended the song. I wrote a song about him when he was having marriage troubles, because he was the kind of man who would always have a wife and a mistress, and because he had this way of getting very emotional and taking it out on the ones he loved. The song went: *Did I come too soon, or did I come too late, because now I am in the middle of your heartbreak, and your heartbreak will become my heartbreak—* very deep, below Dietrich, completely gut-wrenching. One day I will record it.

Pavarotti's father was dying during the early rehearsals, so the atmosphere was extremely heightened. He died two days before the performance, but he had told Pavarotti on his deathbed to carry on with the show and to on no account cancel it. "I will be with you on the stage," he told his distraught son. Pavarotti had been suffering from a bad flu and was not very well at all, and mostly sat down for the rehearsals. The melodrama in all the songs we were singing was hanging heavy over the entire production, and there was a real sense of what it takes to perform these very overwrought, technically complex pieces.

During our rehearsal on the day of the show, I was a nervous wreck.

There was nowhere to hide, no room for emotion, which was odd, considering opera is all about the expression of the deepest, wildest emotions. I started to sing my part, and Pavarotti immediately waved for me to stop. He was not looking me in the eye, and he appeared deeply distressed. I instantly thought that after all my preparation I had fucked up. I was hurled back to Philly and the disaster with Gamble and Huff. *I have failed. I am not a singer. The master has passed judgment.*

Eventually, after a considerable, tense pause, he sat in his chair, looked up at me, eyes filled with tears, and waved his hanky at me to continue. Later, a local journalist who was seated next to Pavarotti's sister in the stalls told me what had happened.

Apparently, when I started to sing, his sister shrieked in alarm, "That is my father's voice!" My voice had the exact timbre of their father, who had died two days before, promising that he would be there onstage with Pavarotti. That was why he stopped me. He heard his father's voice too, coming out of my mouth, and was completely unnerved.

After the rehearsal, I am with Casanova in the dressing room, which is a tent that is open to the stars clustered in an inky black sky. All around us there are trained opera singers all going through their preshow vocal exercises, practicing their scales: *Whoo aaah uuuhh eeee ohhhhh. La-la-la ooh ooh ohh.* All these whooping, bleating, blowing noises as they warm up, a chorus of abstract tunings and vocal stretching. Casanova and I are very caught up in the moment, the stars shimmering above us, feeling part of an amazing evening, the tension dispersed after a draining rehearsal, cooing at each other how much in love we are, overwhelmed with the romance of the setting.

Suddenly, he takes hold of my ankles, pushes my legs apart, and starts to passionately lick my pussy. I am wearing a huge billowing skirt, and he easily disappears inside it between my legs. Anyone looking on would not see him, and assume I am on my own. He is giving the tongue action his most sophisticated Casanova attention, and I start joining in with the vocal stretching and tuning going on around me. I scream and whoop, *La la la ooh ooh ooh eeee ee eeee,* higher than them all, make noises that pierce the sky and reach the stars, clearly considered by those near us to be the most enthusiastic and liberating vocal exercises ever. My orgasm is operatic. Fireflies scatter into the night, each with its own incredible story to tell. Casanova has set me up in the way he knows best for my performance.

The duet went perfectly, and those who never thought I had it in me stared openmouthed at how I sang. I wore what I considered an operatic hat—fabulously big, designed by Philip Treacy, a flowing white number that made me look like a Dalí flying nun. A little religious undertone. In opera, either you are big, or everything else is. It had to be a big, show-stopping hat.

I have put all my discipline and strength into this single point. All of the searching and anxiety I went through to find a voice explodes and implodes as I sing this intense suicide song with one of the greatest singers of all time. After the show, Pavarotti doesn't let go of my hand as he moves around his guests. He doesn't let me go for an hour.

Casanova has gone. He has left me alone. Perhaps he thinks his work is done. Or he had to go back to his wife.

The next morning, when I woke up in my hotel in Venice, everyone else had left, everyone I had invited: Paulo, my mother, my friends, all the people I wanted around me on such a night. I was totally alone. I had been on such a high, had reached such a pinnacle, having done something that was down to my singing—not to my image, my partying, or my appearance—and now I felt completely devastated.

I think everyone left because their way of interpreting what I had done was that it was a triumph, and that I had proved that side of Grace Jones that people assume is all of what I am. The confident, immune, strong, unshakable Grace, who doesn't need any moral support, who has gone to such a powerful place there are clearly no doubts, and no fears. I am fiercely independent, but I suppose I am scared of being abandoned.

They thought I didn't need them around. I obviously believed in myself. I had proved I was a singer in the most taxing of circumstances. It never occurred to them that this was the moment I needed them the most. I had reached the summit. This was everything I had ever wanted and now I had done it. There are moments when you have nothing left to give. I needed them to help me come down from the high I had reached.

I sat stunned on my own for a while. I looked at the canal outside my window, which had looked exactly like that for hundreds of years, representing the slow, slow passage of time. A small thought entered my mind that I should jump in and disappear into all of this time, and then the thought immediately vanished. I got dressed and went to find out where everyone was.

18

Issue

I come from the underground. I am never comfortable in the middle of the stream, flowing in the same direction as everyone else. I think people assume that's where I want to be, famous for being famous, because as part of what I do there is a high level of showing off, but my instinct is always to resist the pull of the obvious. It's not easy, especially when you have had any sort of success, because then people want you to repeat what it was that made you a success, even if your instinct is to move on, or to want to change, or have other ideas.

My biggest success came not because I was chasing it but because I was following through on my impulse to change. What was exciting about those early Compass Point sessions was that we were making something that sounded new, that came from the outside. We weren't chasing fashion. Later, that kind of sound seemed fashionable. At the time we recorded it, it sounded almost uncannily, riskily fresh.

The industry always wants you to play it obvious. The way a corporate company works can never involve the kind of flexibility and spontaneity that encourages the innovation that leads to the biggest sort of commercial success. Capitol Records was very corporate that way, and that world does not work when it gets involved with creative decisions. The employees are working for the company, not for the artist, and their loyalty is always to the company. Their interests are in satisfying the financial needs of the business, not in allowing the artist to develop and perhaps make the sort of music that ends up making a lot of money. The truly creative artist succeeds and makes a profit in ways that the corporate mentality can never anticipate, because that success is based on completely new ways of doing and seeing things.

Sure, following trends, singing the obvious, might make you wealthier. But does it make you happier? If your goal is to make a lot of money and it doesn't matter how you do it, then fine, that is your goal.

You can listen to the label, and sometimes you can follow their advice, or bear it in mind, but in the end you have to remember what the seed was you planted in the first place. What it was you intended to become as you started out. *What was that seed you planted? A rose, an orchid, an apple, a plum, a lemon—what?* You have to remember that. You cannot interfere with that process; what it was you wanted to be has to be what you keep being even as others try and make you change.

You can get sidetracked. A hurricane can wash you away. Trends comes along and people say, *Follow that trend.* A big act emerges, and the advice comes in: *Why don't you follow them?* Even if it was a trend you might have set in motion thirty years ago, and you don't really want to do it all over again. There's a lot of that around at the moment. Be like Sasha Fierce. Be like Miley Cyrus. Be like Rihanna. Be like Lady Gaga. Be like Rita Ora and Sia. Be like Madonna. I cannot be like them, except to the extent that they are already being like me.

I have been so copied by those people who have made fortunes that people assume I am that rich. But I did things for the excitement, the dare, the fact that it was new, not for the money, and too many times I was the first not the beneficiary.

Every now and then a little devil sits on my shoulder and says, *If you had done it that way,* or *If you were white, well . . .* Now and then that comes into play, if you didn't mind that the music was industrial and formulaic, and then I think, *Oh no, then I would be like all the rest.* All these little babies I have had.

Rihanna . . . she does the body-painting thing I did with Keith Haring, but where he painted directly on my body, she wears a painted

bodysuit. That's the difference. Mine is on skin; she puts a barrier between the paint and her skin. I don't even know if she knows that what
she's doing comes from me, but I bet you the people styling her know.
They know the history.

My advice to them is: *Why don't you find your own voice?!* It all
backfired on me, because I set out to inspire other people, but those
I inspire tend not to be inspired in that they do their own thing, but
in that they do my thing, a little their way, but not much. Take out the
me—the dressed-up me, the disco me, the post-disco me—and there
is not a lot left.

I couldn't sell out, but I created the space for others to be able to
make it, without the pressure of being the pioneer. They can play the
pioneer without taking the actual risk. Because to take the risk means
to never soften enough that you can become truly successful. It means
saying no to things that might give you success . . . but not necessarily.

I am to this day a radical about not going with the flow. I decided
after disco that I would not follow the formula, that I would create
something else. If I had followed the crowd, by now I would be as rich
as people think I am.

Perhaps I worry too much about integrity. Perhaps that is now an
old-fashioned concept. Worrying about it too much means that I become a Norma Desmond character, stuck in my ways, despairing that
the world is leaving me behind.

What is integrity? I think it's about identity. I worked so hard finding myself that I don't want to lose myself by becoming a caricature.
It's so easy to lose yourself by following others and joining a gang. It's
a constant fight, and people around you can be very convincing, so it is
easy to say yes.

I remember when one of the singers on the list of those who came
after me first said that she wanted to work with me. Everyone around
me is going, *You have to do it, you have to do it, it will be so good for you, it will
introduce you to a whole new audience, you will make a lot of money. . . .* I had
to put my foot down before I suddenly found myself pretending to take
risks, singing something stupid with her in some cheap, surreal setting.

No! It will be good for *her;* she will draw from everything I have built and add it to her brand, and I will get nothing back except for a little temporary attention. No one could believe that I said no, but I am okay on my own. I am okay not worrying about a new audience. If the fuck don't feel right, don't fuck it.

My instinct is that such a collaboration will not work. I don't completely shut the door, but I want her to show me what she can do that will make it worthwhile. I have been through the jungle, through stormy oceans of time, to find myself and I can't throw that away so easily. I would be a traitor to myself if I worked with someone only because they were the biggest thing on the planet, not because it made collaborative sense. And the biggest thing on the planet these days can very quickly become a normal-size thing on the planet, a shrunken-size thing, and they might drag me with them on their rapid decline.

I do a lot of collaborating, but I like to collaborate with people I can learn something from. I didn't think there was anything I could learn from this person, or from those others who ask me all the time, the kind that have periods in the middle of their names.

With this one, who I will call Doris, I thought she was trying on other people's outfits: She's a baby in a closet full of other people's clothes, a little girl playing dress-up, putting on shoes that don't fit. I could see what she wanted to be when I watched her doing something when she started out that was starker and purer. Deep down, she doesn't want to do all the dressing-up nonsense; she loses herself inside all the playacting. All this other stuff, it was the act of someone who is lost, and saying yes too quickly, and trying on the clothes of others— she'll have that following her for the rest of her life.

That's all it would be: business. Well, I've turned down so much business—you wouldn't believe the business I have turned down—if I give in now, that makes a waste of all the time I stood my ground because I believe in something. I say no more than I say yes in my career. I am the worst person to work with if you want your ten percent. I say no to most things. I'll turn up at a corporate event and spring out of a cake or an animal in full Grace Jones mode, but that is clearly a business transaction. There is no pretense that this is a creative act, and yet doing such a thing seems more creative than performing a duet for the sake of getting attention.

My power comes from standing my ground—empowerment, it's where my strength comes from. It's not meant to intimidate anyone but me. It's respect for the journey I have taken where I did not do things I felt were wrong. It makes me more stubborn now not to give in, even though I'm told, *If you don't do such and such a thing, then you are a has-been.* I never feel like a has-been, only a been-to.

I am disco but I am also dada. I am a sensualist but also a surrealist. That underground spirit—from the Beats, hippies, civil rights pioneers, punks; from the experimental artists, technicians and designers—dissolved into what became known as independent, as alternative, and that's become less and less subversive, and less resistant to a co-opting commercial pull.

The mainstream absorbed the idea of the underground, and in the process made it difficult for there to be an underground, because if there is, it is quickly spotted and undermined. It is difficult to explain what it was like back then, to be so careful about the kind of work you did that you didn't feel like a sellout. A lot of people now do not get the concept of the sellout. This is another thing that sometimes makes me feel a little Norma Desmond—that I am still wary about doing something that puts me in the middle of the current MTV/streaming flow, which all looks like something I did back in the twentieth century, at five in the morning in 54 or the Garage, or with Jean-Paul and Keith Haring, or on a red carpet leading to the sort of delirious humdrum glamour now being endlessly recycled.

I am wary, because to recycle myself means becoming a cartoon. I'd rather be a memory of something fantastic than join in with the party as it is now, filled with people copying something that happened before they were born.

There is stealing, there is inspired by, there is nothing new under the sun, which means that if you live to be a hundred, you realize the same things come and go, come and go. There is a lot of shortsightedness now. I always saw myself as a long-distance runner. The problem with the Dorises and the Nicki Minajes and Mileys is that they reach their goal very quickly, and there is no long-term vision, and they forget or never understood that once you get into that whirlpool as the performer constantly shifting identity, the entertainer creating shock, the singer acting larger than life, then you have to fight the system that solidifies around you in order to keep being the outsider you claim you represent. There will always be a replacement coming along very soon—a newer version, a crazier version, a louder version. So if you haven't got a long-term plan, then you are merely a passing phase, the latest trend, yesterday's event.

My goal was never to be controversial for the sake of publicity, of self-promotion. I wore what I wore—or didn't wear—and acted like I acted because it was who I was, and I was making myself into a performance. I acted the same way before I was famous. I did it when I was a no one, when no one was looking, and I would have kept doing it even if I had stayed a no one. The craziness was there. I went to extremes. That didn't come with fame. It became part of the fame, because that was me already. It was how I had learned to guard my body from evils. The craziness was the fire I lit to keep danger at bay.

Once you have the attention, once people know your name and think they have you figured out, that's when the work really begins. To only be known for a year or two because you are outlandish, extreme, and nakedly in people's faces is relatively easy. It's what comes next that is difficult. That is really where it becomes conceptual. How you maintain the momentum, how you develop yourself, how to keep from drowning in it all. From disappearing.

I feel sorry for a lot of them. They lose their minds. They lose their way. They get pushed around by the system. They are not driving the system, as much as they like to act as though they are. The system is driving them, which in itself completely contradicts the concept of the artistic freedom these performers claim to embody. They are not free, for all their apparent wildness. They are controlled, and living up to a very narrow set of expectations. And many of them do repeat poses and wear costumes that some of us were striking and wearing forty years ago, without the risk attached that it is for the first time, that it does symbolize outsider energy that the mainstream finds provocative and dangerous.

They dress up as though they are challenging the status quo, but by now, wearing those clothes, pulling those faces, revealing those tattoos and breasts, singing to those fractured, spastic, melting beats—that *is* the status quo. You are not off the beaten track pushing through the thorny undergrowth finding treasure no one has come across before. You are in the middle of the road. You are really in Vegas wearing the sparkly full-length gown singing to people who are paying to see you but are not really paying attention. If that is what you want, fine, but it's a road to nowhere.

I had many chances to take the easy road and become a safe, predictable entertainer, but I always chose to reject doing the obvious because that was never part of the original vision. If I didn't like something, if it did not make me feel comfortable, I didn't do it. So sue me. Most of all I have to be happy in what I am doing. If I don't like something that you are making me do, then I will make your life hell. If I am miserable doing something, I am going to let you know.

My guard is always up when it comes to my work and my performance. I keep my eyes wide open, because to stick around in this business among all the people who want to lobotomize you and fuck you up takes a lot of inner strength. Maybe this all comes from those early, monitored acid trips, a certain clarity I have about what makes me tick, and what makes me happy.

I've been told that I have been an influence on many of these new singers—on how they appear, their manner, their style. That was never my intention. I never really thought about anyone else. I was narcissistic in a militant sense. *Oh, I like that, that's different. I want that, because I want to be different.* Difference attracted me. Being different was natural to me. And I was immediately attracted to people who were different.

I look at Doris and I think, *Does she look happy?* She looks lost, like she is desperately trying to find the person she was when she started.

She looks like really she knows she is in Vegas, now that Vegas is the whole entertainment world filtered through the Internet, through impatient social media. I don't mind her dressing up, but when she started to dance like Madonna, almost immediately, copying someone else, it was like she had forgotten what it was about her that could be unique. Ultimately, it is all about prettiness and comfort, however much they pretend they are being provocative.

I would like to be a tutor for some of these singers. I would like to help them avoid becoming a piece in the system. It would only take five minutes. I would say to them, *Get out! Quick! Don't go back for your possessions! Run! There is only hell ahead, the hell of having to cling onto fame by doing what others tell you, the hell of losing fame because they don't really know what they are talking about, and are not interested in you, who you really are, or who you will be in five, ten, fifteen years. They will replace you if you don't do what they say. They will replace you if you don't want to be as commercial as they want you to be. They will replace you when you are not sexy anymore, and if what you are is nothing other than about being sexy, you are doomed. Get out! Run! There is more to life and entertainment than sexy, the sexy organized around you by the system, which is the system set up by men. Take time out and reflect on what inspired you in the first place that came from within you. Jump off the merry-go-round.*

I don't want it to look as though I am moaning about them because I am jealous or feel replaced. With these singers, it's not that they are new and amazing that bothers me. I love seeing new talent. It can be an inspiration. I like to be inspired. It is more that I am disappointed with what has happened to them, that they have fallen into the same old traps. They didn't really learn from those of us who went there before. I'd rather be defaced by them than meekly followed.

Some of them do have something, but they never stay true to what that is, because they get distracted by those urging them to shed those parts of their character that are truly interesting, not simply commercially attractive. Doris in her provisional, original state is the closest she gets to herself, and her public persona reflects who she really is, but she is getting further and further away from that. This other thing, the second-, thirdhand dress-up thing takes over.

I sometimes think even though she doesn't sing or perform in a conventional manner, Kate Moss is more of a rock-and-roll star, a pop star, than most of the singers playing that role. Certainly more than the likes of Doris. In terms of power and mystery, Kate has more going for her, and she's a real survivor with whatever is thrown at her. The way she stays positive in dealing with all the shit is often a big help to me when I feel down. I often help her out with man trouble, women problems, with her children, with work.

I've known her for twenty years. Because we are hard workers traveling the world from job to job, we would always bump into each other on airplanes. When you do this kind of job, in whatever form it takes, there are plenty of people, brands, companies, and magazines keen to suck out of you whatever it is that they need to fuel their own energy and presence. They don't care if they suck everything out of you and leave you stranded, alone—or worse. They just move on to the next source of energy. It's very difficult to survive for long periods of time without losing your sense of purpose.

Kate is very good at dealing with it all. My way is often to lash out. If something hurts me or someone tries to rip me off, I hit right back, I get it out my system so that I don't become a victim. If I don't hit back, that's when I end up ill, or with a nervous stomach, or worse. It's the fight in me. I take the punches but I punch back. I don't become defensive, I go on the offensive. I know how to fight! And I can fight dirty. . . .

Kate has the thing I have, and Jessica, and definitely Jerry—more sometimes than me—which is why we have all survived many years in what is mostly a battering, unforgiving business that really wants to use you up, take what they need from you, and then move on to the next specimen. We end up a little warped, and probably misunderstood, but we refuse to be sucked dry.

Kate often says to me that I am the only performer around at the moment who deserves to be called a diva. That gets us arguing, seemingly a little too serious if anyone hears us. I hate that word *diva*. It's been so abused! Every singer given a makeover or a few weeks on a talent show seems to be called a diva these days! Christ almighty. Where's the exclusivity? It's so commercial now. Call me something else. Call me by my name. For me, a diva is like the great opera singer . . . the great film star . . . out of reach, in their own world, with a real gift for invention, even if it's just their way of entering a room, fame in the purest form, attention-demanding performance artists with a flamboyant, compelling sense of their own importance, so special and inimitable it verges on the alien . . . and of course the word is usually used to describe an apparently erratic female whose temperamental qualities, survival instincts, and dedication to perfection are seen as weaknesses, as self-indulgent, not a strength. So, Kate, I am not a diva. I am a Jones!

Doris came to see me backstage at a concert once after a show. I was surrounded, so we never got a chance to really talk. Ever since, she has sent messages that she wants to work with me. They keep coming, although she never directly contacts me. She tries to get to me through my management, through my brother Noel.

People are surprised that I am not interested in collaborating, but the idea does not immediately inspire me, it does not seem attractive. What would it be the point? What has she got to offer me that I haven't got already? What would I learn?

One thing she has got that I haven't got is the way she plays an instrument, and that might be a way forward to a serious collaboration. A basic, unexpected musical collaboration. But I don't think that's what anyone is looking for from a collaboration between us—they want the wildest, crudest, most monstrous Grace Jones along with the wildest, goo-goo Doris, to satisfy a cheap expectation, a clash of egos, of costumes, of tits and crass, of managed extremes, and it would be a fuss for a day or two, analyzed to death for a few hours, recycled in pictures and headlines, and then it would be all over.

What would that mean? It would certainly be a waste of my time. And what would she get out of it? I'm not sure, really. She would demonstrate perhaps that she is a fan, but I think she has already shown that—as Rihanna has—in the way she dresses and performs. Is she looking to pick my brains, ask me questions about why I've done what I've done the way I've done it? Well, we can do that in private.

One way of collaborating would perhaps be some kind of performance, to be seen by no one, where we talk about fame. I could speak
about my experiences, and how they're really disconnected from who
I am and why I do what I do. I have never done anything to be famous.
Fame is awful. Fame is the worst part of this. People don't realize this
until it happens, and usually they're not ready for it at all. When you're
famous, everyone has an opinion about you, mostly wrong and abusive,
and if when fame hits you are not absolutely rooted in the very earth,
then it can ruin you. You have to be absolutely focused before you become famous to be even a little focused after.

Everything comes at you when you are famous. Even the most talented and grounded people can get swept away unless they have the
right sort of people to turn to for help. I was extremely lucky that I had
Chris Blackwell. I say *lucky,* but there was an element of destiny about
it. He got me, and he understood that I was not contriving to seek publicity, or chasing fame. He understood why I made the decisions I made,
and what I wanted beyond the fame, which passes through you as you
pass through.

If you can meet someone like that, it helps you make the transition
from being someone who behaves in a certain way for a certain amount
of people, to becoming someone who behaves the same way you always
do, but now in front of lots and lots of people. I sometimes think it
would have been good to have had the private conversation I could have
with some of these new fame-crushed singers with Michael Jackson.
Fame distorted his life, so that because he was good at something, singing and dancing, he then had to deal with this other thing, for which
there is no real training.

I talked with him for a while during one of those moments where
we happened to be in the same place. We had a tiny bit of time to talk
when we were both in a recording studio at the same time, with not
a lot of other people around. There was that unusual quiet where you
actually talk about real things that might be on your mind, a quiet you
felt he very rarely got. He shyly asked me about breaking away from
the family, because that was something he knew I had managed to do.

When your world changes so much and yet you are still bringing the family with you into this new state of being, it only adds to the problems.

Michael asked me how I had managed to break away from all the obligations and expectations. He wanted to know how to go out into the world, whatever the dangers, without that extra complication of the family watching over you, sticking close to you, stopping you grow. It was a big pressure on him. My family was deeply religious, and there were a lot of siblings. There was a certain resemblance to his situation. I was, in my small God-fearing Spanish Town setting, the equivalent of a child star, performing on behalf of my family, who effectively managed me, who never wanted me to grow up.

"How did you get away?" he asked. My answer was very simple. I said, "I just did it. You just have to do it. Don't think about it. If you do, you hesitate, and it becomes a problem. Once I was free of their influence, I couldn't think about how I was the daughter of a preacher, and I had a responsibility to behave how they wanted me to. I was out there crazy."

I remember being on *The Merv Griffin Show* in a full-body flesh suit, and my father, he told me later, was appalled. He thought I was naked. In his eyes, I was. As naked as the devil spitting fire, dripping with sleaze and grinning for the hell of it. This was who I was going to be, and I was going to enjoy myself; I couldn't think of what my family would think. It wasn't about them. It was about me.

I had to follow my own path, or I would always feel held back, and frustrated.

I told Michael to do it, to walk out on them and let the chips fall where they fall. If you think about it too long—think about it and think about it—then you get torn apart while you are waiting to make a decision. By the time you make your mind up, it can be too late. Michael could never really make those decisions in time, and by the time he did, it would lead to more problems for him to deal with, and that meant he found it even more difficult to make decisions that could help him.

If Doris and I had that conversation, I would tell her that fame is not inside you, it is outside you. It comes from outside, and you cannot control it. Everybody wants to be somebody, but at the same time, now that everyone is acting like they are someone, there is something more special about being anonymous. Fame doesn't make you somebody. You are already somebody.

There are only a few things I enjoy about being famous. Meeting other famous people is one! So you can talk with each other and say, "Isn't being famous a drag? Don't you wish you could still do what you do without being famous?" When you walk through that door, through to the other side, where there is fame, you cannot believe how different it is.

You can get all the pussy and dick you want. Everything becomes available. It goes to your head. But how do you know how to deal with all the people suddenly around you who are only really interested in you as a famous person? How do you work out who likes you because of who you are, not who they think you are?

You drink too much. You take drugs. You get arrested. You are in a situation where your new position is always being celebrated. Every day is like a wonderland. You start spinning.

You see your fans look at you—*Oh my God, oh my God*—and it's not clear how to handle that. I remember when I was on my first *Tonight* show with Johnny Carson, and everyone was going, *Ooh, you've made it now, your life will never be the same again.* For me, it was a part of my job, which I liked doing. It didn't make me into a goddess or anything; it didn't make me immortal. It was just a good way of telling a lot of people who you were and what you did. You don't want to make a record and have no one know about it. There was plenty of promotion I didn't want to do, but there were some things I couldn't turn down.

I like chat shows. I like the feeling they have of private conversation. You can make a connection. I always wanted to interview the person interviewing me. Sometimes, doing big shows, it's like you are connecting with no one. I never really like a huge audience. I find that I have to have fun on my own, by myself, and hope the audience does too. I find it very hard to get fifteen thousand people to enjoy what someone is doing in unison. Arena-sized venues never suited my minimalist approach.

I am not a big mover. I like to move in slow motion. As slow as possible. I prefer the power of stillness. I prefer the power of the preacher, who is more about getting you to listen, to focus on what you are doing. I don't go in for distraction. I don't want anything to distract the audience but me.

This is what I would say to my pupil: *You have become only your fame, and left behind most of who you were. How are you going to deal with that? Will you lose that person forever? Have you become someone else, without really knowing it? Do you always have to stay in character for people to like you? Do you know that you are in character?*

Doris, I would say, *fame is all well and good if you want to take it to another level. If you have some greater purpose. Me, I am just a singer, on one sort of stage or another, who likes to have an audience, but not all the time. Listen to my advice; I have some experience.*

In a way, it is me being a teacher, which is what I wanted to be. I still feel I could go into teaching. What is teaching but passing on your knowledge to those who are at the beginning? Some people are born with that gift. With me, the teaching side morphed into the performing side. It's in there. And these are my pupils—Gaga, Madonna, Annie Lennox, Katy Perry, Rihanna, Miley, Kanye West, FKA twigs, Doris . . . and Russell Harty: I think he would have liked being in that class.

I wonder if sometimes this really is an inevitable Norma Desmond moment. "I *am* big. It's the *pictures* that got smaller." I am being replaced, now that the movies are in color and have sound, rather than simply mourning a loss of subversive power and deeper meaning. I am isolating myself, cutting myself off from new influences, as opposed to continuing what I have always done, craving the next, from occasion to occasion, event to event, day to day.

Am I holding on to the past? I don't feel that I am. I don't ever feel that I think of time as being past, present, and future, so I don't feel like I am yearning for better days. I still think of better days as being then, and now, and soon. I am as young as I ever was, because I can move and think, in the real world and the unreal world, exactly like I always have done. If I am from another era, everywhere I look, at the electric sheep all around me, it all seems to indicate that we are still inside that era. There is no new era, only the one I am still part of being stored and restored.

If I were Norma, that would mean I have already retired. I will never retire. When I retire, I'm dead, and even then, I will be reincarnated. I will remain on the move. Even death won't stop me. It never has. You can find images of me from centuries ago. Faces that look like mine carved in wood from ancient Egypt, Roman times, the Igbo tribe of southern Nigeria, and sixteenth-century Jamaica, fierce enough to turn people pale, to shrink their hearts. I have been around for a long time, heart pounding, ready to pounce on my prey, blurring borders, speaking my mind, believing that the world is full of visible and invisible forces, crossing the water, tripping, grieving, loving, hunting, conquering, seducing, fighting, dreaming, laughing, and I always will be.

19

Grand

I hate being vulnerable, but sometimes to feel vulnerable is actually to be strong. To write this book is being vulnerable, and it is the only way it will work—not to close off, but to open up, which takes a lot of strength. People think I am very tough and, sure, I can be very tough, but to be really tough, you need to be vulnerable. Sometimes you need a good cry. In private. Not necessarily about yourself, but about others who you have known and loved, who you still know. It makes you feel, and sometimes when you shut yourself off so much, you stop feeling. I don't think of time passing, but it does, and I don't get sentimental about that, but I feel it, and notice it.

People I know from twenty, thirty years ago look older. They look at me, and I don't really look older, for whatever reason. They ask, *Have you sold your soul to the devil?* I think it's because I don't believe in time, I don't believe in age, I don't believe in getting older. I believe in getting wise. I believe in having more memories.

I'll never forget this *Twilight Zone* episode I watched where all the faces looked like the faces of the women in the *Housewives* programs: bloated lips, ballooning cheeks, distorted, warped, sliced up, oddly proportioned. People today often look like they are from this episode of the *Twilight Zone* where the idea of being so facially maimed was a living hell. There are people I knew thirty years ago whom I now don't recognize because their faces have gone through so many changes. They are attempting to retain their youth, but their efforts don't make them look younger, only stranger.

People ask me if I have had work done to my face. I say, "No, I fucking haven't." *Would* I have work done to my face? No, I fucking wouldn't. Why would I want to look in the mirror and not recognize myself again? Why would I want to see myself in the mirror and wonder, *Who is that?* That sounds like the definition of madness. Of course, I am also very afraid of needles. And pain.

Then people say, "Well, one day you will have surgery, when your face finally does start to age."

I say, "Well, no I won't. Absolutely not."

I am not sure what people think they are doing. The pressure in certain worlds and professions has become that if you don't have Botox, filler, a face-lift, you don't belong. It's like peer pressure at school trying to keep up, but it's a global peer pressure among adults. The individual spirit has been devoured. Everyone starts to look the same as well, which makes you think that in thirty or forty years there will only be about thirty or forty separate looks. The world will be full of monocultural clones, all adopting and repeating an apparent, ultimately very stale, ideal.

There is a mass panic among women, especially, and it seems to lack humor and wit—it's a form of self-destruction. Those who surgically alter themselves seem indifferent to how grotesque it makes them look. Attacking their own faces is a hostile act of self-hate, not an act of love. They used to say my lips were too big; now they would be saying they are too thin and telling me to pump them up.

It's troubling that people put their trust in this kind of mind-set. It is all so permanent and addictive, whereas how I would change myself, and manipulate age and time, was through imagery. I didn't literally cut into the skin and move around the muscle in my face. I was stretched, fractured, crushed, expanded, liquefied, but always as a performance, as an effect, a consciousness, never as a real human being.

Versions of me were manufactured, as real as anything, but they emerged out of me, and didn't scar me. At the center of all these multiple versions of me, there was always a mystery, my mind, where the truth about me really exists, which remains beyond all this interference. My body is a language, but it's not the only one I speak.

Perhaps in the future, where life is imagined more than lived, you will be able to separate and decorate yourself in the ways you can in performance, sending an altered and adjusted variety of selves out into the various spaces of the world, while at the center of it, you remain untouched—yourself, pure spirit, staying in your own skin, close to your soul. In one world you age, in another you exist inside a fantasy.

These Housewives and those fetishizing youth who pursue a reshaping of their faces and bodies are taking too literally the techniques that have been used in the production and retouching of image in entertainment. The face and body can be twisted out of shape, or given the illusion of perfection, on film or video, but there are those who actually do it to themselves, to their flesh and bone. I loved the idea of metamorphosis in my performance, of my persona being infinitely malleable, able to transmit the notion that anything is possible, but I never had the urge to do that to my actual body.

I would say to those women plumping up their lips and cheeks, *Eat more pumpkins.* Healthy skin begins from the inside out. The beauty products made from aloe vera—eat them, don't slap them on yourself. We've been eating that in Jamaica since we were kids. Red wine, honey. That keeps you young. Eating the pumpkin. The melon. Don't put all this shit on your face, eat it.

Don't do those quick fixes. It's like doing heroin. You become addicted to something that in the long run will harm you. Don't they see it in the mirror, that they look distorted? Or do they keep doing it to themselves to correct the mistakes? It's like one thing breaks, you fix that; then something else breaks, you need to fix that.

I would never consider cutting into myself to pretend to stay young. It's bad enough going to the dentist or the doctor for a shot. If I ever need a shot, I say, "Hit me as hard as you can where the needle goes into my flesh. I do not want to feel the needle go into my skin. I want to feel numb there. Hit me. Harder! Harder! And don't show me the needle, I don't want to see it." They think I am a masochist. Can you image the pain of all those needles in the service of smoothing you out and pretending you are still young and attractive even as death gets closer?

When I became a grandmother, it still didn't make me think, *Now I must burn away the wrinkles, lift the breasts, pump up the lips.* There was no sense of panic. How could there be? Becoming a grandmother was simply another stage I was moving through. Paulo became a father at the same age that I became a mother. His daughter Athena was born in Paris, and I happened to be there on the day she was born doing some promotional work for the *Hurricane* album, including a photo shoot with Jean-Paul. The day she was born, the album entered the British charts.

I got to the hospital not long after she was born, and when I first saw her, she had her eyes closed. I had to leave soon, and I was begging her to open her eyes. *Before I leave, please open your eyes!* A few moments before I had to leave, she opened her eyes—and my God, what a shock. I shouldn't really say it, but it was like a *Rosemary's Baby* moment. She had these deep purple eyes, and this little spray of red hair, and her skin was so white (her mother is half Italian, half Finnish) it was almost transparent. She was like Elizabeth I in wrinkled miniature. Her blue-purple eyes locked right on mine. It was an extraordinary moment.

I rang Jean-Paul when she was born and said, "If you don't get down to the hospital immediately I won't do the photo shoot." He still had that fear of the newborn, but he came down. It was one great ending to our story, and of course another beginning: to become grandparents and feel how much that stretches reality.

Paulo had a group with the mother of Athena, Azella, called Trybez, and they supported me when I did the *Hurricane* tour. I would look after Athena while they were on tour in much the same way I would have Paulo with me when I toured after he was born. I would have her in my dressing room as I was putting on my makeup. It was continuity. You could see Athena respond to the music as it came through the dressing room walls, and notice how she was reacting to something she had been hearing when she was inside her mother's womb. There was a definite connection with a noise and rhythm she was familiar with.

I am glad that I had a boy and that Paulo had a girl, which means that, in a way, I can have a girl. I never wanted a girl, because of how I had to compete with all my brothers, and how they can be boxed in and denied freedom. Girls are treated as inferior; it just seems to be the way things are, however much you fight. Now she's here, I want her to be tough and work out how to do well in a man's world.

When she was born, there was some debate about what she should call me—Nana, Bonne Maman, Aunt Grace. "No," I announced. "I deserve to be called Grandmother, with emphasis on the *grand*." I never really had a grandmother, not in any traditional, nurturing sense. Athena made me feel grand. I definitely wanted to be Grandma.

20

Bare

As I finish off this book, as far as it goes, I am also finishing off a film that I have been making for a few years with the director Sophie Fiennes. She made a film, *Hoover Street Revival,* about my brother Bishop Noel and his ministry at the City of Refuge Church in Los Angeles, making a connection between the idea of the church and what theater must once have been like, the pure performance at the heart of both. She treats Noel as an artist as well as a priest, sampling his sermons, speeches, and the uplifting sound of a gospel choir, and watching how he inspires a troubled black community through sheer force of will. It's amazing to watch how Noel transforms the idea of God, and the word of God, after how he was brought up, making it something that can do good, whatever the circumstances. Chris Blackwell saw him deliver a sermon once and said he was the greatest performer he had ever seen.

Sophie also made two films with the Slovenian philosopher Slavoj Žižek, *The Pervert's Guide to the Cinema* and *The Pervert's Guide to Ideology,* which will blow your mind if you love film, dreams, fantasy, and reaching out to the edge of thinking. I think the film we have been making together will completely contradict this book, or confirm it, or complement it, or all three—it will be about one of the Grace Joneses in this book, or some of them, or none of them.

I am also finishing a short film with Chris Cunningham, who directed mesmerizing videos for Autechre, Aphex Twin, Björk, and

Madonna. This will be astonishing, if we do finish it, and in that sense working with him is like working with Trevor Horn and Jean-Paul Goude. The project could go on forever—there is perhaps no limit to a piece that is about there being no limit, to thought, to art, to dreams. I feel he could modify and manipulate me forever, looking for some impossible sweet spot, or some obscene end point, just like I think Jean-Paul could. They are both chasing the definitively unfinished, and in a way keeping what they do secret. I share that sense of delaying the end of something, of working on something over years and avoiding having to complete it. If someone asks me what scares me, I will reply: *Finishing.* If you are reading this, then I did finish this book. Or at least, I pretended to. Ultimately, you never really want to be finished.

The film with Chris is based on a fashion shoot, what I called an anti-fashion shoot, which we did for *Dazed and Confused* magazine. If those glossy Scavullo *Cosmo* covers in the 1970s of split, doomed Gia and shiny, happy Christie Brinkley symbolized the world of fashion that pretends everything is fine, these photographs dig into the pressure and violence of the truth. They represent how I survived the superficial and often sick modeling world because I was interested in photography and image as a method of telling stories about my relationship with reality, in analyzing the shady processes of a devious world. I was never interested in selling myself, but in discovering myself, and how I am always on the move whether anyone knows or not.

These photographs were themselves based on a truly revealing short film Chris had made called *Rubber Johnny* about a hyperactive, shape-shifting, mutant child. Ugliness bends around to beauty and back again. A book he compiled to accompany a DVD release of that film was rejected by the Italian printers, who said that they flatly refused to print it on moral grounds. They said they didn't want their workers to catch even a glimpse of some of the images. Such a reaction makes me very optimistic about the future of art and film.

In these photos, I become the stripped-bare, shape-shifting freak of nature somewhere between a speck of dust and a landscape. They are bleak, wounded nude photos in the tradition of Francis Bacon, some of them showing me pressed against glass, capturing yet another sticky, shape-shifting birth. The series is Helmut Newton from hell. It shows how photography, and image, and the telling of a story, even in fashion and entertainment, can still move on and don't need to recycle other styles and fashions. Chris does not fake or glamorize the depraved, but he does celebrate it. I love how Chris doesn't copy what I once did but refers to it, and explores where the story, where my mind, has moved since my first images and performances. His photos of me represent volatile continuity, not dreary, nostalgic senti-mentality. He's investigating how, through my body and mind, I try to make sense of the material and spiritual world around me.

The film and photos are about power, in the way the Jean-Paul pic-tures were. They're photographs that are at the service of the mind. They are about how the body speaks a completely different language, a continuation of the Haring body paint. They're about how I know more than words can express. I might meet the Queen, scream for the tennis players, and charm the pants off today's chat show hosts, but I don't let go of the dark, of the skin of me, the ageless age of me, the riotous comedy of me. All the things that have always interested me in terms of inventing who I am, making myself up from scratch and always adding to that invention. Chris is a black comedian like me, really: He giggles a lot; he has fun with his work however disturbing it gets, and the best comedians go to the darkest places because they thrive on breaking taboos. (One thing I often think I should try that I haven't yet is some stand-up comedy. I'll bring my whip in case no one laughs.)

Also, as I finish this book, I am recording a new album with Ivor Guest. We split up during the recording of "Hurricane," but there was enough creative momentum and togetherness for us to complete it. We remained close friends, but I don't think we thought that we'd make another album together. Then one day at about the same time we both had the same idea. Africa. The rhythms of Senegal, Congo, Mali, Nigeria mixed up with my life. It was too good an idea to resist. The disco trilogy was followed by the Compass Point trilogy; and then *Slave to the Rhythm,* with Trevor Horn, which was out on its own, was followed by two al-bums on Capitol Records that never became the third trilogy. The album I am making now is perhaps the second in a trilogy that started with the *Hurricane* album. The last one in this trilogy might be my final album, or I might not make another album and there will be another aborted trilogy, another empty space. Perhaps I'll just stay at home, somewhere, keeping myself to myself, bloody-minded, opening up the next bottle of wine, aiming for the stars. Or I might simply end up singing my favorite arias as a way of studying and celebrating beauty, and analyzing the death of beauty, and how all things slip like sand through our fingers. I will release them one by one, because I've got all the time in the world, until I reach some sort of planet-shaking climax, a final act, a whirling octopus mix of acid trip, tidal orgasm, and the ultimate feeling of being free.

I still talk to Chris Blackwell about my music, as I have done for thirty-five years. We sit on the veranda of his house high in the Jamaican hills, which is so secluded it makes Noël Coward's Firefly seem as accessible as a country pub. We sit under a dusting of stars, taking it slow at the end of a perfect day, on the brink of the unknown. Far away from crowds, schedules, and clocks. The flickering candles will soon be snuffed out. The amazed crickets grow in volume; breezes sweep over the high trees that surround us in the dark, still looking like the looming dinosaurs I used to imagine when I was young. I have to say goodbye in a short while, but there's always something else to talk about.

We both have strong ideas. He is of the persuasion that I play my next shows by mostly concentrating on my old songs. He doesn't think I should play the new songs I am recording. Maybe one song, not the whole album. I want to go on tour and play the whole record, because for me, it is always about what I am doing, not what I have done. I still sing those songs, my favorites, for my fans, and they are a big part of my show. I now go out to play shows not to dwell on my past but to put it in a new context, because of the songs I am doing now, and who I am now. The past should not stay fixed, but should itself move with the times. I do believe you can change the past, and that is one way to change things now.

Chris thinks the audience doesn't care about any new album. Being stubborn, I am determined to prove him wrong. I want another chance to not let him down. I want to be the student who, having learned from the master, now turns around and shows him a new path.

My attitude is: I'll give you some of what you want to hear, because I love that as well. But I am not going to ignore my new album, even if I have to play a three-hour show. I am not going to keep repeating myself without introducing where I have moved to now, visually and musically, which will connect with where I have been, and with where I am going. There are still missing pieces of this jigsaw puzzle to find. I'm still planning my next assault.

I refuse to believe that people only want to hear my old songs. They want a show, and I will give them one, like I always have. I am going to go out onstage naked except for some Haring-inspired body paint and a grass stalk, like a member of the Igbo tribe, a loner following her own pattern of thought and feeling straddling many ancient cultures and multiple assimilations. There will be a tree onstage, looking like an octopus, with long, thin, brown tentacles bare of leaves hanging down from a twisted root. Surrounding the stage, stars, as though we are spinning through space.

I've never been one to chase hit singles, to do the bleeding, boring obvious. In the end, it is how I perform it. It is all about the theater. The theater is where I belong, across whatever stages, whatever screens, whatever spaces, pages, and sites, always taking revenge on reality, and I will do it in such a way that I will make Chris Blackwell eat his words. He taught me to stand up for myself. Well, that's what I am doing.

I will get Issey Miyake to design something for me that is Igbo-Japanese-Jamaican. Future-tribal, pitting opposite sensibilities against each other. Beautiful painted bare bodies and straw and dust and the drama of drum to ward off danger, summoning my ancestors, creating links with the wisdom of the world, and taking the old music with me into this new vision. There will be no place for the hoola hoop in my depiction of Africa. The hula hoop will be put aside.

When I am onstage, I am not hiding behind a band, behind a lazy medley of obvious greatest hits. I am doing what I have always done. I have to have total confidence to do what I do onstage, because I am standing there on my own. I am not sharing it with a stage full of other characters, with repetitive magic tricks. I am performing alone. That's where I thrive. No distractions. Me. Focused. On me. Perfecting my ideas. There is no other energy flowing around me from other places so that I can simply wave my hands in the air and get everyone to sing along with me like we are at a kiddie party. I am performing, with my deep simplicity, and from that simplicity comes the power. It all comes from me and out of me.

I don't scatter myself. My image is scattered but I am not. I grew up using my imagination to make reality work for me. In order to make a connection with reality, I made up a world where I could live. I fought to generate self-confidence. I worked hard to feel safe. That's what I do now. I stand out, because that's what I had to do when I was young, to make sure that I existed.

In films that has been a problem. They won't cast me to be part of a group, because I stand out too much. I can't be part of an ensemble cast, because I stand out too much. *Why didn't I get that part in that film? It was only a small part!* They say, *You stand out too much.* I really do try sometimes to blend in, but it doesn't bloody work. I stand out too much. I don't fit in.

That's okay. I'm not like anyone else. It's too late to change.

I think of myself as someone who is always adding to what they do, as part of a never-ending story, and the latest chapter is as valid as anything else. I am always becoming something. I am always turning into something else. That's how I started, and that's how I want it to be now. Otherwise, it's like I have given up on the energy that made me what people wanted to see and hear, that I now simply live off what I was, not what I am. I planted a seed, and I watched it grow.

If people complain that I am not doing enough of my old material, not performing all the hits, I will stand in front of them, a formlessness that engulfs all form. I will put on another hat, crack my whip, scatter fireflies, fix them with a five-thousand-year-old stare, fit to fight to the bitter end, becoming a ghost with the passing of time. I will be ready for the afterlife, for my bones to be buried in the mountains of Jamaica, or the canals of Venice, or the dark side of the moon, or under the ground in the cities I've lived in and loved. And I will say: Do you want to move forward with me, or not? Do you want to know where I am going next?

It's time for something else to happen.

GRACE JONES

RIDER—PLEASE READ CAREFULLY!

THIS RIDER IS HEREBY MADE PART OF THE ACCOMPANYING PERFOR-
MANCE AGREEMENT FOR **GRACE JONES.** PURCHASER AGREES TO MEET
THE FOLLOWING REQUIREMENTS AT PURCHASER'S SOLE EXPENSE.

1. All contractual commitments supersede this agreement and the ARTIST has the
   right to cancel or move a performance up to 7 days prior to event to fulfil these
   commitments.

2. SECURITY—PURCHASER agrees to provide adequate security to ensure the
   safety of all performing ARTISTS, auxiliary personnel, instruments, equipment,
   costumes, and personal belongings, before, during and after the performance. Security personnel shall keep the stage free of any persons other than those directly
   involved with the performance. Security personnel shall be stationed outside
   dressing rooms from ARTIST arrival at venue, continuously through ARTIST'S
   departure and especially when ARTIST is on stage. A member of the security staff
   will be provided to meet and escort ARTIST upon arrival and lead ARTIST into
   the venue and dressing room. Under no circumstance will ARTIST be led through
   the public prior to the show.

3. DRESSING ROOMS—PURCHASER agrees to provide dressing rooms: including
   one (1) large dressing room for the sole use of ARTIST. The keys are to be given to
   Artist's Road Manager upon the time of arrival at venue. No person other than ART-
   IST and Artist's entourage shall have access to the dressing room without the prior
   permission of Artist's Road Manager. If possible, dressing room should be located in

No Smoking area of venue. Dressing room will be comfortable and clean with heating or air-conditioning as appropriate to climate and will be furnished with comfortable chairs and couches, table, lined trash can. Dressing room will be located within easy access of hot and cold running water and private toilet (not public restroom).

GRACE's dressing rooms shall be equipped with:

Dressing Room 1:

6 Bottles of Louis Roederer Cristal Champagne

3 Bottles of French Vintage red wine (e.g. St Emilion, Medoc, Bordeaux)

3 Bottles of French Vintage white wine (e.g. Sancerre, Pouilly Fuisse)

2 Dozen Findeclare or Colchester Oysters on ice (unopened)—(Grace does her own shucking.)

2 Sashimi and Sushi platters for 8 people

6 Fresh lemons

1 Bottle of Tabasco sauce

1 Fresh fruit platter for 8 people

6 Bottles of Coca Cola

12 Bottles of still and sparkling water

12 Bottles of fresh fruit juices

Wine glasses, champagne flutes, tumblers (all glass, no plastic)

Cutlery and sharp knife

1 Oyster knife

1 Make up mirror (no neon strip lighting, only opaque white bulbs)

Fresh towels, clothes hangers, clothes rail

3-4 Bunches of flowers—prefer lilys and orchids

Sofa and arm chairs

Wardrobe Room (next to Grace's dressing room):

1 Iron and ironing board

1 Steamer

1 Clothes rail

Clothes hangers
1 Full length mirror

Dressing Room 2:

2 Cases of decent lager beer, chilled
1 Case of still water
1 Case of sparkling water
Large selection of carbonated soft drinks
Large selection of crisps and snack foods

Production Office:

Phone line, desks and chairs
Free high speed internet access via wireless / Ethernet connection
2 Cases of still water (for stage and crew)
Selection of chocolate / sweets including Minstrels, Maltesers
Catering must also be provided on site, at regular meal times, at all times
Grace's band or crew are on site. Buffet breakfast and cooked lunch and
   dinner where appropriate, with vegetarian options available.
   Purchaser agrees to pick up bar tab for Artist and entourage

4. PRODUCTION—PURCHASER agrees to provide a professional sound system
   with sufficient speaker and amplification systems to produce top quality house
   and on-stage sound without distortion or feedback. System to include:

5. GROUND TRANSPORTATION—PURCHASER agrees to provide first class
   ground transportation for Artist's entourage to and from airport, hotel, and
   venue from Artist's arrival through departure. **Transportation must be a
   Stretch Limousine to be used at GRACE's discretion.**

6. MERCHANDISING—ARTIST shall have the right but not the obligation to sell
   souvenir programs, posters, and other merchandise and to retain 100% of the
   receipts. ARTIST reserves the right to confiscate part or all of any unauthorized
   "bootleg" merchandise being sold in or around the venue.

7. GUEST LIST: Grace is entitled to a minimum 20 person guest list w/tickets
   available for her to distribute.

8. WORKMAN'S COMPENSATION—ALL PURCHASER employees will be covered by Workman's Compensation and Disability Insurance. No employees of PURCHASER will look to ARTIST for any type of compensation or coverage.

9. AIR TRAVEL—Purchaser is responsible for the airline arrangements for members of the group (Windows and Aisles are mandatory). Flights must be fully flexible.

Grace's flight info is as follows:

2 x First Class roundtrip tickets for Grace and travelling companion (These must be fully flexible tickets)

5 x Economy roundtrip for travel party (1 sound engineer, 2 dressers, 1 musician, 1 manager)

*** Airport VIP Service for Grace and her companion must be provided: on departure (curbside-airside) + on arrival (airside-curbside) for ALL flights relating to the event.***

PROMOTER IS RESPONSIBLE FOR ALL EXCESS LUGGAGE EXPENSES

10. HOTEL—Purchaser is responsible for providing artist with rooming at five star hotel. Hotel must have 24 hour room service. Rooming requirements as follows: Six (6) Hotel rooms for three nights (the night of the show and the night before and after the show)

Grace's room is to be a **presidential suite,** which MUST include:

(2) Large separate rooms

(2) Bathrooms

(24) HR Room Service

Full Spa facilities (steam room)

Management's approval of the hotel is required before booking

11. PER DIEM to be provided upon arrival at Hotel. They are as follows:

€300 (EURO) a day for Grace Jones

€150 (EURO) a day for Crew

NO ONE IS ALLOWED ON STAGE DURING ANY PERFORMANCE, UNLESS PERMITTED OR INTRODUCED BY ROAD MANAGER!

Acknowledgments

I'LL NEVER WRITE MY ACKNOWLEDGMENTS ...

Mom, Dad, Chris/Patrick, Noel, Bev, Pam, Janet, Maxwell, Randy, Aunt Sybil, Hyanthe, Alison, Ma Powell, Aunt Ceta, Grandpa Dan Williams, Grandpa Pat Jones, Bishop Walters, his wife Zina, Mas P, Mas K, Sister Leah, Sister Bobsie, Aunt Sybil, Uncle Roy, Uncle Sidney, Uncle Easton, Uncle Randolph, Cousin Zeke/Norman, Cousin Marie, Cousin Wayne, Uncle Jacky, Cousin Jackie, the Cuban relatives, Spanish Town neighbors, Syracuse neighbors, church friends, church crushes, church singers.

Paulo and Athena.

Sam, Jean-Paul, Dolph, Sven, Chris, Atila.

Andy, Richard, Keith, Tom.

Chris Blackwell, Suzette Newman, Issey Miyaki, Eiko Ishioka, Francesca von Habsburg, John Carmen, Steve Newman, Raphael Santin, Toukie Smith, Natalie Delon, Azzedine Alaia, Jean-Paul Gaultier, Kenzo Takada, Dennis Hopper, Luciano Pavarotti, Glenn O'Brien, Alex Sadkin, Tom Moulton, Trevor Horn, Bruce Woolley, Nile Rogers, Ivor Guest, Barry Reynolds, Mark Van Eyck, Frankie Crocker, Mark Jones, Timothy and Barbara Leary, Danny Huston, Cubby and Barbara Broccoli, Sophie Fiennes, Tony Moses, Chris Cunningham, Greg Gorman, Adrian Boot, Philip Treacy, and Russell Harty.

Taking care of business: Marjorie Grant of L.A., Eric of Ocho Rios, Vanja, Goran, Jane, Amber, and Brendan Coyle.

All my life sisters: Jerry—"Grace, honey, we're in a hell of a rodeo"—Jessica, Mary, Patti, Efva, Antonio, Tara, Lulu, and Kate.

Studio 54 and the Hells Angels, Lion of Pantrepant and Prince Albert and Princess Stephanie of Monaco.

Island Records 1977–1985, the Compass Point All Stars 1980–1982, and Wall of Sound 2008.

All those who made it into the book and this list and to those who didn't but will next time; those who helped me get here on time one way or another; those along the way who captured the moment; those who help me write, sing, perform, and stage my songs; Jennifer Bergstrom, for asking me if I wanted to write a book; and the team at Gallery Books.

The 2009 Bordeaux vintage.

As told to Paul Morley, at the San Marco restaurant, somewhere on the waterfront between London, New York, Venice, Paris, Alligator Head, and Goldeneye, Jamaica.

Xxgr

PAUL MORLEY

Elizabeth Levy, Madeleine Morley, Tricia, Nina, and Jeremie at Gallery Books, Jayne, Carol and Cairo, David Godwin, the North Wales relatives, Chris Blackwell, Suzette Newman, and, wherever she is, whatever the time . . . Grace Jones: "Paul, before we do some work, I need to go for a swim. I need to feel weightless."